Defensive Relativism

PENNSYLVANIA STUDIES IN HUMAN RIGHTS

Bert B. Lockwood, Series Editor

A complete list of books in the series
is available from the publisher.

DEFENSIVE RELATIVISM

The Use of Cultural Relativism in International Legal Practice

Frederick Cowell

PENN

UNIVERSITY OF PENNSYLVANIA PRESS

PHILADELPHIA

Published by
University of Pennsylvania Press
Philadelphia, Pennsylvania 19104-4112
www.upenn.edu/pennpress

Printed in the United States of America on acid-free paper
10 9 8 7 6 5 4 3 2 1

Hardcover ISBN 9781512823318
Ebook ISBN 9781512823325

Library of Congress Cataloging-in-Publication Data
Names: Cowell, Frederick, author.
Title: Defensive relativism : the use of cultural relativism in international legal practice / Frederick Cowell.
Other titles: Pennsylvania studies in human rights.
Description: Philadelphia : University of Pennsylvania Press, [2022] | Series: Pennsylvania studies in human rights | Includes bibliographical references and index.
Identifiers: LCCN 2022011658 |
ISBN 9781512823318 (hardcover)
Subjects: LCSH: International law and human rights. | Cultural relativism. | Human rights.
Classification: LCC KZ1266 .C69 2022 |
DDC 341.4/8—dc23/eng/20220408
LC record available at https://lccn.loc.gov/2022011658

To Rosie for her love, patience,
and all the conversations

CONTENTS

ACKNOWLEDGMENTS

"Cultural relativism . . . well I'd rather you than me," said Peter Fitzpatrick on a cold day in January in 2012. He was looking at three early draft chapters of my PhD thesis, one of which was very tentatively titled "Defensive Relativism." Peter rather deftly explained why this didn't quite fit into my doctoral thesis, but then, as was his wont, pulled about half a dozen photocopied readings off the log canoe from Papua New Guinea that sat in the middle of his office. Many of his former students will recognize this scene, and I was truly sad when revising the manuscript of this book in the spring of 2020 to learn of his death, as his intellectual legacy was invaluable to this book.

The idea of defensive relativism was duly taken out of my doctoral thesis and then sat on my hard drive for a year before I began to shape it at Post Graduate Research conferences at Birkbeck College, School of Law in 2013 and 2014. I am forever grateful to my institution for running these conferences for PhD students and for the feedback I got on the early ideas contained in this book from Stewart Motha, Costas Douzinas, and Jose Bellido at these conferences. When I was a faculty member in 2019, I was enormously grateful for research leave in the spring and summer of that year, which gave me the time to complete the first draft of the manuscript of this book. Eventually the papers presented at those postgraduate conferences were turned into a chapter in the book *Decolonizing the Enlightenment* (Barbara Budrich Publishers, 2014), where an early development of the ideas found in chapters 1 and 8 can be found. The editor of the volume, Professor Nikita Dhawan, showed incredible patience with me and challenged me on several core assumptions which help refine the theory. I also have to re-thank Fletch Williams, now at LSE School of Law, who helped me greatly with my understanding of the literature on anthropology and law at this early stage.

In 2015, I had further refined the ideas and wrote papers on the material in chapters 3, 4, and 8. I was pleased to present them at the "Getting Closure: Human Rights after Human Rights" conference at the Univeristé Libre de

Bruxelles in May 2015 and at the Human Rights Integration Conference at the University of Ghent in December 2015. One of the opportunities conferences like these provide is for experienced scholars and researchers to ask questions, and those I received from Martti Koskenniemi, Eva Brems, Barbara Oomen and Julie Fraser—even if you don't remember asking them—were so important in refining how I approached the entire work. Chapter 3 was born out of this experience, and in January 2017 I presented one of its early drafts at the "Challenging Human Rights Disenchantment" conference at the University of Sussex. When I was editing this manuscript in the midst of the early summer pandemic lockdown in 2020, I missed these conferences so much, and it is not an exaggeration to say that conference questions made this book.

There are some chapter-specific thank-yous that need to be made. Nick Long of LSE's Anthropology Department very kindly took the time to give me comments on chapter 2 and tell me where I had gone wrong on anthropology. Stephanie Berry from the University of Sussex Law School, who chaired the panel where I outlined an early draft of chapter 3, also very helpfully gave me detailed comments on the right to religious freedom in chapter 5. Gayatri Patel, from the University of Aston Law School, gave some invaluable feedback on chapter 6 and women's rights. Giorgia Baldi, formerly my colleague at Birkbeck and now at the University of Sussex, shared a panel with me on an early draft of chapter 4 and offered a myriad of useful suggestions on the introduction. I am also very grateful to have had the opportunity to present a summary of the culture as defense argument at the meeting of the European Society of Law Interest Group on Culture at Athens in 2019; the discussion of different meanings of culture was very helpful for me in redrafting parts of chapter 2, chapter 8, and the Conclusion.

I was very grateful to Peter Agree, formerly of University of Pennsylvania Press, who helped me develop this project toward publication and secured some early peer reviews of chapters which were very helpful while I was still writing the manuscript. The anonymous reviewer who gave feedback on the first draft of this book is a person to whom I owe a bottle (or two) of wine, as their very detailed six-page report in May 2020 enabled a wholescale revision of the manuscript for the better—so if it is you, write and claim your reward! Finally, Walter Biggins and his team at the University of Pennsylvania Press have been very helpful with the long process of keeping this project moving and turning the manuscript into this book.

Finally, an enormous thank-you to a couple of my postgraduate human rights classes in 2017 and 2018, who were occasional guinea pigs for some of the ideas here, and my PhD student Crina Morteanu, who was also very helpful in directing me to sources on the margin of appreciation that I had not thought about. Great patience was shown by my students as I took time to finish this manuscript and was late in answering their emails. Great patience was also shown by family and friends—my wife Rosie and my friend Scott were willing testers for the introductory chapter to check that it all made sense.

All references in this book are accurate as of November 15, 2021, and all URLs (unless otherwise stated) were last accessed by September 10, 2021. I have done my best to make sure all of the law is current as of November 18, 2021. Given the contested nature of different concepts, I have tried where quoting material to use the wording and terms as originally written to give as clear an impression of the original source as possible, which explains why there may be different spellings of certain words. Any subsequent errors identified are mine.

INTRODUCTION

What Is Defensive Relativism?

In December 2009, Steven Monjeza and Tiwonge Chimbalanga held a simple traditional public engagement ceremony in Malawi in front of a group of close friends. Couples the world over that day performed similar pre- and postnuptial ceremonies in front of their friends and family. But what made things different for Monjeza and Chimbalanga was that in Malawi a relationship between two adult males was a crime. Section 156 of the Malawian penal code criminalized "public or private" gross acts of indecency between adult males, and if convicted, the perpetrators were "liable to imprisonment for five years, with or without corporal punishment."[1] Two days after this ceremony the couple were arrested at their home and charged with gross indecency and unnatural practices between males. In May 2010 they were convicted, with the trial judge giving them the maximum possible sentences for both offenses—fourteen years' prison time with hard labor. Handing down the sentence in a packed courtroom in Blantyre, Judge Nyakwawa Usiwa-Usiwa condemned them for setting a bad example to others, and as a consequence he issued what he described as a "scaring sentence."[2] Although international media attention focused on Monjeza and Chimbalanga's case, across Malawi that spring there were a series of arrests of individuals accused of various criminal offenses related to their sexual orientation.

Malawi's penal code originated in colonial-era laws imposed by the British, adopted from model criminal laws in Sudan and Delhi. When Malawi became independent in 1964, these laws were simply incorporated into the postindependence legal system, even though there was a tension between the penal code and the commitment to equality in the country's constitution.[3] Nevertheless, opinion polls showed popular support for the laws criminalizing sexual orientation in Malawi.[4] As a member of the Commonwealth of Nations, the international organization originally formed as a forum for states that had been part of the British Empire, Malawi sent a delegation to the Commonwealth

Law Ministers Meeting—a forum where law reforms and harmonization of common law are discussed. At a pre-meeting in September 2010, the issue of decriminalizing sexual orientation was discussed in response to a position paper from a nongovernmental organization (NGO). During the discussion, the South African delegate to the meeting noted that many of the states present at that meeting—including Malawi were parties to the International Covenant on Civil and Political Rights (ICCPR) which protected the right to privacy and equality before the law. In 1994, the Human Rights Committee (HRC)—the body charged with monitoring the protection of rights contained in the ICCPR—had decided in response to a petition brought from Australia that criminalization of sexual orientation was a violation of the right to privacy.[5] Even if there was a public interest or a policy reason for such laws, the HRC's view was that criminalization was a disproportionate restriction of rights. Arguably, the South African delegate concluded, the states at the Commonwealth Law Ministers meeting who continued to criminalize sexual orientation were violating the rights they were obliged to protect under the ICCPR.

The Malawian delegate to the meeting, the deputy attorney general, visibly bristled at this point. In response, he said that this was another attack on Malawi over the Monjeza and Chimbalanga case. They were common criminals, he argued, who had staged the entire thing to attack the Malawian government after being provoked by NGOs such as Amnesty International. Dealing directly with the argument that Malawi's penal code violated the ICCPR, he said that the laws were a reflection of Malawian traditions, and that international human rights law should not interfere in matters considered criminal in Malawi. As campaigners later pointed out, the traditions in question were by no means monolithic, and popular hostility to the rights of a minority had previously been rejected by the HRC as a justification for the criminalization of sexual orientation.[6] Furthermore, there was no obligation by the state under the ICCPR to make marriage available to same sex couples; a 2002 HRC decision had made it clear that the covenant did not require the "redefinition" of marriage, and a restriction of the right to marry was not a violation of the covenant.[7] Under the ICCPR, the state's obligation was limited to the decriminalization of sexual orientation and prohibiting discrimination against the LGBT community—practices such as the administration of marriage were matters for states to decide. Yet, the argument made by the Malawian delegated to that Commonwealth meeting maintained in essence that the government's definition of tradition, and the laws which reflected that definition, took precedent over any international legal obligation. Writing up a summary of the day's proceedings for my employer at the time, I struggled to convey what had just happened. I wrote that it was almost as if the Malawian delegate was being a sort of defensive cultural relativist, using relativism like a defending counsel might use an argument about intent in court.

This was an example of defensive relativism—the state practice of cultural relativism to resist implementing human rights law. Cultural relativism is often analyzed within the literature on the philosophy of rights or the politics of human rights. But this misses the distinctiveness of defensive relativism which uniquely emerges only in response to human rights law. All states have the potential to engage in defensive relativism, as it is a response to the obligations imposed by international law on a state. For example, at the same time Malawi was cracking down on the LGBT community, the Italian government had instructed its lawyers to resist a claim at the European Court of Human Rights (ECtHR) that the mandatory display of crucifixes in all school classrooms was incompatible with the freedom of religion of schoolchildren. Under Article 9 of the European Convention on Human Rights (ECHR), Italy was required to protect an individual's right to freedom of religion and conscience. A mother with a child in an Italian elementary school had taken the Italian government to court, arguing that the presence of a crucifix in every classroom violated their child's Article 9 rights, as it constituted an imposition of a particular form of religion. In making its case at the ECtHR, the Italian government claimed a form of cultural exceptionalism, based on Italy's heritage as a Catholic country.[8] Both of these examples dealt with very different issues, involved different legal regimes, and emerged from very different social contexts. In both of these cases, however, the state party was making a relativistic argument to resist an obligation of international human rights law.

This book is an attempt to theorize what has been a part of hundreds of treaty body sessions, meetings of international organizations, and other interstate forums—the state practice of defensive relativism. To convey what defensive relativism is, it is important to first give a brief overview of cultural relativism before examining how defensive relativism occurs in international human rights law.

What Is Cultural Relativism?

To understand relativism, it is first important to understand universalism—the idea that human rights ought to apply to everyone equally. Why everyone has, or, more precisely, should have, human rights is a complex question. Some theorists of rights have either argued that human rights have some form of natural origin, or made the case for the intuitive origin of rights within the common human experience. This was common in early theories of human rights or debates about the rights of man as they were then known at the end of the eighteenth century.[9] Other theorists of rights have pointed toward the widespread acceptance of rights as evidence of some kind of common agreement on the fact that certain rights are universal.[10] Further still, others have argued that rights ought to be universal in a teleological sense because they contain a vision of a better society that protects human interests.[11] As Janet Holl Madigan notes, however, these different attempts to explain universality soon run into a number of conceptual problems, because if rights are truly universal there must be some universal conception of "good" or of what is and what is not moral.[12] Value judgments of this sort vary from society to society, as do understandings about what interests rights ought to protect and the legitimacy of rights more generally.[13] Confronted with the fact of divergence, it is tempting to draw a relativistic conclusion about the universality of human rights.

Relativism basically means that a concept or fact that is of notionally universal application is instead relative to a particular context, time, or place. There are two different schools of relativist thought, epistemic and moral. Epistemic relativism is the position that knowledge of any given object, entity, or idea is relative to a specific context, society, culture, or individual. For example, the statement "chocolate cake is sweet" could be a statement that a chocolate cake contains over two hundred grams of sugar. It could also be a factual judgment that might be relative to a particular context, place, or person—after all, if you have a very sweet tooth, it could be that a cake is not very sweet. Moral relativism is the position that moral judgment, the question of what is right or wrong in a particular situation, is relative to a specific context, society, culture, time period, or individual. This deals with the question of whether it is ethically right to eat a chocolate cake. Is it right to eat the cake knowing that animals suffered to produce the milk and eggs that are an essential component of it? In some societies, the animals that produced those milk and eggs are considered sacred and, therefore, eating the cake might be considered immoral, whereas in other societies the exchange of an appropriate amount of money for the cake would be considered appropriate to address any attendant moral questions.

Generally, moral relativism is the school of thought that is connected to the interpretation of human rights, but in practice relativist arguments about human rights may make epistemic claims. Moral relativism is a complex and multifaceted school of thought and a number of different arguments have been made in relation to its impact upon human rights. These arguments are usually grouped under the banner of "Metaethical Moral Relativism," which contends that the truth or falsity of moral judgments, or their justification, is not universal but relative to the traditions or practices of a group of persons.[14] Neil Levy, in his overview of moral relativism, describes how it is often considered dangerous when taken to extremes, as in essence we find ourselves in a world of total epistemic and moral uncertainty where everything and anything is moral if someone says it is moral from their point of view.[15] What a moral relativist is seeking to explain, in very broad terms, is that the moral norms which guide individuals, over which acts are morally right or wrong, are not universal but relative to a particular context. As Steven Lukes explains, moral relativism starts from the "observer's standpoint" describing the fact of moral diversity in the world.[16] From this observation the conclusion is drawn that it is impossible, impractical, or undesirable to attempt a reconciliation of these different sources of morality. This is in contrast to moral realists, who would assert that universal moral rights and wrongs exist—for example, a moral realist would say that the proposition "it is wrong for an adult brother and sister to have sexual relations even if they use birth control" has a truth value to it, as in, it is a true fact about the world in which we live.[17] A moral relativist would, however, argue that there are variants on core moral questions between societies, and the fact of this variance means there is no moral reality in an objective sense; some philosophers term this the "argument from disagreement."[18]

Cultural relativism is the specific type of moral relativism often used in the discourse around international human rights law. It contends that moral judgments are relative to individual cultures, and it is skeptical of intellectual projects to construct a universal system of morality. The origins of cultural relativism can be traced back to the work of the anthropologist Franz Boas, who in the early twentieth century challenged the dominant view that non-Western societies were on a journey toward some form of civilized state.[19] Other anthropologists built on this work with a variety of fieldwork, and argued that an individual's moral judgments are contingent upon the society in which they live.[20] Claude Lévi-Strauss, in his highly influential 1979 work *Myth and Meaning*, argued that indigenous people were wrongly described as "primitive" because they did not use methods of communication and technical terms to explain natural phenomena.[21] Drawing on a myth from indigenous communities in western Canada about a battle between ancient man and "evil winds," which allowed a southerly life-giving wind to blow, Lévi-Strauss argued that the myth was trying to solve a particular problem—how do you explain a natural phenomenon, such as the change in winds, which has a clear physical effect? The use of myths about fights between imaginary gods was simply a way of explaining the weather in a world where high-tech satellites monitoring meteorological data didn't exist. Lévi-Strauss' thesis was that the differences between cultures were readily explicable. What anthropologists were explaining with cultural relativism was how different societies developed governmental systems and moral codes, which, while different from Western societies, were no less valid as a system of morality. Some anthropologists went slightly further, holding that all morality was contingent upon the culture of that individual.[22] The core difference between moral relativists, who principally were philosophers, and anthropologists was that anthropologists were basing their arguments in part on fieldwork and were attempting to understand social systems, leading them to what can be described as a descriptive relativist position about the societies they were studying. Moral philosophers were principally interested in the structure and coherency of relativistic arguments themselves. This is a broad-brush distinction, but it is useful to appreciate why different academic disciplines took divergent approaches to cultural relativism. It is also important to note that, in spite of many anthropologists dispelling the notion that societies were on some form of journey toward an ideal type of civilization, the assumption that societies were or should be on a path to being "civilized" persisted in international law until well into the twentieth century, with colonial territories being assigned mandate status until they could demonstrate their capacity for independent governance.[23]

Cultural relativism in relation to human rights is often normative rather than descriptive; it maintains that people ought, or ought not, to do something. In 1947, the principal concern of the American Anthropological Association in their statement in response to the Universal Declaration of Human Rights (UDHR), was that "persons, living in terms of values not envisaged by a limited Declaration" would be disenfranchised by the UDHR, and it needed to include a "statement of the right of men to live in terms of their own traditions."[24] This helped shape the concept of cultural relativism as a response to international human rights law, leading to the growth of the idea that communities ought to have different rights depending on their cultural backgrounds. It was true that international human rights law originally reflected a particular set of assumptions about the role of state, the nature of society, and the role of the individual, which were common in Western European states.[25] However, as it evolved, international human rights law came to protect a much broader range of interests, including economic and communal rights, with non-Western states contributing extensively to the creation of human rights instruments and the development of human rights in international organizations. Cultural relativism came to focus on the incompatibility of international human rights law with national traditions gravitating toward the position which Christos Galanos summarizes as "outsiders should never be able to criticize practices within a culture" because any form of intervention into "the affairs of another [culture] to safeguard the rights of individuals is unacceptable."[26]

Among the vast literature on human rights and cultural relativism, some of the leading works that attempted to frame the issues in the 1980s and 1990s focused on relativism emerging from a clash of Western traditions of rights with other non-Western cultures and their traditions.[27] This framing prompted three main strands of critical engagement. Firstly, there were those who argued that human rights had a distinctly Western set of origins, which meant that arguments of the sort generated by cultural relativism were inevitable.[28] Secondly, there were those such as Abdullahi An-Na'im, who argued for a cross-cultural approach to human rights, looking at the traditions of different societies which could protect rights and trying to identify them through what he termed "internal cultural discourse and cross-cultural dialogue."[29] Finally, a more recent strand of scholarship, an example of which can be found in Federico Lenzerini's work, has attempted to view the tension between cultural relativism and human rights through the prism of multiculturalism, arguing that allowing human rights standards to adapt to different traditions over time maximizes their overall effectiveness.[30] In a related vein, the work of Mark Goodale and Sally Ann Merry has made the case for acknowledging different traditions in a pluralist legal framework and for looking beyond standard legal structures to understand how customary or informal practices may advance human rights in some societies.[31]

By the early 2000s, a range of scholars from different disciplines had started to become more critical of the implications of the universalist-relativist divide. Yale Ferguson and Richard Mansbach, in their book *Remapping Global Politics*, argued that relativism makes it "virtually impossible to make and sustain value judgments."[32] Ferguson and Mansbach cautioned that postmodernist philosophers, in their criticism of universality, had not offered any alternative resulting in a situation where "truth would no longer be accessible beyond individual understanding."[33] The practical implications of this position were highlighted by Kamari Maxine Clarke's work on violence in Nigeria following the 2003 riots over the Miss World competition; she noted that "epistemological" relativists concluded that "all kinds of violence [were] foundationally legitimate in their own spheres of meaning."[34] A similar issue had been raised by Alexander Hinton in his study of the anthropology of genocide, which argued that cultural relativism "had likely played a key role in inhibiting" the anthropological study of genocide because it engendered the perception that "the judgement that something is 'horrendous' may be ethnocentric and culturally relative."[35] Discussing comparative law in Southeast Asia, Andrew Harding noted that relativist discourse had a homogenizing effect, obscuring divergence within societies, because it was defined in opposition to universality.[36] This line of scholarship was much more critical of the conflict between universality and relativism and how it framed arguments about ethics. Yet, while much of this work discussed the way that states had made relativist arguments, it did not explore how states used these arguments within international legal frameworks.

Defensive relativism involves states taking the normative conclusion drawn by some cultural relativists—that different standards of rights ought to apply to different societies—and turning them into a legal claim that certain rights (or a particular right) protected by international human rights law shouldn't apply in their state because of the relative incommensurability of a cultural tradition with their obligations. For example, when the 1979 Convention on the Elimination of All Forms of Discrimination against Women (CEDAW) was opened for signature, it attracted a number of wide-ranging reservations to its substantive provisions, which were justified on loose and unspecified cultural and religious differences.[37] Many of these were completely incompatible with the rights contained within CEDAW and went far beyond the sort of latitude given to states to realize rights within their domestic jurisdiction that was permitted under the convention's legal framework. Yet, over the course of a two-year debate between 1986 and 1988 at the UN Commission on Human Rights and UN General Assembly, many states defended this seeming double standard on the grounds that women's rights were a culturally sensitive issue.[38] These states did not necessarily have to become a party to CEDAW. Studies on the motivations of states when joining international treaty regimes or human rights organizations have identified how states often desire to appear human rights–compliant or signal to other states that they meet a certain international standard.[39] What the states opposing CEDAW sought to achieve was a form of legal exemption from implementing CEDAW as required by the treaty, because of their definition of cultural standards and their importance, while at the same time benefiting from remaining a party to CEDAW.

What Is a State Practice?

Defensive relativism is a state practice, meaning that its practitioners are state parties, not communities or individuals. It is a type of argument seen in international practices in international human rights law. A state practice describes the behavior of a state in its relations with other states, international institutions, or international actors. The term "state practice" is used here in its broadest sense to describe common practices undertaken by state parties. In particular it refers to the legal processes of international treaty bodies and tribunals, but it also encompasses some political processes relating to international human rights and their enforcement. This book is concerned with international human rights law because defensive relativism is a response from a state to international human rights law and the existing or prospective obligations it imposes upon that state. Unlike cultural relativism, which may examine the origins of different moral practices in some societies, defensive relativism is a reaction from a state to an obligation in international law; hence it only really has life in the various forums or mechanisms for disputing obligations in international human rights law.

By international human rights law, this book mainly refers to three types of legal regime. Firstly, the major international human rights treaties, some of which codified the 1948 Universal Declaration of Human Rights (UDHR). These include the ICCPR and the 1966 International Covenant on Economic, Social, and Cultural Rights (ICESCR), collectively known as the International Bill of Human Rights.[40] Later human rights treaties such as CEDAW and the 1989 Convention on the Rights of the Child (CRC) contained much more complex formulations of rights and obligations as they aimed to address patterns of discrimination. In total, there are nine core human rights treaties which are open to all states to become party to them, and state performance under the treaties post-ratification is governed by expert panels known as treaty bodies.[41] These treaties oblige states to follow their terms as a matter of international treaty law. Under the framework of the 1969 Vienna Convention on the Law of Treaties (VCLT), state parties are meant to enter into a treaty in good faith and understand that they are under an obligation to implement its substantive terms.[42] The HRC, the treaty review body of the ICCPR, has interpreted this to mean that all levels of government are bound by the terms of a human rights treaty and are required to make "such changes to domestic laws and practices as are necessary" to comply with that treaty.[43] Concerns had been raised during the drafting of the ICCPR about the scope of limitations of rights that could be justified by an appeal to morality.[44] However, human rights treaties such as CEDAW are governed by the principle of legality, meaning that states are bound to follow the legal framework under the treaties in relation to the implementation and limitation of the substantive rights contained within them.[45]

The second institution is the case law and instruments of regional human rights tribunals. Regional human rights organizations vary considerably, but their basic feature is that their membership is restricted to states within a particular geographic region, and the tribunal often has a legal relationship to a regional organization promoting political or economic integration. The European Convention on Human Rights (ECHR) has a regional enforcement mechanism (which includes the ECtHR), with which member states are obliged to comply as a matter of international law. The relatively powerful nature of the ECtHR can be explained by its historical origins at the end of World War II and later by its role as a guarantor against totalitarian rule in Europe.[46] Other regional tribunals operated in a different context; the Inter-American Human Rights System evolved slowly, but by the 1990s the Inter-American Commission on Human Rights was regularly issuing decisions, including a number of decisions in connection with the regionally sensitive issue of human rights in states emerging from military rule. The other significant regional human rights tribunal—the African Commission on Human and Peoples' Rights—has a much more limited set of powers but, crucially, still has the right of individual petition and the capacity to issue decisions against states.[47] This is not the case with other regional human rights bodies such as the Association of Southeast Asian Nations (ASEAN's) Intergovernmental Commission on Human Rights, which, as chapter 4 shows, has no real powers to protect human rights. The third institution, the UN Human Rights Council, is not an institution with formal legal powers but has an important role in the development and protection of human rights. In particular, the Universal Periodic Review (UPR) process has, in the decade since its creation, played an increasingly important role in monitoring the implementation of human rights obligations through the review process and in encouraging states to adopt new human rights commitments or comply with existing commitments.

Defensive relativism occurs during the course of four separate established practices within these institutions. These practices describe an area where a defensive relativist argument may be raised by a state to justify the limitation, nonacceptance or nonimplementation of a particular right or set of rights. Firstly, state parties can use defensive relativism to justify a reservation to a treaty. Article 19 of the Vienna Convention on the Law of Treaties allows states to enter a reservation to a provision of a treaty entailing that the provision in question does not apply to that state.[48] The "object and purpose test" in international law requires that reservations not undermine a treaty's core purpose. If a reservation does so, it is considered impermissible and the state party is still expected to abide by that treaty's terms regardless of the reservations.[49] A version of the object and purpose test is employed by treaty review bodies, but is somewhat constrained in its effect by the nature of human rights treaties, which prioritize the inclusion of state parties and give treaty bodies limited powers to deal with impermissible reservations.[50] This means that treaty review bodies, and more recently the UPR process, try to encourage states to remove reservations through dialogic processes. Defensive relativist arguments manifest themselves either in the course of this process or in the text of reservations themselves.

The second and third practices both concern the justifications advanced by state parties either to explain limitations of rights or noncompliance with a treaty's substantive provisions. A number of the provisions containing substantive rights in human rights instruments contain either qualifications or limitation mechanisms allowing the state party some scope for implementing rights in a manner particular to its national legal and social traditions. Developed at the ECtHR, the margin of appreciation—the second practice where defensive relativism occurs—refers to the room for maneuver that international institutions are prepared to accord national authorities in discharging their human rights obligations, which gives states some latitude to interpret rights in line with national legal and cultural traditions.[51] The doctrine provides a framework for a tribunal to assess the validity and proportionality of the limitations imposed by states on the rights in a human rights instrument.[52] Protocol 15 of the ECHR has incorporated the doctrine into the text of the ECHR, and other human rights bodies have developed similar processes for scrutinizing the limitation of rights.[53] Defensive relativist arguments can be used to contest the limits of the margin of appreciation, arguing in essence that the state ought to be given an unlimited discretionary scope to apply certain rights as it wishes, to reflect its cultural traditions. In practical terms, this either takes the form of submissions by state parties before international tribunals or of arguments made by the representatives of state parties justifying their state's position in international forums more generally. In a similar fashion, defensive relativist arguments also appear when a state defends its nonimplementation of a particular right or noncompliance before human rights institutions. The defense of nonimplementation and noncompliance—the third practice where defensive relativism occurs—can be seen in state reports to treaty bodies and in the interactive dialogue between states and treaty bodies or at the UPR. In both of these practices, a state is not seeking to change, withdraw, or decline to become a party to a particular instrument, but rather wishes to remain party to that instrument while claiming a form of legal exemption from complying with a particular obligation or provision.

The fourth type of state practice concerns the acceptance or creation of new legal obligations or institutions. The process of creating new instruments or institutions protecting human rights is referred to in some of the literature as organization or regime design, and it describes how states shape future legal regimes according to a variety of different preferences.[54] Within this process, states can create legal regimes to acknowledge their relativistic preferences, effectively enshrining defensive relativism into the framework of an international instrument. This can create a regime with limited scope for protecting rights, but one which preserves the outward signs of a rights instrument and organization. As with other practices, there is the possibility with this type of practice that defensive relativism's impact is to weaken its capacity for rights protection.

Other areas of international law have also experienced states using relativistic arguments in relation to existing or prospective legal obligations. One of the lawyers who helped shape the 1948 Genocide Convention, Raphael Lemkin, became increasingly skeptical of the way states attempted to use forms of nationalist relativism to resist the universal nature of the convention.[55] As recent histories have noted, the development of the Genocide Convention was characterized by the fourth type of defensive relativist practice from the Soviet Union, which tried to shape the obligations in the convention in a way that would minimize its obligations.[56] Contemporary international criminal law, both at regional human rights tribunals and the International Criminal Court (ICC), has also had states use relativist arguments in a variety of different ways.[57] Even when regional tribunals were specifically constructed to adapt to the country in question, as Jane Stromseth describes it, they often were seen as "alien spaceships."[58] All of this describes the complexities of realizing universal legal principles on the ground. Some studies on environmental law, particularly in relation to human rights and the environment, have noted relativistic objections from states.[59] Kathryn Hochstetler, Ann Marie Clark, and Elisabeth Friedman's study, which analyzed state behavior at the 1992 United Nations Conference on Environment and Development, in Rio; the 1993 World Conference on Human Rights, in Vienna; and the 1995 World Conference on Women, in Beijing, noted how states fused together their cultural concerns and sovereignty in a similar fashion across the different conferences.[60]

Many of the themes discussed in this book can be seen in other relativistic discourse. Defensive relativism is, however, specific to international human rights law, in part because of its subject matter—it attempts to shape social policy in order to protect rights—but also because the universality of international human rights instruments attempts to fuse together moral objectivity with legal obligation.[61] International human rights law's legal processes also create a functional system of monitoring and opportunities for the contestations of interpretations of rights, which, as chapters 1 and 3 outline, either allow individuals to contest a state's domestic laws on human rights, or allow international human rights bodies to provide some form of qualitative judgment on a state's restrictions of human rights. The practical impact of this can be quite limited, but it challenges an important conception of state sovereignty triggering a reaction from states. The tension between an international institution and state sovereignty is what distinguishes defensive relativism from relativistic argument in constitutional courts—the state is defending its sovereignty in the process of international legal argument. Other areas of international law often involve cultural relativism, but, as discussed in chapter 8, it is the system of argument and specific version of defending sovereignty caused by international human rights law which distinguishes defensive relativism.

Defining Defensive Relativism: Some Clarifications and Caveats

Defensive relativism is the state practice of a particular kind of cultural relativism in response to a prospective or existing international legal obligation requiring a state to protect human rights that consists of three basic elements. Firstly, defensive relativists claim that supranational or extracultural human rights standards must be resisted, not because of their content but because of their attempt to formulate universal standards. Secondly, defensive relativism maintains that a state's self-defined cultural standards are the only relevant ethical standards. It is this construction of culture that defensive relativism defends. Finally, defensive relativism is a legal practice, so the antiuniversalism and state-constructed culture in a state's arguments are instrumental in delivering a specific set of legal outcomes. In this sense, it is important to understand a defensive relativist's antiuniversalist arguments not as statements of fact about the world, and their arguments about culture not as an account of the value of a tradition in a particular society, but as pillars of a case advocating a tangible result, such as justifying a reservation to a human rights treaty. Unlike cultural relativism in a philosophical sense, as outlined above, which aims to challenge dominant or ethnocentric assumptions about culture and values, defensive relativism has a distinct, practical end goal. This is a summary of the practice of defensive relativism as one would observe it in an international organization such as the UN Human Rights Council. Yet, it is important to set out five caveats and clarifications to the arguments advanced in this book about the nature and existence of defensive relativism.

Firstly, to utilize Upendra Baxi's terminology from *Human Rights in a Posthuman World*, defensive relativism is not a "theory of human rights"; it is a "theory about human rights." A theory of human rights, Baxi argues, is a social theory that "attends primarily to the ethical" and foundational questions of human rights, such as where they come from and to whom they apply, and which rights should have hierarchy over others.[62] Relativism, as it is often discussed in relation to human rights, often concerns these questions. A theory about human rights, Baxi argues, is a social theory of rights examining their legal form in the "jurdico-political sphere" and how rights protection develops within an institutional framework.[63] Crucially, a theory about rights assumes that many of the questions posed by theories of human rights, such as the ethical foundations or the historical basis of rights, are, as Baxi puts it, "rather well done," and the essential issue in understanding how rights affect a society is their legal form.[64] Relativists and critical theorists of human rights might well object to such a distinction, noting that the legal form of human rights is inseparably linked to the origins of human rights. Yet defensive relativism only really exists in relation to international human rights law and the legal forms it currently occupies. Almost all states are party to one or more of the nine major international human rights treaties, and as consequence it is reasonable to assume that most states have concluded that human rights law is of some importance, regardless of its origins, and that the major issues are the form, scope, and nature of the states' duties which flow from those treaties.[65] Thinking of defensive relativism as a theory about human rights law does not negate the importance of questions about the origins of rights, the holder of rights, or whether the juridical forms of rights are appropriate as vehicles to protect human interests. Rather, when seeking to understand defensive relativism, it is important to keep in mind that it does not concern these issues but is a theory about the law and its application.

The issue of how the law should be applied raises the question of what international human rights law is for, which introduces the second caveat/clarification. This book takes the position that international human rights law is an important means of constraining the state in order to protect the dignity, desires, and interests of the individual, although in this role it is far from perfect. Many of the arguments presented in this book about limiting the scope of human rights law made by states by implication involve strengthening the power of the state at the expense of the individual or group. Human rights in their legal form, Andrew Vincent argues, are part of the "configuration of the civil state" either because the ability to use rights against the state guarantees the ability to access other rights (in the sense that Hannah Arendt talked of the "right to have rights") or because the rights act as a constitutional form of self-limitation to state power.[66] As the nation state was exported through colonialism and decolonization, and, crucially, states participate in the international system through a system of international law predicated on the sovereignty and power of the nation state, the concept of rights being tools against the state can therefore be utilized in a variety of different cultural contexts.[67] International human rights law has also expanded to protect a wide range of different interests that go significantly beyond the narrow liberal paradigm in which human rights came into being in late eighteenth-century Europe.[68] For example, the 1989 Convention on the Rights of the Child contains rights protecting the material security of the child, a child's right to health and education, and a variety of collective rights pertaining to children.[69] This was, in part, a reflection of the concerns of states from the Global South who had long argued that human rights did not meet the needs of developing states. Rights also need commitment from states for their implementation, and consequences for their nonimplementation, in order for any protection of individual interests to be meaningful—otherwise the very notion of rights becomes a meaningless piece of political terminology devoid of all substantive content.[70] The notion that there exists a tension between the rights of the individual and the state can, according to critical legal theorists, preclude the possibility of potentially radical political solutions to social issues and can result in the ossification of political power in the legal form of rights.[71] However, while there are many informative critiques of the nature of rights, with which some relativist texts have engaged directly, international human rights law concerns the power of the state and what the state ought to do with that power; therefore an analysis of any limitation of rights from that perspective is appropriate, as it reflects what can loosely be described as the overall function of international human rights law.

Thirdly, and related to the above caveat/clarification, defensive relativism needs to be situated in relation to attempts to reprioritize or reform human rights law, or literature critical of the notion of human rights law. It is possible for there to be a genuinely local or regional conception of human rights, differing from the existing cannon of international human rights law that protects individuals, and giving a distinct sense of regional ownership to human rights. One notable example is the 1981 African Charter on Human and Peoples' Rights (ACHPR), which contains alternate formulations of rights prioritizing collective rights and conceptions of communal duty in its substantive provisions.[72] There is a range of scholarship, discussed in chapter 2, inspired by Alison Dundes Renteln's work arguing that in order create a genuinely universal concept of human rights, cross-cultural research should be undertaken to examine equivalent practices across different societies that may then form the basis for a new form of universality.[73] This work seeks to offer a template for answering much of the criticism cultural relativists have had with the origins of human rights law, but it is not an account of state practice within international human rights law.

Defensive relativism is not principally concerned with the reprioritization of human rights as much as it is concerned with defending existing state laws and justifying restrictions on human rights. Although states practicing defensive relativism might tactically suggest that reprioritization or reform of human rights are important to pursue defensive relativist aims, they use the language of rights to undermine their protection; an example of this is the ASEAN Human Rights Declaration discussed in chapter 4. This is problematic, as the term "human rights," by invoking the legal notion of a right, infers the existence of enforcement, and the creation of a legal framework that has no intention of doing this weakens the overall political cache of human rights law.[74] Equally, while critical theories of human rights, such as those outlined above, highlight the way human rights are abused by sources of power, this is not, as chapter 7 makes clear, something for which defensive relativism provides a solution, as it simply advocates the replacement of the imperfection of human rights with the limitations of a state-defined culture. The principal role of defensive relativism, as demonstrated in chapters 4 and 6 and at other points in part I of the book, is to protect the role of a state's power and its current practices from the notional protection offered by international human rights law to individuals and marginalised communities. Therefore, while there might be a case to argue, as William Paul Simmons does, that human rights law ought to be deconstructed and refounded within the struggles of the "marginalised other" in society, it is not clear that defensive relativism is a meaningful part of such an exercise.[75]

Fourthly, defensive relativism is a type of argument which appears in a number of different legal practices, such as the application of the margin of appreciation, the interpretation of treaties, and the consideration of the permissability of reservations, all topics where there is a burgeoning doctrinal and critical literature. At several points, some of the discussions raised in this literature will be engaged with, and in a few areas developed, but this book does not have the room to contribute to all of these particular debates, absent identifying how the three elements of defensive relativism appear within certain legal practices. For example, the debate over the process and limits of evolutive interpretations of treaties, engaged with in chapter 3, is wide ranging, but its consideration is mainly focused on states using relativistic arguments to dispute the court's use of this method of interpretation.[76] But, defensive relativism's existence within the law also speaks to the way in which international law has constructed a form of belief system in which broader philosophical contestations of the meaning of the universality of human rights and the legitimacy of cultural practices are fought out in legal language and frameworks. As Jean d'Aspremont argues, international law can be characterized as a form of self-referential belief system which allows lawyers to claim that international law is based on the functioning of fundamental doctrines whose authority is, in essence, circular.[77] Self-referentiality has given international legal forms both an epistemic and discursive power, and states behave in a manner that acts as though the outcome of legal argument matters.[78] This means that international human rights law's role as law encourages states to treat its structures and institutions as authoritative. Even if the compliance mechanism of a given international regime is weak, or there is a high degree of noncompliance, being seen to fulfill international legal commitments, as Onuma Yasuaki argues, plays an important external communicative function for a state.[79] International legal commitments of all types are an important mechanism for legitimating states in the eyes of other states, and as a consequence some degree of convergence of interests between a state and a human rights regime can occur from the mere fact of participation in a regime, even though there might be noncompliance in certain areas.[80] As outlined in the final chapter of this book, there are political reasons connected with a state's reputation as to why states value being party to international human rights treaties and try to avoid becoming noncompliant with human rights regimes.[81] Hence, defensive relativism is both evidence of the belief, from the state practicing defensive relativism, of the authority of international human rights law and a recognition of the of the impossibility of human rights instruments to fully realize juridical universality. As an argument, defensive relativism is tactical; it is a tool for maintaining notional legality and compliance with human rights law on the international plane while avoiding making domestic social changes to certain traditions which interfere with the realization of human rights.

Finally, the perspective of defensive relativism focuses on the limitations of human rights "from above," as it is a state practice in international human rights law. There is a significant literature on what is termed "human rights from below," a term describing how social movements within countries can advance human rights and even use the language of international human rights law to achieve particular social outcomes.[82] Some theoretical and empirical models of how state behavior changes to protect human rights acknowledge the role of human rights "from below."[83] Relativistic arguments can come into this literature to understand both the limits of human rights law's universalism and the role that alternative practices can play in protecting the same interests that human rights law protects. Yet, for the purposes of assessing defensive relativism, human rights "from below" are only relevant insofar as they are reflected in, or alter a state's human rights practice at, the international level, and that is the lens through which this book will consider any human rights movements "from below." This raises a related issue of how representative governments are when they claim that a right is incompatible with a cultural practice of their state. At first glance, it would seem that a government is performing a notionally democratic function if, say, 70 percent of its population disagrees with the existence of a particular right. The fact that this objection might overlap with a tradition that has deep historical and cultural roots is often highlighted as being of particular significance by defensive relativists. Yet at its core, this argument simply acknowledges the existence of a specific pro-violation constituency within a state, and is a common argument made by all sorts of governments claiming that a particular right should be restricted in their country.[84] For example, for many years (prior to 2018) the Irish government maintained that there was widespread support, as evidenced by a 1983 referendum on the issue, for a prohibition on access to abortion in the country, due to its incompatibility with the country's interpretation of Catholic traditions. Even though the HRC found that this violated the right of women to be free from inhuman and degrading treatment and to access medical care, the Irish government maintained its position.[85] Equally, the Egyptian government maintained that reservations to CEDAW allowing for the restriction of the rights of women in matrimonial proceedings were based in Sharia law, and thus implicitly enjoyed the support of large numbers of population.[86]

The point is that governments of all types of can point toward the existence of a pro-violation constituency of some form or another as a justification for restricting certain rights, in the same way that all governments can cite security concerns for committing certain abuses of rights. Given that the protection of rights in international human rights law is not governed by individual national plebiscites on the acceptance of each individual right, it is not clear why a willingness to limit rights in a manner that goes far beyond what is proportionate or justified in international human rights law should be accorded special status if such a restriction happens to be justified within a cultural framework or by reference to prevailing cultural sentiment. As chapter 3 demonstrates, from a legal perspective, there is nothing necessarily different or exceptional about these arguments being given this added dimension. In the same way that a state ought not to be able to raise "national security" or "the popular will" as a blanket justification for restricting a particular right, there are ample grounds for believing that "cultural tradition" should be treated the same way. Again, to return to the refrain of the third caveat/clarification, it is perfectly possible to argue that international human rights law ought to be changed to become more democratically grounded, but that is slightly beyond the scope of this book. In any event, it is not clear that defensive relativism would necessarily come to the aid of anyone making such an argument.

The Structure of This Book

In recent years, the scholarly consideration of cultural relativism in human rights law has retreated somewhat. In part, this is because some work has demonstrated that the concerns relativists have had about the universalizing nature of rights has been addressed by accounts of universality that accommodate differences and disagreement about moral values.[87] Others have argued that the sharp distinction between relativism and universalism is either conceptually unwieldy or that there are models of human rights practice that can be adopted to circumnavigate the practical problems posed by attempting to implement human rights law universally.[88] As a result, there has been some speculation as to whether there has been a broader change in state practice. Jack Donnelly has argued that, in the 1980s, when "vicious dictators regularly appealed to culture to justify their depredations," it was necessary to adopt perhaps an "over-heavy emphasis on universalism."[89] Donnelly's "over-heavy" reliance on universalism in his 1980s work was critiqued by Alison Dundes Renteln for its "unnecessarily rigid view" of rights as an exclusively Western concept and for its restrictive approach to the content of rights.[90] By 2007, however, Donnelly felt justified in developing an "account that gives somewhat greater emphasis to the limits of universalism" because, as he notes, "few states today directly challenge international human rights . . . [and] contend that large portions of the Universal Declaration do not apply to them."[91] Yet the assumption that fewer states contend that human rights apply to them ought to be challenged—these arguments still exist, albeit in much subtler forms, and have been institutionalised within new legal frameworks.

Writing in 1997, Rhoda Howard looked ahead to human rights in the next century and warned that there was a "real danger that culturalist social movements [would] have increasing influence," and that, were they to ally with various kinds of "authoritarian governments," they would be able to supress human rights, claiming them to be an "inauthentic, non-indigenous, Western cultural imposition."[92] Howard was partially correct in predicting that "culture wars" would continue to be a factor in arguments about the universality of human rights, but missed the form that this would take.[93] In the 1990s, when significant scholarly attention was paid to cultural relativism's response to human rights, there was also a growth in ratification of the core human rights treaties.[94] Human rights bodies at the regional level became more influential, with the European Court of Human Rights acquiring compulsory jurisdiction in the 1990s, and reform of the UN human rights system in the 2000s leading to the creation of the UN Human Rights Council. The growth of formal legal structures surrounding human rights, the increase in treaty ratification, and the growing importance of demonstrating human rights compliance as a mark of legitimate statehood both increased the political importance of compliance with human rights law and the incentive of states to seek out legal ways of limiting the scope of their legal obligations while remaining human rights-compliant. In the 2010s there was a growing body of literature about the concept of "backlash" to human rights law which touched on some of these developments.[95] But the use of culturally relativist arguments in legal forms to try and resist international human rights law had been going on for some time prior to this, with the arguments over CEDAW reservations in the mid-1980s arguably being the first major episode of defensive relativism.

This book's core thesis is that defensive relativism—the state practice of cultural relativism—is and remains an important phenomenon in international human rights law, which can significantly limit its capacity to protect individuals and groups. In this respect, the claims defensive relativists make are not indistinct from other arguments made in favor of restricting rights—as David Penna and Patricia Campbell noted, along with concepts such as "zealotry, patriotism or ultra-nationalism," governments can use the concepts of "culture" or "tradition" in a manner that is a "danger to human rights."[96] The arguments between universalists and relativists, Adamantia Pollis cautions, often ignore the "role of the modern state in defining the rights of and for its people," and claims of culture made by states are often used to "rationalize the arbitrary exercise of power."[97] All states, regardless of whether they are Western or non-Western, have the potential to engage in defensive relativism, in the same way that all states may make claims to limit rights in the name of security. Defensive relativism is, as the final chapter of this book argues, a phenomenon generated in response to international human rights law's attempts to balance the complex and contradictory claims of modern sovereignty and universal rights. This is not to say that all states are defensive relativists; rather, that the capacity exists for such behavior in all states. Because defensive relativism emerges in response to international human rights law, most of its examples occur after the growth in the ratification of human rights instruments in the 1990s, and most of the examples and case studies in this book look at the first two decades of the twenty-first century. Whether defensive relativism occurs or not is down to a number of factors, such as a state's internal political situation and the nature of right being disputed. Defensive relativism is not a "bug" in international human rights law; it is inherent to the entire project of constructing a functioning legal regime to deliver universal rights.

Part I of this book sets out the three crucial components of defensive relativism. Each chapter examines the philosophical basis of each of these arguments in turn, looking first at their intellectual origin and then at examples in practice, at treaty bodies, tribunals, and other international organizations. Firstly, as chapter 1 sets out, defensive relativism is antiuniversalist in that it attacks the notion that human rights law or particular types of rights can have a truly universal application. Antiuniversalism comes from two sources: anticolonialism, which is specific to defensive relativism from states in the Global South or with a history of Western intervention, or anticosmopolitanism, which is common to all states and built on the notion that international human rights law promotes a particular political agenda. The second component of defensive relativism, chapter 2 argues, is a state-constructed culture—which is what defensive relativism "defends." State-constructed culture describes a state's definition of its moral values, which are presented as static and closed to outside influence. It is linked to a state's overall sovereignty because, as this chapter shows, when a state defends cultural values, it is in fact referring to its domestic laws and practices. This makes defensive relativism a means of defending state sovereignty in international law, which, as chapter 3 demonstrates, takes a specific legal form. Defensive relativism aims to use existing frameworks of legal arguments or processes to achieve a form of exemption for a state from its obligations in international human rights law. It is the presence of all three of these features that differentiates defensive relativism from other arguments about international law, and from cultural relativism in wider social and academic discourse. In these chapters, a distinction is drawn between the theoretical basis of an argument, as expressed in academic literature, and the manifestation of the argument in state practice in international law, in an attempt to form a coherent sketch of the core elements of defensive relativism.

Part II looks at three case studies of defensive relativism from the 2010s, which move away from the examples discussed in part I. All of these case studies highlight how different groups of states use defensive relativism in a particular legal practice and demonstrate how defensive relativism is an ongoing contemporary concern. Chapter 4 looks at the formation of the ASEAN Intergovernmental Commission on Human Rights in the late 2000s to show how defensive relativism was used in the process of designing a legal regime. Chapter 5 examines cases involving freedom of religion before the ECtHR to show how states use defensive relativism in their submissions to international tribunals. This chapter discusses the so-called "burqa-ban" cases from France and Belgium, demonstrating both how state parties to the ECHR can use secularism as a form of state culture.[98] Chapter 6 examines the rejection and acceptance of recommendations in the UPR process at the Human Rights Council in the 2010s concerning impermissible reservations to human rights treaties and the use of defensive relativist arguments in this process.

Part III of this book looks at the practical role of defensive relativism in international human rights law. Chapter 7 situates defensive relativism within the debates had by both philosophers and practitioners about the reform of human rights law. Defensive relativism, while enjoying a seemingly superficial relationship with some of these debates, is in fact distinct from all of them due to its principal tactical function of defending state sovereignty within the framework of international human rights law. In chapter 8, the meaning of defensive relativism's defense of sovereignty is unpacked with reference to different concepts of sovereignty. The role of human rights institutions in evaluating whether a state has fulfilled a particular obligation can be in tension with a state's domestic-legal sovereignty, which is intimately connected to conceptions of a state culture. But states often wish to remain in a human rights regime because of the benefits to their interactional sovereignty, such as the reputational benefits of being members of a human rights regime. Defensive relativism, as this chapter argues, reconciles the tension between the two types of sovereignty. The different varieties of defensive relativist argument all implicitly or explicitly lead to the conclusion that human rights law should operate in a manner which is completely deferential to state interests, but which still retains the notional frameworks and labels of human rights law. Yet, as the conclusion outlines, while defensive relativism is an inherent and possibly necessary feature of human rights law, it does not need to operate in the way that defensive relativists might want it to. The book concludes by sketching out some ideas for human rights practitioners to engage with and to use in managing defensive relativism.

In analyzing defensive relativism, one needs to be conscious of Renteln's warning that ratification of an international instrument by a state should not mean acceptance of the legitimacy of rights in society.[99] In some cases, defensive relativist arguments are very popular, and in some societies, certain rights do not enjoy widespread legitimacy. But this can be the case with many human rights issues. For example, in many societies there is a reasonably high degree of support (sometimes among up to 40 percent of the public) for torturing terrorists in certain circumstances.[100] Even in societies such as the United Kingdom, where polling shows a notionally high level of respect for rights, such as the right to a fair trial, in cases involving terrorist suspects there is considerable support for removing these rights.[101] In circumstances such as these, it would be relatively easy to make the case that protecting the human rights of terrorists and terrorist suspects does not enjoy broad-based legitimacy. Whether a right is considered legitimate in society is not the same as arguing that that right ought to be considered legitimate or that it is important to protect the rights of a particular group. Defensive relativism doesn't often involve rights relating to questions of life-or-death issues, as counterterrorism does, but often involves questions about who can get married and which religious symbols people can wear in public. These are issues which can be steeped in traditions but which are also fundamental to a person or a community's entire well-being. It is completely beyond the scope of this book to provide or advocate for a comprehensive sketch of what a "good life" is or what should be important for individuals, but the protection of very basic rights, such as the right to privacy, intersects with the wider philosophical and political questions behind how a society operates. While the role of international human rights law as a form of law has been criticized for turning the entire notion of human rights into a quasi-disciplinary framework, it nevertheless exists as a body of law which can afford a measure of protection to individuals.[102] The extent to which a state complies with the law, implementing and realizing rights, can therefore be assessed in relation to the frameworks and parameters set out by human rights law, as imperfect as such a scheme of law may ultimately be.

PART I

Defining Defensive Relativism

CHAPTER 1

The First Element of Defensive Relativism: Antiuniversalism

As World War II entered its third year on 1 January 1942, the "Declaration by the United Nations" was signed in Washington, DC, committing Britain, the United States, and the Soviet Union, along with twenty other states, to work for "complete victory over their enemies."[1] The declaration was a simple statement of war aims but looked beyond the war's end, committing the allies to preserving "human rights and justice in their own lands as well as in other lands." This marked the beginning of universalism in international human rights law—the idea that human rights ought to apply to everyone, regardless of the country in which they live. The declaration was one of many instruments and summits culminating in the conference of the United Nations in May 1945, which opened the UN Charter for signature on 26 June 1945. There was no real reference in the declaration as to why human rights should be applied in all states. Instead, it was simply taken as a given; human rights would apply in all states because it was part of a new international order of which human rights was an essential component, which was being imposed because the allies had won the war.

After 1948 and the passage of the Universal Declaration of Human Rights (UDHR), through the UN General Assembly the promotion of human rights was characterized by a growing emphasis upon the universality of human rights as derived from a natural law tradition. Opposition to human rights law from Soviet states in the 1940s and 1950s was sometimes predicated not on a disagreement with the principle that rights could be universal but rather on the nature of the rights protected. The Soviets objected to the lack of material protections in human rights law and the separation of economic social and cultural rights from civil and political rights. Serious criticism of universality began in 1968 at the first International Conference on Human Rights, where many newly independent states from Africa and Asia were openly skeptical of the universal application of human rights across different societies.[2] This challenge probed the unresolved philosophical tension that had remained dormant in international human rights law—why should human rights be applied in every single state and society? The technical requirements of structuring international instruments brought this tension to the fore in the drafting and ratification of human rights treaties and at the UN Commission on Human Rights in the 1970s and 1980s. At the second World Conference on Human Rights in 1993, the Vienna Declaration and Programme of Action reaffirmed the universalism of human rights but included a clause directly recognizing the role of cultural relativism in the implementation of human rights.[3]

As set out in the introductory chapter, the state practice of cultural relativism in international law—defensive relativism—has three core elements to it: antiuniversalism, a state-constructed culture, and legal exceptionalism. This chapter looks at the first of these elements, antiuniversalism—the opposition to the idea that the values contained in international human rights law should be applied universally. Antiuniversalism is different from a defense of culture or tradition, and that element of defensive relativism—state constructed culture—will be covered in the next chapter. Antiuniversalism describes the arguments made by state parties that problematize or attack the assumptions behind the provisions in international human rights law requiring its universal application. These arguments are, to a large extent, rooted in the structure and origins of contemporary international human rights law. As the protagonists of defensive relativism are the governments of states and state representatives to international organizations, different examples of antiuniversalism from treaty bodies or international discussions about the creation of legal obligations show antiuniversalism at work. Sometimes there is a deeper philosophical basis to some of the arguments advanced by state parties, but defensive relativism is primarily a reaction to the obligations imposed by international human rights law. Whether antiuniversalism can ever be successfully answered or counteracted by the creation of new forms of human rights instruments is a subject for discussion later in the book. This chapter instead focuses on unpicking the nature of antiuniversalism by first addressing how universality is framed in international human rights law before going on to examine the different strands of antiuniversalist argument.

The Meaning of Universality

Universalism describes the process of making human rights applicable to all people within a state. Human rights instruments usually contain statements of universality within their provisions outlining a state's duty under that instrument; for example, Article 2 of the International Covenant on Civil and Political Rights (ICCPR) requires signatory states to "respect and to ensure to all individuals within its territory and subject to its jurisdiction the rights recognized in the present Covenant."[4] This means that as a matter of law a state party to the ICCPR needs to fulfill the terms of Article 2. It is a juridical statement of universalism because it declares what a state should do to make rights apply to everyone in its jurisdiction. The legal obligation on a state to do this arises out of the principle of *pacta sunt servanda* in international law, which requires that states implement treaties in good faith. In practice, compliance with all of the terms of a human rights treaty is normally of a somewhat patchwork nature, but the assumption is that, as a matter of law, a state will implement all the terms of a treaty unless it has entered a valid reservation to a particular treaty provision or is granted some form of opt-out, because it has consented to the treaty by the act of signature and ratification.[5]

Beyond international and regional human rights treaties there are obligations that are binding on states without their consent, such *jus cogens* norms. These are norms protecting rights often considered core human rights, such as the prohibition of slavery, torture, and genocide.[6] In justifying their obligatory status, the judges at the International Court of Justice (ICJ) have often used language highlighting the importance of *jus cogens* norms to the international community, describing them alternately as the "collective juridical conscience" of the international community or as necessary for international public policy.[7] Formulations such as these explain the juridical universality of *jus cogens* in terms of their functional necessity for the effective functioning of the international legal order. Constructivist theories of international law and international relations have highlighted how norms and the maintenance of norm-based behavior are vital to maintain interstate interactions.[8] Universality is also a feature of international criminal law which attempts to maintain that certain actions should be treated as criminal no matter the cultural context and is a feature of the instruments underpinning institutions such as the International Criminal Court (ICC).[9]

However, statements or provisions on universality in international instruments explain why there is a legal obligation on a state to either realize a particular set of rights in its jurisdiction, desist from a particular practice, or undertake a particular course of action. It does not necessarily explain why a particular set of rights ought to be universally applicable. This is the difference between juridical universalism and justificatory universalism. Behind the juridical universalism of a human rights instrument, Seyla Benhabib argues, there is a justificatory universalism which seeks to explain why rights should be applied across all societies.[10] Yet international human rights law does not always draw such a distinction; as Philip Alston describes it, the international human rights legal regime has been characterized "by a determined, and often single-minded, commitment to universality," which has drawn "strong support from the ranks of those victims of oppression" but has not necessarily resolved the underlying issue of why rights ought to be universal.[11] Almost inadvertently, this viewpoint led to a strong emphasis being placed on the fact of the ratification of a human rights instrument as proof or evidence of the universality of the rights contained within that instrument.[12] This is, however, insufficient to account for an instrument's legitimacy because, as Alison Renteln explains, treaty ratification is often undertaken by the governmental elites in pursuit of specific political interests; there is no express obligation on elites to adopt a particular philosophy about the importance of rights.[13]

To assess the justificatory universalism behind legal obligations, it is necessary to distinguish the universal aspiration and the universal realization of human rights. Universal aspiration is the idea that rights *ought* to be or should be universal. The preamble to the UDHR contains a statement of universal aspiration, where it states that human rights are a "common standard of achievement for all peoples and nations."[14] At the time of the UDHR's drafting, the preamble was justified in terms of human rights being a shared utopian project for the betterment of humanity.[15] In 1945, over twenty-five states called for the creation of a bill of rights to be part of the UN and saw such an instrument as vital for the future functioning of the organization. The justification for this kind of universalism, Benhabib argues, can be found through a "discourse-theoretic framework," which reasons that all humans ought to have rights because of a "moral universalism" based on "equal respect for the other [human] as a being capable of communicative freedom."[16] This is a cosmopolitan form of reasoning that is broadly teleological in its declarative statements—it explains the basis for rights being universal, or for why they ought to be universal, without necessarily providing a rationalization or justification for how they became or can become universal.[17]

This justification is, however, specific to the UDHR and the circumstances of its creation. Between 1945 and 1948, there was a relatively high degree of international consensus on both the importance of human rights and the necessity of a rule-based order. Subsequent international human rights instruments utilized slightly different justifications for their universality. For example, the preamble to the Convention on the Elimination of All Forms of Discrimination against Women (CEDAW) acknowledges the importance of the UDHR and other human rights before noting, "despite these various instruments extensive discrimination against women continues to exist."[18] Because of that discrimination, the preamble continues, "the welfare of the world and the cause of peace require the maximum participation of women on equal terms with men in all fields."[19] CEDAW, therefore, uses a much more specific set of justifications than those used for UDHR, as it is predicated on acknowledging systemic discrimination against women and the necessity of its elimination. This emerged out of a growing international movement at the UN in the 1970s aimed at recognizing the importance of eliminating discrimination against women in order to help states develop economically and politically; in some states, feminist movements were successful at getting their governments to adopt the elimination of discrimination against women as a priority to pursue in international human rights law.[20]

The arguments used to construct the justificatory universalism of a particular human rights instrument are often a reflection of the ideological assumptions behind that instrument. As Wade Mansell and Karen Openshaw argue, human rights can "never be a politically neutral concept," and arguments about the content of human rights or the application of human rights law are often subject to the "economic interests and ideology" of those "making or rejecting demands in connection with such rights."[21] The process of establishing the justificatory universality of a particular human rights instrument, therefore, is an ideological contestation, although it is often not treated as such. As Renteln notes, the philosophical foundations of international human rights treaties are often not adequately demonstrated, and natural law reasoning in the Western philosophical tradition is simply assumed to be the basis of human rights instruments.[22]

International law is not merely an ideological treatise or manifesto, as it presents legal norms, principles, and rules as superior to other international political norms because of the legal obligations imposed upon states to implement those principles.[23] Contesting justificatory universalism is therefore a necessary part of contesting the juridical universalism of a human rights instrument and the legal obligation that entails. As justificatory universalist arguments are, in essence, arguments about why a particular scheme of morality ought to be universally applied through a system of international human rights law, this makes culturally relativist arguments, which contend that the authority of moral norms is relative to time and place, vitally important.[24] After all, if it can be successfully established as a matter of principle that there is no universal moral consensus in a particular area, it becomes much easier to argue that it is not necessary to fully comply with a legal obligation designed to protect the rights that are a component of that moral consensus. This argument gains a lot more traction given the consent-orientated legal framework of much of international human rights law.[25] States can argue that they acknowledge certain rights or certain interpretations on the scope of rights as being universal, through the process of entering reservations or applying limitations to rights when implementing them in domestic law.[26]

Technically, defensive relativism is not a clash between universal values and culturally relative values but rather a clash over moral realism. Moral realists maintain there are some objective moral facts and that particular factual scenarios or situations have the properties of "wrongness," and therefore can and should be judged as wrong.[27] Realism does not entail that all moral disputes between different value systems are not genuine, but maintains that in some situations, other systems may use moral terms in a way that shows those systems are, as Mark Balaguer puts it, "simply mistaken about what the moral facts are."[28] An international human rights instrument, by containing both a justificatory universal reference to why the rights within it ought to be universal and a juridically universal reference as to why there is a legal obligation to implement those rights, is an instrument of moral realism. A defensive relativist seeks to advance their own alternate moral realism pertaining to a particular situation or practice seemingly threatened by international law. It is therefore necessary for defensive relativists to implicitly challenge the justificatory universality of international human rights law, which, as Jack Donnelly states, gives "priority to the demands of the cosmopolitan moral community" over any one particular community.[29] Defensive relativists use two broad lines of argument to challenge the justificatory universalism of international human rights law, which are considered in turn later in this chapter. The first line of argument challenges the origins of universality in international law more generally, focusing on international law's association with colonial imperialism and draws a direct line between the origins of universality in sixteenth-century international law and contemporary international human rights law. The second line of argument maintains that universality in international human rights law is in fact a cover for a political project, or that international human rights law is smuggling in political values under the guise of universal rights.

Anticolonialism and Antiuniversality: Criticism of the Origins of Universality in International Human Rights Law

The universal ordering of the world into different territories, which was an important part of colonialism, allowed the projection of a universal morality across cultures.[30] What Carl Schmitt termed the nomos of colonialism, which "considered Christian nations to be the creators and representatives of an order applicable to the whole earth," allowed for the construction of a universal law to regulate and control the nomos.[31] A basic history of Western colonization, Neil Levy argues, reveals that in many cases "exploitation [was] often justified by invoking morality," which is the basis of the "colonial origins" school of antiuniversalism.[32] This is essentially an argument trapped in human rights origins, concluding either that a line can be drawn from colonialist universality through to present day international human rights law or that the idea of universality involves a projection against a constituted other—often non-Western states or non-Western societies. Both variants of this argument are used interchangeably by defensive relativists, although this variation of the antiuniversalist argument applies principally to non-Western states or postcolonial states.

To understand the "colonial-trace" argument, it is important to understand the early development of international law in relation to the colonization of the Americas. The sixteenth-century legal theorist Francisco de Vitoria used an early version of universality in his writings when he argued that although indigenous Americans were "barbarians and as a consequence slaves" they should not excluded from the human race even though they "were of a lower status"; they should be protected and civilized.[33] Here began the association between the civilizing mission of colonial-imperialism and juridical universality. Manuel Barreto notes that Bartolomé de Las Casas, a Dominican monk writing in the sixteenth century, created the concept of universal jurisdiction specifically to oppose other writers who justified the slaughter of indigenous Americans by the conquistadors.[34] Las Casas was involved in the debate at the

Council of the Indies in Valladolid in 1550 on the status of the natives of the New World, and there argued strongly for their protection under the law.[35] Yet as Michael Hardt and Antonio Negri observe, Las Casas's reasoning was based in part on the idea that the indigenous Americans could be converted to Christianity and therefore saved.[36] Vitoria took a different approach to dealing with the status of the new territories as he argued that there was a new form of secular law created and administered by the Spanish sovereign. This usurped the role of the Pope and divine law and essentially rooted the emerging doctrine of international law in the European sovereign.[37] Later writers on international law, such as the seventeenth-century Dutch theorist Hugo Grotius, who envisaged the creation of international law in natural terms, argued that international law was universally applicable, as it was a reflection of the natural order of states—although the states in question were European states.[38]

There is evidence of this Eurocentric notion of universality permeating into international human rights law. The UDHR's creation was motivated in part by the legacy of the Second World War and the horror of the Holocaust, but this motivation and cultural sense of guilt was located primarily in the experience of European states, which was not directly shared by postcolonial states.[39] For example, Article 30 of the UDHR was a rights abuse clause, which was specifically designed to prevent totalitarian political movements using the rights of political participation and free speech to gain power in a democratic society. This was a largely European concern and was an issue that was dealt with in the laws of many European states.[40] In the ICCPR's drafting process the inclusion of a rights abuse clause was justified largely in terms of preventing extremist political movements of the type that were common in European states from taking power. During the drafting of the 1965 Convention on the Elimination of All Forms of Racial Discrimination, delegates from the Middle East objected to a European proposal that specifically referred to Nazism as "the most flagrant manifestation of racial discrimination."[41] The Saudi delegate to the drafting committee argued that Nazism had been an "affliction" of Europe but, for the rest of the world, "it had . . . been colonialism" that had been the most significant "affliction of racial discrimination."[42] As a general historical critique this argument has some merit, but in defensive relativism it mutates into a notion that international human rights law reflects a set of interests that automatically diverge from the interests of developing states, justifying partial compliance with or implementation of international human rights law. This can be illustrated with a few examples where states highlighted their status as developing states to justify open-ended limitations or restrictions on rights. When China was addressing queries from the Committee on the Elimination of All Forms of Discrimination against Women (CEDAW Committee) about the political freedom of women and employment rights, they responded that women's rights were "one aspect of human rights" and that as a "developing country" they were doing their best to implement the convention.[43] When it ratified the Convention on the Rights of the Child (CRC), India filed a broad-ranging declaration emphasising its status as a developing state and arguing that this justified the implementation of provisions surrounding child labor and social rights according to an unspecified timetable of its own definition.[44] In 1998, when justifying an open-ended reservation on every provision of the CRC, Kuwait stated that it had to handle certain issues with "considerable political sensitivity," as it was a "developing and traditional" society.[45]

The other area where the colonial-era origins of international law had an impact on antiuniversalist arguments was in the assumption that universality entailed the subordination and civilization of others. From around the seventeenth century onward, the process of colonialism explicitly defined universality with reference to colonized peoples. The foremost theorist of this process was Edward Said, who argued in *Culture and Imperialism* that colonization was not just a "simple act of [territorial] accumulation" but was an "impressive ideological formation" which justified ongoing domination.[46] The ideological tool for domination was the construction of an alterity or otherness in East Asia against which the Occidental virtues of "civilisation" were defined.[47] This justified "a right of conquest" for the colonizer, later providing the moral and cultural legitimacy for the project of colonialism.[48] This permeated into eighteenth-century thinking. Immanuel Kant's concept of perpetual peace, as John Hobson noted, was predicated on the removal of the "threat to civilized states" from "uncivilized societies."[49] Kantian perpetual peace had significant implications for the eventual intellectual project of international human rights law and was intertwined with the general idea of establishing universal rights.[50] John Locke's ideas of liberty, which were significant in establishing the theoretical justifications for certain rights, such as the protection of property, excluded the subjects of colonial rule and different races from consideration as rights holders.[51] These views were reflected in the writings of nineteenth-century legal theorists, who described international law in terms of rules governing civilized nations, with the assumption that non-European states could be civilized through exposure to the law.[52] This was part of a wider colonial ideology; the French *mission civilisatrice*, the philosophy defining

France's administration of colonial territories, depended upon the "fundamental assumptions of the superiority of French culture and the perfectibility of humankind."[53] Contemporary theorists on globalization and the law have echoed a similar cautionary critique of universality, claiming that the UDHR promoted, as a common concept across the world, a culture of the rule of law which supported globalization.[54] A similar theme was taken up in Hardt and Negri's seminal work *Empire*, which argued that human rights law was intertwined with other legal regimes which helped cement a diffuse form of global hegemony.[55]

This led to the claim that the colonialist concept of a universal civilizing mission had found its way into international human rights law; Article 28 of the UDHR described the creation of a "social and international order" that could realize human rights.[56] This seemed to imply that human rights were a new form of civilizing mission and inspired the American Anthropological Association's (AAA) 1947 declaration in response to the UDHR, which was heavily critical of colonialism, arguing that international human rights law would in a similar fashion disregard non-Western cultural standards.[57] This particular critique has come under some attack, not least because it seemed to suggest that as the idea of universality was colonial-imperialist, any appeal to universal values as a defense against oppression was redundant.[58] Nevertheless, the interconnection between juridical universality and a universal standard of civilization permeated into the framework of human rights law: the preambles to the ICCPR and the International Covenant on Economic, Social, and Cultural Rights (ICESCR) seem to describe a civilizing mission when they refer to the creation of the "conditions" to enjoy human rights.[59] As Makau Mutua concluded, because international human rights law required the construction of an uncivilized "other," this made it difficult for it to gain universal legitimacy.[60] Mutua framed this in part as a response to the work of Abdullahi Ahmed An-Na'im, who had argued that it was possible to construct a cross-cultural conception of universality through an analysis of traditions of dignity in different societies.[61]

The notion that human rights law contains a civilizing mission can be seen in responses from states to the Committee on the Rights of the Child, the CRC's treaty body. Some states, in particular Jordan, Morocco, and Sudan, have been hostile to what they perceive as the lack of respect shown by the committee to traditional or religious practices limiting the rights of female children.[62] The Moroccan delegate to the committee described the potential changes brought about by the convention's implementation as a form of "hasty modernization" with the potential to disrupt society.[63] The delegate from Benin went even further, arguing before the committee that it could not "force . . . alien ideas" upon its citizens by altering its laws and practices to comply with the CRC.[64] That was precisely what was expected from signatories to a human rights instrument, and the argument appeared to be that fulfillment of obligations under the convention would cause damage to society because they represented an imposition of outside values—inverting the logic of the colonialist-imperialist argument described above. This is echoed in the defense of reservations; Kuwait, justifying its reservations to the CRC, said that they were necessary to avoid "social fabrics [coming] under intolerable strain."[65] Reservations such as those originally entered by Pakistan and Djibouti allowed unlimited restrictions on rights in line with Islamic Sharia without ever defining what those restrictions were or what was included in their scope, in a manner that was largely incompatible with the convention.[66] Pakistan initially justified its reservation by arguing that it was "difficult to accept anything tantamount to a challenge to the basic ethos of a people," which again appeared to be justifying a reservation that was impermissible as a matter of law, on seemingly open-ended grounds of antiuniversalist cultural incompatibility.[67] However, Pakistan was to later withdraw its reservations, and in later interactions with the committee was prepared to outline precisely how it incorporated Sharia law into its family law and how it was implementing its CRC obligations by tackling child marriage.[68] In both versions of the anticolonialist argument, a reductionist version of a historical, legal, or philosophical critique of the human rights argument is used by state parties to assert either the Western origins of a right or set of rights or their cultural incompatibility, challenging their justificatory universality.

"Hidden Meaning" or "Hidden Good" within International Human Rights Law's Claim to Universality

This version of the antiuniversalist argument is not confined to a particular class or group of states, as it maintains that international human rights law advances a specific set of values that represent a specific political project. The universality of international human rights law is open to the criticism that it is a series of practices grounded in a particular culture which has been exported. To some extent this is inevitable; as Peter Fitzpatrick argues, the universal does not exist in abstract, and the rights that are claimed to be universal necessarily "correspond to some particular practice somewhere."[69] In a similar vein, Judith Butler argues that claims of universality are bound by "various synaptic stagings with culture."[70] Much scholarly attention has been given to common conceptions of dignity that intersect different cultures; some, such as Renteln, have argued that "empirical research" should be undertaken to "validate universal moral standards" as a basis for human rights.[71] However, international human rights law was not constructed through an exercise of this nature.[72] Although representatives from India, Jordan, and a few other states from Africa and Asia were involved in the UDHR's drafting, claims persisted for many years afterward that it reflected a Western set of values. This claim was later effectively reversed when, from the late 1960s onward, non-Western states gained more power in the UN Commission on Human Rights. During the 1980s, the United States fiercely criticized the commission as "anti-Western" and was hostile to initiatives such as the creation of a right to development, which it criticized as being a political project from states in the African and Asian blocs at the UN—or the third world bloc, as it was then referred to.[73]

It is important to realize that both views are the product of the same critique of human rights law—that it substantively reflects a particular set of political views rather than a set of universal principles. The content of human rights law often relies on some form of implied agreement or recognition of a common set of values identifying what Charles Beitz terms the "non-parochial core" of human rights, which are truly universal and apply to all persons equally.[74] The identification of these values is, however, performed not by an anthropological or empirical exercise of the sort envisaged by Renteln, but with reference to a form of universalized person, from whom common interests can then be extrapolated. The universalized human self was an eighteenth-century construction that allowed rights to be decoupled from citizenship to create a universalized humanity.[75] Even though some histories of this process cite earlier forerunners of the notion of the individual as a rights holder, the version which came to be central to international law came from the European Christian tradition and arguments about natural law in the 1700s.[76] But, as Costas Douzinas argues, highly reductive conceptions of humanity alone cannot "act as the *a priori* normative source" of universal law and morals.[77] Therefore, a presumption has to be made that human interactions defining the self beyond immanent agency have a reductive, universal quality to them. This is a conclusion which, as Rom Harré demonstrates, does not square with anthropological and historical evidence which points to "wide variations . . . in the degree of singularity with which persons organize their experienced thoughts, feelings, premonitions and plans of their own."[78] The concept of the universalized human is also open to an epistemic criticism. Attempts to derive human rights from extrapolating the behavior of a hypothetical agent, Alan Gerwith points out, involves making conclusions on what that agent would or would not do in a given situation, and these conclusions are ultimately dialectically contingent—they are predicated on people agreeing to come to the same conclusion in a hypothetical scenario.[79]

This means that it is possible to reject the justificatory universality of a particular set of rights as being representative of a particular political ideology rather than a universal set of values. There are several examples of this type of argument in opposition to human rights more generally; the United States' long-term opposition to economic and social rights and the ICESCR was built around the idea that these rights were reflections of the political priorities of other states rather than human rights which ought to be protected.[80] In relation to defensive relativism, claims that universality reflects a particular ideology can be seen in state arguments in response to human rights cases brought by LGBT individuals. In response to initiatives on the protection of LGBT rights by the UN Human Rights Council, the Russian government claimed such initiatives constituted an assault on "traditional values" and risked distorting the "traditional concept of the family as a union between a man and a woman" attitudes that also underpinned the Russian government's responses to cases brought against the state at the European Court of Human Rights (ECtHR) by the LGBT community in Russia.[81] The notion and language of tradition in Russia's responses to these cases was used to make the argument that LGBT activists were using human rights to advance a specific political agenda.[82] As well as making cultural claims (which will be discussed more in the next chapter) there was a specific antiuniversalist claim also seen in responses from other states locating interpretations of human rights law as providing protections for the LGBT community as a specifically Western construct.[83] In other cases, this form of antiuniversalist argument is deployed in reverse against attempts to change what is considered universal, which can be seen in state responses to cases arguing that the right to marry, as protected in some human rights instruments, entails that same-sex marriage should be lawful. As Linda Hart notes, these cases are defined by the applicants' attempt to alter the constellation of what "family life" is considered to be, using a "human rights rationality"—where arguments about what human interests are, are grounded in positivist law—but that these interpretations then collide with "deeply held moral and historical cultural understandings of 'family'" advanced by the state party.[84] The contestation over the meaning of concepts such as family life and marriage often sees the state party arguing that heterosexual marriage is the de facto universal meaning of marriage and that other readings of the law are attempts to advance a particular political conception of what marriage should mean.[85] In *Joslin v. New Zealand*, the applicants were a lesbian couple who claimed that the refusal of the domestic authorities in New Zealand to grant them a marriage license constituted a discriminatory application of Article 23 (the right to marriage) of the ICCPR.[86] The state party argued before the Human Rights Committee (the ICCPR's treaty body) that the restriction on same-sex couples marrying served the "purpose of protecting the institution of marriage and the social and cultural values that that institution represents."[87] But the state party also contended that marriage was "universally understood as open only to individuals of opposite sexes," implicitly pushing back at the attempt of the applicants to redefine what the state claimed was a universally understood meaning of the term "marriage" at the time the case was heard (the events in the case happened in 1995 and it was submitted to the Human Rights Committee in 1998).[88]

Another version of this argument maintains that the political dimension of universality is more totalizing and subtle in the ways it tries to construct a universal set of human interests. Because the provisions of justificatory universality in international human rights law rely on the basic assumption that there is a universal form of humanity that can stand free from cultural particularities, this has led to suggestions from communitarian philosophers that advocates of universalism are responsible for "smuggling in a hidden conception of good" to the "human" of human rights law, which was overtly Westernized or reflected particular political priorities.[89] The abstract projection of humanity attempted by international human rights law did create some assumptions and presumptions of a universal common good. Upendra Baxi argues that human rights based on a universalized humanity acknowledges "abstract particularities" by protecting the rights of particular groups, such as women and refugees.[90] Homi Bhabha makes a similar argument, concluding that international human rights law, by containing provisions emphasizing the need for minorities to "preserve their cultural identities," implicitly creates the image of a majoritarian "human artifice."[91] The universality of rights such as women's rights, children's rights, and minority rights was achieved by abstracting members of these groups out of their political and social contexts and giving them a homogenous identity and a set of rights in the furtherance of a designated teleological end, such as the elimination of structural discrimination against women.

Critics of cosmopolitanism give another twist to this argument contending that existing institutions shape the meaning of universal humanity to reflect and perpetuate existing power structures.[92] Supranational institutions, such as the UN Human Rights Council and the World Bank, have in some specific ways been responsible for advancing common conceptions of economic personhood through their resolutions and policy instruments.[93] Even though many international institutions, particularly those created to promote and protect international human rights, do not have much direct power, they are, as Martha Nussbaum argues, important vehicles of persuasion and can shape an international consensus on how societies ought to operate.[94] Alexander Hinton's work on transitional justice has observed how the universalism of international criminal law depends on envisaging a form of teleological transformation of society.[95] Critiquing some of the literature on human rights compliance, Hinton describes how it and the literature on transitional criminal justice is predicated on a "typology on conversion," where the universal is presented not as a description of the world but as something states are supposed to evolve into.[96] Thus, the cosmopolitan foundations of universal human rights are located within positivist legal instruments that reflect a specific set of moral propositions which are often shaped by the culture of those drafting such instruments.[97]

The hidden good argument can be seen in discussions over the scope of Article 5 of CEDAW, which places an obligation on states to "modify the social and cultural patterns of conduct" in society to achieve the "elimination of prejudices and customary" practices based on the idea "of the inferiority or the superiority of either of the sexes or on stereotyped roles for men and women."[98] India issued a declaration in relation to this provision stating that it would implement it "in conformity with its policy of non-interference in the personal affairs of any community without its initiative and consent."[99] Justifying this declaration, India argued that in its multicultural society traditions were "too deep and too entrenched" and that laws—referring to both domestic laws and the implementation of its international obligations—could not, in its view, bring about "enduring changes in an ancient social fabric such as India's."[100] There was an indication that India would pursue these goals by other means such as education programs, but as the CEDAW Committee noted in 2000, the failure to engage in lawmaking processes in the manner envisaged by Article 5 "perpetuates sexual stereotypes . . . and discrimination against women."[101] The Indian government's justification of this declaration seemed to indicate that this provision was not applicable to its highly conservative society, implicitly challenging the universalism of this provision on grounds of its content.[102] Yet, as the committee noted again in 2007, the broad wording of this declaration was in essence evading the implementation of Article 5's substance.[103] In interactive dialogue with other states, the committee has had to highlight areas as diverse as ritualized slavery for brides in West Africa and Caribbean traditions of machismo, with states sometimes reluctant to use legal mechanisms to tackle these seemingly deeply embedded cultural practices.[104] As Rikki Holtmaat notes, Article 5 is not designed to address only "exotic" or "backwards" cultures but is focused on all human rights relations, institutions, or structures where detrimental gender stereotypes inhibit the realization of women's rights, and highlights a series of comments from the CEDAW committee relating to European societies with respect to Article 5.[105] Yet Article 5 is vulnerable to this antiuniversalism precisely because a case can be made by defensive relativists that its ambiguous wording means it contains a hidden conception of what society ought to look like that is incommensurable with the reality of other particular societies.

The Incommensurability of Antiuniversalism

The two strands of antiuniversalist arguments set out in this chapter are not exclusive to defensive relativism. There are a number of important historical critiques of the UDHR and the subsequent trajectory of international human rights law. It is worth noting that some arguments, such as the critique of cosmopolitanism, are aimed at criticizing the way that states construct values through institutions and do not necessarily support a state's construction of morality to oppose human rights law—which is the principal project of defensive relativists. What differentiates these general antiuniversalist arguments is that generally defensive relativism is framed in a manner ultimately incommensurable with the concept of an obligation in international human rights law.

International human rights law has various structural mechanisms for acknowledging divergences over the application of particular rights in individual contexts. For example, the margin of appreciation doctrine, which allows international courts and tribunals to err in favor of a state party's interpretation of the application or limitation of a particular right, can acknowledge genuine cultural divergence. Although this will be explored in much more depth in subsequent chapters, it is worth examining these mechanisms in the context of antiuniversalism. In the case of *Handyside v. United Kingdom*, the ECtHR held that the UK government was best placed to assess the interpretation and application of Article 10 of the European Convention on Human Rights (ECHR), which protected free speech but allowed laws limiting speech in the interests of preventing "disorder or crime. . . . [or] the protection of health or morals" as long as it could be shown that this was "necessary in a democratic society."[106] In *Handyside*, the applicant had protested that UK laws had prohibited him from circulating a nonfiction book which, among other things, promoted underage sex, pornography, and drug taking to young adolescents. The UK government successfully argued that it was entitled to restrict the publication of a book that encouraged adolescents to watch pornography on the grounds that state authorities were better placed to resolve these sorts of moral questions about the limitations of freedom of speech.[107] This acknowledged divergent standards of morality across the different state parties to the ECHR, yet the court was careful to stress that this did not mean states had "unlimited power of appreciation" and that restrictions in speech were in principle undesirable, but where that did occur they should be "hand in hand with European supervision."[108] This did not grant the state unlimited license to restrict the right to freedom of expression, but rather gave primacy to the state party on the application of rights in particular areas. The ECtHR has also ruled against state parties who argued that restrictions on free speech in their jurisdiction fell within the scope of their margin of appreciation.[109] The decision about the margin of appreciation all takes place within the framework of the interpretation of the ECHR, which has its own justificatory universalism based on its role in maintaining liberal democracy, as set out in the preamble and Article 1 of the convention. Not all human rights bodies use the margin of appreciation doctrine, and chapter 3 explores the application of the doctrine in more detail.

While legal doctrines such as the margin of appreciation appear to acknowledge the limitations of certain rights due to cultural differences over moral questions, they still require that the basic justificatory universality of an instrument is accepted. Antiuniversalism, as practiced by defensive relativists, however, seeks to undermine the basis of a human rights instrument's justificatory universalism. An examination of reservations entered by state parties to CEDAW gives an insight into how the antiuniversalism of defensive relativism drifts toward claims of incommensurability. For example, the reservations originally entered by Singapore to Article 16 of CEDAW, which protects the freedom of women to enter into marriage, stated that Singapore's "multi-racial and multi-religious society" meant that the Singaporean authorities had to "respect the freedom of minorities to practice their religious and personal laws" and therefore freedom of marriage would not apply "where compliance with these provisions would be contrary to their religious or personal laws."[110] As several other state parties pointed out, this had the practical effect of undermining the entire rationale for the protection of the right to marriage—and, indeed, the convention itself.[111] This criticism had some merit, as Article 28 of CEDAW states that any reservation "incompatible with the object and purpose of the present Convention shall not be permitted."[112] Furthermore, when the Economic and Social Council commented on a draft of CEDAW in 1976, they noted that there was an agreement among the delegates from a number of different countries that the new convention should contain "anti-discriminatory measures" relating to a variety of social practices (including marriage) and "a number of positive and constructive steps designed to advance the status of women in different fields."[113] If this is taken as an indication of the justificatory universality of CEDAW, then a reservation of the sort originally filed by Singapore can be read as an indication that the state party viewed the entirety of Article 16 as incommensurable with its cultural objections.

The incommensurability of antiuniversalism is what distinguishes relativism as a concept from other seemingly analogous concepts such as pluralism, which is instead focused on providing a framework for acknowledging indigenous or hybrid institutions which provide justice.[114] Relativists do not consider themselves to be relativists. Instead, as John Tilley summarizes it, they believe that "although for every culture some moral judgments are valid, no moral judgment is universally valid . . . every moral judgment is culturally relative."[115] Relativists are interested in their own moral universe in opposition to other moral universes, which they would hold not be moral, whereas a pluralist, Paul Berman argues, will recognize that "alternative normative universes" exist and attempt to mediate where normative systems and communities overlap and clash.[116] Defensive relativists—the state parties engaging in cultural relativism—take a modified view of this argument, maintaining in essence that while some rights might be applicable within their state, they can only be applicable if they are relative to the society within the state. This strays toward an epistemic claim which Claudio Corradetti summarizes as: "what is true for a culture X is false for a culture Y."[117] Among philosophers of human rights, there is some skepticism about the epistemic relativist case supporting the existence of incommensurable systems of morality, in either linguistic or descriptive terms, because it is highly inconsistent and prone to logical incoherence. Tilley notes how arguments of this nature easily dissolve into fallacies such as the "true for them fallacy," which reasons that if a community believes something to be true it automatically justifies its morality.[118] Different systems of morality are also not necessarily incommensurable with one another; as Alasdair MacIntyre notes, a tradition "can be rationally discredited by[,] and in the light of appeal to[,] its very own standards of rationality in more than one way."[119] Yet, for the defensive relativist, any such inconsistencies can be resolved by reference not to the coherency of their own moral argument but by criticizing the universality of international human rights law.

Crucially, this means that antiuniversalism does not need to be applied consistently, as it rebuts the claim to universality made by a given instrument; it is not an attempt to defend an alternate conception of morality. When, for example, states defend their reservations to CEDAW or the CRC on the grounds that the provisions claimed to be universal within both instruments are incompatible with their cultural traditions, there is no real obligation to articulate or justify the morality of the cultural tradition. This was noted in a report from the CEDAW Committee in 1996 that was highly critical of some of the reservations entered by state parties noting that their "terms . . . sometimes do not explain their legal and practical scope," and that none of the reservations acknowledged "the divergence of views among Islamic scholars or that Shariah [law] may be subject to evolving interpretation and practice."[120] The lack of explanation or justification of a limitation of rights was a common theme of opposition to CEDAW which either attacked the convention or portrayed debates over CEDAW as another incident of the "west versus the rest."[121] All these arguments were antiuniversalist, as they were predicated on attacking the universality of CEDAW rather than necessarily defending a particular cultural tradition. Not all reservations to CEDAW have to follow an antiuniversalist framework undermining the convention. At the CEDAW Committee in 1999, Algeria acknowledged the "changing nature" of Sharia law, gave detail of how the convention's obligations could be achieved within its national legal framework, and detailed at length how it intended to modify its reservations, and in its 2015 report to the committee gave details of how its reservations had been significantly limited in scope.[122]

Both strands of antiuniversalist argument presented earlier are a reaction to the juridical universality of a particular instrument manifested as arguments designed to attack its justificatory universality. By focusing on an instrument's justificatory universality, either by arguing that it represents a particular political agenda or that universality is a reflection of colonialist tradition, states can maintain that their position on the protection of particular rights is simply incommensurable with the provisions of a human rights instrument. This allows states to cherry-pick which areas or which obligations they wish to subject to a defensive relativist argument and then use that to assert their own moral realism.

Conclusion: Antiuniversalism

In answering the question of why rights ought to be universal, scholars, philosophers, and practitioners have reached for religious, anthropological, ethical, and even biological arguments to explain why rights should apply universally.[123] This is distinct from the legal question of why the rights contained in international human rights law have a universal application which takes the form of jurisdictional debates, arguments about personhood in law, questions of sovereignty in international law, or arguments about interpretation of treaty law. International human rights law has somewhat neglected the first question, meaning that the justificatory universalism of human rights instruments have implicitly relied on a line of argumentation stretching back to the UDHR, premised on the importance of human rights to the international order following World War II. The antiuniversalist claims of defensive relativism are in part inspired by the limitations of these arguments, but these are also arguments which, as the last section of this chapter indicates, serve the interests of the states making them.

Antiuniversalism is not, strictly speaking, an ideological position, but rather uses ideological arguments to unpick the justifications behind legal obligations. The main strands of antiuniversalist argument outlined above are not fixed schools of thought as much as they are frameworks within which states contest the justificatory universality of prospective or existing obligations in international human rights law. Importantly, because defensive relativism is a response to international law, the type of antiuniversalism in any defensive relativist claim varies according to the state making it and the nature of the obligation being contested. When antiuniversalism is coupled with the state construction of culture, described in chapter 2, a defensive relativist claim is created.

CHAPTER 2

State Construction of Culture: The Second Element of Defensive Relativism

The Aztec empire was one of the most ferocious powers in Central America. Not only did it have a disciplined military machine, it also maintained a complex economic system based on tribute from its neighbors. An observer from the twentieth century might see, in the Mexico valley of the sixteenth century, something akin to Tsarist Russia or the Hapsburg empire. Yet, in the popular imagination, the Aztec empire is often dominated by one abiding image—one that provided a convenient moral justification for the Spanish conquest—the human sacrifice. The morality of the Aztec human sacrifice has become a staple in arguments on cultural relativism. As one professor of anthropology observed in his undergraduate classes, it was common when asking the question of whether a society that practiced human sacrifice was moral to hear refrains such as "Who are we to say that it was wrong?" or "It was their culture, right?"[1] It is a historical fact that the Aztecs engaged in mass ritualized slaughter, but at the same time the homeland of the invading Spaniards was also engaged in ritualized slaughter as it executed heretics of the Catholic faith.[2]

The human sacrifice argument, John Tilley notes, is attractive to proponents of cultural relativism. An external observer may find the practice immoral, the argument goes, but reason that the individuals carrying it out may be justified in doing it because they "never had occasion to question the practice" and see it "as their only way to avoid divine punishment."[3] This confuses judgments of blame and moral judgments; it focuses on whether or not a society ought to be condemned for carrying out a particular practice, not on whether that practice is itself moral. As a form of reasoning it allows for moral decision making to be contextualized to a particular society.[4] The rigid adherence to the notion that anything practiced by a culture must itself be moral is a feature of what Michael Brown calls "classical cultural relativism."[5] It explains why different societies make different moral judgments, in some cases making the normative claim that they ought to be treated differently—although from a modern anthropologist's perspective, Brown notes, this is not necessarily a defensible or relevant definition of cultural relativism.

Yet, the argumentative templates created by highly reductive versions of cultural relativism play an important role in defining the values that defensive relativism "defends" in response to the obligations of international human rights law. The previous chapter examined the first component of defensive relativism, antiuniversalism—opposition to the claim that rights ought to be applied universally. This chapter looks at what defensive relativists champion as a source of morality, the state construction of cultural values. A more accurate definition would be that defensive relativism defends a state's claim that certain domestic laws or practices are important cultural values. This can be summarized as "state constructed culture," the second element of defensive relativism. When drawing on cultural traditions in society, state-constructed culture is not necessarily representative, or even inclusive, of the cultural values of a society. State-constructed culture can be identified in the places where defensive relativist arguments are made, such as in the text of treaty reservations, state submissions to international tribunals, and reports to the UN Human Rights Council.

It is important to briefly define what is being referred to by the word "culture" in this chapter. One of the first attempts at defining the meaning of culture came from Edward Tylor, a nineteenth-century English anthropologist of the cultural evolution school who argued that the knowledge, beliefs, customs, laws, artistic habits, and, indeed, almost every other aspect of a society should constitute its culture.[6] As David Perusek argues, while Tylor's definition of culture was often criticized, it was significant in democratizing the notion of culture away from being the private property of the aristocratic few located solely in "the music of Mozart and Bach, the art of Michelangelo and Rembrandt."[7] Culture in Tylor's formulation is understood as the property of a whole society. But the concept of society should be treated with circumspection here. In the context of defensive relativism, and, indeed, a lot of early writings on relativism, it is principally referring to a nonorganic, bounded community defined by law, either as the nation-state or as a territory of "peoples."[8] The 2001 UNESCO Universal Declaration on Cultural Diversity defines culture as the "distinctive spiritual, material, intellectual and emotional features of society" which can be articulated both through forms of artistic expression and through "ways of living together, value systems, traditions and beliefs."[9] Other attempts by UNESCO to define culture have often aimed to take a holistic definition of culture, which includes both the tangible and intangible aspects of culture.[10] References to culture in the literature on relativism often relate to the whole of society, including legal and social institutions, which make decisions on moral values and create an overall values system. David Wong's work on this notes that it makes sense to think of societies as forming systems of rules, of which the legal system is a large part, which then shape moral values.[11] Culture, therefore, in this chapter is taken to refer to the legal system and other institutions performing social functions, such as a religious institution performing marriage ceremonies.

What a state practicing defensive relativism is doing in constructing a version of culture is twofold. Firstly, they are attempting to fuse culture and sovereignty as a unitary entity. As will be shown in the second section of this chapter, the connection between culture and conceptions of sovereignty actually have quite a long history, but in defensive relativism this often turns into an argument about the sovereignty of a state's lawmaking powers. Secondly, as illustrated in the final section of this chapter, states practicing defensive relativism present state-constructed culture in certain distinct argumentative forms, such as referring to cultural values as being static or describing cultural practices in internationally vague terms, all of which are designed to allow the state total discretion in determining what is and what is not considered a cultural value. Before doing this, however, it is important to look at some of the broader intellectual concepts behind defensive relativism by analyzing cultural relativism's response to international human rights law.

Cultural Relativism's Reaction to International Human Rights Law

The discussion of cultural relativism across different disciplines such as anthropology and philosophy has been wide-ranging and complex. Rather than attempt an exhaustive survey of the different meanings and usages of cultural relativism—other fine works undertaking this project exist—it is instead useful to analyze defensive relativism's intellectual pedigree.[12] While states do not explicitly cite their intellectual source material when making a defensive relativist argument in a submission to an international tribunal, it is possible to identify how some major strands of cultural relativist thought underpin the assumptions behind defensive relativist arguments. Most of this emerges from the history of cultural relativism's response to the political and intellectual project of international human rights in the latter part of the twentieth century. Some histories of cultural relativism begin their analysis much earlier. Derek Robbins, for example, begins with an analysis of French Enlightenment thinkers such as Montesquieu and Comte, and others begin their works even earlier with an analysis of ancient Greek thinking on morality.[13] However, because defensive relativism as a practice takes place in a state's response to international human rights law and the obligations it entails, it is useful to take the responses of classic cultural relativists to the Universal Declaration of Human Rights (UDHR) as the starting point of this analysis.

"Classical cultural relativism," as Brown terms it, emerged in anthropology and was used to frame some of the concerns anthropologists had with international human rights law. Franz Boas, a German American anthropologist, is widely considered the intellectual godfather of cultural relativism. He undertook his early fieldwork on Baffin Island in Canada in the 1890s, observing patterns of language and value systems within indigenous communities. In his letters, he detailed how fifteen months in the "sublime loneliness of the Arctic" confirmed his conviction that the idea of a "cultured individual" is relative.[14] Boas's work challenged the prevailing assumption in the social sciences at the time that cultures were in a process of evolution toward a civilized end state and concluded that different societies could have their own traditions of morality that were no less valuable than each other.[15] Central to Boas's thinking, Kwame Anthony Appiah notes, was a cautious rejection of ethnocentricity; he was also careful to acknowledge how traditions could be used in society to limit human freedom, once remarking that his "whole outlook . . . [was] determined by the question: how can we recognize the shackles that tradition has laid upon us?"[16] Boas was not the first anthropologist to explore ideas such as these, but his fieldwork and intellectual synthesis was to prove highly influential for among some of his students who would go on to expand cultural relativist thought. One of his students, Ruth Benedict, would argue in her 1934 book, *Patterns of Culture*, that there existed "equally valid patterns of life formation in all societies" and went on to further develop what is now understood as the Boasian tradition.[17]

Benedict's work was to have a considerable impact on the international legal scholar Raphael Lemkin, who believed that cultural relativism would foster respect between societies and could serve as the basis for a common conception of human rights.[18] As Lemkin's biographer Douglas Irvin-Erickson noted, Benedict's work framed Lemkin's thinking on the necessity of preventing the destruction of cultures, which was, in turn, influential in his work shaping the definition of genocide.[19] Another disciple of Boas, Melville Herskovits, argued that a discussion of relativism focusing solely on ethics and differing values ignored the fact that the "human individual is always provided with some culturally constituted means that are among the conditions which enable him to participate with his fellows."[20] In an effort to deconstruct the colonial-era assumptions about the absence of ethical values in non-Western societies, anthropologists emphasized the complex nature of what were thought of as primitive societies, and in doing so endorsed relativism by contextualization.[21] This was predicated on the idea of promoting tolerance and understanding between cultures; Peter Winch argued in his 1964 paper "Understanding a Primitive Society" that an "important feature of any human society [is] conceptions of good and evil in human life" but that an investigation or contextualization of that society is necessary to understand those values.[22]

Herskovits was chairman of the American Anthropological Association's (AAA) Committee on International Cooperation, which in the summer of 1947 was invited to comment on an early draft of the Universal Declaration of Human Rights (UDHR). Herskovits largely drafted the AAA's statement in response to the UDHR, and it was unclear how much other members of the association had contributed to its development or agreed to its content.[23] In the winter of 1947, the final version of the statement appeared in *American Anthropologist*. The introductory passage set out in broad terms the problems associated with defining how societies and groups operate before noting that due to the social nature of learning, an "individual cannot but be convinced that his own way of life is the most desirable."[24] It then set out three principles about human rights, the third of which was that "values are relative to the culture from which they derive," leading to the conclusion that any attempt to formulate universal moral postulates, such as the UDHR, were destined to fail.[25] This can be described as the default position of cultural relativism toward human rights—agnosticism about the existence of universal values and a deep hostility to any attempt to juridify human rights for fear that it will turn into a mechanism of wider intolerance toward different societies, leading to the dominance of the Western enlightenment tradition of rights over all others. After 1949, there was scant reference to human rights made in any AAA publication until the late 1980s.[26]

It is important to note that the chief concern of anthropologists—that the UDHR would lead to a lack of tolerance but that relativism could not sufficiently confront fascism or other forms of systemic intolerance which were justified on cultural grounds—would later cause some embarrassment among anthropologists and legal scholars.[27] In 1987, reflecting in *American Anthropologist* on the forty-year period since the statement, Wilcomb E. Washburn noted that anthropology had moved from "a naive faith in cultural relativism" to an "embarrassed and skeptical unease" of the whole doctrine.[28] One of the principal reasons why this happened, Elvin Hatch observed a decade later on the fiftieth anniversary of the statement, was that cultural relativists easily became caught in the impossible position of being morally neutral with respect to "intolerable situations" such as "political executions, genocide [and] genital mutilation."[29] Despite this widespread, latter-day skepticism from anthropologists, the central idea of the statement—that values are relative to the cultures from which they originate—proved highly influential in shaping arguments by states about human rights law. Even though the precise arguments advanced by the Boasians, especially the concern about the tolerance of diversity, were abandoned in defensive relativist argumentation, the idea that human rights were Western-centric, and hence intolerant of cultural difference, persisted.

The ascent of epistemological relativism in the 1970s helped frame the idea that cultural value systems are incomprehensible between different communities and hence incommensurable with one another. As Elizabeth Zechenter summarizes it, all standards against which cultural practices may be judged are deemed meaningless because different cultures are assumed to be mutually incomprehensible.[30] Renato Rosaldo states this position as, basically, "my own group aside, everything human is alien to me"—a position that is ultimately intolerant of diversity.[31] This line of argument reasons that the causative way by which people acquire moral values is through a process of "enculturative conditioning" within their own communities, and as such the value systems of different cultures are, in effect, incomprehensible to each other.[32] Duncan Pritchard, in an overview of epistemic relativism, notes that it is based on the premise that two parties to a dispute about a matter of fact may be equally correct even though they reach different conclusions, because their dispute can be explained through a divergence of epistemic clusters.[33] For example, someone of religious faith would accord a central role to the testimony of scripture because it would be treated as a reliable source of true belief on particular subjects. However, if all epistemic standing is framework-relative, then, as Pritchard argues, "it follows that there can be no framework-independent way of conducting an epistemic assessment of an opponent's framework."[34] This effectively renders any form of universal standard of morality irrelevant.

John Tilley's analysis of the "polygamy argument" shows how this thinking works in practice.[35] This argument maintains that, as no standard can be found to arbitrate the morality of different types of marriage due to the variance of practice across human societies, there must therefore be no universal standard for the arbitration of morality; hence all forms of marriage are morally justified. Taken at its highest, the polygamy argument is an argument for recognizing different practices as potentially being equivalent, not an argument for their morality. The polygamy argument quickly breaks down into what Williams terms "vulgar relativism," where all competing values are pronounced ethical by default.[36] There may be valid reasons for defending the ethical nature of polygamy within the context of a particular society, but the polygamy argument as typified by Tilley does not do that; it says that any form of marriage is moral because it exists as a practice in a society and is deemed to have "cultural value."[37] The polygamy argument also allows for a high level of generalization over what is and is not cultural and relies on an ongoing conflation of the moral and cultural. Richard Shweder, drawing on a range of anthropological sources, notes that just because differences between societies over social practices exist, that does not mean such differences are moral or in any way susceptible to rational defense as moral practices; they may well be simply practices that evolved over a number of years.[38] Even those, like Xiaorong Li, who carefully reconstruct the "culture concept" in relation to human rights, arguing that people's everyday interactions with cultural practices are important for understanding ethical questions, are careful to note that cultures are far from homogenous and therefore claims about moral hegemony should be treated with caution.[39]

The concept of cultural absolutism outlined in Rhoda's 1993 article "Cultural Absolutism and the Nostalgia for Community" explores the idea that relativism tends toward a form of absolutist thinking, inverting the assumption made by many relativists that cultural relativism resists the absolutist thinking of universalists.[40] Cultural absolutism, as Howard describes it, is the belief that "a society's culture [is] of supreme ethical value" and an ethnocentric adherence to one's own cultural norms is the only ethical position.[41] Cultural absolutism has three basic principles: inferring that universal rights do not really exist, maintaining that human rights are culturally Western, and concluding, therefore, that "indigenous cultures supersede human rights as a social good."[42] Howard's theory received a significant degree of criticism not least because it relies on, or implicitly defends, a form of default universalism. As Peter Fitzpatrick notes, the idea of universality does not exist in the abstract; it necessarily "correspond[s] to some particular practice somewhere," which usually means that human rights are situated in the West, and in reality, what Howard is arguing for is a set of competing universals.[43] Others objected to the relatively abstract nature of universality in her account of cultural absolutism and the sharp distinction drawn between it and cultural values. Howard's framing of culture and universality as opposites, as Ann-Belinda Preis argues, led to the debate about human rights and relativism becoming "highly antagonistic" and taking place at an "extremely abstract level."[44] Even though Howard's concept is flawed, the epistemic position that competing ethical values are pronounced ethical by default because a society's culture is the only ethical position is one that has been used by states advancing defensive relativist arguments.

Because of the capacity of relativism to be used in the promotion of widespread intolerance, some anthropologists have instead argued that cultural relativism and human rights can be reconciled either by seeking to identify some kind of middle ground or by looking at empirical approaches to understanding cultural differences.[45] Others, such as Alison Renteln, have defended relativist ideas and argued that it is possible to look for cross-cultural universals in different societies, which can validate international human rights standards.[46] Margaret Jolly, in her commentary on women's rights in the Pacific nation of Vanuatu, noted the existence, and almost inevitability, of a tension between universal notions of rights and local cultures.[47] But Jolly concluded that the language of rights could help women in Vanuatu and Papua New Guinea to negotiate competing claims to their identity, both from the authority of the state and traditional or communal forms of authority, to create new discourses on human rights. Related to this work is Tom Zwart's development of the "receptor approach," where the social-cultural situation in a society is taken as a starting point and existing cultural institutions are utilized to drive reforms to protect human rights.[48] Zwart's project is to look at alternative mechanisms in society for promoting and realizing the human rights obligations a state has in institutions such as religious authorities or women's groups.[49] This is not necessarily an entirely new theoretical concept; Sally Engle Merry's analysis of how human rights can be translated into different cultural traditions is based on a variety of fieldwork looking at women's rights organizations in India and Hawaii and demonstrates how community leaders can help human rights become "vernacularized, or adapted to local institutions and meanings."[50] But defensive relativism, by virtue of emerging in response to legal obligations that a state already has, is by design focused on explaining the difficulties a state-constructed culture poses for human rights implementation, or on the incommensurability of a state-constructed culture with certain rights, rather than finding mechanisms to implement human rights law.

Some political and cultural theorists have responded that much of the criticism of cultural relativism ignores the circumstances within which cultural relativism emerged more broadly as a response to claims of universality. Most notably, Clifford Geertz, in a seminal article entitled *Anti Anti-Relativism*, argued that relativism was being unduly targeted and that there was a risk of forgetting that anthropological relativists had shown "that the world does not divide into the pious and the superstitious; that there are sculptures in jungles . . . [and] the evolution of morality [was] not consummated in England."[51] This parting rhetorical flourish illustrates the persistence of relativism as an intellectual framework—it shows the culturally contextual nature of certain value claims—but, crucially, Geertz's argument does not examine the contestation of the ethical meanings of cultural practices within societies and relies a little too heavily on the assumption that cultures are in some way fixed.[52] Philosophers seeking to defend relativism from the criticism that it promotes intolerance have noted various ways that a notion of tolerance of different value systems could be reconciled with relativistic thought.[53] However, as Hye-Kyung Kim and Michael Wreen caution, these forms of argument would entail that "a self-conscious relativist" becomes an amoralist because to treat all moral codes as equal is "to preclude the commitment essential to having a moral code in the first place."[54] The state construction of cultural values, explored later in this chapter, relies heavily on the idea that because all cultural values are fixed, a position of default amoralism is appropriate in response to universalizing claims of human rights law. In summary, the defenders of cultural relativism from various disciplines would be correct in arguing that defensive relativism cherry-picks a number of ideas from various schools of thought, often utilizing some quite reductive versions of the arguments presented with them. But defensive relativism's principal project, as later chapters show, is tactical; it provides the state the tools to defend itself in an international legal argument and therefore can rely on some quite reductive versions of the concepts involved in the academic literature on cultural relativism.

The State Definition of Culture and the Sovereignty of Lawmaking as a Cultural Value

What links the theoretical ideas described in the section above to the real-world application of defensive relativism described in the section below is the idea that lawmaking by the state is a reflection of cultural values which are important to the state. This is not necessarily a conscious or coherent process of norm selection, or a defense of laws or institutions consciously deemed to be culturally significant. Rather, it most commonly emerges through defensive relativist arguments defending particular laws or policies, which are potentially in tension with obligations in international human rights law. Crucially, defensive relativism relies on the fusion of the culture, or cultural values, and the legal issue of sovereignty in international law.

The way that nations evolved into states, which then claimed sovereignty in international law, shows how the interconnection between cultural values and the legal doctrine of sovereignty emerged. The formation of nations as entities, Benedict Anderson's seminal work *Imagined Communities* contends, was facilitated by the creation of a shared language and the formation of written laws in a rudimentary public sphere.[55] More generally. the clustering of communities based on shared language groups was the start of the shaping of shared value systems. As Azar Gat argues, this was a common feature of kinship communities across the world and meant that when modern states formed, their shared values were rooted in systems of language and conceptions of culture that often overlapped with ethnicity or other demarcating factors.[56] The concept of sovereignty as distinct from nationhood emerged in the European context following the Peace of Westphalia in 1648.[57] As with many other concepts in international law, it was construed in narrow terms in the aftermath of a war—in this case, the Thirty Years' War that began when the Holy Roman Emperor attempted to forcefully convert the religious denomination of his subjects in Bohemia. This unleashed a complex, interrelated series of wars which devastated central Europe as outside powers intervened, notionally to protect and defend religious minorities, resulting in a higher death toll per capita than the First World War. The Peace of Westphalia was intended to resolve the question of which religion would be practiced in which princely state, as that had been the original cause of the conflict. As the historian Peter Wilson observes, when reviewing the key terms of the treaties signed in Westphalia it is hard to conclude that they inaugurated "a fully secular international order," yet that was precisely the significance many histories of international law later assigned to Westphalia—both the treaties and the idea.[58]

Westphalian sovereignty, as it came to be known, was characterized by the ability of the state to exclude external forces from intervention into its domestic affairs.[59] It evolved as an international legal doctrine later in the eighteenth and nineteenth centuries, becoming an operating assumption of international law.[60] This understanding of sovereignty was then exported around the world in the process of colonial-imperialism, initially by defining other societies as uncivilized (and lacking sovereignty), then by trying to shape statehood for territories under colonial rule, and finally by granting independence to them as legally recognized states.[61] The notion of Westphalian sovereignty grew in prominence precisely because the notion of excluding outside forces became such a core tenet of the international legal doctrine of sovereignty.[62] In the *Island of Palmas* case, the Permanent Court of Arbitration, when trying to resolve a dispute about who controlled an island off the coast of the Philippines, defined sovereignty as the "right to exercise therein, to exclusion of any other State the functions of a State," essentially endorsing the Westphalian model of sovereignty.[63] The Permanent Court of International Justice, in the *Eastern Greenland* case, drew upon exclusion as a key attribute of sovereignty but also held that a sovereign power would be able to control activities such as scientific experiments, hunting, and commerce on a territory.[64]

These early rulings framed sovereignty as a form of exclusionary power in international law, largely neglecting the legitimacy of the authority of the state wielding that power.[65] By the early- to mid-twentieth century, the dominant concept of sovereignty in international law was that states had a virtually unlimited power of lawmaking within their own jurisdictions and that their participation in international organizations was a means of pursuing their own set of interests.[66] Even though the mid-twentieth century saw the rapid growth of international law and international institutions with far-reaching powers, the common understanding of what sovereignty was remained fixed on a quasi-Westphalian notion of sovereignty premised on the exclusion of outside authority.[67] Westphalian sovereignty needs to be distinguished from what can be termed domestic legal sovereignty—the power of a state to make laws governing its domestic sphere.[68] Both types of sovereignty are important and, to an extent, interdependent. On the international plane, an entity's control of national lawmaking—its capacity for domestic legal sovereignty—is an important marker of it being seen as sovereign by other powers, which is, in turn, important for recognizing its Westphalian sovereignty.[69] Where defensive relativist arguments are used in international human rights practice, a state is generally defending its domestic-legal sovereignty and reasserting a sense of Westphalian sovereignty. When states are justifying a reservation, defending a limitation of rights, or arguing against a particular human rights obligation, they are either implicitly or explicitly defending their domestic legal sovereignty by arguing that state laws are justified and reasserting a Westphalian sense of sovereignty against the external pressure of international human rights law.

It is necessary to also examine the nature of domestic legal sovereignty to understand how sovereignty and culture are fused in defensive relativist arguments. The German political theorist Carl Schmitt, discussing the works of influential seventeenth-century writers on sovereignty, such as Thomas Hobbes and Jean Bodin, notes that modern sovereignty depends on the law to both promote its power and secure its legitimacy as sovereign.[70] The formation of law through the democratic political process was treated with some skepticism by Schmitt, who was critical of the institution of liberal democracy—which, given that he was writing in Weimar and later Nazi Germany, led to understandable criticism of his work's authoritarian tendencies. Yet, Schmitt's account of sovereignty is important precisely because it gives an account of the constituent power of sovereignty without relying on democratic or representative principles.[71] The state, Schmitt argues, constructs a political theology—a civic "god" of sovereignty—which is a form of constituent power. Lior Barshack, refining this further, differentiates the communal body, the sovereign collective in the moment of its enactment, from the corporate, which is the imaginary form of the community residing beyond the group as a form of existential entity. The corporate formation "secularizes the social," grounding the sovereign's power within the law that is then capable of being projected externally and recognized by others.[72] For Schmitt, in the penultimate chapter of *Political Theology*, sovereignty is dominated by the quasi-theological "metaphysical image" of the sovereign, which is necessary to provide the "organic unity" and a "national consciousness" of a people as a whole.[73] The existential body-corporate embodying a national community incorporates the culture and values of its constituent parts to create a single, unified sovereign. In Schmitt's view, this is not necessarily democratic or representative but rather a process of secularizing the formerly transcendent godlike figure that has both acted as the lawmaking sovereign and bound the various traditions of a nation together.

Therefore, using Tylor's definition of culture, outlined in the introduction to this chapter, a state's laws are not only representative of its society's culture but also representative of the power of the sovereign as a lawmaker. Laws do not necessarily need to be representative in a democratic sense for this to hold true; it is perfectly possible for a government to claim to an international body that a law, which its citizens have had no input in making and are unable to change through the democratic process, is representative of that government's values, because as a sovereign it constitutes the existential figure representative of that nation's culture and values. This is not to say that a state is justified in making such a claim but rather to illustrate how such an argument is possible, given the interconnection of culture with domestic legal sovereignty. The construction of laws, therefore, needs to be seen as part of the process of constructing culture. This point is explored by Annette Marfording, who, drawing on her research on Japanese culture, argues that Japanese education policies and laws on employment rights, some of which were enacted in partial fulfilment of their obligations under the Convention on the Elimination of All Forms of Discrimination against Women (CEDAW), reflect cultural assumptions about gender equality which have, in part, been constructed and shaped by the state.[74] A similar exploration is undertaken by Phil Chan, who argues that Singaporean laws criminalizing sexual orientation and sex between two adult males reflect a particular construction of Singaporean culture as defined by the state authorities.[75] By their nature, laws regulating the rights of individuals and their personal behavior are expressions of a collective morality in that they shape the behavior of individuals and society, creating ethical dividing lines. But this collective morality is not an organic fact of society; rather, morality is constructed in the process of lawmaking by state authorities as a means of constructing a national identity.

This means that when a state makes a defensive relativist argument, defending a domestic law or policy which is incompatible with international human rights law, it is making a claim about the legitimacy of the cultural practice it has chosen to defend, but also more broadly defending its domestic legal sovereignty and its construction of culture. Anne Bayefsky's concept of "cultural sovereignty," which she outlines in a 1996 paper, explains how states have claimed international human rights should be limited because of the "state's sovereign or superior authority to define the cultural needs of its citizens and the cultural parameters of their lives."[76] Bayefsky draws on a number of developments in the early 1990s to show that defenses of culture during the construction of declarations such as the 1993 Vienna Declaration and Programme of Action were aimed at permitting "no external critique of the substance of legal (or moral) rules."[77] Bayefsky's concern is that there has been a "certain romanticism" associated with cultural sovereignty because of its association with ideas of tolerance of other cultures and traditions, when in fact it is simply a means of attacking human rights law.[78] The problem with Bayefsky's thesis is that it treats all forms of argument relating to cultural differences with a very broad brush when it is not clear that every instance where cultural differences are cited is an example of cultural sovereignty. For example, Fiji has explained to a number of international human rights bodies why it experiences difficulty in implementing human rights obligations involving domestic violence and violence against women due to domestic cultural factors, but it does not present this as an insurmountable barrier to implementation and has used traditional justice mechanisms to try and advance rights in this area.[79] As the next chapter shows, the third element of the defensive relativist argument—the argument that a state should be exempt from a legal obligation—is where the weakening of human rights obligations actually occurs. Where Bayefsky's work is important is in its analysis of how the representation of cultural and moral values can be instrumentalized by states, which had been a concern of some anthropologists working with indigenous communities in the Americas.[80] In international human rights law the instrumentalization of cultural values uses the vehicle of a state's responses to an international body or international process to articulate the interconnected nature of cultural values and lawmaking.

One particular case study about reservations to CEDAW illustrates how the state construction of culture works. When it ascended to CEDAW in the 1980s, Egypt entered a reservation to Article 16 requiring states to "eliminate discrimination against women in all matters relating to marriage and family relation," which was far reaching in its scope allowing the state party to place unlimited restrictions on Article 16 in line with Sharia law.[81] As noted in the previous chapter, reservations such as these were often imprecise and did not specify which school of Sharia applied or to what extent the right would be restricted, becoming a vehicle for the state to insert whichever interpretation of the term it chose. Justifying its reservation, the Egyptian government stated in a letter that the reservation reflected the "sacrosanct nature of the firm religious belief which govern marital relations in Egypt and which may not be called in question."[82] This argument wrapped numerous divergences and nuances in religious doctrine into a blunt defense of sovereignty, and subsequent acts of the Egyptian government highlighted this still further. When in 1986 the issue of impermissible reservations to CEDAW arose at the UN General Assembly, states such as Egypt framed the issue as an attack by the West upon states in the developing world.[83] In 1991, when the Arab Women's Solidarity Association started arguing that Islam was being used as an excuse by the government to restrict women's rights, the Egyptian government banned the organization.[84] In Egypt's third periodic report to the CEDAW Committee in 1998, reservations were defended as necessary for preserving "the national particularities of Egyptian society along with those of its historical and cultural customs."[85] In 2000 the National Council for Women (NCW) was established, but as several NGOs noted, this led to the "governmentalisation" of rights claims with groups not favorable to the government's position, including its approach to CEDAW, being ignored or denied funding.[86]

Egypt kept its reservations in place, yet by its fourth and fifth report in 2000 there was some indication that domestic procedures were being altered to improve the formal equality of men and women in marital law.[87] Nevertheless, in its report for the CEDAW Committee in 2010, the Egyptian Association for Community Participation Enhancement—a coalition of women's rights activists based in Cairo—noted that laws on equality were not widely understood and de facto discrimination persisted in many places; some of that discrimination was linked to the absence of laws that the government would have been obliged to implement were it not for the reservations to Article 16.[88] The Egyptian government was clearly prepared to take some steps to modify other domestic customs that were incompatible with the protection of rights under CEDAW. In its third report, female genital mutilation (FGM) was described as "one of the customs and practices that have been inherited," and the report goes into detail on "state efforts to suppress this custom."[89] Also in its reports to the CEDAW Committee, the Egyptian government details the measures it has taken to implement the convention in a number of different areas. As Jasmine Moussa notes, in an extensive survey on Egyptian secular and Sharia laws it is possible to harmonize many aspects of Sharia-based law code with CEDAW obligations, and the CEDAW Committee has issued a recommendation dealing with these issues.[90] In its 2010 concluding observations, the committee welcomed Egypt's "progress in withdrawing reservations" but reiterated its concern over the reservation to Article 16, reaffirming it as "incompatible with the object and purpose of the Convention."[91]

In the process of contesting obligations under CEDAW, the Egyptian government was not only defending its domestic legal sovereignty but implicitly constructing a version of culture where laws protecting marital traditions were "unquestionable."[92] The construction of culture was based on Egyptian society, but the selection, recognition, and, ultimately, defense of cultural tradition in arguments to the CEDAW Committee was in the hands of the Egyptian government. As Yvonne Donders and Vincent Vleugel note, resistance to the CEDAW Committee from state parties and the presentation of cultural values as impediments to the implementation of particular rights is common, and not limited to arguments over Sharia.[93] Understanding this as a contestation over sovereignty helps explain why certain practices are defended by states and others aren't. It is perfectly possible for states to rationalize weakening domestic legal sovereignty in a particular area in order to comply with a human rights treaty.[94] When making a defensive relativist argument, however, a state is doing the opposite of this, selecting a set of traditions which it then designates as immutable and inherent to its sovereignty in international law. The claim being made by states uses a modified version of the principle of the cultural defense, originally developed by Renteln in the context of municipal law, which maintains that when an individual commits a crime in the context of a culturally motivated act they may, as a defense, raise the cultural context that inspired or shaped their actions.[95] This theory has been criticized for being highly deterministic about the nature of individual actions, assigning cultural traditions the responsibility of shaping and controlling individuals.[96] When this argumentative framework is used in international law, it not only advances a deterministic vision about the nature of society (maintaining that traditions shape society and can't be changed) but also maintains that this determinism makes any attempt to incentivize a change of cultural values an infringement of a state's sovereignty.

Later chapters demonstrate how defensive relativism can be used as a tactical argument to maintain human rights compliance while at the same time resisting the domestic reforms to laws and institutions required by international human rights law. The state construction of culture is a crucial part of that process because of the link between sovereignty and culture. As discussed in the beginning of this section, culture is always the subject of construction in political disputes—and the arguments by the monarchs prior to the Thirty Years' War over the churches at which their subjects worshiped relied on the head of state constructing an argument about the nature of religious and cultural practices in society. The principle established in seventeenth-century Europe that rival princely states should not try and interfere with another state's appointed church and the worship of their subjects is in essence the ancestor of the argument in the twenty-first century that international human rights bodies should not try and interfere with the cultural values that states deem important.

Identifying the State Construction of Culture in Defensive Relativists' Argument

The state construction of culture in defensive relativist argument manifests itself in three central forms. While there are other forms of claim about cultural values, these are, as subsequent chapters will highlight, the three most common. As defensive relativism is a form of cultural relativism advanced by states in international legal practices, defensive relativism can be identified in the arguments made by a state party in response to an international tribunal or human rights body, or in the text of instruments created by states. Within these legal practices, defensive references to a state's construction of culture are three common argumentative forms. It is the role of the next chapter to analyze the legal implications of these arguments; for present purposes, it is important to focus on the way references to culture are presented as a form of claim about state and the nature of moral values in a society. Each of these claims is summarized in the title of each subsection below and followed by an unpacking of their theoretical origin and an illustrative case study.

Cultural Values are Static and Resistant to External Change

Many anthropologists have criticized the perception that culture and cultural values are naturally closed and therefore antagonistic to human rights as an attempt to create an artificial "us versus them" dichotomy.[97] Traditions and practices in most, if not all, societies are continually emergent; social life is always happening in the present, so active decisions are being made about whether a way of living should be maintained or transformed in the face of economic, cultural, and political changes affecting it.[98] Attitudes toward the legitimate roles of violence, state coercion, and the role of women have changed over time in many societies.[99] Yet defensive relativists often draw on absolutist ideas about the relative incommensurability of cultural values in constructing their arguments. This involves the construction of what Seyla Benhabib describes as an interpretation of culture that is "hermetic, sealed," reflecting a "reductionist sociology of knowledge."[100] Epistemically, this is what Neil Walker terms "thick particularism," as it does not acknowledge divergent strands of opinion but rather protects a set of values as a uniform and closed system of morality.[101] This is remarkably reductive and does not assign individuals any real agency—the underlying assumption being that moral values are entirely contingent upon the culture of an individual's birth. Individuals in these arguments are, as Bhikhu Parekh notes, rendered "passive and pliant material devoid of independent thought."[102] Decisions on morality become simply a matter of consulting the prevailing social standard of the society in question. James Rachels poses the following thought experiment to illustrate the limits of this argument: "Suppose in 1975 a resident of South Africa was wondering whether his country's policy of apartheid was correct . . . all he has to do is ask whether this policy conformed to his society's moral code."[103]

Examples of this assumption are the arguments raised in opposition to the repeal of laws criminalizing sexual orientation. At the time *Dudgeon v. United Kingdom* was heard at the European Court of Human Rights, the nineteenth-century law criminalizing "buggery" was still in force in Northern Ireland some years after it had been repealed in the rest of the United Kingdom, and was being used to criminalize private homosexual behavior in Northern Ireland.[104] The applicant argued that this violated his right to a private life under Article 8 of the European Convention on Human Rights (ECHR), but the British government responded that this was a legitimate restriction given that religious communities in Northern Ireland strongly objected to homosexuality.[105] The fact that some other groups in Northern Ireland had argued strongly in favor of decriminalization was not taken into account in the state party's submissions, which argued that criminalization reflected the dominant cultural sentiment. Other states behaved in a similar fashion when defending the criminalization of sexual orientation in response to the now widely acknowledged obligation in international human rights law to repeal such laws due to their incompatibility with the right to privacy. Governments from some of southern African countries argued in the late 1990s that homosexuality was simply incompatible with their countries' traditions and later used such arguments to resist international calls to repeal their laws criminalizing sexual orientation.[106] It is an open question in these cases as to how much the state parties actually believed these conceptions of culture were genuine, or how much the state simply utilized a closed conception of culture in order to tactically mount a defensive relativist argument.

In some cases this has gravitated into a quasi-epistemic claim; the Nigerian national report to the UN Human Rights Council in 2009 as part of the Universal Periodic Review (UPR) process stated that the LGBT community was "not visible in Nigeria" and that LGBT rights were not a human rights issue in Nigeria.[107] There is an LGBT rights community in Nigeria that at the time was experiencing numerous human rights issues, not least the ongoing criminalization of sexual orientation in federal law, and the presentation of this issue in the national report seemed to support the sentiment echoed in domestic political discourse that homosexuality was alien to Nigerian culture. This kind of moral claim, Bernard Williams notes, utilizes the concept of incommensurability from the philosophy of science, which in its more extreme form maintains that two separate theories of the same phenomenon cannot be combined.[108] This is, in essence, the position adopted collectively by states in the Organisation of Islamic Cooperation (OIC) group at the UN Human Rights Council who have refused to consider LGBT rights as a human rights issue, citing cultural incompatibility.[109] When in 2003 Brazil proposed a resolution on LGBT rights to the UN Commission on Human Rights, five states that criminalized sexual orientation attempted to amend the resolution to remove a reference to the LGBT community or sexual orientation.[110] As Williams notes, arguments based on incommensurability often labor under the "artificial" assumption that there are "two clearly self-contained cultures" that do not intermingle with "one another [or] exchange and modify practices and attitudes."[111] More broadly, the idea of a closed value system draws on the ideas of absolutism and cultural absolutism in the way that Howard defines them, to maintain that value systems cannot, or more accurately should not, be subject to outside influences.[112]

Tradition Needs to Be Protected from International Human Rights Law's Cosmopolitanism

Cultural values can also be defined and defended as a reaction to international human rights law, in particular its cosmopolitan assumptions. Under a cosmopolitan ethical system, as David Held defines it, "allegiance is owned first and foremost to the moral realm of all humanity" and not to any national or ethnic grouping.[113] Cosmopolitanism is reflected in international human rights law both in its substantive provisions, which oblige states as a matter of law to adopt domestic legal reforms reflecting cosmopolitan values, and in the way that human rights law is used in political discourse, which is used as a shorthand reference for a set of transcendental moral values.[114] Critics of cosmopolitan thinking have noted how some of its leading proponents tend toward forms of Eurocentric assumptions about the construction of society.[115] Pheng Cheah situates cosmopolitanism in the context of a much wider project of economic globalization, which both supports and spreads human rights but also turns to them as a moral justification for political projects.[116] As a means of moving away from this dominant paradigm, some have focused on the rooting of human rights and moral values in local demands for justice. Yet, another means of rejecting cosmopolitanism's appeal to a notion of humanity that transcends national identity can also be the reassertion of a dominant state identity. This can take the form of a reactionary argument, which, as Mark Lilla describes it, contends that the "well-ordered state" previously governed by respect for "tradition" is being undermined by the presence of "alien ideas."[117] It can also take on a distinctly conservative form, as Howard notes with reference to debates about multiracialism in Canada, where a defense of cultural values was used to justify positions such as "[no one] would want to live in the same community as blacks," which, while racist, arose as part of a conservative response to cosmopolitan and universalist claims about citizenship.[118] The relationship between relativism and conservative ideas is in some ways obvious, as the unquestioning deference to community as the source of morality implicitly empowers traditional sources of social authority.[119] But reactionary behavior is different from conservatism, as it requires something to react to and is not necessarily an uncritical defense of all forms of authority.[120]

As the previous chapter outlines, the idea that human rights law has a hidden political agenda has been used to question the notion of universality, and the cosmopolitan assumptions of international human rights law can also provoke a reaction from states. The Indian government's reaction to the treatment of the caste system in international human rights law is an example of this argument. India is party to the Convention on the Elimination of all forms of Racial Discrimination (CERD), and Article 1 defines racial discrimination as "exclusion, restriction or preference based on race, colour, descent, or national or ethnic origin."[121] For many years, the Indian government contended that this provision did not apply to caste even though the CERD committee on repeated occasions found that caste, by virtue of being inherited, was a form of descent.[122] The Indian government maintained that it had passed extensive domestic legislation to decrease formal discrimination on grounds of caste, but Dalits—the lowest caste sometimes referred to as "untouchables"—argued that systemic social discrimination persisted, and therefore required not just an end to formal discrimination in bureaucratic procedures but in far-reaching affirmative action.[123] The Indian government maintained, however, that caste was a specifically Indian problem that was not analogous to other forms of discrimination experienced by other countries, despite the 2007 concluding observations of the committee stating it was a form of discrimination.[124] It is important to note that the government's position was not so much a defense of the caste system but a reaction to an international human rights body claiming that caste was its concern.

When, in 2001, activist groups sought to include a statement on caste in the final Programme of Action at the second world conference on Racism, Racial Discrimination, Xenophobia and Related Intolerance, the Indian minister of state for external affairs criticized it as a form of "social engineering" and claimed it was inappropriate for international human rights law to "legislate, let alone police, individual behavior in our societies."[125] In 2016, when responding to a report from the UN special rapporteur on minority issues on caste discrimination, senior Indian diplomats again claimed that caste was unique to Indian society and that this was an inappropriate extension of both the special rapporteur's mandate and the scope of CERD.[126] There have been several other resolutions at the UN Human Rights Council on caste and racial discrimination, all of which have been resisted by India on similar grounds. Political opinion in India was divided on the issue, for much of the 2010s with different values placed on intercaste relations and rights and a very complex ongoing debate taking place among the societies involved.[127] Internationally the subtleties of this debate disappeared, however, turning into a straightforward but antagonistic division, with the cosmopolitan values of human rights law on one side maintaining that it was a form of discrimination and the government on the other side claiming that it was an interference in sovereign matters. Reports at the beginning of the 2020s on caste-based discrimination in India suggested that while a lot of the traditional barriers had evaporated, deep structural barriers in society remained.[128] In this case, the reaction international law provoked ended up cementing the conflation of cultural values and sovereignty.

The Meaning of Culture Is Left Unspecified

In defining culture, defensive relativists often leave a large degree of ambiguity about what the meaning of certain concepts are or how terms are to be interpreted, which enables state definitions of cultural values, or, more accurately, the definitions of cultural values by the elites of states, to gain prominence. Critics of cultural relativism have often been highly skeptical of the way that culture and cultural values are determined, noting the propensity for elite capture in the process of state definition. In an influential 1996 paper, Adamantia Pollis warns that a more significant question than the often narrow debate between universalism and relativism is "whether modern states adhere to the values that they claim inhere in their cultures," or whether the language of cultural relativism is used "to justify and rationalize [a state's] own repressive actions" and the "governing elites'" drive to consolidate or to hold on to political power."[129] In a 1985 article, Fernando Tesón, in an influential critique of absolutist ideas of relativism, describes the idea as "elitist" because it is insufficiently concerned with the role of human suffering and prioritizes the protection of cultural values out of concern about "ethnocentrism" regardless of the state's morality.[130] The argument Tesón hints at but does not explore in detail is that the capacity of elites to define what is and what is not cultural could lead to the use of "traditions as a shield against legitimate demands for basic human rights."[131] In a wide-ranging study in 2007, Anjesh Prasad notes the way relativist ideas, which originated in moral philosophy and anthropological thought, have been "appropriated by third world bourgeois-nationalist elites" leading to them entering into an enabling relationship with oppression.[132]

Vague or imprecise definitions of culture are instrumental in this process. As Li argues, if one wishes to take the cultural context of ethical positions into account, it is necessary to "critically examine culture" and "scrutinize" its "attributes and nature."[133] But in practice it is precisely this level of scrutiny that defensive relativists wish to avoid, hence the resort to a lack of specificity in references to cultural practices. Culture, Charles Beitz argues, provides a "concrete precept" that can create "instability" in a claim of universality by positing the existence of a place with alternate and more "stable" moral norms.[134] The extent to which a claim of culture can fulfill this function is in part dependent on references to culture being a term into which state parties can insert different meanings. One of the most significant issues with reservations to CEDAW, for example, is that there are often deliberately imprecise or vague references to religion or religious practices in the text of reservations.[135] Some of this is more broadly strategic—it allows states to exploit the inherent indeterminacy of certain legal concepts to maintain that a limitation of rights is in fact justified by international law.[136] The capacity of states to control the meaning of what culture and cultural values entail has been critiqued in other areas of international law; as Thomas Eriksen argues, the UNESCO concept of culture, as defined by various UNESCO instruments, has been responsible for the "imposition of homogeneity whether from the state or self-appointed spokesperson of the group."[137] What distinguishes defensive relativist argument, however, is the intentional vagueness of various terms which can, if used as methods of interpretation or as justification for a state to limit rights, give the state virtually unlimited leeway to restrict rights according to its own state-constructed definition of culture.

An example of this is the resolutions on "traditional values" at the UN Human Rights Council. In 2009, a group of countries including China, Russia, and Singapore tabled a resolution following up from the 1993 Vienna Declaration and Programme of Action which, in the title, contained a reference to understanding the "traditional values of humankind."[138] The resolution, echoing the earlier text of the Vienna Declaration, noted that "human rights must be treated in a fair and equal manner" but that "the significance of national and regional particularities and various historical, cultural and religious backgrounds" must be taken into account, and called on the UN high commissioner for human rights to convene an "exchange of views on . . . a better understanding of traditional values of humankind."[139] These concepts were all very open ended, and at a workshop a year later, the high commissioner for human rights, Navi Pillay, warned that concept of traditional values could be used as a shield to erode the authority of human rights.[140] Although many states pushed back at this interpretation of the term "traditional values," there were a number of different practices often associated with, and defended using the language of, tradition identified by the Office of the Human Rights Commissioner, such as forced female genital mutilation, which clearly were human rights violations.[141] Defenders of references to cultural values could not find adequate demarcations in their use of the concept and did not make any concerted attempt to do so. In 2011, a further Resolution, sponsored by Russia, again looked at the issue—as the title put it—of "promoting human rights and fundamental freedoms through a better understanding of [the] traditional values of humankind."[142] Again, the resolution's substantive terms emphasized the universality of human rights and went on to emphasize the importance of traditional values before noting "the important role of family, community, society and educational institutions in upholding and transmitting these values."[143] Although the resolution was clear that "traditions shall not be invoked to justify harmful practices violating universal human rights," there was a distinct lack of any definition of the different concepts mentioned in the declaration and how they were to be interpreted.[144]

The International Justice Resource Center noted in a comment shortly after the 2011 resolution that the concept of traditional values was "without a firm foundation in international law" and that it would be "especially problematic for institutions like the Human Rights Committee"—the treaty body of the International Covenant on Civil and Political Rights (ICCPR)—to use such an imprecise tool to assess "whether a State is complying with their international obligations."[145] As the sponsor of the resolution, Russia's emphasis on "traditional values" also provoked concern among some human rights activists because it came at a time when it was using the rhetoric of protecting traditional values in domestic politics to justify limiting LGBT rights.[146] As women's' rights activists noted, the traditionalism-versus-modernity clash engineered by the resolutions was also at the core of a wider ideological challenge to women's human rights.[147] Yet, the key instrumental factor for many of the states supporting both resolutions was that "tradition" as an undefined concept should be recognized as a legitimate ground for interpreting human rights law, a development which would, if ever put into practice, result in states having interpretative power over both the meaning of the law and what was and what was not traditional.[148]

Conclusion: State Culture

Let us return to the Aztec sacrifice case with which this chapter begins. In common with Brown, I used a modified version of this exercise for law students—my undergraduate human rights law class had to imagine the Aztec empire was a party to the ICCPR and was seeking to defend the practice of human sacrifice within the terms of the convention. The limitations on Article 6 (the right to life) allow for the death penalty, but only when administered by a component court; they also give those sentenced to death the right to appeal.[149] Reading the literature on human sacrifice, it is difficult to conclude those selected for human sacrifice had anything like a trial or a right of appeal.[150] This leads students to argue that the practice is so culturally important to the state that it ought to be exempted from fulfilling that particular obligation—in other words, reaching instinctively for the defensive relativist argument. The nations of the sixteenth century were of course never party to any human rights instrument, and to suppose that such standards could apply to them is unrealistic. Yet, the point of such an exercise was not about the Aztecs but about the students as would-be international lawyers arguing a state party's case—relativistic arguments emerged as a response to the assertion that a state's laws or practices are incompatible with international human rights law and the state's version of culture was constructed and articulated in these arguments. Anthropologists and philosophers might object to this as a highly reductive notion of cultural relativism, but defensive relativism, while drawing on some of the ideas of cultural and moral relativism, does not attempt intellectual coherence because as a form of argument it is primarily a tactical response to international human rights law.

Defensive relativist arguments rely on a construction of culture that emerges via the process of defending legislation, institutions, or social practices in response to the obligations of international human rights law which require changes to be made. This makes "culture" in defensive relativist arguments—the substance of what a state practicing defensive relativism is notionally defending—more a defense of a state's domestic legal sovereignty than a definitive statement about the cultural values of societies within that state. The three most common argumentative forms used by defensive relativists to refer to culture, described in the final section of this chapter, all have the intended end result of placing the state government as the sole authority for defining the nature and meaning of what culture and cultural values mean in the context of that state. As will be shown in chapter 3, this becomes important as references to culture are used to justify limiting rights or an interpretation of a state's obligations which limits rights.

CHAPTER 3

Legal Exemption: The Final Element of Defensive Relativism

"It is the concept of every social order," the renowned jurist Hans Kelsen wrote in 1952, "to bring about certain reciprocal behavior of men," requiring them to refrain from particular courses of conduct and carry out others.[1] The whole point of international law, Kelsen concluded, was to change the behavior of "men," or the male-dominated governments of states who are the subjects of international law. International obligations were, in the eighteenth and nineteenth century, generally understood as consensual commitments from states, at least from those territories recognized as states or as stemming from the law of nations or international custom. When rights began to be codified in international law, such as the right to self-determination in the 1919 League of Nations charter, they were presented in collective terms. The groups that were entitled to enjoy those rights were strictly controlled by the dominant powers of the day according to their ideas of racial hierarchy.[2] Individual rights did not have much of a place in international law, which had traditionally seen the individuals living within states as the subjects of states rather than as stakeholders in the international legal order.[3] International human rights law poses a problem for this understanding of international law, as it seeks to directly create rights for individuals living within states.[4] It does this by placing a legal obligation on states to implement laws and change domestic practices in order to protect the substantive rights contained in international human rights law.

The process of discharging obligations varies considerably, and there are number of different legal mechanisms a state can utilize to protect rights in a manner which responds to divergent cultures and societies within its jurisdiction. These are detailed in the second and third sections of this chapter, setting the context for understanding the third and final element of defensive relativism—the claim to a legal exemption, which is discussed in this chapter's final section. A legal exemption means seeking to exempt a state from the legal obligations of a human rights regime, such as an international treaty or regional human rights organization, in a manner which, strictly speaking, might not be legal but allows a state to remain within the overall legal framework of that regime while maintaining notional compliance with the law. What differentiates defensive relativism from other forms of relativist discourse—which may share the antiuniversalist approach to human rights outlined in chapter 1 or defend the state construction of culture outlined in chapter 2—is that it attempts to achieve a tangible legal outcome. In practice, this involves a state either shaping future legal obligations (which will be discussed more in the specific case study in chapter 4) or, as is set out in this chapter, seeking a form of legal exemption. To understand the meaning of a legal exemption it is important to acknowledge that what a state is attempting to do when advancing a defensive relativist case is remain in a human rights regime. Yet at the same time it does not wish to comply with a particular obligation of that regime (with which other parties are expected to comply) because that obligation would be at odds with a domestic law or practice which the state defends. What a state practicing defensive relativism is attempting to do, therefore, is argue that its limitation, or nonimplementation of a particular obligation, is in fact legal within the framework of a human rights regime.

Defensive relativism as a form of argument emerges from the indeterminacy of international law. Martti Koskenniemi argued in *From Apology to Utopia* that the presentation of international law as an objective discipline, in contrast to forms of political argument, ignores the basic role of courts and legal institutions in rendering the vague standards of the law determinate as they go about the business of resolving the practical problems with which international law has been tasked.[5] In this process, relatively open-ended terms in international law, such as "sovereignty," require a concrete definition, which is less a matter of applying a clearly defined standard than one of construction. Equally, evaluative terms in human rights instruments, such as "undue delay" or "inhuman and degrading treatment," contain elements of indeterminacy which, in order to give a clear and universal meaning, require a degree of intercultural construction.[6] In a commentary on the Convention of the Rights of the Child (CRC), Philip Alston acknowledges that international human rights law might be inherently indeterminate, but this is desirable, as the broad value frameworks of international instruments will provide sufficient coherency for determining rights standards and will not run the risk of excessive antiuniversality of the sort described in chapter 1 of this book.[7] Some schools of thought in legal theory argue either that indeterminacy is structural or that legal rules can only be understood in the cultural context in which they were developed and are used.[8] Critics from the "New Stream" of international legal discourse, as Andrea Bianchi terms it, follow Koskenniemi in arguing that international law's structural indeterminacy reflects its liberal ideological underpinnings, creating recurring patterns of argument characterized by sets of dichotomies (i.e., normative versus concrete norms or communitarian versus autonomous norms), all of which reflect the increasingly incoherent nature of international law as a disciplinary project.[9] The effective conclusion of these different schools of thought is that the structural nature of international law's indeterminacy means attempts to arrive at universal definitions of the terms of international human rights laws end up in the reproduction of the politics of the institutions or states defining them. Alberto Puppo attempts to refine discussions about indeterminacy, which he notes is a somewhat ambiguous term, by separating "deep or radical indeterminacy," which deals with questions regarding the function or purpose of the whole institution of international law, from "normal indeterminacy," which concerns the applicability of a determinate rule to some real situation or the meaning of some particular legal issue.[10] The latter, Puppo argues, is "a normal feature of any domestic legal system" and can be consistent with a formalist approach to interpreting international law, which focuses on decision making by reference to a set of formal rules which are recognized as producing a legal outcome.[11] This form of indeterminacy and determinations by institutions can be part of the way international law maintains its overall framework of authority. Importantly, it is the presence of the former concept—radical indeterminacy—which underdetermines international law's normal indeterminacy; as Jason Beckett explains, it is impossible to "answer the question of what law says until we have answered the question of what law is."[12]

Because defensive relativists are often making a legal argument in order to defend their state's position within an international legal regime, they are not really engaging in radical indeterminacy. To use Upendra Baxi's terminology, they are not theorizing about what human rights law is "for," they are instead trying to play a legal game of interpretation or demarcation within the context of a given international regime to determine what, in practice, their obligations under human rights law "are."[13] An interpretative game, to use Daniel Peat and Matthew Windsor's terminology, is a metaphor for the way states and international bodies contest the linguistic and practical meanings of the terms within certain boundaries; an example of this is discussed in the second case study in the third section of this chapter, which looks at the dispute over the evolutive interpretations of treaties.[14] A demarcation game, or dispute, is where a state contends that an international regime lacks the legal authority to involve itself in a particular matter; an example of this is discussed in the fourth case study in the third section of this chapter, which looks at the way reservations to treaty provisions operate.[15] These games are played by states practicing defensive relativism in order to challenge the limits of legal doctrines designed to allow pluralism in the delivery of a state's obligations under a human rights instrument. Antiuniversalist arguments and arguments about the state construction of culture end up being framed in terms of concepts which would work within the interpretive communities of international law, such as tribunals and treaty bodies; therefore, the process described in the previous chapter whereby notions of culture and sovereignty are fused takes on a precise form in the interpretation and demarcation games of defensive relativists, in order to increase their chances of success before international institutions.[16] The "game" metaphor has its limitations but captures the contests of meaning in international human rights law, of which defensive relativism is a crucial part, and the way that defensive relativism seeks the "prize" from the game of an exemption from the obligation to implement a particular right.

The Nature of a State's Obligations in International Human Rights Law

The seventeenth-century Dutch legal theorist Hugo Grotius described international legal obligations as arising from "the duty of benevolence the duty of keeping faith or the duty of making amends for wrongdoing."[17] This formulation was rooted in the Roman-Dutch legal tradition and was essentially a projection of civil law onto the law of nations, as it was then termed. It was established as a matter of practice after the Congress of Vienna in 1815 that a state was bound by both the obligations made with other states in the form of treaties and by the laws of nations—the web of customs and practices determining conduct between states.[18] States were by and large responsible for upholding these obligations because their enjoyment of sovereignty and the framework of international law was to an extent contingent on reciprocity within the international system; as Judge Huber of the Permanent Court of

International Justice noted in a 1925 decision, "responsibility is the necessary corollary of a right."[19] The 1970 Declaration of Friendly Relations between States made it clear that a state was expected to "fulfil in good faith its obligations under international agreements" and "generally [recognize] principles and rules of international law."[20] The focus on treaties and customary international law omits other sources of law and obligation, leading toward a divide between "soft" and "hard" forms of law, with the latter having a binding character and the former considered to be of a largely political nature.[21] Such a sharp distinction has more of a basis in legal theory than state practice, and many commitments termed soft law have some discernible effect on state behavior. Not all instruments containing human rights law are treaties which create a responsibility upon a state to implement their provisions into its domestic law; for example, the 1986 Declaration on the Right to Development is part of a UN General Assembly Resolution, which is not, strictly speaking, legally binding on states, although the holders of duties under the declaration are international institutions and other states.[22]

Obligations in international human rights law can, at a very basic level, be broken down into those which are mandatory and those that are consensual. Some norms, such as the prohibition on torture, are binding on states regardless of their consent to any particular instrument.[23] Peremptory norms, as they are termed (sometimes referred to as *jus cogens*), are binding on states principally because they represent norms which are important to the international community as a whole, and their preservation allows the protection of the international community as a community.[24] As Oscar Schachter notes, some International Court of Justice (ICJ) judgments inferred the existence of legal obligations using terms such as the "will of the community" or "humanitarian duty," which are used to infer the existence of obligations upon states in a broader sense.[25] These are often quite limited in nature, and while some academic discourse has attempted to expand the range of rights-based issues considered *jus cogens*, in practice many of the rights considered to have *jus cogens* status, such as the prohibition on torture or slavery, largely (although, it is important to stress, not exclusively) deal with prohibited state conduct.[26] Therefore, the level of contestation from defensive relativists is often relatively limited, mainly concerning the implementation of positive obligations to tackle the deeper societal causes of certain types of prohibited practice. For example, in many of the debates around the implementation of programs to combat female genital mutilation (FGM), the dispute is focused more on the means of intervention rather than (beyond a few exceptional cases) an outright justification of practices constituting inhuman and degrading treatment.[27] Even in cases where cultural practices conflict with *jus cogens* norms, the dispute is often more about the limits of the law than an absolutist defense of the practice. For example, in *Hadijatou Mani Koraou v. The Republic of Niger*, where an applicant was held in a traditional form of slavery and was unable to obtain remedies from the domestic courts in Niger, the defendant state did not contest that slavery was a protected cultural practice; it instead argued that slavery was being slowly eliminated in Niger and this was an issue of implementation making the case unnecessary.[28] As a consequence, this chapter is mainly focused on what the introduction to this volume terms human rights regimes—treaty bodies and regional bodies with tribunals—as this is often where a substantial disagreement about the implementation of obligations arises.

The consensual model refers to international treaty law, which places the general obligation on states to perform their obligations under the treaty in good faith, as codified in Article 31 of the Vienna Convention on the Law of Treaties (VCLT).[29] The International Law Commission (ILC), which in the 1960s drafted rules on treaty interpretation, explored the notion of good faith in a 1964 report, arguing that it meant interpretation with respect to the "declared or apparent objects and purposes," and substantive provisions should be interpreted "so as to give them their fullest weight and effect consistent with the normal sense of the words and with other parts of the text."[30] In practical terms, this means that where a state has become party to a human rights treaty it is expected to implement its provisions in line with the requirements of that treaty following a good faith interpretation of those terms. For example, Article 2 of the International Covenant on Civil and Political Rights (ICCPR) requires states "to adopt such legislative or other measures as may be necessary to give effect to the rights recognized in the present Covenant," which on a plain reading requires states to implement laws to protect the rights in the convention.[31] Some obligations are relatively easy for some states to adopt; for instance, one of the arguments used by President George Bush to secure the United States' ratification of the ICCPR in the early 1990s was that it was easy to satisfy its obligations under the treaty since many of its provisions were already protected in U.S. federal law.[32] State consent both explains the existence of the obligation and justifies any perceived weakening of a state's sovereignty after entry into a treaty framework which requires compliance with a tribunal or treaty body's interpretation of a treaty provision—the state is deemed to have consciously willed that state of affairs by consenting to an obligation to follow a particular body's interpretation of the law.[33] Yet, the idea that state consent justifies all obligations is open to question, given that sometimes state consent is time contingent and the scope of obligations a state is consenting to is not always clear at the time of signing or ratifying a treaty.[34] As the UK Privy Council noted, the language of the European Convention on Human Rights (ECHR) is "for the most part so general that some implication of terms is necessary"; the council also cautioned that this needs to be done carefully to avoid "contracting parties . . . by judicial interpretation, [becoming] bound by obligations which they did not expressly accept."[35]

While it may be clear that where an obligation originates has a bearing on whether it should bind a state, there is only a limited description of what a state is expected to do in the discharge of its obligations. The 1975 Final Act of the Conference on Security and Co-operation in Europe set out the principle that "in exercising their sovereign rights, including the right to determine their laws and regulations," states were under a duty to fulfill their international legal obligations—seemingly confirming the obligation to adhere to international legal standards in the creation of domestic law without ever really clarifying what the threshold for discharging such an obligation would be.[36] Some courts, tribunals, and treaty bodies have been careful in developing the scope of state obligation, especially in relation to the positive obligation of states to investigate or prevent violations of rights committed by third parties.[37] For example, the European Court of Human Rights (ECtHR), in its jurisprudence on Article 2 of the ECHR (the Right to Life), has held that the discharge of this obligation can require public authorities, such as the police, to protect individuals from known criminals directly threatening their life, but has been careful to set a high threshold for this obligation so as not to impose onerous obligations on the police force of state parties.[38] Equally, the ECtHR has held that Article 2 requires state parties to maintain environmental standards regarding the disposal of dangerous waste in order to safeguard against accidents which might result in a loss of life, but has not sketched out the precise content of what such environmental laws and regulations would be, leaving member states to do the technical work in this area.[39] Where the obligation on state parties under a human rights instrument only requires states to "progressively" implement the rights contained within it, as is the case with the International Covenant on Economic, Social, and Cultural Rights (ICESCR), this still places a substantial responsibility on a state party.[40] The Committee on Economic, Social, and Cultural Rights clarified that state parties to ICESCR are under an obligation to "use all the means at its disposal to give effect to the rights recognized," ensuring that within the "domestic legal order, appropriate means of redress are available," and remedies are available "to any aggrieved individual or group."[41]

Broadly speaking, the obligation on the state under most international human rights instruments is to alter its laws and domestic practices where necessary in order to prevent a violation of the substantive provisions of an instrument. This does, however, leave some considerable scope for interpretation in key areas as to how extensive such implementation should be or what form it should take. In most non-human-rights-related multilateral treaties, it is other state parties that often take the lead in ensuring that good faith interpretation is being carried out by another party, lest they secure an unfair advantage. For example, under the 1961 Vienna Convention on Diplomatic Relations, states have a direct incentive to police another party's accreditation of diplomats in order to ensure that the other party does not breach the rules and gain an unfair advantage under the treaty's framework.[42] Human rights treaties, however, are not mechanisms for bargaining interests between state parties or for regulating transnational interests. Human rights obligations are, as the Inter-American Court of Human Rights (IACtHR) held, part of a "legal order within which . . . [states] for the common good assume various obligations not in relation to other states but towards all individuals within their jurisdiction."[43] This effectively constructs a third-party interest in the form of the individuals living within the state.[44]

How far a state goes in protecting a right, such as the right to freedom of speech, is open to contestation, precisely because the nature of free speech is open to differing interpretations; therefore, within the scope of implementing a particular right there is room for some considerable divergence in how that right is implemented. Because individuals living within a state have been bestowed rights by a human rights instrument, they have an incentive to contest a state's interpretation of their rights if they disagree with, or are affected by, that interpretation. The legal theorist Stanley Fish once described interpretation as the "only game in town," but the most important part of this famous phrase, Andrea Bianchi argues, is the word "game,"—as the interpretation of all rules takes place within a normative framework for their contestation, reflecting the habits and culture of those involved.[45] The starting point for interpreting treaties is found in Articles 31–33 of the VCLT, which set out the "good faith" and "object and purpose" test for interpreting the individual terms of a treaty. Human rights tribunals can circumscribe the limits of what can be realistically considered in the process of interpretation to deliberately exclude certain considerations. For example, in *Tyrer v. UK*, the ECtHR held that the practice of "birching" young offenders (a traditional form of corporal punishment on the Isle of Man in the UK), regardless of its popularity and acceptance as a practice, could not be interpreted as being compatible with the UK's obligation to prohibit "inhuman and degrading treatment."[46] At a very basic level, as Fernando Tesón observes, this decision affirmed the "proposition that international human rights possesses a transboundary meaning that cannot be modified or ignored on relativist grounds."[47] Therefore, while a considerable degree of discretion can be allowed in the domestic interpretation of an obligation to implement a right contained in an international human rights instrument, allowing for a domestic slant to the realization of rights, the nature of that interpretation is circumscribed by international legal authority.[48] The range of different domestic forms of rights protection that can be interpreted as a legitimate discharge of obligations can be considerable. One study on the implementation of the Convention on the Rights of the Child (CRC) across South American states demonstrates how implementation of the convention can encompass processes as diverse as creating new institutions, repealing laws, or running promotional campaigns.[49] This can make it difficult for treaty bodies to assess compliance, although there has also been some criticism of the lack of a systemic method from the treaty bodies in developing an interpretive schema under the framework of the VCLT leading to inconsistent assessments of states' interpretation of their obligations.[50]

An examination of the patchwork nature of interpretation between different human rights bodies at the regional and international level can end up confirming Koskenniemi's thesis that international law is caught between an apology for following the wishes of states or utopic versions of what the law should be, which is divorced from state practice.[51] For example, some criticism of the ECtHR's process of interpretation has argued that it is too state-centric in cases such as *Bankovic v. Belgium* and *Al-Adsani v. UK*, which involved ECtHR jurisdiction in politically sensitive situations for the state concerned (respectively, war and relations with foreign governments), and that the ECtHR has failed to interpret the ECHR as an instrument of international public order promoting rights protection.[52] Equally, the rigorous work done in the development of the Yogyakarta Principles for the interpretation of the human rights instruments to protect LGBT rights can seem somewhat utopic in the context of the limited powers that treaties give human rights treaty bodies over the enforcement of their parent treaties, and the somewhat inconsistent way they interpret the discharge of obligations by state parties.[53] It is in this landscape that defensive relativism as an interpretive strategy operates. Like other interpretative strategies in what Bianchi calls the "interpretation game", it appeals to a set of principles that are amenable to the "perception of their audience" and accepted by the profession of international law.[54] Defensive relativism strategically packages its antiuniversalism and construction of culture into arguments about sovereignty or arguments within the context of existing legal mechanisms on the discharge of international obligations, making it more likely that these arguments will gain traction with international legal professionals, diplomats, and others involved in human rights institutions.[55] Examples of states engaging in what the introduction to this chapter describes as radical indeterminacy are relatively rare in defensive relativist practice, simply because it is often difficult to achieve the recognition of such arguments. One such instance is the Saudi reservation to the whole of the Convention on the Elimination of All Forms of Discrimination against Women (CEDAW), which states that in the event of a "contradiction between any term of the Convention and the norms of Islamic law, the Kingdom is not under obligation to observe the contradictory terms of the Convention."[56] This goes so far as to neutralize every single obligation under the entire convention—and in effect asks the radical indeterminist question, "What is the Convention for?"—but few, if any, regard this as a permissible reservation.[57] As will be shown, most defensive relativism does not attempt radical indeterminacy; instead, states use interpretation games to advance their construction of culture.

How Does a State Control and Limit the Discharge of Its Obligations under International Human Rights Law?

There are some legal mechanisms that allow a state to control the application of rights in its domestic law, thereby limiting the scope of its obligations under a human rights instrument. There are three principle legal mechanisms: derogations, reservations, and the margin of appreciation doctrine. Denunciation or withdrawal from treaties is not really at issue here, even though it is considered in some of the literature on the subject, because the state is often trying to exit from its legal obligations altogether rather than manage their scope.[58] In all the cases below, states wish to act within the law, or at least be seen to be acting within the law by a human rights body, but not remove themselves from a human rights regime itself. Arguments over the applicability of these legal mechanisms can be called a demarcation game, as they are a contest over the authority of an international regime in a particular area. In this game, states argue about the limits of a treaty in a formalist sense, in terms of the express powers granted to an international regime under the terms of a treaty.[59] They also argue about sovereignty in what Koskenniemi describes as its "self-justifying sense," where sovereignty is treated as a description and a norm, and any limitation on sovereignty can only be justified in terms of sovereignty itself.[60] In a demarcation game, a state aims to get an international body to recognize that one of the mechanisms described below should be available to the state to limit its obligations. Even if they are stretching the application of one of these mechanisms, the argument presented by states revolves around self-justifying sovereignty; i.e., a state is entitled to use a legal mechanism limiting rights because it has engaged in the act of signing up to a treaty which contains mechanisms allowing the limitation of rights. When participating in a demarcation game, a state practicing defensive relativism is, in short, attempting to draw an imaginary line demarcating its authority from the authority of an international regime to which it is a party and under which it has obligations to implement rights. As a form of argument, a demarcation game is distinct from an interpretation game, although both are used by defensive relativists through the legal mechanisms contained in the human rights instruments and organizations. The following will detail the nature of these mechanisms before going on in the final section to look at how defensive relativists use both interpretation and demarcation games to achieve a legal exemption.

Derogations

The derogation or suspension of the rights contained in a human rights treaty in response to an emergency is the most far-reaching power a state has to limit the application of human rights in the instruments which contain them. The rationale for suspending rights in a time of emergency can be found in rights jurisprudence from a number of different countries following the general principle that such an instrument should not be a form of "suicide pact," and temporarily limited suspensions of rights in times of grave emergency can help secure rights more broadly.[61] Derogating from a right goes further than other limitations of rights, such as might be justified under the margin of appreciation doctrine, as derogation involves the complete or partial suspension of the obligation to maintain the right which is the subject of the derogation. This is why some treaties such as the ICCPR take the position that, where possible, states should restrict rights through other mechanisms rather than enter a derogation.[62] As Rolando Gaete points out, derogation clauses are appealing to "dictatorial regimes" that can be induced to become party to human rights instruments through, in effect, the offering of "the right to use emergency clauses."[63]

Although derogation clauses might look tempting to a defensive relativist, their structure places some considerable restrictions on states. Under Article 15 of the ECHR, a state needs to demonstrate that it is facing an "emergency threatening the life of the nation," and the ECtHR has imposed a clear test for ascertaining when such an emergency occurs.[64] The Inter-American Commission on Human Rights has also emphasized that situations must be sufficiently serious for there to be a suspension of the rights guaranteed in the American Convention on Human Rights (ACHR).[65] A derogation is not a carte blanche for a state to restrict rights as they choose, as any rights restrictions justified by a derogation must be limited to responding to the circumstances of the emergency.[66] Finally, the derogation clauses in the ACHR, ECHR and the ICCPR all require some form of supranational supervision or option for review of any such order constraining the traditional sovereign prerogative of deciding and exercising emergency powers.[67] This all significantly limits the power of a state to suspend rights, and the requirement to demonstrate the existence of an emergency does not automatically lend itself to the construction of a state culture described in chapter 2. Therefore, while there are often tensions between a state and a human rights regime over a state's use of derogation clauses, they are not really the sites of defensive relativist argument. They are where a state contests its sovereign prerogatives rather than asserts its cultural identity.

Reservations

Article 19 of the VCLT allows a state to enter reservations to a specific treaty provision, meaning that it will not be required to follow that provision. As the International Law Commission's (ILC) report on reservations makes clear, a permitted reservation's effect is to "exclude or to modify the legal effect of certain provisions" of a treaty as it applies to a state.[68] Partial reservations to human rights treaties allowing for a variation in national law or some other specific circumstance particular to the state entering that reservation can offer a useful way to encourage accession to that treaty.[69] When reservations blanket-cover a whole range of different provisions or are open ended in their wording, this can act as a barrier to implementing human rights treaties. The ILC's report prohibits vague or general reservations, stating that a reservation should "be worded in such a way as to allow its meaning to be understood."[70] As outlined in the preceding two chapters, a number of states have entered reservations to treaties which are sufficiently vague as to allow a state party to claim more or less what it likes in relation to the implementation of a particular right. Reservations of this sort are often held to be impermissible, meaning as a matter of law they should not be permitted—although the exact way in which that determination is made and what the practical consequences on a state are following such a determination has been open to considerable debate.[71]

The object and purpose test, first applied by the International Court of Justice in its advisory opinion on reservations to the Genocide Convention, sets up an arbitral standard for assessing the permissibility of a reservation, by asking whether the reservation is compatible with the overall objectives of the treaty and the changes on state behavior the treaty in question intended to make.[72] The Human Rights Committee (HRC)—the ICCPR's treaty body—has stated in general terms that states should recognize the full range of rights accorded in a human rights treaty because "human rights norms are the legal expression of the essential rights that every person is entitled to as a human being."[73] This is similar to the positions taken by both the Inter-American Court in a 1982 advisory opinion and the ECtHR in an early judgment on the principle of reservations.[74] The HRC specifically noted in its general comment on reservations that where the reservation is on a matter of customary international law that reservation will be considered void; the HRC illustrated this by reference to fifteen different practices, such as allowing slavery, engaging in torture, or presuming a person guilty unless they prove their innocence, that could not be the subject matter of a reservation.[75]

In spite of some early scholarship on the law of treaties weighing in heavily against reservations of any sort being considered permissible for human rights treaties, reservations are generally considered an important component of human rights treaties .[76] As Catherine Piper explains, reservations encourage "greater participation in the agreement" and serve to spread the norms that the treaty seeks to create.[77] For instance, a state which is party to a treaty might alter its preferences over time in relation to a reservation, and in general would be more likely to see a treaty regime as legitimate where it had had some scope in shaping its obligations by being able to manage them through the tactical application of reservations.[78] There are examples of states removing reservations that were once considered essential for their participation in an international treaty after a period of participation in that treaty. For example, Norway, on accession to the ECHR, insisted on a reservation limiting the rights protected under Article 9 (the right to freedom of religion) in relation to Jesuits, to reflect the country's long cultural tradition of excluding Jesuits from public life.[79] Later, it withdrew this reservation, in part because of social changes in Norway and because through its participation in the Council of Europe and its identification as a modern European state it no longer saw the need for a reservation of this sort.[80] Some human rights scholars have described this process of changing state behavior through interaction with international legal structures as state socialization.[81] Yet the flip side of this argument is that a state is being granted the opportunity to participate in a human rights agreement without making any meaningful commitments, something the HRC recognized when it warned that "a tendency of states not to want to change a particular [domestic] law" would quickly lead to a situation where "no real international rights or obligations" are accepted by that party.[82] Jan Klabbers notes that the dilemma faced by human rights treaties has been linked to the failure to properly situate them as reflections of a normative public order, treating them instead as contractual bargains.[83] Yet, as Klabbers goes on to argue, this simply masks a wider dilemma in treaty law—not what he terms the "false dilemma" of the clash between universalism and relativism, but of how exactly alternate systems of values are recognized in an instrument that is designed to be universal.[84] Some reservations to CEDAW, for example, cover subject matter relating to arguments states lost during the drafting process and then subsequently reintroduced as reservations so as to not be bound by a legal commitment to which they had previously objected.[85]

Given that there is no easy answer to the dilemma reservations pose to human rights treaties, the legal framework for assessing reservations takes on a particular importance. There was some discussion during the drafting of the ICCPR as to the competence of treaty bodies to assess reservations; however, in their subsequent practice, treaty bodies have clarified their power to examine reservations in the same way that they deal with other aspects of treaty compliance.[86] International courts with stronger jurisdictional powers have less of an issue when it comes to their capacity to examine reservations, but both have increasingly utilized the severability doctrine, which prevents a reserving state from accessing the benefit of a reservation deemed to be incompatible with the treaty. This was first adopted by the ECtHR in *Belilos v. Switzerland*, where interpretative declarations entered by the Swiss government to Article 6 (the right to a fair trial) upon ECHR accession were held to be "too vague or broad for it to be possible to determine their exact meaning and scope," so the ECtHR proceeded to interpret Article 6 as applying to Switzerland without the benefit of the reservation.[87] This approach was adopted by the HRC when considering a reservation from Trinidad and Tobago to Protocol 1 of the ICCPR, which limited the committee's ability to hear petitions from individuals on death row in that country. The HRC held the reservation was discriminatory and therefore contrary to the object and purpose of the convention.[88] While this poses problems for the doctrine of state consent, as it effectively means imposing a nonexistent intent to comply with the treaty on a state which has entered a reservation indicating its intent to do the opposite, it has nevertheless become increasingly favored across the international community as a means of directly dealing with invalid reservations.[89]

Other mechanisms for dealing with invalid reservations are also prone to legal and practical problems. The opposability doctrine, which is based on Article 20 of the VCLT, maintains that where a state makes a reservation to a treaty, any other contracting state may object to that reservation, specifying that the treaty or that provision does not enter into force between those two states.[90] Given the nature of human rights treaties, opposability has relatively little impact unless all states block the accession of a reserving state to a human rights regime. Most human rights treaties try to encourage participation with their institutions in order to encourage the universalization of human rights.[91] There is little consistency in the objections that states enter against reservations—the far-reaching reservations entered by Libya to CEDAW received only four objections from other state parties—suggesting, as Roslyn Moloney argues, a level of near collusion among state parties to allow certain reservations to go unchallenged.[92] Part of this is due to the political dynamics of objecting to reservations (which are discussed in more detail in relation to CEDAW below), but, as Moloney concludes, this serves to underscore why the permissibility doctrine—that reservations should only be permissible if they meet the object and purpose test—provides the more coherent approach for dealing with reservations. Yet the permissibility doctrine still leaves important questions unanswered, specifically, as Moloney notes, "who has the authority to determine incompatibility," as this is not uniform across treaties or in the practice of human rights institutions, and raises the difficult question of who subsequently applies the doctrine of severability.[93] Human rights treaties are therefore left in a difficult position of attempting to maintain a permissibility test, with little clarity on which forum is to apply this test and what result (if any) occurs after its application.[94] There is a vast literature on permissible reservations to human rights treaties, and because no one effective approach has been established to deal with reservations, the practical ambiguity provides an opportunity for states to advance defensive relativist arguments to justify impermissible reservations.[95]

The Margin of Appreciation Doctrine

The margin of appreciation doctrine, which was outlined in chapter 1, quite simply entails a supranational tribunal or body allowing a state leeway to interpret a right protected in an international instrument in line with its national traditions. Rights considered *jus cogens*, or absolute rights, are granted a limited or no real margin of appreciation, whereas rights such as the right to free speech or freedom of association, both of which are framed in the ECHR and ICCPR as qualified rights, allow a state some considerable leeway in terms of implementation. What this looks like in practice is that, in response to an individual petition alleging a violation of a particular right, a court or tribunal finds that the restriction or limitation of that particular right, as a consequence of a state's domestic laws or practices, is not a violation of the state's obligations in respect of that particular right. This has two basic justifications: firstly, to pay deference to the state's national authorities and the decisions of its political and legal institutions' decisions in the implementation of international obligations, which is a means of acknowledging the sovereignty of individual states and their institutions.[96] Secondly, the margin of appreciation acknowledges the normative uncertainty of certain rights, such as the right to privacy, and the different conceptions of such rights between member states of a human rights regime acknowledging that "the requirements of morals [vary] from time to time and from place to place."[97] The doctrine was developed at the ECtHR but had deeper roots in the principle of subsidiarity in international law.[98] The HRC does not operate a formal margin of appreciation doctrine, holding that the freedom a state has to implement rights in its jurisdiction is "not to be assessed by reference to a margin of appreciation, but by reference to the obligations" undertaken by the state.[99] Critics of the margin of appreciation doctrine note it can easily result in a situation where different standards of rights apply in different countries, and human rights standards overall might be "diluted."[100]

The margin of appreciation doctrine can allow for limitations of rights reflecting the moral traditions within a particular society. For example, there can be such divergent moral standards between states on a particular issue of interpretation, and no clear factual consensus, that it can be difficult to establish a consistent principle. In *Vo v. France*, the ECtHR declined to take a position on whether the fetus was covered by Article 2 of the ECHR, reasoning that "the diversity of views on the point at which life begins, of legal cultures and of national standards of protection," meant that there was no consensus about whether the fetus was "life."[101] Another example would be where there is such a culturally specific version of a harm or interest that is necessary to interpret a right in a particular way. For example, in *Tammer v. Estonia*, a journalist was charged with the criminal offense of insulting a public figure by using a traditional term denigrating the former prime minister for being a single mother.[102] Before the ECtHR, the Estonian authorities admitted that criminal charges interfered with Mr. Tammer's rights under Article 10 of the ECHR (the right to freedom of expression and opinion), but argued that such a charge was justified under the framework of Article 10 as it was proscribed by law in pursuit of the "protection of the reputation or rights of others," a permitted ground for restricting free speech under the framework of Article 10.[103] In reaching its decision that there had been no Article 10 violation, the ECtHR held that the words Mr. Tammer had used "had a very special meaning in the Estonian language" and that it was necessary in such cases to take their "specific nature within the Estonian language and culture" into account.[104] As James Sweeney notes, this was an example of the court giving due weight to the local meaning of the words at issue, rather than the court acknowledging that for cultural reasons free speech was subject to far greater restrictions in Estonia.[105]

There are three important elements to the margin of appreciation doctrine which seemingly make it less amenable to use by defensive relativists seeking to claim that a cultural practice or interpretation of human rights law ought to be acknowledged by an international tribunal or treaty body. Firstly, the doctrine at a fundamental level involves a tribunal's determination of how a law or practice restricting rights was created.[106] For example, in *Jahn v. Germany*, an ECtHR case involving land rights following the reunification of Germany in the 1990s, the court held that the threshold for interference should be where a state's laws restricting rights are "manifestly without reasonable foundation."[107] Even though the nature of this assessment is often highly deferential to state parties, the assessment of state lawmaking in this way runs counter to the absolutist claims about the inviolability of cultural claims outlined in the previous chapter. Secondly, tribunals retain the power to restrict the margin of appreciation in particular areas; for example, the IACtHR has maintained that in cases involving political speech, states have a limited margin of appreciation, meaning that laws restricting the activity of political parties are considered a violation of the right to free speech and political participation.[108] While potentially justified under the general need to protect democracy, this illustrates how the doctrine still involves a supranational tribunal determining the universality of particular rights, pushing back against the antiuniversalist claims about human rights which, as detailed in chapter 1, is an essential component of defensive relativism. Finally, and underpinning the first two points, the doctrine does not automatically respect the sovereignty of lawmaking or the importance of particular sovereign prerogatives (as it is sometimes argued in relation to derogations and national security); it is instead a way of navigating the metaphorical "crossroads" of international judicial supervision and national sovereignty.[109] Therefore, the starting point in any application of the margin of appreciation doctrine is that an institution assesses how a state has balanced certain interests in making laws that restrict rights with its obligations under a human rights agreement. This is in tension with the fusion of cultural values and the sovereignty of domestic lawmaking, in the defensive relativist argument.[110] However, this does not mean that defensive relativists don't attempt to use the margin of appreciation doctrine to gain a legal exemption.

Argumentative Strategies toward a Legal Exemption from Human Rights Obligations

The first section of this chapter sets out in basic terms what a state's obligations under international human rights law are—namely, the implementation of policies and laws to implement and protect the human rights contained in a human rights instrument. There is a degree of flexibility in the interpretation of these obligations, and states can play interpretation games to justify their interpretation of particular treaty provisions. In the second section, the three main legal mechanisms for limiting rights in a state's jurisdiction are outlined, along with the way states might utilize them to make a defensive relativist case in what can be termed a demarcation game—an argument about the limits of the authority of a legal regime under one of the mechanisms to limit the application of rights. Interpretation and demarcation games relating to human rights instruments are, as John Tobin argues, "ultimately an act of persuasion . . . to persuade the relevant interpretive community [a tribunal or treaty body] that a particular interpretation is the most appropriate meaning to adopt."[111] Persuasion, Tobin argues, depends on consistent reasoning within "the system of international law, and [must be] sensitive to the nature of the socio-political context within individual states."[112] States practicing defensive relativism are attempting to work within an existing legal framework, pleading that the framework in question should be understood in a manner that is not merely sensitive but actively deferential to the sociopolitical context in their state. They take a maximalist antiuniversalist position and defend certain practices—the ones at issue in a given case—but use legal language or framings to make these points, enhancing the likelihood of success in context of the interpretation/demarcation game they are playing. The complicated nature of secondary rules surrounding interpretation of legal instruments, or, indeed, the lack of such rules in the case of many bodies such as treaty bodies, is not as much of an issue as the ability of defensive relativists to root their arguments in legal authority; it can be to a defensive relativist's advantage if the rules surrounding interpretation are unclear, as they can be strategically utilized to suit their objectives.[113] What the state practicing defensive relativism is seeking at the conclusion of this is, in effect, a "pass" or exemption for not discharging its legal obligations under the relevant legal framework. It should be seen as an exemption, as the state in question is either not fulfilling an obligation, interpreting a right in a very narrow way, or limiting a right in a manner that would be considered excessive and going beyond the legal mechanisms (described above) designed to qualify human rights.[114] States in these situations want to persuade the interpretative community in question to find that they are acting in accordance with their obligations—in other words, to grant them an exemption.[115]

To understand the concept of a legal exemption, it is necessary to make four clarifications about the precise nature of what is being sought by defensive relativists. Firstly, states are attempting to justify their conduct as legal, or at least claim that it ought to be recognized by an institution with interpretative authority (i.e,. a tribunal or treaty body) as a legal act within the framework of international human rights law. This is a metaphorical "win" of the game in question, and the virtue of thinking of interpretation and demarcation as a game helps highlight that states can also "lose" these games and not be granted a legal exemption. Some of the cases considered below and in subsequent chapters, such as the arguments about the ECtHR's margin of appreciation, involve examples of a human rights body rejecting a state's defensive relativist arguments. Secondly, as already noted, states making the case for a legal exemption are not necessarily arguing that they should leave a particular human rights agreement. This aspect of the argument distinguishes defensive relativism from arguments criticizing the way in which a human rights agreement interferes with a state's domestic lawmaking authority.[116] An operating assumption of most defensive relativists is that entering into and remaining a member of a particular human rights treaty has at least instrumental value to their state; therefore, the argumentative strategies to achieve a legal status (set out below) are designed to preserve that status.[117]

Thirdly, the case for a legal exemption is for the most part implicitly subjective—it argues that an exemption is necessary because of that state's culture. The antiuniversalist elements of the defensive relativist argument, detailed in chapter 1, are often used to support the precise claim at hand rather than establish a general principle of the nonuniversality of human rights. There are cases where defensive relativists make a general legal claim based on cultural particularism, but for the most part a legal exemption is being pleaded in relation to a specific situation and is agnostic about the consistency of the application of legal principles in other cases. All of this can make it difficult to tie down an exact uniform definition of a legal exemption, and can look like a state is engaged in a cherry-picking exercise. But engaging in what some scholars of human rights have described as *à* la carte compliance—where states pick and choose which obligations to follow and treat the substantive terms of a human rights instrument as some sort of menu of suggested legal reforms—would probably be a vision of compliance with international human rights law acceptable to many states making a defensive relativist case.[118] Fourthly, a legal exemption is not the same as the issues raised by the doctrine of legal pluralism, which refers to the coexistence of more than one legal order in a given field of social relations.[119] International human rights law can coexist in a pluralistic legal environment with different bodies applying and interpreting legal standards. Giselle Corradi's work on systems of indigenous justice and fair trial rights demonstrates that international law can provide a crucial set of baseline standards for assessing the nature of diverse legal and social practices, and traditional courts can use internationally recognized standards for a fair hearing, adapting them to their own traditions.[120] Defensive relativists are concerned with an institution recognizing their claim to a legal exemption based on their absolutist protection of a set of practices. While this may involve the recognition of a plurality of legal frameworks, it equally may not involve such recognition if, for example, the state party has decided to prioritize the majority culture to the exclusion of minority cultures in that particular instance.

Most defensive relativist arguments end up using one or more of four basic argumentative strategies to achieve a legal exemption. These are set out below and titled in a way that summarizes the implicit general conclusion states wish to reach. They are all interpretation or demarcation games operating within the legal framework of a human rights regime. Although the consequential legal outcome of these argumentative strategies, should they be recognized by an interpretative body, might be wildly inconsistent or contradictory, a state party making such an argument is simply seeking an exemption for itself in the context of a particular case or issue. To the extent that a state is concerned about the integrity and legitimacy of the international human rights regime in which it is making one of these arguments—a subject discussed in more detail in chapter 8—its concern is focused on obtaining a legal exemption.

The Domestic Law and Practice Surrounding a Particular Practice Supersedes an International Legal Obligation

Under the VCLT, states may not involve the existence of domestic law as a reason for not performing any treaty obligations.[121] This is the logical corollary of the good faith principle underpinning international treaty law and prevents states from claiming they are unable to implement the provisions of the treaty they have just ratified, giving coherency to the law of treaties.[122] In general comment 31, the HRC applied this to the ICCPR, noting that it was binding on states "as a whole," which included every branch of their government.[123] The position where a state party's laws conflict with the substance of the convention means that "changes in the state party's laws or practices" are required.[124] The position in general comment 31 is taken as a guiding principle in the interpretation of other human rights instruments. The domestic law objection is distinct from arguments about incorporation in domestic law—there is no obligation for the ICCPR to become the law of the land and be directly justiciable in municipal courts—rather the obligation is to ensure that existing law can protect the rights contained in the covenant.[125] Although this may arguably lead to a denial of rights in certain situations, as has been claimed with the discharge of obligations under the ICCPR in the United States, especially in cases involving the death penalty, the state party is still attempting to discharge its obligation involving that particular right.[126]

Defensive relativists make the argument that a specific law or practice which contradicts a substantive obligation in international human rights law justifies them not fulfilling that obligation. This can take the form of outright refusal, as was the case with states that resisted decriminalizing same-sex relationships, as detailed in the preceding chapters.[127] It also can take more passive forms, with states claiming it is practically difficult or impossible to implement a particular right. For example, Pakistan has maintained that it is difficult to implement some of the provisions of CEDAW due to the intense religious divisions in society.[128] In some spheres this almost certainly correct: a 2015 law designed to respond to the growing problem of violence in the domestic sphere, which was designed to discharge CEDAW obligations in relation to domestic violence, was attacked by religious political parties as "an attempt to make Pakistan a Western colony."[129] In 2015, there were some Pakistani provinces where there were widespread problems with law enforcement and the police. Yet, such arguments are often used in a sweeping manner by states seeking to limit their obligations by default. As a 2004 article noted, there were frequent delays in implementing recommendations from national commissions and a lack of willingness in Pakistan's country reports to the CEDAW committee to engage with any of the issues involved with the implementation.[130] Although many rights are difficult to implement and require a complex process over many years to realize, some states use the difficulty of implementation, due to prevailing majority cultural norms, as means of playing a demarcation game.[131] They argue, in essence, that their inability to discharge an obligation is a reflection of their present economic, legal, or political weakness, but—in a form of circular logic—that only they as the responsible sovereign authority are able to overcome this weakness. Examples of a state behaving this way would include a refusal to engage with criticisms from a treaty body in relation to restrictions on a particular right or citing difficulties in relation to implementation of rights without specifying the nature of that difficulty.

Interpretations of Rights by a Human Rights Body Should Reflect the State's Interpretation

A static interpretation of an international instrument runs into the basic problem that language is in a state of flux, and therefore the common-sense meaning of the terms of a treaty might change over time. Many international legal practitioners have come to favor a flexible interpretative model, summarized by Ulf Linderfalk as drawing both on the "language and rules that were in existence when the interpreted treaty was concluded, and sometimes upon the language and rules existing at the time of interpretation."[132] Human rights bodies have often utilized an evolutive model of interpretation where the nature of an instrument's terms are accepted to change over time, as the linguistic meaning of words evolves and the social situations they describe change.[133] As Eirik Bjorge argues, there is nothing special about the evolutionary interpretation of treaties, and in fact it is entirely consistent with the process of giving effect to the original intention of the parties to that treaty.[134] The Inter-American Court of Human Rights (IACtHR) has consistently taken the view that human rights treaties should be interpreted in an evolutionary manner, holding in the Consular Assistance case that evolutive interpretation was "consistent with the general rules of the interpretation of treaties embodied in the 1969 Vienna Convention."[135] In the *Mayagna (Sumo) Awas Tingni Community v. Nicaragua*, the court held that human rights treaties have an "autonomous meaning not equivalent to rights as protected in domestic law" and as a consequence "must adapt to the evolution of the times and, specifically, to current living conditions."[136] The ECtHR has developed a method of evolutive interpretation called the "living instrument" doctrine, which focuses on locating the determinate point for interpreting any term of a treaty firmly in the present to acknowledge changing social and legal circumstances.[137] The living instrument doctrine is used both in cases interpreting rights and as a means of assessing the balancing of rights by a member state in relation to laws restricting rights protected under the ECHR.[138]

The IACtHR has also applied the "living instrument" doctrine to the ACHR.[139] In some cases this can be in direct tension with particular interpretations of rights taken by states for moral reasons; for example, when the court ruled that Costa Rica's ban on in vitro fertilization (IVF) was incompatible with the right to life under the convention, the decision to interpret the right in an evolutive manner was criticized for not giving due weight to Costa Rica's moral position.[140] The 2000 ban on IVF was a response to the concerns of the Catholic Church, which were also reflected in significant elements of Costa Rican society and politics, about the destruction of embryos in the IVF process. Feminist and health care campaigners in Costa Rica had been campaigning against the ban and had brought the case to the IACtHR.[141] Some Catholic groups in Costa Rica were hostile to the notion that the meaning of "life" could be interpreted by the IACtHR to include artificial insemination (part of the IVF process).[142] The process of interpretation was also called into question directly in *Atala Riffo and Daughters v. Chile*, where the state party defended a domestic decision from the Chilean Supreme Court upholding a lower court decision over a custody dispute, where the claimant had lost custody of her children because she had entered into a homosexual relationship following her divorce.[143] The Chilean court predicated its reasoning for giving the claimant's husband custody of her children in part on the context of the "heterosexual and traditional society" of Chile.[144] On certain social issues, such as permitting divorce and advancing LGBT rights, Chile differed from other countries in the region, and for a variety of social and cultural reasons, governing political parties had moved slowly on legislative reform in this area.[145] Therefore, in *Atala Riffo* the Chilean government defended the domestic courts and criticized the IACtHR, arguing that states had given their consent to the court with "certain types of violations in mind, and not others that did not exist at the time."[146] Both of these cases are illustrations of an interpretation game, played out both at the IACtHR and in society more generally, about the scope of interpretation permissible for an international body when a domestic institution has made an alternate interpretation of the law in line with dominant cultural traditions. A similar trend can be seen in relation to cases involving the interpretation and balancing of rights in relation to Article 8 of the ECHR, in cases involving LGBT rights, with states arguing against an evolutive interpretation of the ECHR on defensive relativist grounds.[147] The legal exemption being sought in cases such as these is predicated on the grounds that any interpretation of the law by an international body should follow a state's own interpretation, made in line with its conception of cultural values, in a manner not entirely distinct from the defensive relativist conclusions around the margin of appreciation.

The Margin of Appreciation Granted to States Should Have Unrestrained Width

The "width" of a margin of appreciation refers to the relative scale of leeway states will be allowed when exercising the margin of appreciation to limit rights within their domestic law.[148] For instance, where an individual's personal autonomy is concerned, the ECtHR often gives states a far narrower margin of appreciation than in relation to questions surrounding areas of social and economic policy, where a much wider margin of appreciation is generally permitted.[149] The aim of defensive relativists is to try and secure as wide a margin of appreciation as possible, decreasing supranational scrutiny of their laws and enhancing a state's capacity to enact laws reflecting its moral preferences in relation to a particular practice. For example, in *Marckx v. Belgium*, the claimant was a child born out of wedlock who claimed that the principle in Belgian law that maintained there was no legal bond between a child born out of wedlock and their unmarried mother was a discriminatory infringement of the child's rights under Article 8 of the ECHR (the right to private and family life).[150] The state party argued that the law was designed to protect the "traditional family" and therefore fell within the state's margin of appreciation, as this restriction was "founded on objective and reasonable grounds relating to morals and public order," which under Article 8 was a permitted justification for limitations of the right to a private and family life.[151] The court ultimately rejected this position, but the state party's argument that the provision in Article 8(2) that allows states to restrict the right to family life in order protect "health or morals" should allow a wide-ranging limitation of rights justified by a constructed cultural conception of the "traditional family," was an attempt to widen the margin of appreciation.

A successful version of this argument was seen in the HRC's decision in *Leo Hertzberg et al. v. Finland*, where the decision of the state broadcaster to censor a program on homosexuality, on the basis that it breached provisions in the Finnish penal code (now long repealed) on sexual morality, was held not to be a violation of the ICCPR. The applicant complained that this was a restriction of Article 19 of the ICCPR (the right to freedom of expression), but the HRC acknowledged that "public morals differ widely," and in the absence of a "universally applicable common standard" a certain "margin of discretion" would be granted to national authorities.[152] Although the HRC subsequently departed from the *Hertzberg* formulation, the open-ended margin granted to the state party in the decision gave states a potential vehicle for arguing that their restrictions of rights were justifiable on "public morality" grounds.[153] Under General Comment 34, state parties to the ICCPR are required to "demonstrate in specific and individualized fashion the precise nature of the threat, and the necessity and proportionality of the specific" restriction on rights.[154] This formulation makes it difficult for states to justify an unrestrained limitation of rights, and while the ECtHR maintains a margin of appreciation doctrine, notionally allowing states greater freedom in terms of restrictions of certain rights, it subjects the margin to judicial control looking at the right being restricted, the nature and context of the interference, and the aim pursued by the state party in making such a restriction. While the consistency of this scrutiny has been criticized, the court has been willing to restrict states' claims to the margin of appreciation in certain areas.[155] Yet this does not stop states from trying to seek expansive notions of the margin of appreciation. In *Fedotova v. Russia*, the applicant had been fined under an administrative offenses law prohibiting "public actions aimed at propaganda of homosexuality among minors" for putting up a poster saying "homosexuality is normal."[156] When this was challenged at the HRC on the basis that it was a violation of Article 19, the state party relied on a domestic court ruling that the state was entitled to protect "traditional understandings of family, motherhood and childhood," and that the restrictions on rights in laws such as these were justified on the basis of "protecting morals."[157] Although the committee rejected this argument and the applicant was ultimately successful, it is nevertheless indicative of how states can use conceptions of morality to maintain the existence of a margin of appreciation so wide that it amounts to a legal exemption. Treaty scholars draw an understandable distinction between "balancing" rights and the interpretation of a treaty's terms, but this does not stop arguments over the margin of appreciation becoming an interpretation game.[158] In these cases, the state is seeking to maintain that its assessment of the balance of rights in a domestic law restricting rights, which is based on its own assessment of a factual situation, the questions surrounding it, and interpretation of the state's obligations in international law, is ultimately correct.

Reservations Should Be Open-Ended when Referring to Matters of Cultural Importance to the State

The best example of this phenomenon is CEDAW; there are 189 parties to CEDAW, making it the human rights treaty with the second most state parties, but it also is the treaty which has the most reservations. Some reservations are designed to remove rights protection and are designed to permit a state to engage in an unlimited restriction of a particular right or the complete removal of rights in a particular area; for example, some of the reservations on the basis of Sharia law to Article 16 of CEDAW discussed in the preceding chapters effectively remove any rights concerning marriage. Article 28 of CEDAW contains a clause setting out an impermissibility test for reservations to the convention which expressly utilizes the object and purpose test.[159] CEDAW entered into force in 1981, but by 1986 the scale and scope of reservations to the convention had led to members of the CEDAW Committee advocating that they should begin examining the substance of reservations. In 1988, the issue of CEDAW reservations was placed on the General Assembly's agenda, but, as Belinda Clark notes, the ensuing debate quickly dissolved into a broader argument along East versus West lines, with a number of different relativist arguments being used by some states.[160] In 1998, the CEDAW Committee clarified that "traditional, religious or cultural practice nor incompatible domestic laws and policies [could not] justify violations of the Convention," strongly indicating the existence of limits on the way that states could use "culture" to justify reservations.[161] The conclusion of the committee was that it was necessary to reexamine the "self-imposed limitations to full compliance" with CEDAW.[162] In 2008, the CEDAW Committee changed its rules of procedure to give it the power to require states to explain reservations as part of the reporting process. Committee reports began to explicitly highlight where objections had been filed from state parties in relation to the reservations of a state under review and where those objections highlighted the failure of the state party to meet the object and purpose test.

Some states entered far-reaching reservations upon accession to CEDAW, which were designed to block the convention having any meaningful force. One survey noted the correlation between the percentage of a country's Muslim population and the tendency to enter reservations to CEDAW.[163] Many of these reservations made explicit or implicit references to various forms of Sharia law, but there is no uniform structure to these reservations beyond references to Sharia. There is no unified school of Sharia law; it is not, as is the case with Catholic cannon law, subject to a form of hierarchical authority. Sharia schools of thought vary considerably across different regional and national cultures, as well between Sunni and Shiite traditions of Islam. Yet, as former special rapporteur on reservations for the ILC Alain Pellet has noted, this has led to a discourse over "Sharia reservations," the assumption being that they exist as a problematic class because of their references to Sharia, even though, as Pellet says, "the issue was by no means the Sharia by itself but the inacceptable specificities of certain reservations based on the Sharia."[164] As Pellet goes on to point out, the issue with reservations involving Sharia law is not their religious origin but their frequent vagueness, which "makes it impossible to assess [their] compatibility with the object and purpose of the treaty," denying other parties the possibility of reacting to the reservation and accessing information about its impact and scope.[165] As Nisrine Abiad argues, in a study of international human rights law and Sharia law, the tactical use of the notion of Sharia law by some states—as a form of demarcation game—has specifically interfered with the implementation of human rights obligations.[166] As Abiad demonstrates, there are a number of examples where Sharia law has actually been instrumental in advancing rights protection, so perceiving Sharia as an automatic impediment to human rights protection is inaccurate.[167]

Reservations referencing Sharia can use it as a deliberately vague term, a "black box" into which states can claim any meaning that is instrumentally useful for them to advance a culturally absolutist argument in a particular area, thus facilitating defensive relativism. For example, Malaysia, in the text of its reservations upon CEDAW ratification in 1995, stated that where provisions of CEDAW were in "conflict with the provisions of the Islamic Sharia" law and the Federal Constitution of Malaysia, the government did "not consider itself bound by the provisions," and then went on to list the different provisions to which it did not consider itself to be bound, including Article 2 (the legal obligation of states to implement the rest of the provisions of the treaty), Article 9, and Article 16, amounting to reservations to seventeen separate provisions in total.[168] The open-ended nature of the reservation's framing, the lack of specificity about who would determine Sharia law, the lack of detail on equivalent protections in domestic legislation, and the sheer volume of different provisions included in the reservation's text led to the conclusion that this was intended to create a legal exemption in relation to the obligation to provide equal citizenship for women and protect the right to marry. In 1998, as part of the implementation of the Beijing Platform for Action, coming out of the fourth World Conference for Women, Malaysia withdrew six of its reservations, replacing them with narrower declarations.[169] This did not stop the French government from objecting that the remaining reservations were inconsistent with the object and purpose of the convention.[170] Objections to a reservation on the basis that the reservation is incompatible with the object and purpose of the convention have a specific legal status and go beyond mere statements about the convention.[171] The CEDAW Committee was to refer to this on a number of occasions in its concluding observations to Malaysia. In 2018, the committee noted that Malaysia had withdrawn another three reservations—to Articles 5(a), 7(b) and 16(2)—but had kept in place other reservations to Article 16 which were "contrary to the object and purpose of the Convention" and continued to justify this "on the grounds that those provisions are not compatible with the Federal Constitution and Islamic or Syariah law."[172]

Conclusion: The Final Element of Defensive Relativism

The final element of defensive relativism is defined by the conclusion of an argumentative strategy. Hence, the titles of the four types of argument detailed in the final section of this chapter are both a summary of the argument and the conclusion that a state party wishes a tribunal or treaty body to reach at the conclusion of advancing their arguments. Arguing for a legal exemption, even if the state arguing for it is unsuccessful in its demarcation or interpretation game, is vital because it allows a balance to be drawn between appearing human rights–compliant at the international level while at the same time leaving practices that are potentially incompatible with international human rights law untouched in that state's domestic legal system. The entire system of international human rights law is predicated upon the capacity of obligations in international law to change the domestic conduct of a state in relation to the protection of rights.[173] The practical realities of universalism, and to an extent the antiuniversalism detailed in chapter 1, entail that very few obligations in international human rights law require a uniform realization across all states. Existing mechanisms in human rights law can already acknowledge a wide degree of cultural differences between societies, but defensive relativist argumentation pursues a more expansive version of such mechanisms, emphasizing those that inhibit a tribunal or review body reviewing domestic limitations of rights. Exempting a state from the law allows it to remain notionally compliant with human rights law, thus allowing it to conform to the broad notion of legitimate statehood that being party to a human rights instrument brings, while not making changes to its domestic laws or practices.[174]

Defensive relativism uses the language and frames of argument necessary to persuade a tribunal or treaty body that it is acting legally, but is in reality advocating something that is at or beyond the boundaries of what would be considered a lawful restriction of rights. At the same time, this is indicative of the power of international law as a system of belief, which underpins state interaction and the way states frame arguments.[175] Defensive relativist arguments can be unsuccessful—states can lose the games they are playing before international institutions. The consequences of losing the game, which can result in backlash to the institution, are, however, separate from the fact that states feel compelled to play it, which is indicative of the strategic value of human rights law to states and the relative authority of the legal forms of human rights law.[176] A unifying feature of the interpretation and demarcation games outlined above is their reliance upon arguments relating to sovereignty, and, as will be discussed in the final section of the book, defensive relativism can strategically defend certain conceptions of sovereignty. The focus in this chapter has been on the role that ordinary indeterminacy plays in defensive relativism, where states choose to operate notionally within the law as it currently exists. The next chapter focuses on examples in which states design a defensively relativist human rights regime.

PART II

Defensive Relativism at Work: Three Case Studies

CHAPTER 4

The ASEAN Human Rights Declaration: Defensive Relativism by Design

On 30 May 2003, outside the town of Depayin in northeastern Myanmar, the militia group the Union Solidarity and Development Association (USDA) mounted an attack with the intention of assassinating Aung San Suu Kyi. It didn't go to plan, and in the resulting violence up to seventy civilians were killed, some beaten to death with iron rods. The USDA was backed by the leading elements in the Burmese military, and when news of the massacre got out there was mounting political pressure from Western governments and on the Association of Southeast Asian Nations (ASEAN), of which Myanmar was a member, for action against the country's military government.[1] Three weeks later, the ASEAN Ministerial Meeting in Phnom Penh noted "the incident of 30 May," but in the meeting communiqué went on to say that it welcomed the government of Myanmar's attempt to "promote peace and development," and that it was assured restrictions on civil liberties put in place by the government were temporary.[2] Although this language appeared muted when contrasted with the horrific human rights abuses taking place in Myanmar, as scholars of ASEAN observed the 2003, the communiqué marked a significant departure from the normal ASEAN practice of strict noninterference in the affairs of member states, especially in relation to human rights.[3]

ASEAN is an association of ten states—Brunei Darussalam, Cambodia, Indonesia, Laos, Malaysia, Myanmar, Philippines, Singapore, Thailand, and Vietnam—broadly committed to promoting economic growth and regional stability. Founded in 1967, it was for much of its history a loose association of states, with its summits producing broad statements on the nature of political cooperation between governments rather than creating legal structures reminiscent of an international organization. During this period, its operation was defined by the policy of noninterference, with no real public statements or action on human rights. In 2007, ASEAN began a process of constitutionalizing itself as an organization, creating a formal charter governing its powers. It also commenced the process of drafting its own human rights instrument, with the ASEAN Human Rights Declaration coming into effect in 2012 to complement the ASEAN Intergovernmental Human Rights Commission (AIHRC). The AIHRC was widely criticized by legal professionals and human rights advocates for its ineffective and highly deferential legal structure, which seemingly allowed ASEAN to adopt the veneer of a human rights body without making practical commitments to protect human rights. Its legal structure essentially continued and institutionalized the noninterference doctrine. Yet others argued that given the nature of societies within Southeast Asia and the structures of ASEAN as an institution, the AIHRC and the Human Rights Declaration reflected commonly held norms about human rights, and that the AIHRC's powers were likely to evolve over time.[4]

In fact, the ASEAN declaration reflected a collective set of ideological assumptions about the role of the state in international law, championed by ASEAN states in the process of regional integration. The principle of noninterference was a core component of this ideology which was advanced by political actors in ASEAN and drew on conceptions of common cultural values among ASEAN states. It gained particular prominence during the "Asian values" debate of the mid 1990s, and in the 2000s provided the conceptual underpinning for regional integration and the formation of the ASEAN human rights system. All three elements of defensive relativism—antiuniversalism, the state construction of culture, and legal exemption—can be seen in the process of designing the ASEAN human rights regime and are institutionalized within the declaration's structure. This chapter is the first of three in-depth case studies on defensive relativism. The role of defensive relativist arguments in constructing new legal regimes is examined in this chapter and, as the first section sets out, the design of a legal regime can be understood as a form of legal practice, even though it relates to prospective rather than current human rights commitments. As the latter two sections then demonstrate, ASEAN states designed the ASEAN human rights regime to be structurally defensively relativist, which facilitated non-interference and reflected some of the core ideological arguments about human rights in ASEAN from the mid-1990s.

Organizational Design as a State Practice

International legal regimes exist for a multitude of different purposes, such as controlling inward investment, regulating the environment, or promoting human rights. The legal powers those regimes possess, in a formalist understanding of international law, is dictated mostly by the act of delegation where a state formally accords powers to a legal regime through a constituent treaty.[5] The act of delegation then dictates what that regime's powers are and limits its future competences. But this, as many scholars of international organizations and international relations have noted, does not explain how the powers of international organizations evolve over time.[6] Although a core distinguishing feature of international organizations is the creation of a "body corporate" which is able to operate, independently from its member states, the precise dimensions and level of power, in particular the implied powers an organization has, is often a focus of dispute between states.[7] There are a few theoretical models in the literature on international organizations which have sought to explain state behavior in relation to the formation and evolution of their powers.

Functionalist theories of international organizations contend that international organizations are a reflection of processes of mutual cooperation between states to achieve a particular aim, and that all the legal capacities of an organization can be traced back to that underlying aim.[8] But this theory was somewhat utopian in its assumptions and has difficulty explaining why so many legal disputes occur around the steps states take to keep an organization's powers in check if such mutual cooperation exists.[9] Neo-functionalism takes these insights further, contending that the "low politics" of day-to-day welfare issues of states in the international system create the conditions for cooperation, which then evolve over time, increasingly settling political arguments in the language of legality.[10] While a plausible theoretical framework for understanding how certain organizations have expanded their legal competences beyond the boundaries of delegation, it offers a less coherent explanation about the limitations states attempt to put on the growth of organizational power, relying heavily on teleological notions of the inevitable growth of organizational power and treating the growth of institutions as a self-sustaining process.[11] Rationalism, or rational-institutionalism, draws from realist arguments about state behavior which maintain that states participate in international organizational structures to achieve particular ends, and that organizations, far from being simply vehicles of their member states as maintained by standard realist accounts, become powerful precisely because of their utility in achieving particular outcomes.[12] All institutionalist theories are unified by the belief that institutions themselves alter the ways in which states act, in contrast to liberal theories which focus on the domestic forces within states that determine the way states act in organizations and comply with them.[13]

Rational design theories maintain that the design of an international organization is best understood by understanding the underlying cooperation problem that a legal regime has been created to solve.[14] Rational design theorists seek to construct a more nuanced account of the formation of international organizations that differs from constructivists, who argue that international organizations play a role in diffusing norms by noting that international organizations are rarely exogenous outside actors situated completely outside the state but are specific creations of state parties.[15] That does not mean that rational design theories subscribe to realism, seeing organizations as merely ciphers of state power, as this oversimplifies the nature of organizations which pooled state power or were designed to constrain state interests in particular areas.[16] Rational design theory has been criticized for focusing insufficiently on the ideas, or ideational politics, that lie behind institutional cooperation, and for treating institutional formation as a means of simply knitting together a series of different interests.[17] Equally, an agreement between parties may not be a reflection of shared values or priorities; it may be that the institution is seen by some states as a mechanism for achieving instrumental outcomes, or as a mechanism for realizing an isolated political priority.[18] Yet, an analysis of the shared value systems of states in a human rights organization can be a guide as to what states intend the organization to do and what its powers are, and rational design theorists argue that rational design as an analytic framework can help understand why mechanisms do or don't contain enforcement provisions.[19] This can be particularly important in relation to tribunals or other review bodies which form part of an organization's broader structure, as the legitimacy of such a body's interpretative powers are often intrinsically linked to an organization's original design.[20]

For example, the growth of the European Court of Human Rights' (ECtHR) competencies and the interpretation of the European Convention on Human Rights (ECHR) as a living instrument in the 1970s and 1980s, while sometimes controversial, arguably did reflect the broader set of preferences among states at the time of the convention's drafting.[21] Equally, the enhancement of the court's powers with the introduction of Protocol 11, making its jurisdiction compulsory for all members of the Council of Europe, was part of a conscious decision of state parties to improve the way the court functioned in the post–Cold War political climate of the 1990s.[22] An example of where a human rights body was expressly designed not to have expansive jurisdictional powers was the African Court on Human and Peoples' Rights, where during the drafting of the court protocol certain states were able to successfully argue that in order to stop NGOs or other pressure groups from using the court against member states interests, it needed to have a tightly limited jurisdiction.[23] State behavior in the design stage of organizations can "future shadow," effectively dictating or defining the future evolution of a tribunal and its parent organization. Behavior in this area can be underpinned by a variety of factors, such as the level of concern from a state about the cooperation problem the organization was created to solve, or its domestic audience and their likely reception of organizational action.[24] It can also reflect shared ideological expectations and preferences, yet the choices states make concerning the frameworks of cooperation can be understood as a type of legal practice and not just a reflection of the normative preferences of states.

When designing a regional regime, such as ASEAN in its post-2007 iteration with its own charter, one of the objectives of the process is to demonstrate to a wider international audience that there is a functional regional order.[25] The constitutionalizing of ASEAN centralized the authority of the organization, something which rational institutionalists argue is a core component of a successful international organization.[26] ASEAN's charter, which came into force in 2008, declared itself to have international legal personality as an organization, which not only meant that it was seeking recognition as organization in the same way that other bodies with legal personality are recognized, but also signaled that it was committed to operating within a broader framework of international law.[27] As the International Law Commission's (ILC) report on the fragmentation of international law noted, legal regimes such as regional organizations should not be completely isolated from one another, as by virtue of being legal regimes there are certain common expectations placed on them.[28] Therefore, when in 2007 ASEAN member states took the decision to move the association from a club of nations onto a more formal legal footing, it was being taken at least notionally with reference to the wider framework of international law.[29] The ASEAN human rights framework can also be comparatively assessed alongside other human rights regimes—legal structures which aim to alter the behavior of their member states.[30] The ASEAN human rights regime was set up as a regional regime that was designed to play a similar role to other regional human rights regimes and was also part of a wider project to refocus ASEAN into a more people-focused organization in the late 2000s.[31] Yet, the shared organizational ideology underpinning the design of ASEAN more generally was to develop a regional legal system founded on the principle of nonintervention, which was an instrumentally useful organizational principle, as it preserved the power of various elite forces in ASEAN states, but also reflected certain shared social and cultural ideas between member states.[32] Understanding the ASEAN form of noninterference—sometimes described as the "ASEAN way"—is important, as this was the cooperation problem that the human rights regime was designed to solve—namely, how to make a regime that resembled other transformative regimes but left the ASEAN way intact.[33]

Nonintervention as a Shared Organizational Ideology in ASEAN

One of the most interesting aspects of ASEAN is that its member states are strikingly different. Communist states (Vietnam) and avowedly capitalist states (Singapore) coexist in the same organization. Religious monarchies (Brunei), quasi-military regimes (Myanmar), and parliamentary democracies (Malaysia) agree on some shared principles of economic and political cooperation. Compared to other regional groupings there is little shared history, given the very different experiences of decolonization among its ten member states. Shared experiences of colonialism, decolonization, and the struggle against white minority rule and apartheid were significant political factors underpinning the growth of African intergovernmental organizational cooperation and the creation of the African Charter on Human and Peoples' Rights (ACHPR).[34] Nor do ASEAN states share any larger historical moments, such as the end of World War II or the collapse of the Soviet Union, which were essential in shaping the political commitment of European states to European institutions as well as those institutions' legal structures.[35] ASEAN's founding instrument, the 1967 Bangkok Declaration, stated that one of ASEAN's aims and goals was "'respect for justice and the rule of law" in interstate relations.[36] There was no direct reference in this instrument to human rights or the protection of human rights in ASEAN member states. Most of the states involved in founding ASEAN had also been involved in the 1956 Bandung Conference, the first conference of

African and Asian nations, which supported the importance of human rights in international relations more broadly but stopped short of supporting any commitments or legal frameworks to protect human rights.[37]

ASEAN's insistence on noninterference as a guiding doctrine of interstate cooperation, according to one commentator, prevented destabilizing secessionist conflicts and insurgencies from escalating in the 1960s and 1970s, by requiring states to adopt a self-denying ordinance on commenting on those conflicts in multilateral settings.[38] ASEAN's role in Myanmar in the 1990s and 2000s was an example of how noninterference could protect human rights abusing states. "Constructive engagement" with the government was focused on an attempt to encourage it to engage in reforms to open its internal market to other ASEAN states, but in a manner that wouldn't politically offend the new government.[39] Although much was made of political engagement between ASEAN and Myanmar before and after it joined in 1997, there was little evidence of what this actually achieved.[40] However, in 2006, following increasing concern about the treatment of the civilian population after the 2003 Depayin massacre and growing instability within Myanmar, ASEAN states were able to block the military regime taking up the rotating Chairmanship of the Association.[41] Earlier, in the 1990s, Cambodia's ASEAN membership had been delayed following a coup, but the delay was in part a defense of a 1991 peace agreement in the country which was at risk of being violated by the coup, rather than a major organizational change in policy.[42] Noninterference is often framed within the broader context of the ASEAN way, which describes a system of intergovernmental cooperation based on cooperation and harmony, with a focus on informal dispute solving mechanisms predicated on achieving an interassociation consensus.[43] Noninterference also had a distinctly ideological element to it which was instrumental in the design of the ASEAN charter and the human rights frameworks it initiated.

The Theoretical Foundations of "the ASEAN Way" and Noninterference

There is some evidence that noninterference within ASEAN is not merely something akin to a doctrine of subsidiarity, common in most regional organizations, but was a reflection of a broader ideological program framed in what appears to be the language of cultural relativity.[44] As Hiro Katsumata notes, the absolutist defense of sovereignty in ASEAN instruments is described in the neo-Confucian language with references to "harmony" and "peace."[45] Commentary on ASEAN within print and broadcast media often uses the terms "harmony" and "cooperation," reflecting the same set of values which both justify noninterference and appeal to a form of collective solidarity between states.[46] In this respect, the ASEAN way is often situated in contrast to Western or European multilateralism's insistence on legal and political confrontation, almost as a form of counter-Orientalism.[47] In the mid-1990s, there was some attempt by different official bodies and think tanks to develop a synthesis of the different values comprising the ASEAN way, which included "politeness, non-confrontation and agreeability," all implicitly justifying noninterference as a reflection of shared values.[48] Noninterference was not just an organizational doctrine for the administration of the organization but, as Acharya argues, helped refine the participating states' identities.[49] Another element of the noninterference doctrine, explored by Gillian Goh, is that it had its roots in collective elements of the political culture in some ASEAN states, with their emphasis on the politics of patronage and personal agreement between a small number of elites.[50]

Defenders of the noninterference doctrine in the charter have justified it in terms that reflect elements of the "Asian values" debate of the mid-1990s (which is discussed in more detail below). Tan Sri Ahmad Fuzi bin Abdul Razak, an ambassador for the Malaysian Ministry of Foreign Affairs at the time of the ASEAN charter's drafting, said that noninterference was being criticied for not being "progressive or forward looking," and went on to defend the use of "consensus" in decision making.[51] Some scholars have questioned the rigidity of the noninterference doctrine, noting it was used flexibly; it could for instance be malleable where the interests of the political and commercial elites with ASEAN were at stake, and that its most important feature was cementing the idea that the interests of individuals within states was a matter for state governments only.[52] Daniel Seah takes up this argument, noting some softening of the doctrine, but framing the argument in explicitly realist terms, he also notes that "ASEAN members continue to regard the rule of non-intervention as fundamentally important to their national interests."[53] When it comes to human rights protection, John Arendshorst notes that references to "constructive engagement" within ASEAN were used to protect the doctrine of noninterference and were seen as preferable alternatives to more interventionist mechanisms, such as a human rights court.[54]

While ASEAN was politically committed to promoting economic growth there was no express commitment to economic integration as an organizational goal.[55] In other regional organizations the promotion of economic integration has been a way in which commitments to the protection of human rights have been advanced. As the promotion of economic integration by an organization is often premised on a state's laws being open to some sort of review by that organization's tribunal, and the protection of human rights can be reviewed in the context of the promotion of economic well-being for individuals, this can lead to the development of organizational powers to protect rights.[56] However, ASEAN economic integration appeared to be based upon a limited notion of cooperation which envisaged ASEAN acting more as a facilitator rather than a stand-alone organization.[57] Furthermore, there was a series of references to independence in pre-charter ASEAN instruments which all seemed to point toward a rigid definition of nonintervention.[58] The 1976 Treaty of Amity and Cooperation declared that Asian states had a mutual respect for "independence . . . and territorial integrity." Equally, the 2003 Bali Concord II reiterated the principle of a broad commitment of noninterference as the premise of regional order.[59]

Noninterference and the Design of the ASEAN Human Rights System

ASEAN's noninterference doctrine was directly reflected in the ASEAN Human Rights Declaration, which was an illustration of the rational design thesis, described in the first part of this chapter, that an organization's legal structure can be understood by way of the cooperation problem it was designed to solve. In this case, the cooperation problem was how to make a regional human rights instrument work with the ASEAN doctrine of noninterference. Article 14 of the 2007 ASEAN charter mandated the creation of an ASEAN human rights body "in conformity with the purposes and principles of the ASEAN Charter relating to the promotion and protection of human rights and fundamental freedoms."[60] In July 2009, the terms of reference for a human rights mechanism were finalized.[61] The terms of reference committed the future AICHR to respect the principle of "non-interference in the internal affairs of ASEAN Member States."[62] This meant that the AICHR would be designed to reflect noninterference as a value. There was nevertheless some disagreement between member states in ASEAN about the power that the future human rights organization would have. The Philippines, Indonesia, Malaysia, and Thailand argued that the AICHR's functions should include monitoring of human rights standards; however, Cambodia, Laos, Myanmar, and Vietnam argued that it should be limited to a consultative status. Proposals for a court or commission that could offer human rights protection to individuals were ultimately rejected because they were not compatible with "the ASEAN way."[63] Paragraph 2 of the AIHRC terms of reference limited it to "constructive and non-confrontational approach[s] and cooperation to enhance promotion and protection of human rights," which along with other provisions essentially precluded the development of its own independent authority.[64] The terms of reference for the AIHRC showed how the body was designed to operate within the bounds of ASEAN's noninterference doctrine.

The final version of the ASEAN Human Rights Declaration is broken into six sections, two of which group the civil and political Rights and economic and social rights contained in the declaration together. There are two other sections at the end of the declaration containing the third generation, or collective rights covered by the declaration—the right to development and the right to peace. The final section, titled "Cooperation in the Promotion and Protection of Human Rights," contains references to human rights protection. The terms of this section explicitly protect the doctrine of noninterference; Article 40 states that the nothing in the declaration could be interpreted as allowing the "undermining of the purposes and principles of ASEAN."[65] When read in tandem with the numerous provisions in the ASEAN charter protecting the sovereignty and noninterference in the internal affairs of other member states, this appears to directly undercut all the other rights notionally protected in the charter.[66] Read alongside the absence of any real reference to enforcement in the declaration, or any attempt to create frameworks which went beyond the relatively weak frameworks of the AIHRC, it meant that the ASEAN human rights system as a whole was designed to be unable to meaningfully protect human rights.[67] Civil society groups had hopes that the regular five-year reviews of the body's competencies would offer an opportunity for the AIHRC's powers to be developed, but by 2021, the tenth anniversary of the declaration, this had yet to materialize.[68]

The substantive rights contained in the declaration represent a significant attempt to regionalize human rights norms. The declaration explicitly does not call for a rejection of individual rights and situates states as the responsible agents for protecting human rights, making it in substance more akin to instruments such as the ACHPR. In so doing, it maintains a version of antiuniversalism that tries to adapt to local particularities rather than reject human rights outright. This fulfills the first element of defensive relativism, set out in chapter 1, but as already outlined in earlier chapters of this book this is not necessarily in tension with the idea of human rights protection. However, the declaration needs to be seen in the light of several declarations from ASEAN summits in the early 2000s, situating human rights within the context of inter-organizational development, which, as Shaun Narine notes, reflected short-term political calculations, in particular ASEAN's wider international image, rather than a collective change in attitudes toward human rights.[69]

Defensive Relativism in the Design of the ASEAN Human Rights Declaration's Substantive Provisions

The relative weakness of the ASEAN system in terms of its practical powers to protect human rights, compared to other regional human rights systems, such as the Council of Europe, the European Convention on Human Rights (ECHR), and the Inter-American Human Rights system, is a reflection of the organizational design of the ASEAN human rights system. Some scholars argued around the time the ASEAN declaration was being drafted that it was possible that the AIHRC could evolve and become "a formidable body with wide ranging powers."[70] But these assumptions rested heavily on statements coming from government officials and bore little relation to either the AIHRC terms of reference or the substance of the declaration. As well as drafting the declaration, the AIHRC was to use it to develop "a framework for human rights cooperation" and promote "the full implementation of ASEAN instruments related to human rights."[71] There is no reference to the AIHRC in the declaration, and the interrelation between the two is somewhat opaque. The AIHRC was not granted any power to consider individual petitions, and the declaration did not give the AIHRC any capacity to interpret its mandate more broadly. Defenders of the promotional role of the AIHRC, such as Hao Duy Phan, are quick to concede that the AIHRC was designed by states specifically not to have a protective function; however, they are keen to emphasize the benefits of its promotional work.[72] Although Phan does not go as far as others in arguing that the AIHRC has the capacity to evolve, the conclusion reached regarding the significance of the declaration and the AIHRC is that human rights is to no "longer be considered a solely domestic affair" in ASEAN.[73] Yet, the design of the general principles section of the declaration, which provides the framework through which the rest of the declaration is to be interpreted, situates human rights as a distinctly domestic concern.

Furthermore, even if the AIHRC were to acquire the capacities of a human rights tribunal capable of issuing decisions against states, the defensive relativist structure of the general principles is designed to limit the capacity of the declaration to protect human rights. Harsh Mahaseth and Karthik Subramaniam's study of ASEAN integration makes the compelling case that a major problem with ASEAN at an organizational level is its overreliance on and proliferation of its "soft law" instruments, and absent a broader institutional structure built on "hard law" it would be prone to incoherence.[74] Yet, the problem with the declaration is not its status as a "hard" or "soft" instrument, but the way its provisions were structured; regardless of the nature of the obligation in the declaration, it is constructed to facilitate defensive relativism and exempt states from having to comply with an international human rights instrument or the decisions of a human rights organization. There are two specific provisions in the general principles section which showcase how the declaration was designed to promote a defensive relativist interpretation of the human rights it contains.

Article 6: Duties and the State

Article 6 of the declaration states that the rights contained in the rest of the declaration are to be interpreted in light of "the performance of corresponding duties" which exist toward the "community and the society where one lives."[75] This is a somewhat ambiguous and open-ended clause, as it is not clear what the content of such duties are and what effect, if any, they have on the application of rights in the rest of the declaration. For example, Article 24 states that "every person has the right to freedom of peaceful assembly."[76] It is not clear if Article 6 acts as a limitation clause on the exercise of this right, allowing the state to legislate to restrict the right to freedom of expression in cases where it can be shown that on balance a particular speech act causes harm to the community, in the way that the European Court of Human Rights (ECtHR) allows states to place some limitations on the right to free speech using the margin of appreciation doctrine.[77] Equally, it is not clear if Article 6 requires that any exercise of the right to freedom of assembly be in accordance with community interests. If this is the case, it would effectively render the right meaningless, as rather than being exercised by an individual or group of individuals as an expression of their own interests, it would be something that was simply utilized by the state. Provisions relating to the duties of individuals are also contained in the ACHPR in Articles 27-29, which list a range of duties upon the individual, including "duties towards his family and society."[78] Although these provisions have been criticized as being somewhat open-ended, they are not framed in a way that expressly limits other rights, and the ACHPR has not held that these rights constrain the application of other rights in the ACHPR or that state parties are in the position to determine the scope and content of duties.[79] Article 6 of the declaration, however, allows governments to have an unlimited scope to limit rights under the broad framework of duties, as the state party is the sole determinate of what those duties are. The design of this provision reflected an ongoing series of debates about the nature of society within Southeast Asia, and its eventual codification represented a relative victory for one side of this argument.

All governments want to establish some form of authority and control over their populations, and human rights instruments are constructed to allow some leeway for state authorities to use lawful forms of coercion to carry out state policy. However, at a cross-regional level the "Asian values" debate of the 1990s advanced the thesis that societies in Southeast Asia were more suited to authoritarian forms of governance—which was taken as meaning a nondemocratic government, limited civil space, and a constraint of individual freedom (usually with heavy custodial penalties for minor criminal and civil offenses), all of which were justified by an appeal to traditional forms of cultural authority. The Asian values debate began around 1993, and in form was a mix of the speeches from politicians, articles from leading public intellectuals, and, very occasionally, references in official declarations.[80] It coincided with rapid regional economic growth in the area, leading some politicians to argue that this was a unique societal model that had emerged which, although dependent on neoliberal forms of growth, also placed an emphasis on values, broadly understood as traditional.[81] It would be incorrect, however, to see the Asian values debate solely through the prism of universalism versus relativism, as that misses some crucial ideological elements about the arguments put forward by its proponents, which were not merely descriptive about society or a reaction to the imposition of Western values, but were an ideological statement about how Southeast Asian states ought to be governed.[82] Instead, the Asian values debate was a political ideology advanced by some leading politicians in ASEAN states about how to organize their societies, and should be interrogated as such. It was very different from the often deterministic and culturally reductive notion of "oriental despotism," which was a racialized caricature of some colonial-era texts of international law and has influenced some subsequent political analysis.[83]

One key component of the "Asian values" debate was a strong emphasis on deference to authority, in particular the authority of the state, over the rights of the individual. Mahathir Mohamed, former prime minister of Malaysia, argued that although democracy was useful, Asians "should respect authority because it guarantees stability" and that political processes, such as challenging political leaders, was "treachery" according to Malay tradition.[84] These arguments were echoed by former prime minister of Singapore Lee Kuan Yew, who argued that Singaporean society valued "discipline more than democracy" and that other Asian societies should follow its example.[85] Mohamed and Yew maintained that they were critiquing a Western conception of democracy and individual rights rather than defending authoritarianism, but the centrality of these two figures to the Asian values debate led to some speculation that it was more a reflection of the politics of the contemporary Malaysian and Singaporean governments than a pan-regional ideology.[86] Asian values advocates were, broadly speaking, in favor of a form of "soft authoritarianism" that ostensibly favoured the reprioritization of rights rather than their elimination; in practice, however, the Asian values thesis was used by the governments of Malaysia and Indonesia in the late 1990s as a justification for human rights abuses.[87] This was again packaged within a quasi-cultural set of justifications; as Amartya Sen noted in a 1997 lecture, Confucianism and other religious values in the Asian values debate had been turned into a "monolithic authoritarian image" used by states to justify control over their populations.[88]

Neo-Confucianism in the Asian values debate tended to politicize morality, using the collective and duties toward the collective as shorthand for deference to authority which, as Inoue Tatsuo notes, was a highly controversial interpretation of Confucianism, diluting down the complex debates over individuality within Confucian thought.[89] Communitarian values were often bluntly advanced by politicians in the ruling political parties who heavily blurred the line between representing cultures within their society and claiming cultural exceptionalism in opposition to Western values—of which human rights was one.[90] Although the Asian values debate had largely petered out as a phenomenon by the mid-2000s, it created a set of "discourses" on authoritarianism that came to provide what Leigh Jenco terms an "enduring vocabulary for articulating 'Asian' characteristics as challenges that transform, rather than traditional values which supplement, 'Western' processes of modernization."[91] Empirical research on some of the distinct claims advanced by the proponents of the Asian values debate, such as valuing authoritarian forms of government, showed that they had little basis in fact.[92] What the Asian values debate did was shape the assumptions of ASEAN states in relation to the role international human rights law ought to play both in terms of ASEAN integration and an overall system of constraining state action.[93]

These assumptions about the role of cultural duties and their relationship to rights formed the context within which the declaration's substantive provisions, such as Article 6, were drafted. During the mid-to-late 2000s the Working Group for the Establishment of an ASEAN Human Rights Mechanism had helped normalize the notion of human rights among states involved in ASEAN by situating it within the context of institutional values and regional integration.[94] When it came to setting the terms of reference for the declaration, which the AICHR adopted in 2011, there were state parties who were keen to draw a link between the Asian values debate and shared values. During the drafting there was a split between the conservative group of states (Vietnam, Laos, and, to varying extents, Malaysia and Singapore) and states who were more liberal in respect to what a future human rights regime could look like (Thailand, Indonesia, and, to varying extents, the Philippines).[95] The former group was heavily influential in the shaping of the general principles section of the declaration, and what came to be known as the Malaysian draft, which was leaked in the summer of 2012, contained direct references to duties.[96] In November 2012, before the declaration was due to be adopted, Amnesty International issued a press release warning that requiring rights to be interpreted in light of unspecified duties could result in rights being "restricted on a wide array of grounds including 'national security' and 'public morality'".[97] That same month, the UN Human Rights Council, in an open letter, noted that the reference to a "balancing" of rights and duties in the text of Article 6 would almost certainly create "much greater scope for Governments to place arbitrary, disproportionate and unnecessary" restrictions on rights.[98] In December 2012, the International Commission of Jurists criticized the duties provisions as they appeared to give an almost unlimited freedom to state parties to restrict human rights.[99]

In response to these concerns, some argued in part that the duties section was necessary to give the regime legitimacy, and Tan Hsien-Li makes the case that the "preponderance for 'duty' alongside rights should not be seen as a detraction of the latter."[100] However, the states that appeared to have the most influence in the shaping the general principles were the same states who had supported the incorporation of the "Asian value'" agenda into the development of ASEAN structures more generally. Furthermore, absent specifics within the declaration's text on the source and scope of duties, and absent a body capable of issuing decisions about the limits of interpretation, there is nothing to prevent a state from claiming that any restriction of rights is the performance of a duty. The wording of the duty provision allows a state to present its own conception of culture as being the sole determining factor in the protection of rights. Furthermore, the phrase "corresponding duties" appears to perform a similar function to treaty reservations with intentionally vague wording—of the sort described in chapter 3—allowing the state to project onto it any values it choses as a duty.

Article 6 appears to be tempered by Article 8 of the declaration, which contains what appears to be a proportionality provision, as it requires that limitations of rights are "determined by law" and limited to specific cases—in a manner not entirely dissimilar to the ECHR.[101] However, Article 8, like Article 6, reaffirms the capacity of ASEAN states to make unlimited restrictions on rights in two specific ways. Firstly, it reaffirms the duty provisions of Article 6 by stating that exercise of rights is subject to "due regard" to others, which is a sufficiently broad provision to allow a state party to argue—in the event the AIHRC was tasked with enforcing the declaration—that any restrictions on a right to free speech, association, or political participation are simply a reflection of having due regard for the wider interests of the population. Issues surrounding the interpretation of free speech in domestic law in Malaysia provide an example of how this might happen: from 2013 to 2018 the government of Najib Razak used a series of open-ended sedition laws to criminalize civil society groups and journalists, justifying them on the basis of open-ended concerns about the need to promote social cohesion, and domestic judges were often unwilling to probe these restrictions.[102]

Secondly, Article 8 allows rights to be restricted in the interests of "public morality."[103] Some other human rights instruments have similar-sounding restrictions; Articles 8 and 9 of the ECHR, for example, are able to be restricted on the grounds of public morality, but these limitations are constrained to specific rights and subject to judicial oversight from the ECtHR. As the Malaysian delegate noted during the drafting process, Article 8 was designed to reflect domestic laws which allowed restrictions in relation to public morality. But civil society groups countered that given the far-reaching restrictions on rights justified in the domestic law of ASEAN member states, particularly in relation to the rights of minorities and the LGBT community, the inclusion of a provision designed to reflect domestic legal practices was not conducive to the development of an organizational culture of rights protection.[104] Absent AIHRC powers to issue decisions about the interpretation of the declaration this is a hypothetical exercise; yet it is clear that Article 6 is constructed in a manner which would allow a legal exemption to be claimed in relation to a rights restriction because that restriction was necessary to perform some kind of duty. Article 6's structure is evidence of the declaration's defensive relativist design, as the provision solved the collaboration problem of building a human rights declaration which protected the ASEAN way and the additional problem of adequately reflecting the conclusions of the Asian values debate over the function of human rights, which were clearly important to some states at the time of the declaration's drafting.

Article 7: Cultural Limitations

Article 7 of the declaration reflects crucial assumptions about the universality of rights outlined in the Asian values debate; again, it is designed to reflect prevailing assumptions about universality and the defense of cultural values. Article 7 includes a general statement of universality which states that rights are universal as well as "indivisible, interdependent and interrelated," but goes on to say that "at the same time, the realization of human rights must be considered in the regional and national context bearing in mind different . . . cultural, historical and religious backgrounds."[105]

This has a distinct echo of the 1993 Bangkok Declaration, which came out of the Asian regional human rights conference that convened in April during the buildup to the second World Conference on Human Rights in Vienna in June 1993. The Bangkok Declaration recognized the importance of human rights and their interdependence but stressed that they were subject to an "evolving process of international norm-setting" and that "the significance of national and regional particularities and various historical, cultural and religious backgrounds" should be taken into account when applying human rights standards.[106] It was not a legal declaration but was a founding text of the Asian values debate in part because it explicitly linked regional cultural exceptionalism with a noninterference doctrine in relation to human rights.[107] The Bangkok meeting was often quite fraught, with some states arguing for a broader rejection of human rights altogether, so the final declaration which made its way to Vienna in 1993, was a significant achievement in and of itself.[108]

What was significant was the language that made it into the final text of the Vienna Declaration and Programme of Action. Paragraph 5 stated that human rights are "universal, indivisible and interdependent and interrelated" but that "national and regional particularities and various historical, cultural and religious backgrounds" needed to be "borne in mind" in the interpretation and implementation of human rights.[109] The declaration was a somewhat confused document; at paragraph 8 it states that the "protection of human rights and fundamental freedoms at the national and international levels should be universal and conducted without conditions attached," reflecting the political trade-offs in its construction.[110] It wasn't a legally binding document, but it was to prove influential as a set of norms guiding the evolution of human rights law, and the meaning of paragraph 5 was heavily contested. Some have argued that paragraph 5 was a "rejection" of cultural relativism, but the requirement that cultural practices be "borne in mind" created an opening for states to argue a defensive relativist case.[111] This is certainly the way that paragraph 5 has been interpreted by states—when the Organisation of Islamic Cooperation (the OIC group of states) objected to a debate about LGBT rights at the UN Human Rights Council in 2012, it cited paragraph 5's text, arguing that this entailed that cultural objections or cultural incompatibility should trump human rights.[112] Yet, paragraph 5 also contains a requirement for states "regardless of their political, economic and cultural systems, to promote and protect all human rights and fundamental freedoms," indicating that the interpretative scope of the provision was more about finding an appropriate balance between cultural particularities and universalism rather than culture being used as a means for attacking universalism.[113]

As the Vienna Conference concluded, the Asian values debate—which very much saw nationality, sovereignty, and community as synonymous with one another—was getting underway. As Catherine Renshaw argues in an overview of the declaration, the genesis and interpretation of Article 7 of the declaration needs to be seen in this context.[114] The emphasis on community reflected a crucial component of the Asian values debate, which as Bruun and Jacobsen note sought to "explicitize" cultural values "in the face of rapidly modernizing and globalizing forces."[115] The language of culture and collective values was used to infer a common set of shared values across states with Asian values advocates advancing a harmonized, unitary model of society which rooted its ethics in the supposedly prepolitical values of an interpretation of Confucianism and other religious traditions.[116] An emphasis on the importance of community values is not necessarily an impediment for the protection of human rights, but, as Donnelly notes, the terms of the Asian values debate often came close to advocating a conception of human rights that was essentially meaningless, as it saw the state controlling the exercise of rights.[117] The language of exclusionary collectivism crucially survived the decline of the Asian values debate in the early 2000s and became embedded in thinking about ASEAN. For instance, commentary on ASEAN within state media is often framed in terms of "harmony" and "cooperation," reflecting the sort of neo-Confucian values presented in the justification for noninterference but also appealing to a form of collective solidarity between states.[118] Additionally, the absence of any reference to indigenous rights in the declaration and the terms of reference, as well as no explicit recognition of cultural diversity within a state, pointed toward the role of the state government's exclusive role in defining what a culture would mean with little space provided for a cultural counterpoint to its authority.[119]

Article 7 appears to be a continuation of this exclusionary interpretation of culture, emphasizing the "regional and national context" of cultural values. Commenting on Article 7, Mathew Davies notes that its linguistic framing was a direct "reawakening of the Asian values debate" which, he claims, was surprising, as the relativism of the Asian values debate had been largely absent during the 2000s.[120] Since the early 2000s, overt comparisons with "Western values" to position Asian values as a relativistic counterpoint had diminished in public discourse, and its relativistic discourse had morphed into a defensive discourse on national sovereignty as a form of resistance to outside interference—international human rights law being a prime example of outside influence. Some have argued, as Anthony Langlois does, that despite the institutional shortcomings of AIHRC the way that the declaration encourages forms of "rights talk" can be instrumental in the development of human rights more generally.[121] But this is where it is important to understand the impact of provisions such as Article 7 in terms of institutional constriction on the entire development of the notion of rights. While there may be improving rights consciousness in the region—the development of rights and scholarship in the early 2020s has begun to identify the increasing role that civil society groups are playing in shaping human rights norms—at an institutional level, in ASEAN, human rights protection was intentionally designed to be limited by provisions such as Article 7.[122]

Civil society groups at the time of the declaration's drafting criticized Article 7 as a provision that would allow member states to avoid human rights obligations, with Human Rights Watch Thailand going so far as to call it a "tragedy for the region."[123] Such rhetoric made sense, Renshaw argues, in the context of how those civil society groups and other human rights campaigners had seen the terminology of Article 7 defined during the Asian values debate.[124] Article 7-like language had been a recurring theme of discourse about human rights in ASEAN, used either to emphasize a distinct regional identity or to underscore the notion of noninterference.[125] During the declaration's drafting process, some states, such as Thailand, expressed repeated concerns about the declaration falling short of accepted international standards in the context of discussions about Articles 6, 7, and 8. It was suggested that the wording from paragraph 5 of the Vienna Declaration, which unlike Article 7 contained a requirement to protect human rights regardless of "cultural systems," should be included in the final text of the declaration. This was, however, rejected at the instance of states in the "conservative" grouping.[126] Much like the construction of Article 6, the final text of Article 7 reflects a core assumption about human rights in the Asian values debate, which, during the declaration's drafting process, at the instance of some states, morphed into a collective ASEAN-wide statement of cultural absolutism. Equally, much like Article 6, were Article 7 to be used by the AIHRC in an interpretative capacity, it would be very easy for a state party, due to the construction of Article 7, to argue that it gave them an unlimited license to restrict rights in their jurisdiction out of defense to their national culture.

Conclusion: Defensive Relativism by Design

The ASEAN Human Rights Declaration and the AIHRC have been the subject of considerable criticism for essentially creating a human rights regime that was little more than window dressing to make ASEAN appear to be adopting a human rights instrument when it was in fact consolidating organizational power. This is an understandable view, but it misses an important nuance; there clearly were ways in which human rights were instrumentally useful. The adoption of the declaration was a mechanism which improved regional cooperation and provided a framework for action on issues such as preventative health care—ASEAN's work on strategies to combat HIV/AIDS being a prime example.[127] It also provided an implicit response to external criticism ASEAN received in relation to its noninterference over systemic human rights abuses by the military regime in Myanmar.[128] In fact, there is a case to be made that the Myanmar crisis, following ASEAN's response to the

2003 Depayin massacre (described in the introduction to this chapter), began to act as a driver for change within ASEAN, making it more open to exerting pressure on the military regime, which in turn led to Myanmar beginning to improve its human rights record in certain areas.[129]

There is, however, little evidence ASEAN intended to create a functioning human rights regime with the capacity to issue decisions against states, and the declaration and the AIHRC's terms of reference are designed to preclude such a possibility.[130] Organizational design is not a legal procedure of the sort described in chapter 3, but needs to be understood as a process where states perform in relation to external expectations and can be risk averse over what they anticipate a regime will do in the future. The ASEAN Human Rights Declaration, particularly the general principles section, was designed to deal with the cooperation problem posed by adopting a human rights instrument and maintaining the ASEAN way as an institutional framework. The comparisons with the European human rights system described above were not intended to advance a Eurocentric conception of human rights; the African human rights system was constructed to reflect a distinct sense of regional identity. Unlike the ASEAN human rights system however, the African system, as demonstrated further in chapter 7, has a functional protective mandate and is capable of issuing decisions against states and of hearing individual petitions from people claiming rights abuses by state parties. The construction of the declaration was an example of utilizing the language of human rights to an external audience—invoking what Jack Donnelly describes as the "global script of legitimacy" given by the language of human rights—and attaching it to a legal framework which does not actually offer any meaningful protection for individuals living within states.[131] As Davies describes, ASEAN's approaches to human rights represent a form of institutional ritualism, which combines notional support for human rights with structuralized nonintervention, which has the net effect of seemingly acquiescing in human rights violations.[132] The Rohingya crisis in Myanmar in the 2010s, which saw only a limited political response from ASEAN and no institutional support for the victims of human rights abuses, arguably demonstrated the persistence of the noninterference doctrine and how limited any human rights reforms to ASEAN had been.[133]

The declaration was designed to be a defensive relativist instrument. Articles 6 and 7, through which all other substantive rights are to be interpreted, explicitly allow a state party to invoke a construction of state culture as a defense to any limitation of rights it is undertaking in its domestic law. This was a form of culturated sovereignty, which fused existing tropes from the Asian values debate about the role of human rights and culture with a legal structure that was deferential to state parties. Looking at regional human rights regimes through the lens of the fragmentation of international law, differing regional regimes do not necessarily pose a particular problem for the protection of rights, as they can acknowledge divergent historical origins of rights and often enjoy their own forms of localized legitimacy.[134] In spite of this, some have argued, conceding that the ASEAN human rights system does not have protective capacities, that it performs an important promotional function and helps mainstream human rights concerns with ASEAN.[135] Yet, as chapter 8 outlines, the way that the ASEAN Human Rights Declaration is constructed to institutionalize defensive relativism represents a form of false fragmentation, as it is designed to shield both the legal regime and the state from the notion of legal obligations to the individuals in that state.

CHAPTER 5

Defensive Relativism in State Submissions to the European Court of Human Rights on the Freedom of Religion

In March 1998 Leyla Şahin, a fourth-year medical student at Istanbul University, attempted to enter her oncology exam. At the doorway, the university officials stopped her from entering the exam hall because she was wearing a hijab. Earlier that year, a university circular had officially prohibited the wearing of the "Islamic headscarf," but this was the first time Leyla had been stopped for wearing it.[1] Leyla was to embark on a seven-year legal battle which culminated in the Grand Chamber of the European Court of Human Rights (ECtHR). The court held that her individual right to express her religious beliefs was subordinate to the Turkish government's maintenance of a secular higher education system. The case revolved around the extent to which it was legitimate for the state to police the public sphere in order to enforce its secularist cultural doctrine.[2] When, six years later, the Grand Chamber considered Soile Lautsi's claim that the presence of crucifixes in her child's classroom in Italy violated her family's right to freedom of conscience, the court held that the display of crucifixes in every classroom originated from traditions reflecting the country's majority Catholic faith and therefore, despite concerns about the neutrality of state education, the Italian government was justified in imposing this requirement.[3] These two cases had two seemingly different outcomes: in the former case, the religious freedom of an individual was not protected by the court, and in the latter case, a specific religion was protected by the court. What united them was that they were both examples of defensive relativism being successfully used by state parties at the ECtHR.

The margin of appreciation doctrine, discussed in chapter 3, describes the leeway the court gives a state party in its interpretation of the qualified rights in the European Convention on Human Rights (ECHR). The court has been heavily criticized for its lack of doctrinal coherence and for its deference towards the state party's presentation about how particular rights are balanced.[4] As Marie Dembour observes, the margin of appreciation is where the court effectively permits a form of cultural relativism in relation to domestic laws in state parties which limit particular rights.[5] In cases involving Article 9 of the ECHR—the right to freedom of thought, conscience, and religion—the submissions of state parties before the court attempting to justify limitations of the right often use defensive relativist arguments. Article 9 of the ECHR is located among the family of qualified rights, contained in Articles 8–11 of the convention, protecting, in turn, the rights to private and family life, religious freedom, freedom of "opinion and expression," and freedom of association. They can be described as a family of rights, as they are all framed in the same way: the first paragraph of the provision defines the right, and the second paragraph sets out the circumstances and framework by which the right may be subject to limitations by a state party in domestic law. As the first and second sections of this chapter demonstrate, the framework in which limitations of Article 9 are contested before the ECtHR is antiuniversalistic in nature, but notionally restrained by the legal practice of the margin of appreciation doctrine.

What states are attempting to do when making a defensive relativist argument in these cases is seek as wide a margin of appreciation as possible from the court in order to defend a state's construction of culture. This explains the seemingly contradictory nature of some of the case law in this area, as the defenses of established churches and defense of anti-veil laws, described in the latter two sections below, emerge as responses to a challenge from a particular minority religious interest about the restriction of its rights.

State Submissions Justifying Limitations of Rights

State submissions to the ECtHR on the scope of a restriction of a qualified right are the specific legal practice within which states make defensive relativist arguments. In order to take a case to the ECtHR, an individual needs to demonstrate that there has been a violation of their convention rights in the jurisdiction of a state party and that they have exhausted all available domestic remedies in that jurisdiction.[6] A variety of mechanisms allow the court to declare applications impermissable, and there are friendly settlement procedures contained in the convention, encouraging state parties to resolve the matters prior to the court deciding the case. Oral proceedings are the exception rather than the rule, and the majority of the advocacy before the court takes place in writing. Once the applicant demonstrates they have satisfied the admissibility requirements for their claim, they are able to present their case in writing, and the state party is invited to reply.[7] In the case of absolute rights, or rights such as Article 5 and 6, which contain restrictions on the rights of the detained and the administration of justice, state party submissions will often involve arguing that a domestic law or practice is in fact compatible with the precise framework under the ECHR and in line with previous interpretations of the right. Known as the "rights principle" in the court's method of adjudication, the ECtHR attempts to ensure that its decisions effectively protect rights as they are set out in the convention.[8]

In the case of qualified rights, the case being advanced by the state party is somewhat different under Articles 8–11, as the first part of those provisions determines the scope of the right and the second part sets out the limitations states may apply to those rights in domestic law.[9] Therefore what a state party is doing in cases involving these rights is arguing that its restrictions of rights in domestic law fit into those limits. The precise factual circumstances for which a limitation of rights may be justified are contained in a closed list in the second paragraph of Article 8–11; these include circumstances such as "national security" or "the protection of health or morals."[10] Compared to the rights to private and family life, "opinion and expression," and association, there are fewer circumstances in which the right to religious freedom can be restricted by state parties—for example, Articles 8, 10, and 11 can be restricted in order to prevent "crime and disorder," whereas Article 9 can't. It is not enough for the state party simply to claim that a limitation of rights is being undertaken for one of the reasons in the second part of the provision, it needs to demonstrate that it is in accordance with the law—to avoid the arbitrary exercise of power—and that the measure limiting rights is "necessary in a democratic society."[11] This is what Stephen Greer calls the democracy principle in the court's method of adjudication. The test the Court uses is to make an assessment as to whether the interference with the right in question is being made "in pursuit of a 'legitimate aim' proportionate to a pressing social need."[12] The proportionality assessment is a matter-of-fact assessment made in relation to the balancing act that is theoretically carried out by states in making laws in relation to the circumstance detailed in part 2 of the provision (the societal interest) and the statement of the right in part 1 (the individual right). There have been some criticisms of the doctrine because proportionality assessments question the means rather than the ends of restrictions to rights and can turn human rights into justifications for the exercise of political power, rather than constraints on their exercise.[13] Where the doctrine is pursued in a systemic faction—deferring to the state party not on the merits of their decision in balancing certain rights, but due to the mere fact that they have made a decision on rights in the form of a law or policy—this can amount to an unlimited deference toward the state about the legitimacy of its restrictions on rights.[14]

The margin of appreciation doctrine is explicitly pluralistic in intention. It does not associate the universality of rights with conformity of implementation, and it acknowledges the divergence between societies over the protection of rights.[15] In this respect, a state party defending a restriction of rights before the ECtHR with a submission that requests the court to adhere to the margin of appreciation doctrine is implicitly appealing to an antiuniversalist position, fulfilling the first element of defensive relativism outlined in chapter 1. The margin of appreciation doctrine, while practically permitting limitations of notionally universal rights, does this in part because it recognizes the ECtHR's role as a supranational court, and also because it acknowledges that societies, values, and customs differ from country to country and therefore a controlled antiuniversalist doctrine aids the interpretation of the abstract rights in the ECHR and helps build the authority of the ECtHR as an institution.[16] Protocol 15 of the ECHR, which inserts the margin of appreciation doctrine into the text of the ECHR, was designed to clarify the scope of responsibility on state parties for the implementation of ECHR rights without altering the substance of the doctrine.[17] As outlined previously, the antiuniversalist element of defensive relativism (outlined in chapter 1) is not, in isolation, problematic for the protection of human rights and is a reflection of the limits of universalism. However, the subsequent two elements of defensive relativism—the state construction of culture and a legal exemption (outlined in chapters 2 and 3)—do result in the margin of appreciation being used in a manner that significantly interferes with the protection of human rights.

In relation to Articles 8–11, the margin of appreciation doctrine takes two basic forms: firstly, the substantive margin of appreciation, which is where a state argues that a restriction of rights is justified because it is pursuing a collective good or goal listed in the second part of Articles 8–11 in a proportionate manner. The aim is to devolve to the domestic level the balancing of human rights with the ECtHR overseeing the limits of that process.[18] The second conception of the margin of appreciation, the structural margin of appreciation, refers to the deference that a court ought to accord a state party in terms of the assessment of the balance of interests involved in a particular decision; what a state party is arguing in making a structural margin of appreciation argument is that the ECtHR lacks the authority to supplant the judgment of the national government on this issue.[19] The latter conception is the one often advanced by state parties making a defensive relativist argument, as it allows the greatest width of the margin of appreciation and therefore provides them the intellectual room to defend their conception of state culture. The ECtHR's seemingly deferential approach toward states in a number of cases involving Article 9 has been criticized by some scholars and judges as an abdication of its stated "task of discerning and articulating the criteria" for the balancing of religious rights with other societal interests in such cases.[20] Cases over the course of the 2010s (some of which are discussed below) have led some scholars to question whether the court is in effect hiding behind the doctrine in order to avoid conducting a proportionality assessment of domestic restrictions of Article 9 rights.[21] However, this is also a reflection of the fact that Article 9's text and the jurisprudence of the article indicates that the provision is structurally disposed toward defensive relativist arguments.

The Scope of Article 9 of the European Convention on Human Rights

What freedom of religion substantively entails has been open to considerable debate. Disputes about the interpretation of the First Amendment to the United States Constitution, which commits Congress to not making any law that infringes upon the freedom of religion, have covered this terrain with some scholars speculating over the intent of the U.S. Founding Fathers.[22] On the international plane, the freedom of religion evolved partially as a mechanism for protecting religious communities dating back to the Peace of Augsburg in 1555, which allowed princes in the Holy Roman Empire to determine whether Catholicism or Lutheranism would be recognized in their territory.[23] Freedom of religion also developed as means of protecting minority rights; Article 14 of the Treaty of Utrecht of 1713 ensured that French-speaking Catholics in American territories, who would as a result of the treaty be ruled by Britain, would still have the right to practice their faith.[24] The minority treaties after the First World War sought to protect the rights of religious minorities as well as ethnic and linguistic minorities, protecting their freedom of worship as a matter of international law. The freedom "of every person to worship God in his own way—everywhere in the world" was listed by President Roosevelt as one of the "four essential human freedoms" that U.S. foreign policy would aim to protect around the world, recasting freedom of religion as a universal right.[25] When the Universal Declaration of Human Rights (UDHR) was being drafted there was considerable disagreement over what eventually become Article 18—the right to freedom of thought, conscience, and religion—because the Saudi Arabian delegate to the UN objected to the implication that the freedom to change one's religion was a universal right, given that it was incompatible with the principles of Sharia law as practiced in Saudi Arabia.[26] Not only was this arguably the first instance of cultural relativism in international human rights law, but it also highlighted an important tension within the concept of freedom of religion: if "freedom" implies the absence of government coercion over religious practice, it also entails a positive obligation on the state to facilitate religious freedom. The 1981 UN Declaration on the Elimination of All Forms of Intolerance and of Discrimination Based on Religion or Belief, while not a binding instrument, set out the positive duty of states to "enact or rescind legislation" and use all "appropriate measures to combat intolerance on the grounds of religion."[27]

From a conceptual perspective, the freedom of thought, conscience, and religion is a somewhat meaningless protection because at the individual level, as Caroline Evans notes, absent a mind control machine of the sort found in science fiction comics, a state cannot control the content of an individual's personal thoughts.[28] It is at the external or communal level where freedom of religion matters, as a state can interfere directly with people's ability to exercise their rights by restricting worship, teaching, and other forms of observance which are necessarily public. This is acknowledged in a general comment from the Human Rights Committee (HRC), the treaty body of the International Covenant on Civil and Political Rights (ICCPR). The comment states that the part of Article 18 of the ICCPR which protects "the freedom to have or adopt a religion or belief of one's choice" is "protected unconditionally."[29] The classically liberal notion of freedom to engage in religious worship can be seen as simply an extension of general liberal freedoms—what philosophers such as Isaiah Berlin define as noninterference by others—in that all that is required by a state to ensure religious freedom is not to interfere with a manifestation of beliefs and to retain legal agnosticism about the merits of any faith.[30] Yet, approaching religious freedom from this perspective ignores the practical reality of many societies where dominant religions may put direct or indirect barriers in the way of other faiths, or through the democratic process instruct lawmakers to keep immunities and privileges historically accorded to the dominant religion.[31] Also, given the nature of some religious ideologies, one individual's exercise of their religious freedom can reduce the rights of another individual—this is a particular concern with regard to religious proselytization, which can in some cases aim to reduce the freedom of thought and conscience of others, and in circumstances where the freedoms or interests of minors are involved there are legitimate concerns about the exercise of their freedom of religion and conscience.[32] Practically, therefore, protecting religious freedom requires trade-offs and potential restrictions of rights in order to enable a broader societal protection of religious freedom, which is what is notionally captured in the second paragraph of Article 9 of the ECHR.

Discussions surrounding Article 9 during the ECHR's drafting broadly reflected the ECHR's origins as an anti-totalitarian instrument, designed to respond to the concerns of the late 1940s about the growth of Stalinist Communism and potential for a reemergence of fascism. A number of delegates at the Council of Europe conference which drafted the ECHR were concerned about banning or persecuting religions, with references being made to the Nazi persecution of Jews and minority Christian faiths. Conservative politician and British representative to the Council of Europe David Maxwell-Fyfe's exhortation to "revere the great family of Western Europe and Christian civilisation" was not just a rhetorical flourish but a reflection of the predominantly Christian nature of the vast majority of the countries drafting the ECHR.[33] The relatively high level of Christian homogeneity led to the discussion on Article 9 becoming dominated by rather simplistic statements about the importance of religion and religious freedom without really considering the practicalities of protecting the right to freedom of religion.[34] Sweden and Turkey, in an early example of an attempt to shape rights to reflect the dominant culture of a state, did attempt to amend the convention to create an exemption for national laws that might be considered incompatible with the freedom of religion, but these amendments were later withdrawn.[35] Beyond that, however, there is scant evidence of any broader consideration about the limitations of the right to religious freedom and the sort of interests states would be required to balance. This fit the broader pattern of the ECHR's drafting where, as Ed Bates describes it, states were keen to include rights "already protected thoroughly" within their domestic legal systems, seeing the convention as a form of safeguard for the status quo in their jurisdiction.[36] Appeals to "Western" human rights standards in the political language surrounding the convention in the 1950s promoted relatively orthodox notions of protecting dominant established churches, which were often intertwined with social organizations and the dominant Christian Democratic Parties in many countries, as well as notionally safeguarding the rights of minorities against the state.[37] This was seen mostly through the lens of countering Fascism and other totalitarian ideologies, rather than with an understanding of how these rights might help adjudicate the relationship between the individual and the state.[38] In fact, there is little evidence of much consideration about how a future court would function and protect rights. As A. W. Brian Simpson observes, had states in 1950 foreseen the future "intrusiveness" of the ECtHR "into what were once viewed as purely domestic matters," the process of the ECHR ratification may have been far more fraught than it was.[39]

It wasn't until 1993 that the ECtHR first found a violation of Article 9, and in its first half century the ECtHR only found violations of Article 9 in thirty-four cases, which as an overall sample was a lower ratio of violations-to-claims than with Article 8 or 10.[40] Although this is not a particularly conclusive statistic, as it gives no real insight into the merits of individual cases, it is noteworthy that as an overall percentage of the ECtHR's caseload there were far fewer cases alleging violations of Article 9 prior to the mid-1990s compared to those involving Articles 8 and 10. As the role of the ECtHR evolved in the 1990s, due to the advent of its compulsory jurisdiction in 1998, the growth of the evolutive interpretation of the convention in ECtHR jurisprudence, and applications to the ECtHR increasing due to the Council of Europe expanding in size, there was an overall general increase in claims before the court.[41] Social changes within member states and the composition of member states led to an increase in Article 9 claims in the 1990s and 2000s. A number of states from Eastern Europe joining Council of Europe had dominant national churches and a recent history of being denied religious freedom under Communist rule. There was also a growing number of issues arising from the domestic polices of some Western European states designed to respond to the increasing multicultural nature of their societies. In part because the right to freedom of religion is subject to overlapping conceptual issues, and also because there was never much serious consideration of the parameters of limitations to the right to freedom of religion by the court prior to the 1990s, arguments about the scope of Article 9 were particularly prone to states making defensive relativist claims in their pursuit of the widest possible margin of appreciation.

That said, from ECtHR jurisprudence on Article 9 there are three principles relating to its interpretation which, while often set out by the court as being essential components of Article 9, are not necessarily followed in cases where defensive relativist arguments are used by state parties. Firstly, the court places a strong expectation on the state to encourage pluralism of beliefs and religious freedoms, seeing this as an important component of a democratic society.[42] There is a strong presumption against national regulatory restrictions which would limit religious pluralism; in *Moscow Branch of the Salvation Army v. Russia*, the court noted that any restrictions on Article 9 needed to be justified by "convincing and compelling reasons" that reflected a "compelling social need," and there was no flexibility for a state to impose restrictions which were merely "'useful" or "desirable."[43] Secondly, even though it is arguable that Article 9 affords primarily a protection to the private exercise of religious freedom, the court has on a number of occasions recognized the communal importance of religion, noting that under Article 9(1) manifestations of belief "either alone or in community with others" were protected and could not be considered mutually exclusive.[44] These points are difficult to balance with an expectation or policy of secularism which, as the fourth section of this chapter outlines, can take the form of a state cultural practice at odds with these two principles. The third significant principle is that states must be neutral when it comes to individual religions.[45] This is a particularly complex position to reconcile with the relative power of established religions, which are part of a state's constitutional framework or otherwise highly dominant in society, as the next section outlines.

Defensive Relativism as a Justification for the Protection of the Dominant State Religion

European states differ considerably on how they constitutionally seek to establish a church or form of Christianity, reflecting the complex evolution of modern statehood. In some states there is a clear institutionalized church or dominant church with ties to the state recognized within its constitution. In other states, there is a numerically dominant church that, by virtue of the size of its support, is able to be politically powerful. In many Western European states after World War II, Christian Democrat parties with strong informal ties to socially dominant churches were both common and relatively successful.[46] Having a dominant established or state church is not necessarily incompatible with the protection of the right to freedom of religion. As the HRC made clear in concluding remarks to Argentina and Chile, in relation to their obligations under Article 18 of the ICCPR, the fact that such a church exists should not entail that it should be privileged to the exclusion of other religions.[47] This is a relatively simple principle but Article 9 cases have highlighted some of its complex dimensions. For example, in San Marino, parliamentarians were required to take an oath where they swore "on the Holy Gospels ever to be faithful to and obey the Constitution of the Republic" in order to take up their parliamentary seats.[48] Some politicians argued that the overtly religious nature of the oath contravened their individual right to freedom of conscience, and as a consequence they specifically requested to take a version of the oath omitting the reference to the Gospels—but this request was refused. In proceedings before the ECtHR, the state party argued that the oath "was not religious but, rather, historical and social in significance and based on tradition," and throughout its submissions framed the oath as an essential reflection of state culture which was now secular but had religious roots.[49] In the submissions from the state party, the different elements of defensive relativism were apparent, but the court found a violation of Article 9 due to the requirement to "swear allegiance to a particular religion on pain of forfeiting their parliamentary seats" being effectively coercive.[50] The ruling did not address the substance of the state party's broader claim about the place of religion within state culture and its necessity in a democratic society under the framework of Article 9.

In Greece, the Orthodox Church enjoys constitutional protection and is an important social and cultural institution which has survived political upheavals, wars, and the colonization of Greece by various powers during the nineteenth and twentieth centuries.[51] As Adamantia Pollis explains, Orthodoxy and the Orthodox Church were often presented as part of a collective identity, or "ethnos," which made Greek society a united and "transcendent holistic entity," but one which could also easily provide the "rationale for restrictions on the exercise of individual rights."[52] Orthodoxy was central to the military regime's promotion of a Greek identity in the 1960s and 1970s. Even though Greece rejoined the Council of Europe in 1974 and the European Economic Community (the forerunner of the European Union) in 1981, a network of laws and state practices put the Orthodox Church in a highly privileged position regarding other religious minorities.[53] Until the decision in *Kokkinakis v. Greece*, the ECtHR had not made a finding of a violation of Article 9. Its decision that an antiproselytization law, which had criminalized a couple who were Jehovah's Witnesses, had violated their right to freedom of religion was justified by the court on the basis that the prosecution of the applicants was not "justified in the circumstances of the case by a pressing social need."[54] What the court did not challenge was the defensive relativist arguments made by the state party about the special status of the Orthodox Church. The Greek government defended a domestic court decision at the ECtHR which justified the antiproselytization law in terms of prohibiting "activities directed against the dominant religion, that of the Christian Eastern Orthodox Church."[55] As preaching and proselytization was an essential part of the applicants' faith, the law effectively restricted the rights of a minority in order to protect the power and social status of a dominant cultural institution, undermining the pluralist nature of the rights protected by Article 9.[56] The judgment did not unpick this, and the applicants' success in *Kokkinakis* was due in part to the law's disproportionate sanctions. As Dunne notes, the ECtHR's conclusion was that a proselytization law could in theory be justified in a democratic society, therefore implicitly favoring the entrenched status of the Orthodox Church—which can be read as part of a general deference on the court's part toward laws protecting "state-established religions."[57]

A less-overt way in which dominant religions assert their status is through administrative laws requiring places of worship to be registered or to meet a standard of certification not required by dominant religions, which may be difficult for smaller religious groups to meet. In *Metropolitan Church of Bessarabia v. Moldova*, the ECtHR made clear that refusing recognition of a church under registration laws—in this case the church in question was refused registration because the state party held it was a schism in a recognized church—was incompatible with Article 9.[58] Unless the state could demonstrate an actual, not hypothetical, compelling necessity, such as a threat to security, which would justify the refusal of registration in a specific case, refusing to register a church would be a violation of Article 9.[59] As the court has made clear elsewhere, because of the implications of Article 11 (the right to freedom of association), as well as the restriction on religious freedom, there is a high threshold for using registration laws to limit freedom of religion.[60] This has not stopped states from attempting to do this and to justify their actions in distinctly defensive relativist terms. In *Savez Crkava "Riječ*

Života" v. Croatia, the Croatian government contended that it had refused to register the applicants in part because of their lack of "historical or cultural relevance" in Croatia, but was willing to recognize other religious groups which belonged to what it described as the "historical religious communities of the European cultural circle."[61] The way that registration laws for religious buildings were used by state authorities to maintain the privileged position of the Greek Orthodox Church was noted by the court in *Manoussakis v. Greece*, but the Greek government in its submissions defended the centrality of the Church to Greek cultural life, arguing that it "had kept alive the national conscience and Greek patriotism during the periods of foreign occupation'"[62] In these registration cases, state parties often fused together concerns about security, social cohesion, or the protection of vulnerable individuals alongside defensive relativist arguments in an effort to satisfy the somewhat narrow margin of appreciation accorded in cases involving criminal penalties and the restrictions of Article 9 and 11.[63]

Sometimes the way a state accords privileges to a dominant religion is not overtly antipluralistic, as was the case in *Lautsi v. Italy*, where the mother of a child in the Italian school system challenged the mandatory display of the crucifix on the walls of classrooms.[64] The display of the crucifix was part of the Italian tradition of *laicità* which, although originating within Italy's dominant Catholic faith, had evolved in the 1980s to recognize the symbolic importance of the Church in society while maintaining neutrality toward different religious faiths.[65] In the first hearing of the case before the ECtHR in 2009, the Italian state defended the presence of the crucifixes in terms of the *laicità* doctrine, arguing that they represented "a humanist message which could be read independently of its religious dimension" and hence had no bearing on the exercise of religious freedom.[66] Yet, this was somewhat in tension with the state's later submissions, where it claimed it had "decided to keep crucifixes in classrooms for various reasons, including the need to reach a compromise with political parties having Christian leanings" and to recognize religious feelings in the country.[67] When the court found against the state party there was a significant social backlash in Italy, with politicians across the political spectrum defending the practice as an essential part of Italian culture and Pope Benedict XVI stressing that it was a religious symbol which reflected religious values in Italian history.[68] On appeal to the Grand Chamber of the ECtHR the Italian government reemphasized both the nonreligious nature of the display of crucifixes and the importance of the practice as an Italian cultural symbol. The Grand Chamber rejected the notion that the crucifix was a nonreligious symbol but concluded that the "decision whether or not to perpetuate a tradition falls in principle within the margin of appreciation of the respondent state."[69] As Malcolm Evans and Peter Petkoff observe in their commentary on the case, religious neutrality in *Lautsi* was turned by the court into a form of "sovereignty-driven political exceptionalism"; whereas neutrality had been previously understood as a duty on the state to "ensure religious neutrality and impartiality," it was now being interpreted as a duty to ensure the state was left alone to make its own determinations.[70] In effect, this turned rights protection into an exercise of justifying the status quo as it was constituted, rather than changing the law to protect freedom of conscience and religion.

The Defense of Secularism as State Culture: The Veil Cases

Constitutional secularism, András Sajó argues, is the notion that the state should take "no specific position regarding the truth of religion nor any preliminary position regarding the proper place of religion in society."[71] This means that a position of broad neutrality should be adopted by the state in order to promote the maximal amount of religious freedom—which differs considerably from atheism or secular humanism as a principle, which makes value statements about religious faiths.[72] The ECtHR does not maintain that in order to protect Article 9 secularism needs to be enforced. Decisions such as *Wingrove v. United Kingdom* and *Otto-Preminger-Institut v. Austria* make it clear that specific protection for religious communities can be afforded to them through laws restricting the exercise of Article 10 rights (freedom of opinion and expression), such as the laws governing film certification.[73] The ECtHR requires that states maintain religious pluralism, while acknowledging that religious cultures and the importance of religion varies considerably from society to society.[74] Secularism, in the way it is outlined by Sajó, is different from the multiplicity of ways in which the term is used to describe the interpretation of the ECHR, which has a variety of different culturally contingent meanings.[75] There are significant differences between the historical origins of secularism in Turkey and France, and differences in the restrictions imposed by countries across Europe in relation to wearing religious symbols. However, far from analyzing secularism in the same light as other cultural traditions, the ECtHR has instead been implicitly deferential to states justifying restrictions of religious freedom on the basis of promoting secularism, the presumption seemingly being that it assists with the promotion of pluralism.[76] Some have suggested that institutional changes at the ECtHR, such as the increased caseload and compulsory jurisdiction, have led to the court implicitly promoting a form of institutional secularization as the simplest means of maintaining consistency of interpretation.[77] Insofar as the ECtHR has done this, its effect has been to—almost unconsciously—favor the hard forms of state-enforced secularism in certain countries.

Pluralism, or, more precisely, the ECtHR's construction of pluralism, also acknowledges that restrictions on religious freedom may be necessary to "reconcile the interests of differing groups and to ensure respect for the convictions of all," the presumption being that any such restrictions are justified by objective criteria.[78] Cases involving headscarves or veils worn by practicing Muslim women—which have involved assessing whether the restrictions on religious freedom from domestic laws imposing criminal or civil penalties on an individual for wearing religious clothing fall within the margin of appreciation accorded to states under Article 9—have one or both of the following features. Firstly, there is a direct concern with the vulnerability of individuals from either the same class as the applicant or from some protected group in society, which justifies restrictions of religious freedom on the grounds of necessity. For example, in *Dahlab v. Switzerland*, where the applicant had been dismissed from her employment as a primary school teacher after converting to Islam and starting to wear a hijab, the court concluded that the case met the necessity test, given that the applicant was working with very young children who would be curious about her attire and hence would be proselytized to by default as their teacher explained her faith to them.[79] Although the separation between church and state in the Swiss canton (state) where the applicant worked was commented on in the decision, the case turned on the vulnerability of the children under her tutelage; other authorities have also acknowledged some latitude for state parties where restrictions on religious dress are imposed in educational settings.[80] Where this gets more complicated is where secularism is presented by the state party as a means of protecting women more generally, as this creates a conflict between the autonomy of the individual making the choice regarding the expression of their religion and the presumption that cultural secularism protects against any form of social coercion.[81] It would be incorrect to see traditions of secularism as synonymous with women's rights; as Amelie Barras observes in her research on

French activists, the tradition of secularism, or *laïcité*, had not historically been in favor of female emancipation and had been used to exclude women from full citizenship, including the right to vote, for large parts of the twentieth century.[82]

Secondly, the wearing of religious symbols is treated differently from other speech acts in that a clash is engineered between religious symbols which have political content, and dominant cultural secularism, which is treated as being neutral. In *Şahin v. Turkey* it was explicitly noted that supporters of secularism treated the applicant's headscarf as "a symbol of political Islam."[83] Beyond this reference to political symbolism, Yussef Al Tamimi notes, there is scant reference in the court's judgment to the "politicality of the headscarf" and what the consequences of it as a political symbol actually were, allowing the court to simply conclude that to "preserve the secular character of educational institutions" it was necessary to enact a ban on the wearing of the headscarf.[84] The decision effectively then became a clash of political norms—the applicant's "political Islam" versus the state's secularism, which was not value-neutral, as its choices explicitly reflected political traditions in Turkey and the state's view of Islam as a religion, creating an effective secularist double standard.[85] In *Eweida v. UK*, the ECtHR upheld the Article 9 complaint of a British Airways worker who had been dismissed from her job for wearing a cross with her uniform, noting the value to an "individual who has made religion a central tenet of his or her life to be able to communicate that belief to others" seemingly recognizing the speech component of wearing a religious symbol.[86] The UK was not an officially secular society, and the case had arisen in the context of a private law dispute between the applicant and her employer (a private company), who had set a uniform code prohibiting her from wearing a cross. Her failure to get sufficient redress in the domestic tribunals led her to take her case to the ECtHR. *Eweida* can be contrasted with the cases involving secular restrictions on the headscarf, which lack an analysis of the headscarf as a speech act and do not interpret the legitimacy of any restrictions on the public act of wearing a headscarf through the lens of an individual deciding to make a speech act.[87] This is a reflection of how deferential the margin of appreciation doctrine is toward state secularism when it is presented by the state party as a cultural important value. Judge Tulkens's dissenting opinion in *Şahin* raised these concerns, noting the state party had failed to establish as a matter of fact that there was any compelling social need for such a restriction. The majority of the court, Judge Tulkens argued, by finding that "wearing the headscarf contravenes the principle of secularism" took up position on an "issue that has been the subject of much debate" in simple deference to the state party's conclusion on that debate.[88]

The tensions over cultural secularism and Article 9 became particularly apparent in the cases coming from France in the late 2000s. The origins of French secularism—the principle of *laïcité*— came from societal values dating back to the French Revolution in 1789, and laws from 1905 onward had required the removal of religious symbols from public buildings and other symbolic acts designed to highlight the separation of church and state. Prior to the 1990s, *laïcité* had been understood to generate legal obligations only on public bodies, and even after a 2004 law which prohibited the wearing of religious symbols in public schools, some defended this as simply an application of liberal principles designed to protect the rights of children to education.[89] But, as Stéphanie Hennette Vauchez argues, this moved the principle of the law to asserting legal obligations on an individual, and subsequent litigation in French courts established that restrictions on public displays, even if not posing any practical impediment to the discharge of a job's responsibilities, applied across vocational training programs and among staff in public preschools, or nurseries.[90] The symbol of wearing a headscarf had become a site of contestation of a distinctly French identity, with some politicians increasingly using negative stereotypes about Islam and identifying female face covering as antithetical to French culture.[91] It was in this context that the law banning the full-face veils (the niqab and burqa) in public was passed in 2010—and then challenged in a test case in the French courts and, finally, taken to the ECtHR.

The Conseil d'Etat, the highest French constitutional and administrative court, had held that state secularism in isolation was insufficient to justify restricting the right to freedom of religion, but that the broader social imperative of encouraging social cohesion could justify the ban. This, as was the case with Article 9 cases involving dominant state churches, effectively bolted weak cases for restrictions on rights based on social necessity onto defensive relativist arguments. In a memorandum attached to the bill before the French Parliament in May 2010, the wearing of face veils was described as "the sectarian manifestation of a rejection of the values of the Republic," but the memorandum went on to state that the ban was justified on security and antidiscrimination grounds without giving any details of why this was the case.[92] Before the ECtHR the French government played down the defense of secularism, arguing instead that the law banning the burqa was a conscious choice in the organization of society and the full face veil was antithetical to that choice as it represented a "break [to] social ties and to manifest a refusal of the principle of 'living together' (i.e., 'vivre ensemble')."[93] The principle of "living-together" was unclear, although some have argued that this comes close to what is sometimes described as a principle of "*ordre public*"—the principle in international law describing the sum of rules which ensure the functioning of society.[94] Yet, the concept of "living together" as it was presented by the French government in the case was so open ended as to amount to little more than the imposition of majority views on a religion.[95] The state party framed what were obviously social and cultural questions arising from the arguments about the status of the veil in relation to French cultural secularism, a debate that had being going on for over 10 years when *SAS v. France* came to the ECtHR, under general concept of "living together," which almost read as an attempt to escape the questions involved in the dispute.[96]

As Thomas Hammarberg, the Council of Europe Commissioner for Human Rights, notes, those seeking to ban the burqa had "not managed to show that these garments in any way undermine democracy public safety, order or morals." Hammarberg went on to warn that a blanket restriction on the burqa would undermine pluralism, giving the impression that a "particular religion is being targeted."[97] But the ECtHR, while acknowledging some of these concerns, was content to draw the margin of appreciation widely, saying that it needed to have regard for "any consensus and common values emerging from the practices" of a state party—which in this case meant acknowledging that France's version of *laïcité* necessitated a burqa ban—and concluded by agreeing with the French government's submissions that a "systematic concealment of the face in public places" could be contrary "to the ideal of fraternity" which the French government prioritized.[98] A year later, when the ECtHR ruled that the headscarf ban was applicable to the entire public service—meaning that even the hijab, which did not cover the face, could be banned—the French government maintained that this was necessary to "preserve the constitutional principle of secularism," and the court accepted that the ban "involved a fundamental principle of the state."[99] This decision was almost certain to have a discriminatory effect on employment in the public sector, which was now legitimately able to exclude any job applicant for wearing a religious symbol.[100] In these cases, a dominant cultural value was being expressly prioritized by these decisions, and the court was using an increasingly strained construction of the margin of appreciation doctrine to attempt to reconcile the decisions with the principle of religious pluralism as protected by Article 9.[101] Yet, in subsequent cases involving a burqa ban in

Belgium, the court, pursuing its subsidiarity doctrine, found that the bans were compatible with Article 9 because appropriate debate and the weighing up of different interests had taken place at the national level before enacting the law.[102] This illustrated another way of justifying a burqa ban to the court, outside of defensive relativist arguments over the application of the margin of appreciation doctrine.

Conclusion: The Limits of Religious Freedom

There are times, Malcolm Evans rather pithily observes, when one wonders if the ECtHR "secretly subscribes to some doctrine of infallibility."[103] The *Kokkinakis* principle that "freedom of thought, consciences and religion is one of the foundations of a 'democratic society'" has been so often quoted in subsequent cases on Article 9 that it has become a near-trite statement of the obvious, but the actual application of the law in a variety of different scenarios has struggled to reconcile the competing demands of democracy and religious pluralism.[104] The seemingly contradictory approach of the court to interpreting Article 9 in different cases is, in fact, readily explicable—the cases set out in the third and fourth sections of this chapter are cases where the state party was attempting to defend its domestic laws and practices with defensive relativist arguments. *Lautsi* and *SAS* are both examples of successful defensive relativism. The consequences of defensive relativism's success in these cases is that human rights law, far from protecting a plurality of different identities, instead ends up as a justificatory mechanism for domestic laws compelling adherence to the dominant identity of the community in question, which is usually state-backed or favored by the state.[105] Much mirth was had in 2020 when in order to combat the coronavirus pandemic the French government made face mask wearing compulsory, but the fine for not wearing a face mask was lower than the fine for wearing a niqab. As Fatima Khemilat, a fellow at the Political Science Institute of Aix-en-Provence, said, this "asymmetrical reading of the same behaviour" was "arbitrary at best, discriminatory at worst."[106] But this seeming contradiction made sense in the context of the 2010 ban being a means of privileging a dominant institution. What's more, the highest human rights body in Europe had given coherence to this contradiction through the margin of appreciation doctrine, finding that the discriminatory nature of the niqab ban was in pursuit of a legitimate purpose.

Part of the reason for the preponderance of defensive relativist arguments in freedom of religion cases at the ECtHR was that the construction of Article 9 was a somewhat uneasy reflection of unquestioned Christian hegemony in the political climate at the time of drafting. Discussions during the drafting of Article 9 never anticipated how an interventionist supranational court would interpret it or how it would work as the social and religious makeup of different European societies evolved. The origins of Article 9 clearly facilitated defensive relativist arguments as the increasingly wide margin of appreciation doctrine allowed states to argue that their laws and practices that discriminated in favor of a particular religion of belief system, allowing a culturally hegemonic construction of culture, did in fact balance relevant societal interests. The margin of appreciation doctrine was designed to address the concerns about universality that, as chapter 1 of this book argues, have dogged international human rights law. Yet, contestation over its relative width has meant that over some issues, its application has provided a virtual legal exemption, justifying open discrimination against a particular minority. As Eva Brems notes, given that between a fifth and a quarter of all jobs in the French labor market are in the public sector, the impact of granting a wide margin of appreciation in *Ebrahimian v. France* was to create a systemic disadvantage toward French Muslim women in terms of their prospective employment.[107] At the time of finishing this book in the summer of 2021, the case of *Mikyas v. Belgium* had yet to be heard by the court, but as the text of a third-party intervention from the Human Rights Centre in Ghent University made clear, laws restricting the wearing of religious symbols in Belgian schools were influencing "choices of schools, higher studies and employment."[108] The wave of increasingly skeptical scholarship on the margin of appreciation doctrine in the late 2010s was indicative of growing concern surrounding the doctrine and its consequences.[109]

States are often willing to embrace defensive relativist arguments because they give an argumentative template to justify resisting human rights claims that could cause domestic political problems, while retaining notional compliance with supranational human rights standards. Among European states there is a relatively high degree of expectation of compliance with the ECtHR, so defensive relativist arguments justifying a wide margin of appreciation in these cases have clear strategic advantages.[110] Equally, the ECtHR can be unwilling to rule decisively in situations where there is a lack of a European consensus over particular rights restrictions; it can therefore be receptive to defensive relativist arguments, as they seemingly provide proof of this lack of consensus by highlighting both the diversity of social traditions and their importance to the state party.[111] Although defensive relativist arguments appear elsewhere in ECtHR jurisprudence, the complexities of trying to reconcile the somewhat abstract concept of religious pluralism with hard social questions around changing cultural identities presents particular difficulties for the ECtHR. Since *SAS*, the court seems to lean toward a position where, because of the difference between "one country to another according to national traditions," and out of deference to the "specific domestic context," it is willing to give a wider license to defensive relativist arguments in religious rights cases.[112]

CHAPTER 6

Defensive Relativism in the Justification of CEDAW Reservations in Universal Periodic Review

In March 2014, representatives of the Saudi Arabian government at the UN Human Rights Council (HRC) fully accepted 65 percent of all the recommendations offered to the government during its review in the second Universal Periodic Review (UPR) cycle. These included commitments to abolish torture and codify criminal laws to improve rights in the criminal justice system. The regional director for Amnesty International, commenting on the outcome of the review, was, however, skeptical, saying the Saudi government needed to prove "that its acceptance of these recommendations [was] more than a mere public relations exercise designed to deflect criticism of its human rights record."[1] Four years later (while a draft of this chapter was being written), Saudi Arabia was undergoing its review as part of the third UPR cycle, having just admitted its security services had tortured to death the dissident journalist Jamal Khashoggi in its embassy in Turkey. For critics of the UPR and the UN Human Rights Council (HRC), incidents such as these are seen as proof that their whole approach, which places an emphasis on an interactive dialogue between a state undergoing review and the voluntary acceptance of human rights standards, is fundamentally flawed and overly politicized. However, over the UPR's first decade there have been advancements in human rights protection in key areas, such as LGBT rights, migrant rights, and the rights of children, directly as a result of the review process.[2] Moreover, the politicized nature of the review was a design feature of the process, intended to create a political sense of equality between states, to address criticisms of the HRC's predecessor, the UN Commission on Human Rights.[3]

Any assessment of the UPR, therefore, is quite complex, as since its creation in 2006 it has undertaken three review cycles of all 193 UN members, with thousands of recommendations made to states about changes to their domestic laws and practices in order to protect human rights, as well as their international treaty commitments. It has also emerged as a new forum for defensive relativism, as states have sought to defend their existing laws and practices restricting rights contained in treaties to which they are a party. One specific area where the review process has become a forum for defensive relativism is in relation to reservations to the 1979 Convention on the Elimination of all forms of Discrimination Against Women (CEDAW). As noted in earlier chapters, CEDAW is the human rights treaty with the most reservations entered to it and contains a specific test for the permissibility of reservations in Article 28, rendering impermissible reservations "incompatible with the object and purpose of the present Convention."[4] The CEDAW Committee—CEDAW's treaty body—has faced a series of criticisms about its lack of consistency in dealing with reservations, which is part of a wider criticism about CEDAW processes and the inconsistency of the committee's reports.[5] After some initial doubts about its legal capacity to handle reservations, the committee has attempted constructive dialogue with states in relation to reservations and has achieved some success in getting them to withdraw reservations.[6]

Reservations to human rights treaties can represent a means of reconciling the "transcending" nature of a state's legal obligations with the reality of changing laws or policies in its legal and political systems, so by their very nature reservations are antiuniversalist.[7] As the first chapter of this book outlines in its examination of antiuniversality (the first element of defensive relativism), antiuniversalist devices, such as reservations, can be a way of persuading states to implement the substantive provisions of a human rights instrument. The text of a reservation is where the second element of defensive relativism—the state construction of culture (as outlined in chapter 2)—can be seen in the way that the reservation is substantively justified and what specific concepts or practices are cited in the text as a justification for limiting rights. The third element of defensive relativism—a legal exemption— which is outlined in chapter 3, shows how treaties can use the object and purpose test to develop a standard of permissibility for reservations. There are some states which persist in reservations to CEDAW which are incompatible with the object and purpose test set out in Article 28. In some cases these reservations are designed to remove any duty the state has under the treaty; at the time of writing there are six states that have open-ended reservations relating to Sharia law applying to the whole of Article 2, which sets out the duty of a state to implement CEDAW, entailing that their reservation effectively exempts them from their duty to implement the terms of the treaty.[8] The UPR process has provided another forum for states to be confronted about their reservations. As the latter two sections of this chapter set out, the response from some states when their obligations under CEDAW have been raised as part of their review at the UPR has been to restate, and in some cases, amplify, the state construction of culture justifying their reservations.

The Universal Periodic Review and Reservations to Human Rights Treaties

In 2005, UN Secretary-General Kofi Annan published a report on UN reform titled "In Larger Freedom," which noted that at the UN Commission on Human Rights, double standards had cast "a shadow on the reputation of the United Nations system as a whole" and recommended the creation of a new entity, the Human Rights Council.[9] Annan also called for the treaty bodies of the major human rights treaties "to be much more effective and more responsive to violations of the rights that they are mandated to uphold."[10] There were a number of different proposals for reform of the then-ailing UN Commission on Human Rights in Annan's report, including a renewed focus on membership of human rights bodies and membership criteria for the new Human Rights Council. There was, however, little reference in the report to what was later seen to be one of the most the most significant developments in the shift from the commission to the council—the development of a peer review system.[11] During the HRC's creation the role of the UPR was the subject of many disagreements. Although most states agreed on the idea of an objective peer review mechanism along the lines of other peer review mechanisms such as the Development Assistance Committee of the Organisation for Economic Co-operation and Development's (OECD) peer review process, others wanted it to go further.[12] The obligation of states to participate in the UPR process was never seriously contested, but at the same time there was little indication of what would, or could, happen to a state that refused to engage with the review process or what powers, if any, it would have.[13]

UN General Assembly Resolution 60/251, which formally replaced the commission with the council, described the review process as a "cooperative mechanism based on an interactive dialogue" which aimed to assess the "fulfilment by each state of its human rights obligations and commitments."[14] Every state has its human rights record reviewed once every UPR cycle, usually a period of around four years. The review is conducted based on documentary evidence from the state under review, reports from treaty bodies, stakeholder reports, and reports from domestic civil society groups, international NGOs, and other consultative bodies. The intention of this process is to engage in a targeted dialogue with the state under review on its human rights.[15] It is at this stage that recommendations can be issued by other states to the state under review about changes it ought to make in its laws, practices, or domestic policy, in order to improve its overall human rights record. A major advantage of the UPR process over its institutional predecessors was its emphasis on equality—all states can participate in the process, both to be reviewed and to subject others to review. At the opening of the twenty-sixth session of the council the delegate from Cuba praised the UPR process for creating real "equality between states."[16] The importance of sovereign equality between states undergoing the review has been welcomed by NGOs, who have played an active role in the review process—an area where the UPR process has in practice generally lived up to the expectations of its creators.[17] States are also free to advance their own priorities in relation to human rights; for example, Malaysia was able to emphasize at length the importance of economic and social rights when it was first under review.[18] These points are worth noting, as they implicitly answer some of the criticisms surrounding the universality of international human rights law, set out in the first chapter of this book, in relation to the content of universality. Others have, however, noted that the UPR has all the features of an "audit ritual," with states seeing this as a form of test to be passed once every four years rather than as a forum for meaningful dialogue on human rights.[19] Research among key stakeholders in the UPR process conducted at the beginning of third cycle identified that many perceived the recommendations as highly politicized when compared to other international legal processes, such as the concluding observations of treaty bodies.[20]

With regard to reservations, it is worth noting that the presumption that treaty bodies did not have competence to examine reservations has now moved toward a broader understanding that human rights treaties, by virtue of their subject matter, involve a much wider set of interests; therefore, consideration of the validity of their reservations can be undertaken across a wide range of different forums.[21] Alain Pellet, the special rapporteur to the International Law Commission (ILC) on Reservations, noted in a 1996 report that the framework under the Vienna Convention did not assign any particular body for monitoring the reservations, and argued that as a consequence bodies such as the Human Rights Committee—the review body of the International Covenant on Civil and Political Rights (ICCPR)—had effectively assumed that competence for themselves, justifying this position on the basis that such a power was necessary to check treaty compliance.[22] Pellet went on to acknowledge the possibility of a "coexistence of several mechanisms for determining the permissibility of reservations," arguing that considering permissibility in different forums might even strengthen the reservations regime.[23] The ILC report concluded that the regime under the Vienna Convention on the Law of Treaties (VCLT), while premised on state parties objecting to impermissible reservations, and through their objections or subsequent practice being able to determine the consequences to a state for an impermissible reservation, did not preclude bodies other than states from assessing the permissibility of reservations.[24]

What classifies the UPR as a legal practice, in accordance with the template set out in chapter 3, is that the process can act as a forum for reviewing the legal obligations of states and exerting soft power on them to comply with their treaty obligations. As the UPR is both an institutional process and a forum for states to express their own views about any human rights–related issues, there is nothing to preclude the permissibility of reservations from being a feature of the UPR process, but any legal implications arising from the consideration of reservations would need to compliment or reinforce the work of treaty bodies.[25] Yet this can also go beyond attempting to enforce existing obligations of states under a treaty to comply with a treaty's terms. Constructivist scholars of international law have argued that through states' interaction with one another and their socialization within an international body, obligations can emerge.[26] International relations theorists have long argued that an institution's creation of intrainstitutional practices can itself create a sense of obligation, which some legal theorists have argued is evidence of "soft law"—a labeling used to differentiate the creation of these forms of obligation from "hard law," which includes obligations governed by *pacta sunt servanda*.[27] There is evidence that states act as though the review process matters, and the growth of targeted recommendations, as well as a heavy emphasis on the implementation of recommendations from one review cycle to the next, have created a process which is having effects on state behavior with respect to a variety of human rights issues.[28]

Women's Rights in Universal Periodic Review Recommendations

To understand how reservations concerning CEDAW fit into the UPR process, it is important to see them in the wider context of how women's rights are raised in the review process. The UPR was designed to move states toward changing their state practices and laws, but in a manner that moved beyond the paradigm of "naming and shaming" toward a more dialogic framework where periodic review would encourage states to assess how they are implementing their human rights commitments.[29] The interactive dialogue stage of the review process notionally provides an opportunity to raise issues that would otherwise be politically or culturally sensitive, such as women's rights, without the types of negative reaction that would characterize a more confrontational process. The aspect of the process that has had the most discernible impact on the behavior of the state under review is the issuing of recommendations by other states after the interactive dialogue stage of the review process, recommendations which can be supported (UPR terminology for accepted) or noted (rejected). At time of writing in the winter of 2021, there have been just under ninety thousand recommendations, 20 percent of which concern women's rights in some form or another, making this the second most common subject matter of recommendations. Edward McMahon has developed a useful system for differentiating recommendations by the type of language they use. The system divides recommendations into five categories. Recommendations in categories one through three are generally political statements. Recommendations in category two are aimed at emphasizing continuity, continuation, or practice; these recommendations use words such as "continue," "maintain," "persevere," "persist," or "pursue."[30] A large number of recommendations in categories one through three simply offer support for the state or praise it in some way or another.[31] Recommendations in categories four and five involve legal language, and category-five recommendations frequently involve legal verbs such as "abolish," "enforce," "implement," or "repeal."[32] Recommendations relating to international treaties that the state under review is already a party to are usually found in these last two categories. Of the recommendations on issues relating to women's rights, over 80 percent are in categories four or five, and most recommendations on CEDAW reservations fall into these categories.

One of the most obvious successes of the UPR process has been encouraging increased reporting from state parties to all treaty bodies. Some smaller states such as Solomon Islands and Tuvalu submitted their first country report to the CEDAW Committee after their first cycle review, in response to the review's outcome report and recommendations on CEDAW reporting.[33] Recommendations on issues relating to women's right have been accepted by states across all major regional blocs in the UN and from states with a variety of different cultural traditions.[34] Activists and those representing otherwise marginalized voices in particular areas, such as women who have been victims of human trafficking, have been able to use stakeholder reports to influence the review process, enhancing the consideration of particular issues.[35] There has also been some success in promoting women's rights in relation to specific policy areas. For example, there has been some evidence that recommendations on access to reproductive health have been generally accepted by states under review.[36] Equally, a study of recommendations relating to violence against women noted that the specificity and volume of recommendations mattered greatly in whether recommendations actually resulted in substantial change on the ground following a state's review.[37]

There are, however, a number of issues with the ways in which recommendations are framed and the substance of the overall dialogue at the UPR process. For instance, although the overall data on recommendations concerning a woman's right to health care shows high levels of acceptance from states, the text of many of these recommendations is vague or simply draws attention to existing policies.[38] Some of the recommendations on women's rights are framed in such a way as to only require publicity campaigns or very limited action by the government, making it easy for some states to accept most of the recommendations offered to them.[39] Many states also accept recommendations relating to maternal health care or a women's right to access health care without fully considering the different barriers of implementation for some of these recommendations; as Gayatri Patel notes, the only state in the UPR's first decade (2008–2018) to even discuss cultural barriers to the implementation of reproductive rights was Paraguay.[40] This may have deeper structural causes, as while there are a large number of resolutions relating to women's rights, and gender is treated as a specific category in the UPR final report, many of the delegations from states under review are male, and sufficient resources are often not devoted to gender issues at the UPR or in other UN forums.[41]These arguments have also been reflected in a variety of scholarship critical of CEDAW, some from a feminist perspective, arguing that the structures created to enforce it reflect the marginal status of women's rights.[42]

Of all the recommendations relating to women's rights up to July 2020, fewer than 10 percent relate to CEDAW directly, but almost all of these are category four and five recommendations. Only a handful of recommendations—355 in total—directly concern reservations to treaties, and while these are almost exclusively in category four and category five, only a third have been accepted by states under review. Set in the wider context of recommendations this is not particularly atypical; the majority of category five recommendations across the first and second review cycles—60 percent and 55 percent, respectively—were rejected. The way some states have responded in relation to recommendations and UPR midpoint reviews is strongly demonstrative of a general expectation that recommendations are important, and that when a state accepts a recommendation there will be pressure placed upon it to implement its substance. Yet, only 24 percent of all category five recommendations concerning CEDAW are accepted, so it is not so much an indictment of the UPR process but a reflection of how it is simply another human rights mechanism subject to defensive relativism, and it highlights the overall politics of double standards surrounding CEDAW.

Defensive Relativism in Relation to CEDAW Reservations at the Universal Periodic Review

Roger Lloret Blackburn's 2011 study on cultural relativism in the UPR, drawing on the first review cycle, finds two groups of states engaging in what he terms "cultural relativism"—states with a revolutionary background and states engaging in relativism to defend their domestic Sharia law systems.[43] Although somewhat reductive, in part due to a limited data set, this study nevertheless makes the important observation that the neutrality and dialogic inclusiveness of the UPR process have made the UPR a distinct forum for states to contest culturally relativist ideas. Edward McMahon and Marta Ascherio's study notes that regional groupings have played a significant role in relation to the formulation of recommendations which essentially defend the cultural relativism of the state under review.[44] Other studies on the treatment of issues surrounding polygamy and laws concerning sexual orientation at the UPR, which in other international processes have been subject to defensive relativist resistance from states, have identified state constructions of cultural values in state responses and reports.[45] What these studies have not done, however, is examine the interplay of the UPR with treaty bodies and the obligations to which the state party has already maintained a defensive relativist position. There were relatively few recommendations on treaty reservations in the first three cycles, but there was a clear trend emerging in the way that recommendations on treaty reservations were complimenting and enhancing the work of treaty bodies.[46]

As noted in chapter 3, there are a number of reservations from states to CEDAW referring to Sharia law which are impermissible, due in part to their open-ended nature, and subject to a defensive relativist justification from the state party when challenged on their validity. Reservations citing Sharia law are not necessarily a reflection of a cultural set of values, as they rarely specify what precise school of Sharia they are referring to or the nature of the practice they are seeking to protect, and are more often framed to protect the power of existing centers of authority within a state, such as religious courts. The CEDAW Committee has emphasized, as have NGOs from Muslim communities, that Sharia law is compatible with CEDAW and it is possible to shape reservations to protect particular cultural practices, as some majority Muslim states have done, while remaining compatible with the convention.[47] Some states have accepted recommendations or made pledges in relation to the removal of reservations to CEDAW; Mauritania, in its first review cycle, accepted a recommendation and made a voluntary pledge, requiring it to remove a blanket reservation to all provisions of CEDAW—a reservation which stated that the convention would only apply insofar as the state deemed it to be compatible with Sharia law.[48] By the second UPR cycle, Mauritania had withdrawn this reservation and entered more targeted reservations to Article 13, which, on a plain textual reading, did not contradict CEDAW's object and purpose, and to Article 16, which was still potentially in tension with CEDAW's object and purpose.[49] Other states have also responded positively to recommendations relating to their reporting obligations to the CEDAW Committee, and to recommendations relating to CEDAW reservations on the national status of women or state obligations under Article 2.[50]

Other states, however, have used the UPR as a forum to defend reservations which the CEDAW Committee has already concluded fail the object and purpose test and are sufficiently open ended so as to be incompatible with the ILC's guidance on reservations. The reserving state in each case has justified the reservation using defensive relativist arguments at the CEDAW Committee. Defensive relativism can be seen in the areas of the UPR process where the state under review has an opportunity to make its case—the national report (part of the documentary review), the state presentation (the first part of the review hearing), and the responses during the interactive dialogue to the comments or questions of other states. The review process is usually scheduled to last three to four hours so that multiple reviews can be fitted into an HRC session; since there is a finite amount of time for the interactive discussion, defensive relativism in one area can mean that human rights issues in another area are not discussed. Defensive relativism, as the third section of this chapter notes, can also be seen in the way other states react to defensive relativism from state parties.

Defensive Relativism's Amplification through the UPR Process

At a basic level, states simply duplicate their defensive relativist behavior from other international forums through the UPR process, effectively amplifying their defensive relativism. Upon CEDAW ratification in 2002, Bahrain entered reservations to Articles 2, 9, 15, and 16 of the convention. The reservations to Article 2 (the section on state obligation) and Article 16 (the right to marriage) simply stated that the reservation was only in relation to "its implementation within the bound[s] of the provisions of the Islamic Shariah," but effectively Bahrain treated them as reservations to the provision as a whole.[51] The Supreme Council for Women—the domestic body in Bahrain with the responsibility for following up on policy in this area—maintained that it was committed to implementing these provisions without violating domestic Sharia law, and the government argued before the CEDAW Committee that these rights were substantively protected by domestic law already.[52] Yet, as a coalition of local (mainly Muslim) NGOs noted in relation to the reservation to Article 2, the "status of women is one of the main objectives . . . [of] Islamic Sharia," and as a consequence argued that this justified removing the reservation to Article 2, as it simply was not necessary for the protection of human rights or the maintenance of Sharia law.[53] Other human rights organizations within the country also argued that the reservations restricted the implementation of CEDAW; for example, one group noted that the absence of personal status and family laws meant that "cases concerning issues such as marriage, divorce, alimony and child custody" would be transferred to Sharia courts and exposed to "contradictory" rulings based heavily on the "personal opinion" of some judges.[54] The absence of such laws was in part a consequence of the blanket reservation to Article 16, which meant that even if the state were to make a commitment to fully implementing CEDAW within its domestic legislation, as the CEDAW Committee had requested, reservations would effectively exempt the state from any obligation to implement equal divorce laws between men and women because of its open-ended reservation to Article 16.

In 2008, the CEDAW Committee acknowledged the acceptance of a recommendation by Bahrain in its first UPR cycle review to withdraw its reservations, but "remain[ed] of the opinion that these [Bahrain's] reservations [were] contrary to the object and purpose of the Convention."[55] What the committee was referring to was a general commitment made by Bahrain in its national report to review some of its existing obligations and an accepted recommendation made by Slovenia that it should initiate a "campaign with the view to removing reservations to CEDAW, ratifying the Optional Protocol and harmonizing national legislation" with CEDAW.[56] In its second UPR cycle review, Bahrain's national report defended the state's overall progress, saying that the relevant authorities were "studying the possibility of withdrawing or reformulating several reservations" and were examining "narrowing the scope of the reservation to article 2 to the status of women in the family."[57] Whilst emphasizing the importance of Sharia law in the presentation and national report, there was a partial acknowledgment about the need to review the way in which Sharia was compatible with CEDAW, and Bahrain accepted two additional recommendations in relation to the removal of reservations.[58] In November 2013, the Bahraini parliament opposed a package of law reforms designed to implement CEDAW, warning that it would have "dangerous repercussions."[59] This meant that a 2014 royal decree lifting and modifying recommendations did not fully remove reservations to Article 2 or Article 16; instead they were replaced by a declaration stating that the implementation of these articles would be "without breaching the provisions of the Islamic Shariah."[60]

Substantively, this still had many of the problems of the previous reservations. Sharia was presented as a blanket justification for a reservation to most of Article 2, meaning that it could operate as a justification by the state for not implementing large parts of the convention. The justification for this new formula of reservations presented to the CEDAW Committee in their fourth state report was pretty much identical to the ones advanced previously, with the government claiming that its domestic law "fulfils its obligations" under Articles 2 and 16.[61] The 2014 concluding observations of the CEDAW Committee said that this new formula was not compatible with the object and purpose of CEDAW and that Bahrain needed to narrow the scope of the reservations to come to bring them into line with the object and purpose of the convention.[62] At its next UPR review in 2017, during the third review cycle, Bahrain highlighted the action it had taken in connection with CEDAW reservations and the royal decree in its state presentation.[63] In the interactive dialogue CEDAW wasn't mentioned by most states, and apart from a recommendation from Spain to withdraw its reservations to CEDAW, there was no real engagement on the issue, so Bahrain never restated its provision concerning reservations.[64] The UPR process here simply provided another forum for amplifying and restating the state's defensive relativist position with respect to reservations. The format of the UPR did not substantively add or facilitate the practice of defensive relativism in the way that it did in the next two case studies.

Defensive Relativism as Context Setting

Some states use defensive relativism by way of context setting in order to demonstrate their relative unwillingness to move in relation to treaty reservations or on certain human rights issues. Singapore, in its state presentation during its second cycle review, outlined the general context of rights protection in Singapore, stating that the country "protected human rights and preserved social harmony" while taking "a practical and not an ideological approach to human rights."[65] Echoing the language of "Asian values"—described in chapter 4—Singapore went on to note that countries in the "West had to review some of their more liberal policies" in relation to human rights and that each country should develop "human rights in its own way, taking into account its unique social and cultural context."[66] This framed the rest of the review process, and during the interactive dialogue the state was able to justify restrictions on LGBT rights as necessary to avoid the "fracturing of society."[67]

At the time of its first review in 2010, the Maldives had a number of reservations to CEDAW, including one relating to the whole of Article 16 (the right to marriage), which limited the right "without prejudice to the provisions of the Islamic Sharia, which govern all marital and family relations of the 100 percent Muslim population of the Maldives."[68] This was very far reaching, justifying unlimited restrictions from the state on a complicated right, one which reinforced an official, antipluralistic message about religious inclusion, which was criticized during the country's first cycle review. Originally, upon accession to CEDAW in 1993, the Maldives entered a reservation to any CEDAW provision "contradictory to the principles of the Islamic Sharia upon which the laws and traditions of the Maldives." This was formally objected to by Finland shortly after accession.[69] When the Maldives withdrew the reservation in 1999, the Finnish reiterated their objection in relation to reservations to Article 7 (the duty to eliminate discrimination in public life and politics) and Article 16, which the Maldives preserved. During its first UPR review cycle it accepted five recommendations in relation to the withdrawal of CEDAW reservations; these were of varying specificity, including one from Spain to "withdraw reservations to ICCPR, CEDAW and CRC."[70] In its country report it noted that women continued to suffer from "discrimination in most walks of life," which, they claimed, stemmed "from both religious influence" and the culturally patriarchal features of the previous administration.[71] However, a stakeholder report from the UN Development Programme drew different conclusions about the causes of discrimination against women, noting that the Ministry of Islamic Affairs had recently started approving and promoting sermons which promoted harmful gender stereotypes, and governmental officials had spoken approvingly of domestic violence.[72] The acceptance of a recommendation on this topic was simply a mirror of state practice, as a few months prior to the Maldives' review in March 2010 it had written to the UN secretary-general formally withdrawing its reservation to Article 7, which related to constitutional provisions limiting women from being political candidates.[73]

However, there was no movement on withdrawing its reservation to Article 16. In 2012, concern was expressed by NGOs in the Maldives that the government ministry responsible for CEDAW—the Ministry of Gender, Family, and Human Rights—was unaware of the commitment made at the UPR to withdraw the reservation, publicly admitting that the ministry lacked the "capacity to attend to this issue."[74] The failure to take action on Article 16 was noted in March 2015 in the concluding observations from the CEDAW Committee, which urged the state to remove this reservation due to its incompatibility with the object and purpose test.[75] During its second UPR cycle review four months later, the Maldives used its state presentation to warn that the Maldives' "social framework and historic and traditional values" meant that it could not "introduce values and practices that were contrary to the values" of Islam.[76] Although these comments were with direct reference to LGBT rights, this was a broad, culturally absolutist framing designed to apply to a range of legal commitments, as the next part of its state presentation made clear. Human rights, it stated, were "a matter of belief that needed to be carefully cultivated and nurtured" and needed "time to grow organically and become valued and cherished traditions" within the particularities of that society.[77] This was a direct statement of defensive relativism, and by using its state presentation in this way it enabled the Maldives to broadly position itself in relation to all of its other human rights obligations. The appeal for a legal exemption in its state presentation had distinct linguistic echoes of the 1993 Bangkok Declaration (which was attended by representatives from the Maldives), which stated that human rights need to be considered in relation to "national particularities" and take into account cultural values and religious backgrounds.[78] Because the UPR process requires a state to talk about its progress in relation to its human rights record, it gives the state under review the ability to exclude areas where it is not willing to engage in human rights reform, even if it relates to legal obligations it is bound to comply with.

Coordinating Noncommitment to CEDAW

One feature of the UPR process, which has been effectively carried over from its predecessor, the UN Commission on Human Rights, is the presence of regional blocs of states, or more importantly, blocs of states with a common set of interests in relation to international human rights law, effectively defending and supporting one another through institutional processes. For example, during Tonga's first review, Bangladesh commended it for maintaining laws criminalizing consensual same-sex relationships and issued a recommendation stating that it should "continue to criminalize consensual same sex, which is outside the purview of universally accepted human rights norms."[79] Some states had a distinct interest in maintaining the argument that LGBT rights were an overreach of international human rights law, as it supported their defensive relativist position.[80] Overt defensive relativism and coordination of arguments supporting these positions is less common than tactical positioning by states within the UPR process. Writing in 2009 during the first cycle, Gareth Sweeney and Yuri Saito note that some countries, in particular Tunisia and Bahrain, were able to turn their review into "an exercise in filibustering" by only receiving questions praising their human rights records from other like-minded states.[81] Blackburn's study on relativism in the UPR, observed that some states came to the defense of others using defensive relativist argumentation and that there were, based on their actions in the review, two types of state: those willing to directly challenge the state under review with specific recommendations and those willing to implicitly agree with the state under review's cultural relativism.[82] Coordination of questions and comments during the interactive dialogue are important because the process is time-limited (due to the constraints of the review process) and because a large part of the pressure from the UPR process is cumulative—change occurs as the result of escalating political pressure. Defensive relativism, therefore, can be cross-coordinated among the states that wish to practice it in a particular area. Much of this coordination happens informally, by making agreements with each other in relation to agendas, delegates speaking orders, and other procedural matters.[83] By comparing CEDAW reservations as they are commented on in CEDAW Committee reports, state presentations, and records of the interactive dialogue at the UPR, it is possible to see some coordination of defensive relativism.

One such example is the United Arab Emirates (UAE), which currently has reservations to a number of provisions of CEDAW, including reservations to Article 2(f) (duty to abolish discriminatory laws), Article 15(2) (equal rights in civil law), and Article 16 (the right to marry) on the basis of Sharia, following a similar formulation to the reservations detailed above. In 2005, the Danish government objected to these reservations because of their incompatibility with the object and purpose of the convention.[84] In relation to the reservations entered against Articles 2(f) and 15(2) this conclusion seems correct, as Article 2(f) requires states to take "appropriate measures" to "abolish existing laws, regulations, customs and practices which constitute discrimination against women," but the UAE's reservation stated that it "violate[d] the rules of inheritance established in accordance with the precepts of the Shariah."[85] Other reservations, such as the UAE's reservation to Article 9, were not framed explicitly in defensive relativist terms, and while the reservation to Article 16 did use cultural framings it was less open ended in nature than others. In its 2010 and 2015 reports, the CEDAW Committee emphasized that the UAE's reservations were incompatible with the object and purpose of the convention, recommending that the state redraft its reservations, narrowing their scope.[86] In its 2015 report the committee went further, noting that the UAE "should take into consideration the practices of countries with similar cultural backgrounds and legal systems that have successfully harmonized their national legislation" with their commitments under CEDAW.[87] In its country report to the committee, the UAE committed itself to constantly reviewing reservations to ensure that it struck the correct balance between respect for Sharia law in its domestic legal system and its obligations under CEDAW, but gave scant detail about how it was doing this beyond these very general statements.[88]

In its first cycle UPR review in 2009, it rejected three recommendations on the withdrawal of its reservations to CEDAW. It did not mention any justification for refusing these recommendations in its state presentation, but did note in response to concerns during the interactive dialogue that some states had perhaps misunderstood "stereotyping of the role of women" in the UAE.[89] Egypt, during the interactive dialogue, without directly mentioning CEDAW, commended it for its strategy toward, women's rights saying that the UAE should "continue to refuse to apply any standards or principles" that were outside those it had agreed to and should resist "any attempt to impose foreign values and customs on the Emirati people."[90] During its second cycle review, the UAE accepted three recommendations on the withdrawal of reservations, and in its state presentation made a considerable effort to highlight some of the steps it had taken in relation to nationality and female advancement in central government.[91] In the interactive dialogue it again clarified it was looking at removing reservations but only in the context of the "relevant cultural and religious values"—and provided no further details.[92] There were a large number of comments simply praising the UAE, noting its positive record on women's rights but not mentioning CEDAW, with about six comments praising the UAE for every one comment actually analyzing its practice under CEDAW. In the third cycle, seven recommendations were again made to the UAE on withdrawing its reservations to Article 16 and Article 2 of CEDAW, but no states during the interactive dialogue referenced the previous accepted UPR recommendations on CEDAW.

Conclusion: Defensive Relativism at the UPR

The UPR process has both amplified existing defensive relativism toward CEDAW and, by virtue of the interactive dialogue and the practice of friendly recommendations and supporting comments, provided new avenues for defensive relativism. This can be set against the backdrop of the broader context of the UPR process, where there is a high degree of interregional cooperation over the issuing of recommendations and relativistic positions are incentivized by the nonconfrontational nature of the review process, which puts more emphasis on continuing dialogue than "naming and shaming."[93] When it comes to reservations, the UPR process affords states a unique forum for defensive relativism because there are no legal obligations toward the UPR process specifically. Unlike a treaty body, states are not subject to a panel of experts reviewing the discharge of their obligations; instead the UPR is a forum where states are instead asked to explain the discharge of their human rights obligations to their peers, some of whom may be willing to directly support that state's defensive relativism. Unlike human rights courts, described in chapter 5, no direct judgment is passed on a state, so it does not have to defend itself against the institution. The cumulative effect of recommendations on state parties has, over the three review cycles that have occurred to date (at the time of completion in the summer of 2021 the fourth cycle had just begun), shown some impact on state behavior which may have legal consequences. This is why states wishing to practice defensive relativism in relation to a particular matter often avoid recommendations referencing specific legal obligations or explicitly use defensive relativist arguments when such issues are raised in the interactive dialogue section of the review. There is, as Patel argues, a danger in the way the UPR process operates, as it allows particular interpretations of human rights, such as defensive relativist interpretations of reservations, to go virtually unchallenged. The process can almost implicitly endorse the legitimacy of such interpretations, even where the reservation is impermissible and in practice grants a state party a wide, unlimited legal exemption to a treaty such as CEDAW.[94] This is difficult to assess because the justifications of state parties for their treaty reservations often takes place in the interactive dialogue, or can be evidenced when reading rejected recommendations in tandem with treaty body sources; however, it does show how states making defensive relativist arguments can use the interpretive communities of international institutions to legitimize their case.

Defensive relativism toward CEDAW has been extensively detailed in the preceding chapters. While reservations are explicitly antiuniversalist in nature and important for the functioning of international law, the exclusionary construction of culture and impermissible nature of many reservations to CEDAW render state commitment to it meaningless in certain key areas, such as the right to marry. Feminist criticism of CEDAW has long argued that its weaknesses as an instrument are a reflection of the patriarchal nature of international law in general.[95] The experience of women's rights over the first decade of the UPR has shown some isolated policy successes, but in relation to CEDAW defensive relativism has often simply found a new forum.

PART III

Situating Defensive Relativism

CHAPTER 7

Conceptually Positioning Defensive Relativism

In June 1993, delegates from 167 countries arrived in Vienna for the second World Conference on Human Rights. It was intended to be a rethink of human rights after the Cold War and the seeming triumph of liberal values, but at the conference center there was a palpable tension between the scripted statements of political leaders and the activists and NGOs seeking to highlight injustices from around the world.[1] The final conference declaration, with paragraph 5 declaring that when human rights are interpreted "the significance of national and regional particularities and various historical, cultural and religious backgrounds" must be "borne in mind," is seen by many historians as a key moment in the history of relativism in human rights.[2] Given the background to the conference, with the 1993 Bangkok Declaration strongly asserting a structurally relativist position and U.S. Secretary of State Warren Christopher warning that relativism should not become a "refuge for oppression," the declaration was always going to be a difficult balancing act.[3] As Kevin Boyle notes, while the text of the declaration was subject to numerous revisions, used a lot of abstract language, and even was arguably unfinished in some areas, it was a useful document in that it was the end product of an important period "of international diplomacy" on human rights and consequently was "a significant means of making sense of the world."[4] The Vienna Declaration, in both reinforcing the universality—early in paragraph 5 it says that human rights are "universal" and "indivisible"—and supporting relativism, arguably recognized the context within which debates about human rights were taking place in the early 1990s.[5] But importantly the Vienna Declaration also clarified the context in which defensive relativism could be a successful tactical argument for states.

In part I of this book, the core elements of the defensive relativist argument—antiuniversalism, the state construction of culture, and a claim to legal exception—are set out in relation to defensive relativism as an international legal practice. This is drawn from existing practice in international human rights law to show how the core tenets of the argument have been advanced by the proponents of defensive relativism, namely states engaged in defending their human rights records. As the case studies set out in part II of this book demonstrate, defensive relativism is a practice which can be used by all states in different circumstances and contexts. States from the Association of Southeast Asian Nations (ASEAN), described in chapter 4, have different concerns about human rights law than states from the Council of Europe, described in chapter 5, but at a basic level they are united in their reaction to the possibility that human rights law would require them to change their own domestic laws and practices in areas they deem culturally sensitive.

Having defined and explored defensive relativism, the purpose of this chapter is to situate it alongside other discourses on the philosophy and practice of international human rights law. This is important for understanding the overall argument advanced in chapter 8, that defensive relativism is a tactical tool for states in pursuance of a wider strategy of protecting their sovereign interests while maintaining a degree of notional compliance with human rights law. The Vienna Declaration was one of the most significant examples of the way defensive relativism has been used as a strategic tool. As noted in the introduction to this book, broader theories about the nature of what human rights are and who ought to possess them are not really relevant, as defensive relativism is a theory about human rights law, examining how the structures within such rights operate and the way they are recognized by states.[6] Theoretical discourses about the history and ontology of rights are important to these questions—as the first section of this chapter notes, the colonial-imperial origins of international law are highly relevant to the way human rights have been codified in international human rights law—but in order to understand defensive relativism and its use it is necessary to look at theories about the law and international legal regimes more generally. Furthermore, to understand its use as a tactical tool it is necessary to unpack precisely how it relates to other discourses about the origins and use of human rights. “Discourses” is a deliberately vague term designed to encompass both theoretical disciplines, which have defined contours, and proponents, as well as other broader studies of human rights and human rights law that are worthy of a closer analysis because of their proximity to some of the issues raised in defensive relativism. Furthermore, all three of these discourses respectively deal with arguments over the origins, legitimacy, and power behind international human rights law.

Firstly, decolonial theories of human rights refer to a school of thought about the origins of human rights which maintains that the concept of human rights was developed in the West, excluding from its creation colonized peoples and, later, those in the Global South, which therefore necessitates a reprioritization of human rights law. Decolonial ideas about universality are discussed in chapter 1, but the decolonial critique of human rights is not limited to the argument that the presumption of universality represents a set of Western particularities. Decolonial theories of rights also maintain that international human rights law needs to be substantively reprioritized in order to meet the needs and demands of non-Western societies, and defensive relativism could, with its antiuniversalist focus, offer a means for achieving such a reprioritization. Secondly, there are a number of schools of thought on the legitimacy of human rights and the need to base its legitimacy in the experience of peoples and communities. Human rights from below loosely incorporate a variety of academic work and field research on grassroots or people-powered human rights movements, which demand a more representative form of human rights law, moving beyond its focus on the network of treaties and state compliance. This form of discourse has often proposed alternative structures or advocated frameworks for recognizing rights claims outside of formal legal structures. It is also related to arguments about the lack of democratic accountability in human rights law. Defensive relativism could be a vehicle for protecting these alternate mechanisms of rights and defending bottom-up traditions from the overreach of international human rights law. Finally, there are variety of theories about the power behind human rights, stemming partially from the critical legal tradition, maintaining that the legal form of human rights masks broader structures of power, or that human rights are instrumental in forms of political domination. Viewed through the prism of this discourse, defensive relativism can be seen as a means of resisting domination by international legal institutions. Defensive relativism, while notionally aligned with some of the tenets of all three of these discourses, can be distinguished from all of them and, as the last section of this chapter argues, should be understood more as a tactical device for defending a particular conception of sovereignty.

Decolonizing Human Rights and Defensive Relativism

Postcolonial critiques of international human rights law focus on the way human rights were historically rooted in the European tradition of the Enlightenment, which was then exported around the world during the process of colonization.[7] This more ontological critique can be distinguished from the anti-imperialist critiques of international human rights law which are more focused on how this historical legacy affects contemporary human rights, arguing either that human rights represent an ongoing form of colonial endeavor or are used to justify neocolonialist practices.[8] Other lines of critique in the postcolonial tradition have been sympathetic to the aims of international human rights law but have also noted that it is structurally predisposed to colonialist assumptions. For example, Makau Mutua has argued that international human rights law requires the construction of savages, victims, and saviors, defining itself by the identification of an uncivilized "other" making it difficult for it to gain "cross-cultural legitimacy."[9] Another related branch of this discourse are the arguments advanced by those from the Third World Approaches to International Law (TWAIL) school of thought who maintain that international human rights law needs to be refocused on the developing world and the socioeconomic issues and struggles affecting postcolonial states.[10]

Where all of these schools of thought converge (at least implicitly) is in recognizing that international law, and some of the assumptions that lie behind international human rights law, were constructed as a mechanism to justify colonialism.[11] This is referred to in chapter 1 in the context of universalism, but it is worth briefly examining afresh the parts of the history of international human rights law relevant to these schools of thought. Francisco de Vitoria, the sixteenth-century philosopher and theologian, when addressing the question, "By what right were the barbarians subjected to Spanish rule?" invoked the existence of a law of nations, which was exclusively European in nature.[12] The Christian doctrine of baptism and conversion of non-Christians provided a justification in secular law for the control of the Americas by Spain, a form of post hoc justification for colonization which became particularly important after the Valladolid debate in 1550, where Bartolomé de Las Casas, a priest and social reformer, managed to obtain notional protection for the indigenous peoples of the New World.[13] This was, however, premised on notions of racial hierarchies which, as some scholars argued, fed through into the formation of international law.[14] According to postcolonial and decolonial theorists, this began a progressive exclusion of non-European societies from the construction of international law, which was created to define the world and legal concepts governing the world by way of the European colonial encounter.[15] International law crucially codified a standard of civilization, with reference to nations, non-nations, and "un-civilized" peoples, designed to relegate colonial subjects.[16] Colonialism adapted and evolved, but even under liberal notions of colonialism, international jurists in the nineteenth century expressed concern about the influence of "uncivilized nations," and in the twentieth century decolonization was conducted in the paradigm of colonialism, safeguarding and controlling uncivilized nations.[17] International human rights law, as derived from the Universal Declaration on Human Rights (UDHR), protected Western interests, and the process of its creation had excluded so many competing traditions and narrowed the scope of how rights could be used. Although a broad-brush summary, this account of international human rights law's formation is referenced implicitly or explicitly by all forms of critique arguing that international human rights law excludes states that were the subjects of colonialism.[18]

The Decolonial Critique of Human Rights and Human Rights Reform

The literature on postcolonialism and human rights is vast, and any attempt at a synthesis is prone to simplification, but a few core elements of decolonial theory in relation to the reform of human rights can be isolated, which would broadly align with most of the theoretical claims made in other postcolonial critiques. Firstly, decolonial theory makes an epistemic claim arguing that human rights laws' reliance on rationality in fact represents, as Aníbal Quijano puts it, an attempt to impose "provincialism as universalism"; therefore, there must be a renewed focus on "intercultural relations."[19] What this would mean for human rights law, Peter Fitzpatrick argues, is a move away from the paradigm of universal humanity, which underpins existing legal forms of rights, and the creation of a responsibility to include other cultures, delinking them from universality (which defines them as opposite to the universal in a form of occidentalism) and extending what Jacques Derrida calls the unconditional hospitality to the "other" as a basis for human rights.[20] Some postcolonial critiques of human rights focus on its epistemic claims regarding universality, whereas decolonial theories of rights do not see the epistemology of rights as an insurmountable failing of human rights as a concept.[21] Promoters of a cross-cultural dialogue on human rights, such as Abdullahi An-Na'im, share some of these broad aims, arguing that such a cross-cultural dialogue allows for a reformulation of Western modes of thought about rights.[22]

Secondly, decolonial theory maintains that the existing institutions of international law need to be replaced with bodies that represent the Global South and the citizens of postcolonial states. Walter Mignolo argues that decolonialism attempts to empower the "racialized subjects" of colonialism, helping them "to regain the human dignity that . . . [the] imperial project . . . took away from them."[23] Specifically, this would involve "de-westernis[ing]" existing institutions, which Mignolo, in his engagement with the works of Kishore Mahbubani, describes as meaning "that the rules of the game and the shots are no longer called by Western players and institutions."[24] Finally, the content of human rights would need to be, as Macarena Gómez-Barris argues, "re-purposed" to account for the needs and struggles of the marginalized and oppressed.[25] The various attempts to create a right to development in international law in the 1980s, or to create a New International Economic Order in the 1970s, are practical examples of how rights can be reprioritized, even though both movements were eventually inconclusive.[26] The decolonial critique is more prescriptive than other schools of thought broadly criticizing the colonial origins of international law, and offers something approaching a template for addressing the concerns raised by various postcolonial critiques of human rights.[27] By virtue of its prescriptive nature, it is more amenable than other such critiques of international human rights law, which are more descriptive or ontological in nature, to being examined alongside practices such as defensive relativism.

The African Charter on Human and Peoples Rights: A Case Study of Decolonizing Human Rights

The 1981 African Charter on Human and Peoples' Rights (ACHPR) can be regarded as an example of a decolonial human rights instrument. The Organisation of African Unity (OAU), when drafting the charter, wanted it to reflect pan-regional values; as the Senegalese president put it in 1979, the prospective charter needed to "keep constantly in mind our values of civilization and the real needs of Africa."[28] The epistemic decolonization of human rights, described in the first element of decolonial theory, can be seen in the provisions of the charter which sought to ground rights in an alternative to Western individualism; Articles 19 through 24 protect a series of peoples—or group rights designed to protect communities rather than individuals and address issues arising from colonialism.[29] The jurisprudence of the African Commission on Human and Peoples' Rights reflects this; in *SEAC v. Nigeria*, a case concerning the Ogoni people's right to a clean environment, the commission highlighted the importance of the right to a clean environment by urging the Nigerian government to "restore cooperative economic development to its traditional role in African society" and acknowledge the "painful legacy of colonialism."[30] Equally, the provisions on duties reflected a distinct attempt at epistemic decolonization of rights away from an individualistic—or, some would argue, European—paradigm of human rights.[31] Despite concerns from critics that this would limit the application of rights, in particular Article 27 (which sets out a duty toward "family and society"), which would appear particularly amenable to defensive relativist argumentation, the commission has not really had any call to interpret these powers, and states have not cited them in a defensively relativist manner.[32]

Although the charter utilized the same frameworks of international law as other international instruments, the commission existed under the auspices of the OAU (later the AU), and at first put great emphasis on resolution of issues through nonadversarial mechanisms.[33] This notionally addressed the second element of decolonial critique, that the institutions of international law should be controlled by postcolonial states, and numerous features of the charter framed rights in terms of common African values and institutions.[34] Articles 15 through 17 of the charter protect the right to work, health, and education, treating them as indivisible with civil and political rights, a division engineered between the International Covenant on Civil and Political Rights (ICCPR) and the International Covenant on Economic, Social, and Cultural Rights (ICESCR) largely at the instigation of Western states in the 1950s.[35] These provisions, along with Article 21 protecting the right to natural resources and Article 22 protecting the right to development, notionally address the third element of decolonial theory; a number of commentators at the time the charter came into force argued that in order to have relevance to African societies, human rights needed not just to safeguard abstract legal relationships but also provide material security.[36] Although it was later criticized for its weak and contradictory definitions of certain basic rights and its piecemeal mechanisms for monitoring and enforcement, the substantive rights contained in the charter were decolonial in the sense that the charter attempted a radical reprioritization of existing human rights law and attempted some form of redress for the impact of colonialism.[37]

Distinguishing Defensive Relativism from the Project of Decolonizing International Human Rights Law

The reason for exploring the decolonial origins of the African Charter is to highlight the distinction between decolonial theory and defensive relativism in human rights practice. Defensive relativism, while common to all states, whether they are postcolonial states or formerly colonialist states, sometimes overlaps with the claims made by decolonial theory, particularly in relation to the cultural contingency of universality—a core element of antiuniversalism as detailed in chapter 1. Antiuniversalism is essential to the decolonial or postcolonial critique of rights, in part to demonstrate the contingency of existing human rights law, but this does not mean it is similar to defensive relativism. As Bonny Ibhawoh demonstrates, from an African perspective a distinction can be drawn between the conservative paradigm of cultural legitimacy, which places weight on existing state institutions often dominated by patriarchal figures, and the more dynamic paradigm of cultural legitimacy, which seeks to ground human rights within traditional structures.[38] Using examples of women's rights NGOs in Ghana and Swaziland, Ibhawoh notes that these groups are often critical but supportive of individual customary practices which can be used to empower women, contrasting them with "cultural relativists and the male-dominated groups of African elites" who seek "to maintain cultural legitimacy by tempering" the content of human rights.[39] The Inter-American Court of Human Rights (IACtHR), which has often made evolutive interpretations of the American Charter on Human Rights and other instruments in order to protect indigenous communities and cultures, has also drawn a distinction between affirming the "importance . . . due to cultural diversity" in societies while at the same time "discard[ing] the distortions of the so-called cultural 'relativism.'"[40] Practically, defensive relativism requires a level of deference to state claims of cultural values, and these claims are treated skeptically by decolonial theorists because they perpetuate a misleading clash of values rather than seeking to affirm common ground between different sets of values.[41]

Its decolonial origins did not preclude a range of opposition to the African Charter. In a case before the African Commission, *Association of Members of the Episcopal Conference of East Africa v. Sudan*, claims were made about the forced use of Sharia courts on non-Muslims, and arrests targeting members of the Christian faith, under the general guise of security measures implemented to deal with the ongoing insurgency in the south of Sudan (prior to it forming a secessionist state in 2011).[42] The commission held that this was a serious violation of Article 8 (the freedom of religion) of the African Charter even though the Sudanese claimed it protected the right to religious freedoms through its constitution. Yet in response to Sudan's periodic report to the African Commission five years after this finding, the commission noted that the ongoing "application of some criminal law provisions from shari'a or Islamic law in the whole country entails the risk of extending it to individuals belonging to religious groups other than Muslims."[43] In wider scholarship on the role of religion and public authorities, particularly in relation to gender, many of the defenses of religious institutions often reflect defenses of institutions aligned with the governmental power structures in the state.[44] When in 2018 a case involving child marriage in Mali was heard at the African Court of Human and People's Rights the Malian government defended "the established rules" on marriage saying that they "must not eclipse social, cultural and religious realities" concerning child brides.[45] The protocol to the African Charter on Human and Peoples' Rights on the Rights of Women in Africa, while following some of the decolonial framings of the charter, also contained provisions surrounding the need to eliminate harmful cultural practices, posing an implicit challenge to any defensive relativist attempts to defend restrictions of women's rights.[46]

Human Rights from "Below" and Legitimacy: Defensive Relativism in Relation to Social Movements and Democratic Critiques of Human Rights

Both of these discourses relate to arguments questioning the legitimacy of international human rights law. As the first part of this section sets out, these can either take the form of maintaining that human rights are located away from the structures of international law and in grass roots action, or, as the second part of this section argues, focus on the democratic legitimacy, or lack thereof, of human rights law. Defensive relativist arguments may overlap with both of these arguments, and indeed the third element of defensive relativism, as discussed in chapter 3, involves—to a degree—challenging the legitimacy of the existing structures of international human rights law in their interpretation of the law or on the extent to which a legal institution dictates a course of action to a state. One important aspect of this school of thought, and the ideas of power discussed in the third section, is the role of constituted and constituent power. Originally developed in arguments about the secularization of the state in enlightenment thought, particularly in the work of Abbé Sieyès, the two types of power received their definitive modern outline in the 1920s from the philosopher Carl Schmitt.[47] Constituent power from below describes the population at large and the various ways in which a collective might express its power, while constituted power describes the formalized institutions and structures in society.[48] The concept of human rights, while descending from a radical tradition of constituent demands, also relies on the formal constituted structures of the law in order to give it a legal form in international law.[49] There is, therefore, an inherent tension in international human rights law in that it puts itself forward to provide a defense of the people at large but relies on the constituted powers of states, often the very powers it seeks to challenge, to actually deliver rights protection.[50] In the schools of thought under consideration in this section, this tension is reflected in the overarching concern about the authority, or legitimacy, of the population in determining universal values.

Social Movements and Defensive Relativism

Models of human rights compliance now acknowledge the role of social movements in changing state behavior and ensuring greater human rights compliance.[51] There is also now a wide literature on social change in international human rights law focusing on the practical questions of how social movements can effect human rights change or serve as a means for reprioritizing international law to better reflect the priorities of certain communities, addressing some of the concerns raised by decolonial critiques of human rights law, discussed above.[52] Although it is difficult to incorporate such a diverse field under one umbrella, the sustained and implied criticism in much of this scholarship is that the focus on the existing supranational structures of law ignores the development of rights among the individuals living within the state outside of the formal legal system. Some of this has focused on how grassroots groups can compensate for the deficiencies of international law imposed from above. For example, Kay Warren's study of human trafficking shows how women's rights NGOs were able to use the 2000 UN Protocol to Prevent, Suppress, and Punish Trafficking in Persons to create alternative versions of the protocol through their own interpretive analysis and then mobilize networks of local activists to give a broader voice to the violence associated in people trafficking.[53] Other work has been more focused on social movements, which, in contrast to NGOs, are less formal organizations which advocate for change in existing institutions; the conception of rights that they advocate might not follow existing notions of rights and they may make claims outside of positivist legal thinking about human rights.[54]

Social movements, such as indigenous rights movements or women's activism, can create a form of cosmopolitanism from below which leads to claims for justice to become grounded in the community within which they are made.[55] For example, the Indian "women's courts" (*mahila adalat* or *mahila mandal*) exist as forms of alternate dispute resolution for family disputes, domestic violence, and other matters affecting women. They emerged in the 1980s after widespread disenchantment with the local court system, which was often dominated by male judges who were highly corrupt and steeped in patriarchal values.[56] Although originally created in tandem with state institutions, they increasingly have been run by NGOs and often try to use empowerment models to help women deal with issues such as land disputes, where they otherwise would be at a considerable disadvantage.[57] Some of the literature on institutional forms outside the standard models of court and tribunals has identified how community bodies or commission can engage in truth telling and forms of restorative justice. Laura Arriaza and Naomi Roht-Arriaza's study of communal and indigenous mechanisms in Guatemala have identified how a host of local initiatives, some reviving ancient Mayan practices, have integrated post-conflict justice into society, although the study questions the transportability of such a model.[58]

Can defensive relativism operate as a defense of social movements and the protection of rights from below? It is important to note international human rights law does not preclude social movements making rights claims or seeking to ground rights claims within their own social struggles. The recognition of indigenous rights is an example of how diverse social movements in different countries can potentially form a composite international agenda and gain recognition in international institutions, as happened with the UN Declaration on the Rights of Indigenous Peoples.[59] There is literature on indigenous rights and women's rights demonstrating how grassroots organizations can use the structure of international human rights law to frame their claims, or as instruments in a wider political struggle.[60] Furthermore, social movements from racial, linguistic, or other forms of minorities who wish to advance their own political causes are protected under Article 27 of the ICCPR, which protects minority rights, and the Human Rights Committee has held that Article 27 "must be respected in all circumstances," limiting the scope for reservations to deny minority communities protection.[61] Some of the arguments advanced in relation to restrictions to human rights in response to Sharia law, especially in relation to reservations, can adopt the linguistic form of protecting rights from below, as set out in chapters 3 and 6, but in most cases this involves demarcating a state's authority from the perceived intrusion of international human rights law rather than protecting a system of rights from below. That is not to say that there can't be a system of rights from below predicated on Sharia law, but rather that the overwhelming majority of defensive relativist arguments advanced by states are in this regard an exercise in defending the government of a state, not social movements.[62] While it is theoretically possible for defensive relativism to be used as a defense of human rights from below, there is very little evidence of it being used this way in practice.

Defensive Relativism as a Representation of Democracy

The debates about human rights from below also relate to a broader discourse about the democratic legitimacy of international human rights law. There is a school of thought which concludes that because of the importance of domestic institutions in the realization of rights, and the democratic legitimacy of those domestic institutions, international human rights law lacks legitimacy.[63] Cultural relativism as a doctrine, Adamantia Pollis notes, originated from the seeming unwillingness of the universal principles of human rights to accommodate the fact that different cultures organized their societies along very different lines than Western liberal democracies.[64] Yet, even within the amorphous category of "Western democracies" there is considerable skepticism of the idea of a higher universal frameworks overriding democratically accountable national institutions.[65] Seeking to justify American exceptionalism to international law, Jed Rubenfeld argues that international constitutionalism, typified by human rights law, diminished the commitment to democratic constitutionalism because it was premised on the existence of an "identifiable body of universal law, everywhere binding, requiring no democratic provenance," which was "deeply undemocratic."[66] This is not necessarily an argument for the repudiation of human rights law, or international institutions in general, but an argument that more democratic and accountable institutions exist at the domestic level, a theme which is common in arguments made by British lawyers and politicians in their objections to the European Court of Human Rights (ECtHR).[67] For others, the presence of nondemocratic governments in the formation of international human rights law, and the various trade-offs that take place in international forums during the creation of international instruments, lead to the conclusion that domestic institutions are more likely to produce superior human rights norms.[68] Jean Cohen, seeking to identify the origins of this line of argument, notes that it emerged in part as a response to the third wave of human rights which increasingly justified the exercise of power, at the supranational level or by existing hegemonic powers, against other states as it legitimized the notion of political coercion in order to protect rights.[69] Democracy in this discussion, as critics of this line of scholarship have argued, is often a largely procedural concept focusing on the legitimacy of an institution making decisions rather than the decisions on a particular rights issue enjoying political consent.[70]

This relates to one of the core arguments in cases involving the margin of appreciation doctrine, which is that domestic governments are in principle better placed to decide the limitations of rights and balance them with other competing interests, because they are both proximate to domestic populations and more accountable than an international court.[71] Defensive relativists, when trying to justify a wide margin of appreciation, may make reference to popular validation of their position. In *Open Door and Dublin Well Woman v. Ireland*, where the Irish government attempted to justify far-reaching restrictions on the free speech of proabortion activists at the ECtHR, the state claimed that Irish society took a strong moral position on the subject by referencing a constitutional referendum on the question of abortion held a decade prior to the case.[72] In other cases, defensive relativists openly seek constituent power to resist what they perceive as international human rights law imposing a decision onto their society. In response to the 2018 Inter-American Court's advisory opinion on LGBT rights, which required states to recognize both same-sex marriage and transsexual rights, a conservative candidate in that year's presidential election in Costa Rica pledged to pull the country out of the court's jurisdiction, citing moral reasons for resisting the decision.[73]

Yet, international human rights law is not automatically in an antagonistic relationship with democracy or democratic government; in fact, as Jamie Mayerfeld argues, by protecting basic rights, which are normally mirrored in domestic bills of rights, international human rights law can protect the basic constitutive features of democracy.[74] Importantly, while defensive relativists can bolster their arguments by reference to the democratic support their positions may enjoy, this is not an essential component of defensive relativist arguments. Both democratic and nondemocratic states make defensive relativist arguments, as is illustrated in chapters 4 and 5. What unites them is not the popular consent within which those arguments or the governments making them rests. Instead, the defensive relativist primary targets are the institutions of international human rights law, what Ellen Messer terms "the dominant secular legal-expert culture" of international institutions.[75] References to national culture, and its constituent grounding, serve as the antithesis to this supranational expert culture.

Critical Theory, Power, and the Intersection with Defensive Relativism

Critical legal theory emerged in part as a reaction to formalist legal theory and mid-twentieth-century legal theory which focused on the form of the law, rather than structures of power behind the law. Broadly speaking, critical legal theorists aimed to examine both existence and nature of power behind the law.[76] Early critical theorists drew on the critical theory of Theodor Adorno and Max Horkheimer, who in their seminal work *Dialectic of Enlightenment* argue that the rationality of the enlightenment project was underpinned by a form of domination and violence.[77] From the early 1990s onward, when human rights increasingly began to be advocated by governments as being a nonideological set of universal principles critical scholars began to examine human rights law. In their analysis of the power behind the law, critical legal scholars sometimes overlap with the arguments made by anti-imperialist theorists, in particular their ontological critique about human rights law's origins within colonial-era international law.[78] One key distinction, however, is that critical legal scholars are far more skeptical about the capacity of human rights law to be reformed or reprioritized, seeing it as intimately associated with the justification and maintenance of power.[79]

Critical Legal Theory and Human Rights Law

The critique of human rights law advanced by critical theorists is best encapsulated by the following statement from the introductory chapter to Costas Douzinas's seminal work *The End of Human Rights*: "Official thinking and action on human rights," Douzinas claims, had, by the start of the twenty-first century, become "entrusted in the hand of triumphalist column writers, bored diplomats and rich international lawyers" confined to New York and Geneva, whose experience of a human rights violation was "being served a bad bottle of wine."[80] Human rights are not dismissed in Douzinas's account, but he states that they had become institutionalized in the formal structures of power in the international system and effectively deradicalized. Marie Dembour notes that many critical theorists belong to what she terms the "protest school," in that they have conceived rights as being framed by constituent powers from below through collective action and protest, and as consequence are more skeptical of legal institutions.[81] Illan rua Wall takes this a step further, arguing that the structure of international human rights law, in particular Article 30 of the UDHR, which prohibits the abuse of rights, is designed to constrain radical action and demands.[82] Related concerns had been expressed by those in the LatCrit movement many years earlier, who argued that the frameworks of international law marginalized certain voices from the developing world and that legal discourse over human rights needed to be expanded to include "critical methodologies like story-telling, the mapping of legal terms, and the incorporation of political economy."[83]

Beyond critiquing the form of international human rights law and its institutionalization, there are two significant normative claims about international human rights law. Firstly, critical theorists dispute the value-neutral pretensions of human rights law, noting that the rights contained within human rights law are themselves ideological and the mere process of structuring an instrument to include some rights and exclude others is in and of itself an ideological choice.[84] As John Laughland notes, drawing on the legal and political discourse surrounding humanitarian intervention in the early 2000s, the apolitical neutrality presented by appeals to human rights have often been simply a cover to mask the broader exercise of power, and in the context of humanitarian intervention human rights have often been simply tools to justify and perpetuate forms of power.[85] This analysis draws heavily on Michel Foucault's work on bio-power and governmentality, which argues that humanism itself is a construction and reflection of structural power; despite Foucault's later work on humanitarianism, as Ben Golder argues, he remained critical of the reduction of an essentialized human subject which was the foundation of epistemic claims about rights.[86] The construction of the human subject by constituted sources of power raises broader questions, Jessica Whyte argues, about whether they can be "wrenched away from the role of bestowing legitimacy upon domination."[87] Foucault's assumptions about the historical contingency of concepts such as public reason or other epistemic frameworks used to infer the existence of human rights law are also cited by some theorists, who claim that rights represent a set of contingent, not universal values.[88]

Secondly, critical theorists argue that the content of human rights law reflects a particular consensus about the economic order by excluding material concerns or focusing on civil and political rights. The separation of the two covenants in the 1950s, and the creation of a much weaker standard of legal obligation in the ICESCR, justify this conclusion. But critical theorists go much further, arguing that the liberal bias of human rights is rooted in a set of demands made by the eighteenth-century elite and nineteenth-century petite bourgeoise.[89] This echo's Marxist critics of human rights, who argue that rights were designed to separate communities from one another by promoting an individualistic framework of justice, precluding more collective or communal demands.[90] The specific refinement of the problem identified by critical theorists is that human rights law seems to actively preclude certain types of material claims, either by certain rights conflicting with these aims (such as the right to private property precluding claims to redistribution) or newer claims to rights being extinguished by older, better established rights seeming to take precedence. This argument is advanced by Wall, who notes that new rights claims seem to be confined to what the philosopher Jacques Rancière describes as "part of the configuration of the given," bestowing them with a "predictable and limited power."[91] The problem, as other critical theorists see it, is less with which rights are included in a legal instrument than with the concept of a human rights instrument itself, which constructs an "otherness" and is dependent on the identification of a "good" and "evil" which the human rights defined in a rights instruments are designed to remedy.[92]

A Critical Analysis of Defensive Relativism

To understand how defensive relativism relates to critical theory, it is best to reverse the frame of reference and ask, "How would a critical legal theorist interpret defensive relativism?" Defensive relativists often situate their arguments in the context of a state being dominated by international law and legal institutions, which would correlate with critical theorists' concerns that, as Jessica Whyte puts it, the moral language of concepts such as human rights and humanitarian intervention is a "justification for the domination of less powerful states by stronger ones."[93] It is not just that human rights is used instrumentally by powerful states and institutions, it is that the notion of cosmopolitan humanism upon which international human rights law rests (which is in and of itself a political construction), usually reflects a set of political ideologies rooted in Western Europe.[94] Defensive relativists would agree with this argument by citing paragraph 5 of the Vienna Declaration's call to interpret human rights in light of the "regional particularities and various historical, cultural and religious backgrounds" of societies seemingly endorsing critical theorists' skepticism of cosmopolitan humanism.[95] Critical theorists would point to the fact that this makes human rights law intrinsically prone to replicating patterns of domination, and this interpretation, of the sort advocated by defensive relativists in instruments such as these, would not necessarily alter this underlying problem of human rights law.[96] Despite skepticism of universality, the process of decolonizing human rights law has been defended by Dianne Otto as an "important pragmatic" mechanism, especially when human rights have been used in "struggles against various authoritarian, fundamentalist, patriarchal and otherwise repressive states."[97] In very general terms, the shared project of critiquing universality—in a similar fashion to the issues raised in relation to decolonial critiques of human rights law, above—does not mean that defensive relativism, with its state-constructed culture and its defense of the constituted power of state authority, would be a conclusion that critical theorists were likely to endorse.

More specifically, the claims of defensive relativism aim to defend a set of particular ideological assumptions about the importance of dominant cultural institutions, though, again, it is not clear that this is a position critical theorists would share. For example, the resistance from many African states toward regional mechanisms protecting women's rights, Sylvia Tamale argues, was driven by "fundamentalists" with "a selective view of culture" which reflected existing patriarchal power.[98] Defensive relativism, when used to argue for an unrestrained width of the margin of appreciation, is a claim about how a state should be allowed to construct restrictions of rights in a manner that deliberately narrows the scope of plurality. For example, in some cases involving LGBT rights at the ECtHR, such as *L. and V. v. Austria*, states have argued that the margin of appreciation should allow them to construct domestic laws which deliberately exclude the claims of minorities.[99] Critical theorists would not reach the conclusion that the inherent indeterminacy of international human rights law ought to grant an unquestioning license to the state to legislate as it wishes, as its focus is not only on a critique of the law but on the potential for radical political action that the law constrains. Furthermore, critical race feminists and other activists from critical traditions often attempt to give voice to claims from below—some of which can be reflected in cases litigated at human rights tribunals—whereas defensive relativists often resist such challenges to the laws designed to reflect the cultural assumptions of existing sources of constituted power.[100] Finally, it is not clear how some of the substantive critiques of human rights made by critical theorists in relation to human rights law's exclusion of material claims necessarily sit with defensive relativist arguments concerned with defending laws restricting economic freedom for women.

Understanding Defensive Relativism as a Tool of International Legal Argument

Because defensive relativism is common to all states it can take many different forms; therefore, coherently positioning it alongside existing discourses on human rights can be difficult. Rather, as argued in the introduction to this chapter, defensive relativism is a tactical argument. As Martti Koskenniemi argues, all methodological approaches to international law are, in a sense, designed to achieve "strategic goals" and are dependent on the context in which arguments are being advanced.[101] Koskenniemi's view, as Emmanuelle Jouannet notes, is that the determination of the "best" argument for achieving given strategic ends is never grounded in "purely legal criteria alone" and is instead "made on the basis of an underlying political choice."[102] In the legal and bureaucratic system that is international human rights law, with its range of overlapping—or in some cases, isolated—bodies and instruments, compliance is often achieved through various forms of persuasion, which, while not coercive, creates bounded incentives to encourage state compliance.[103] Defensive relativism is a tactical argument that acts as an explicit or implicit counter to this form of persuasion, aiming to justify a legal exemption of the sort described in chapter 3. Paragraph 5 of the 1993 Vienna Declaration was so significant precisely because it situated relativist arguments in this way—acknowledging the importance of human rights and universality in the abstract, but at the same time providing a framework for a state to argue for its practical nonimplementation in particular circumstances. This way, the broader strategic goal of states to appear human rights–compliant while at the same time not undertaking reforms to protect human rights can be maintained.

All forms of defensive relativism share a skepticism of international human rights law as a legal institution with content-independent legitimate authority (the idea that a legal decision is legitimate regardless of its substance because the decision comes from, or is made by, a known source of law), and instead maintain the idea that human rights should be subject to some form of broader sovereign bargaining/negotiation.[104] In this sense, it is what Christian Reus-Smit terms a form of instrumental deliberation, where actors in international law ask, "'How do I get what I want?' or 'How do we get what we want?'" as opposed to a form of ethical deliberation which addresses the question of "how I [an actor in international law] should act."[105] The political identity of states in relation to international human rights instruments is not fixed, and differs considerably between the commitment stage—the process of acceding to and ratifying a human rights instrument—and the compliance stage, where states are required to implement the substantive provisions of a human rights instrument or follow the decision of an interpretive institution such as an international tribunal or treaty body.[106] At the commitment stage, states tend to express what Reus-Smit terms ideographic politics, where actors "pursue institutional arrangements that permit the construction, stabilization and demonstration of their social identities."[107] This fits with the public comments in relation to the importance of human rights often made by states at time of ratification and the general external reputational signaling effects that many political scientists have identified in relation to treaty ratification.[108]

At the compliance stage, however, states' political identities become more strategically rational and human rights commitments start to be seen as a cooperation problem.[109] Some of the literature on compliance with international human rights law and the lack of compliance in particular areas supports this, noting the variation between different types of states, as well as different types of issues when it comes to implementing their obligations.[110] Various forms of instrumental deliberation come into the process of compliance and implementation. For example, security concerns can often shape the way that the implementation of particular obligations, such as the right to a fair trial, is considered by state parties.[111] The presence of competing cultural values is one of these instrumental deliberative factors to be considered by state parties as part of the overall strategic rational political identity a state adopts at the compliance stage.[112] Defensive relativism is, therefore, a tactical argument to deploy at a particular point or in response to an expectation of compliance. Surabhi Ranganathan breaks down thinking on compliance—what she describes as managerialist arguments relating to treaty law—into three strands of thought: quasi-constitutionalist (the idea that a treaty should be part of a constitutional order), managerial (the idea that treaty bodies should contain or manage adherence to their terms), or public order projects (which envisage a treaty and compliance as part of a political process).[113] In all three strands of managerialist thought, arguments are advanced by states either to contest the limits of the constitutional order of a legal regime or resist a particular outcome which that regime produces.[114] Defensive relativism operates in this "managerial" context, to counter and/or define the limits of legal authority. Most states want to comply with their legal obligations and are keen to demonstrate that they are doing so, but are also keen to set out the parameters by which that compliance will be understood and interpreted by international actors.[115] Managerialist logic has come in for a range of criticism from international relations and international law scholars, but because international bodies are trying to encourage compliance from states, and defensive relativism is a means of responding to compliance processes, managerialism is relevant for understanding defensive relativism.[116] This also means that defensive relativist arguments do not need to be defined by a particular set of ideological suppositions or questions about the inherent ideology of international human rights law, in the way that a lot of critical and decolonial theories about international human rights law are often defined by reference to a broader set of underlying ideological argument. The importance of defensive relativism rests on contesting universalism, in particular the universalism constructed by international institutions.[117]

As the analysis of human rights law from below sets out earlier in this chapter, defensive relativism implicitly supports a nonpluralistic and pro-majoritarian conception of democratic opinion in relation to cultural values. This informs the defense of domestic-legal sovereignty (the authority over domestic lawmaking), enabling defensive relativism to situate the protection of culture in the context of protecting the majority population's interests and as a form of opposition to international human rights law.[118] Not every single case of a divergence between a government and an international human rights tribunal or treaty body will be contested by a state party. Literature on the ECtHR and the IACtHR has identified how in some cases, where there is a conflict between the state and a human rights body or obligation, there may well be a variety of domestic incentives to comply with international human rights law.[119] Where this conflict might lead to backlash or noncompliance—and hence where states might reach for defensive relativism to justify noncompliance with their obligations or the excessive limitations of a right in domestic law—is where there exists what Sonia Cardenas terms a "non-compliance constituency" in a state which would be favorable to resisting international human rights law in a particular instance.[120] Yet, it is also still not clear that defensive relativism necessarily has to emerge from this tension; it is possible, as Douglas Donoho argues, for an institution to tailor decisions to recognize local traditions and democratic decisions.[121] The defense of democracy by defensive relativists is therefore often more of a tactical call that a state might make, depending on the circumstances of a given case, rather than a fixed ideological position about the value of grounding of human rights in communities or democratic decision making.

Insofar as there is a common trigger or factor initiating defensive relativism's use as an argument, it is the perceived challenge to a state's authority in constructing its own internal cultural hegemony or decisions over cultural values from international human rights law. Various forms of political recognition or conditionality in relation to women's rights, particularly in relation to CEDAW ratification, are ways of trying to potentially modify the way a state determines its cultural hegemony by providing external political incentives to undertake such a modification.[122] Equally, privacy rights in international human rights instruments are tactically useful for the LGBT community in states where there are criminal laws prohibiting same-sex relationships, as they provide a means of challenging these laws.[123] In this context, defensive relativism serves as a tactically useful argument, as it operates within the same legal structure in which the arguments challenging a state's cultural hegemony are being made and seeks to reassert cultural hegemony. In the context of human rights law, defensive relativism is a useful argument because it principally focuses on challenging the legal powers and legitimacy of the law rather than the politically more volatile approach of challenging the legitimacy of human rights themselves.

Conclusion

Susan Marks, in her commentary on the Vienna Declaration, argues that it falls somewhere between acknowledging the "nightmare of sovereignty as an impenetrable barrier" to human rights protection and the "Noble Dream that human rights transcend global divisions."[124] Many of the provisions in the declaration can be read in that context, especially paragraph 5's wording. However, the most significant aspect of paragraph 5 is the way it provides a context in which defensive relativism as a tactical argument can operate. Defensive relativism, as the first and third sections of this chapter set out, is not concerned with the reprioritization or reform of international human rights law. Equally, as the second section sets out, as an argumentative form defensive relativism does not necessarily protect human rights from below and has a highly instrumental approach to democratic support for its various positions. Therefore, defensive relativism's position is best explained as a tactical argument in the practice of international human rights law. But all tactics are ultimately in service of the realization of a wider set of strategic aims or the attainment of an objective. That objective, as chapter 8 argues, is the defense of sovereignty, or, more accurately, a particular idea of sovereignty.

CHAPTER 8

End-States: How Defensive Relativism Protects Sovereignty

Shin Hak-Chul is an artist who is part of the Minjung art movement, a South Korean political and populist art movement. In the mid-1980s he was painting a series of pictures about the political climate in South Korea, which was going through democratic transition in the shadow of worsening Cold War tensions. One was a painting called *Rice Planting (Monaeki)* which detailed a picture of the Korean Republic accompanied by variety of images. In the words of the Korean Supreme Court, which heard the case challenging Shin's acquittal on national security charges, these images showed "so-called American and Japanese imperialism, Rambo, imported tobacco, Coca Cola, Mad Hunter, Japanese samurai . . . President Ronald Reagan . . . [and] Prime Minister Nakasone," all portrayed as symbolizing "a fascist military power," which was contrasted with positive images of North Korea showing "farmers setting up a feast in celebration . . . [and] dancing and children."[1] The Korean Supreme Court held that the work was an "enemy-benefiting expression" under the National Security Law, which Shin later challenged as a violation of Article 19 of the International Covenant on Civil and Political Rights (ICCPR).[2] The South Korean government had on previous occasions cited the security situation and tensions with North Korea to justify domestic laws restricting both freedom of speech under Article 19 and freedom of religion under Article 18 of the ICCPR.[3] In Shin's case, the Human Rights Committee (HRC) rejected the state party's submission, observing that "the state party must demonstrate in [a] specific fashion the precise nature" of any alleged security threat in order to be able to rely on this as a justification for restricting Article 19 rights.[4]

The HRC wasn't willing to allow the state an unlimited scope for the claim that security required it to restrict free speech; the council required the state to prove that security concerns necessitated a restriction of Article 19. In so doing the HRC implicitly challenged the Korean state's sovereign decision-making in relation to national security. In a sense, this is built into the design of a human rights instrument which aims to challenge the traditionally understood sovereign prerogative of law making over a population by providing an external standard of grading and assessing lawmaking with reference to the protection of human rights. As the philosopher Jacques Derrida argues with reference to campaigns against the death penalty, when making the argument that a given practice violates human rights, "one is calling into question the principle and the authority of the sovereign of the nation state" by invoking a humanity that is beyond its control or constraints.[5] Derrida describes modern sovereignty as beast-like, drawing on the image famously depicted by Thomas Hobbes in *Leviathan*, where the sovereign provides a sense of security for the individuals in the state in return for protection from external forces in a semicontractarian manner, but retains the power of unfettered lawmaking.[6] International human rights law is one of several components of international law which challenged this conception of sovereignty in the twentieth century.[7] But in so doing, international human rights law eventually opened itself to the claim from states that it was interfering with their sovereignty, resulting first in resistance and then later in backlash.[8] As Sonia Cardenas argues, there are three basic types of argument or claim that states give when they are not meeting their human obligations: security, national exceptionalism, and the existence of a pro-violation of constituency.[9] All three of these arguments at their core involve a defense of a state's sovereignty from exterior assessment. States making these arguments are not necessarily successful—the South Korean government was unsuccessful on multiple occasions before the HRC when it argued that security concerns justified its far-reaching restrictions on rights protected by the ICCPR.[10] It is, however, the nature of the argument that is important here, as defensive relativism, like the claim it is necessary to restrict rights in the interests of national security, is a type of argument used to contest the authority of international human rights law and its impact upon state sovereignty.

In chapter 7, defensive relativism is positioned in relation to theories about human rights law, in order to demonstrate how it operates as a tactical doctrine. This chapter aims to explain how defensive relativism affects the way that international human rights law functions on a day-to-day basis as a mechanism for defending sovereignty. If defensive relativism is a tactic, the protection of sovereignty and the appearance of human rights compliance is the broader strategy it serves. On most days, somewhere in the world, international human rights law is being practiced in that there is a body attempting to ensure a state implements the substantive rights contained in an international human rights instrument. The UN Human Rights Council meets over the course of March, June, and September, the ten human rights treaty bodies meet at least once or twice a year, and individual petitions to regional courts are made throughout the year. Defensive relativism is a reaction to that process, as states seek to reassert an interpretation of their domestic-legal sovereignty, built on the state construction of culture, into arguments about human rights in order to gain a legal exemption which protects their sovereignty. Although the role of defensive relativist arguments in defending sovereignty has already been detailed, the precise meaning of a defense of sovereignty has yet to be unpacked. The first part of this chapter defines the different notions of defending sovereignty with respect to a human rights instrument, situating defensive relativist arguments in the context of disputes about sovereignty.

Defensive relativism's defense of sovereignty, as the remaining sections of this chapter outline, seeks to reach a specific "end-state" of international human rights law. Inherent to the structure of defensive relativist argumentation there are specific visions of how international human rights law should operate from the perspective of states making defensive relativist arguments, which are touched on in the conclusions of chapters 4, 5 and 6. Defensive relativism, as these chapters show, can be advanced as a temporal or procedural argument about the nature of the obligation concerned, where non-compliance with a particular obligation is presented as a practical difficulty in the implementation of the law. But from analyzing the individual arguments made by defensive relativists, it is possible to also see broader comments about how the law ought to operate in general or in perpetuity, beyond the circumstances of a particular case. This is an end-state of human rights law, and the latter three sections of this chapter outline three potential ways—or end-states of the law—defensive relativists suggest the law should operate. The first potential end-state of human rights implicitly advocated in defensive relativist arguments can be described as "maximal subsidiarity." Subsidiarity is the legal doctrine that a human rights issue should be in the hands of the national authorities, who are better placed to deal with it than an international court or tribunal. It underpins the margin of appreciation doctrine discussed in chapter 5 in relation to defensive relativist claims to Article 9 of the European Convention on Human Rights (ECHR). Maximal subsidiarity maintains that international courts should not play a role when it comes to arbitrating matters of morality in law, and that states ought to be able to determine what role international courts play. The second potential end-state of human rights implicitly advocated by defensive relativist arguments is for the abolition or restriction of facilitative enforcement. This describes the review process, which relies on international political pressure, by the imposition of legal mechanisms to limit any human rights bodies' power of review over state parties. It is covered in chapter 6 and elsewhere in this book in relation to the treaty reservations on which defensive relativists often rely. Effectively terminating facilitative enforcement, by reservations which constrain a treaty body's ability to review a state's implementation of substantive rights, moves human rights law from being a system of law capable of affecting the behavior of states toward a set of declarative statements. The third potential end-state of human rights implicitly advocated by defensive relativist arguments is for the creation of legal frameworks institutionalizing defensive relativist arguments. An example of this, the Association of Southeast Asian Nations (ASEAN) Human Rights Declaration, is discussed in chapter 4. As the final section of this chapter notes, the fragmentation of international human rights law into institutions which do not have any meaningful legal powers or capacity to protect rights creates an end-state of human rights where human rights law becomes a declarative series of statements rather than legal obligations.

All three of these end-states enable the protection of different conceptions of sovereignty. These end-states also all challenge the legitimacy or efficacy of human rights institutions and instruments to protect rights. This conception of the role of human rights treaties and international law is distinctly "managerialist" in that it takes the view that instruments are designed to manage the compliance of state parties with their substantive positions through a combination of political pressure and other mechanisms.[11] There are other conceptions of how international law should operate which go beyond a focus on compliance, looking instead at the normative or discursive effects that international law seeks to promote.[12] However, as the focus of defensive relativism is on the arguments made in response to a legal obligation, or to a prospective legal obligation, analyzing human rights law through the lens of the arguments made by states contesting compliance is important for developing an understanding of how states might wish the law to operate. An end-state is very different from the third element of defensive relativism, the attempt to gain a legal exemption, which is described in chapter 3. That relates to a specific argumentative tactic within an existing legal framework which is designed to secure recognition of the apparent compatibility of a state practice with a legal obligation. It does not include the creation of new regimes (as detailed in chapter 4), but instead focuses on how the arguments play within the existing system of law on a case-by-case basis. In a sense, this illustrates the way defensive relativists express a collective belief in international law as a system.[13] What has not yet been done is to examine how, from the arguments they advance, defensive relativists ultimately wish the system of international human rights law to operate. Unlike legal pluralism, defensive relativism is not interested in the existence or recognition of multiple legal orders, but instead attempts to advance a vision of how international human rights law should operate as a legal order.[14] The three visions defensive relativists have of the end-state of the law all envisage a form of human rights law where the state party is shielded from any scrutiny of its implementation of rights, presenting international human rights law as a series of political pledges.

Understanding Defensive Relativism as a Defense of Sovereignty

Defensive relativism, as explained in this and earlier chapters, is a mechanism for legally or politically defending a state's sovereignty from the obligations created by a process in international human rights law, such as a treaty obligation or a tribunal/treaty body determination of the scope of a particular obligation. This summary seems to situate defensive relativism within what Louis Henkin describes as the "dark history" of sovereignty. As Henkin sees it, states only accept human rights obligations "if they wish to" and have often cited the protection of their sovereignty as a justification for noncompliance with human rights law.[15] Sovereignty as a concept in the arguments about the power of international human rights law, even though it does not have the power to directly coerce states, often refers to what Robert Jackson describes as "an assumption about authority" in the arranging of the "contacts and relations of political communities."[16] J. Samuel Barkin draws a direct analogy between sovereignty and the concept of property, arguing that states will defend their right to stop international interference in their lawmaking and domestic practices in the name of human rights because that is an interference with their sovereign right.[17] International human rights law seeks to challenge or define the assumptions about a state's authority in certain specific ways. Defensive relativism's defense of sovereignty makes a couple of key assumptions about its nature, in relation to sovereign consent and the notion of relational sovereignty—the process of maintaining an external form of sovereignty recognized by others. These concepts are two sides of the same coin in that they are dimensions of sovereignty notionally affected by the implementation of an international human rights instrument.

Obligations and Domestic Legal Sovereignty

International human rights law aims to impose some form of international legal obligation upon a state to change its domestic laws. This means that international human rights law attempts to affect what can be termed a state's domestic legal sovereignty, which is the capacity to make laws governing its domestic sphere.[18] Classic notions of domestic-legal sovereignty explicitly or implicitly use the works of European political philosophers such as Jean Bodin and Thomas Hobbes, whose assumptions are often cited in later political and legal works on sovereignty, to generate a composite vision of sovereignty (in a legal and Western European sense) with supremacy, perpetuity over time, and the seemingly boundless capacity of decision making among its key tenets.[19] The notion of the sovereign as an unfettered decision-maker sits at odds with one of the principal aims of international human rights law to impose obligations to affect that decision-making process. International human rights law legitimates its role in relation to domestic legal sovereignty because states in international law are treated as agents to protect the individuals under their control, and their authority over their citizens is subject to a series of presumed limitations when it comes to the restriction of basic rights.[20]

Yet, of more significance in relation to human rights treaties is the fact that international human rights instruments are, formally speaking, consensual, in that states have had to commit to an instrument containing legal obligations.[21] However, the consent of states to human rights obligations is often contested in both form and substance. Formally, the notion of consent becomes problematic, as human rights treaties contain interests which are directed to individuals living within the state, challenging the contractual nature of treaties and the idea that they serve what Vassilis Pergantis calls the "subjective individualistic ideal" of states when conducting international relations.[22] This can be seen in the arguments surrounding the validity of reservations to human rights treaties and doctrines such as the severability rule, which removes the benefit of an invalid reservation to the reserving state, effectively reasserting the substantive provision of the law to the presumed benefit of individuals in the reserving state.[23] The contractarian notion of state consent therefore sits relatively awkwardly with treaties which are quasi-legislative in nature.[24] Human rights treaties entail the enactment of specific laws, whether a treaty is directly incorporated into a country's law or not, and thus entail, to a certain extent, the shaping and constriction of a government's legislative agenda.[25] Other aspects of international human rights law also challenge the contractual notion of state consent; for example, some human rights instruments contain no withdrawal clause, and certain obligations, such as *jus cogens* norms, cannot be derogated from.[26]

By challenging contractarian notions of international law, international human rights law regimes can appear to have a much more powerful effect over domestic-legal sovereignty than their formal legal powers actually grant them, and arguments situating international human rights law as a form of supranational constitutionalism only serve to reinforce this perspective.[27] Therefore, a potentially antagonistic relationship exists between the process of domestic-legal sovereignty and the discharge of human rights obligations. It is a potential antagonism, and not necessarily a certainty, because there will be some degree of alignment between international obligations and domestic-legal sovereignty. Various governments may well have an interest in implementing particular sets of rights; for example, it might appease a domestic political constituency or a social movement to implement certain rights or a particular decision of a human rights tribunal.[28] A state may also believe implementation of its obligations is on balance necessary or desirable for external political reasons, and in such cases be willing to overlook domestic political concerns over implementation.[29] Yet, this does not remove the existence of a potential tension between domestic-legal sovereignty and the discharge of human rights obligations. Legal mechanisms, such as the margin of appreciation doctrine, are attempts to resolve that tension within the legal framework created by international human rights law.[30] Political phenomena, such as backlash towards a human rights regime, is generated when the tension between domestic-legal sovereignty and international obligation cannot be adequately resolved by existing legal mechanisms.[31] Therefore, when describing defensive relativism as a defense of sovereignty, what is being referred to is the protection of domestic-legal sovereignty, in cases where there is a lack of pull factors in favor of compliance with an obligation created by international human rights law.

Relational Sovereignty

Given that states will often not experience direct material or political consequences for failure to implement international human rights law's obligations, they are nevertheless frequently keen to appear as though they are more broadly compliant with international human rights law. The reason for this relates to another aspect of sovereignty, the relational nature of sovereignty. Helen Stacy distinguishes relational sovereignty from both the "Hobbesian account" of sovereignty, which defines the nation-state by its national borders and minimal obligations to its citizens, and the "Lockean account" of sovereignty, which extends the sovereign's obligations to protect its citizens' private property, to argue that globalization has created a third type of sovereignty—relational sovereignty, "based upon a broader notion of the state's responsibilities towards its citizens."[32] One key benchmark for demonstrating responsibility, and indeed one which Stacy highlights as shaping what responsibilities are owed toward citizens, is a commitment to human rights law.[33] While this is often cited as being a recent development of international politics following developments such as the creation of the United Nations in 1945, there is, as some scholars have noted, a much longer tradition of "responsible" sovereignty.[34] Others have argued that human rights and compliance with human rights law increasingly defines the legitimacy of a state's sovereignty, pursuing the constructivist account of international law which maintains that states are ideational and have their approach to legal relationships shaped by their external identity as a state.[35] This general line of argument relies on the broader theoretical contention that what is and what is not considered sovereign is itself a construction of wider international society, granted in part by recognition of a state by other international actors, where recognition refers to both recognition of the fact of sovereignty and the legitimacy of the exercise of sovereign power.[36] The interlinking of human rights with sovereign legitimacy has, since 1989, Jean Cohen argues, served to legitimize the exercise of governmental power against states, in effect making human rights a norm of global governance—something which critical theorists of international law have identified as masking the broader power behind the law.[37] Interactional theorists of the law, and studies into state compliance which draw on socialization, often rely implicitly on the assumption that states are concerned with the external nature of their sovereignty as judged in relation to their human rights compliance.[38]

Regardless of the conclusion one takes in relation to the role of human rights in the legitimation of sovereignty, commitment to a human rights instrument is one of the ways for a state to demonstrate to an external audience of its fellow states and international institutions that it is maintaining the core international norm of protecting its citizens.[39] This can lead to mutual recognition of the legitimacy of states by other states and international actors, which, as Michael Fowler and Julie Bunck put it, gives them "a ticket of general admission to the international arena."[40] Jack Donnelly, encapsulating this argument, notes that human rights law provides a "global script of legitimacy" for states.[41] While this line of argument risks overstating the significance of human rights law, multilateral recognition of a state by an international organization is often contingent upon that state demonstrating that it is complying with human rights norms.[42] It is also important to stress that there is a significant difference between commitment to a human rights regime and compliance with it. As several empirical studies have suggested, there is a difference between reputational incentives to commit to a treaty, where reputational concerns will often lead a state to ratify treaties, and compliance, where reputational concerns are weaker, as indicated by a failure to comply with reporting requirements and other terms of the treaty.[43] This leads to a situation where, as Emilie Hafner-Burton and Kiyoteru Tsutsui summarize it, "weak institutional mechanisms to monitor and enforce" human rights give states a strong incentive to ratify human rights instruments "as a matter of window dressing."[44] This also gives states a positive incentive to argue that their interpretation of the law is a discharge of their obligations, and that as a consequence they ought to benefit from the reputational and recognition benefits flowing from human rights compliance. Therefore, individual acts of defensive relativism, such as arguments justifying an impermissible reservation, are arguments to defend a state's relational sovereignty. This is particularly important, as international review mechanisms often try to utilize concern about the perception of relational sovereignty, which can in turn promote overall compliance with international human rights law.[45]

Maximal Subsidiarity as a Defense of Sovereignty

The principle of subsidiarity in international law can have multiple different meanings depending on which legal regime is being referred to, but broadly speaking it describes the position, inherent within the margin of appreciation doctrine of the European Court of Human Rights (ECtHR), that international courts should defer to domestic adjudication and authorities as a means of regulating the overall distribution of authority between an international regime and the state.[46] The principle of subsidiarity, as used in the European Union, allows European authorities to only act where the objectives of the proposed action cannot be met by member states. This operates in part as a teleological mechanism to facilitate common aims shared by the community of member states.[47] By contrast, the way the ECtHR has justified subsidiarity is principally as a form of deference to the democratic authority of the institutions of the state.[48] As Luzius Wildhaber summarizes, it is much more than pragmatic realism; "it is also a way of paying respect to democratic processes." Wildhaber notes elsewhere that this is an area of discretion which derives from the "expression of the democratic will of their people."[49] In the *Belgian Linguistics* case, the ECtHR clarified that it could not "assume the role of competent national authorities," as that would lose sight of the principle of subsidiarity in the "international machinery" established to enforce the ECHR.[50] A number of authors have drawn the link between subsidiarity and the margin of appreciation, as both are about the allocation of authority to national authorities.[51] Since Protocol 11 to the ECHR, which made jurisdiction of the court compulsory, the more pragmatic rationale for subsidiarity (to encourage compliance from states) diminished, but this led to increasing concern about the growing power of the court with complaints about its lack of accountability.[52] The Interlaken Conference in 2010 and the Brighton Conference in 2012 saw significant restatements of the principle of subsidiarity, with an agreement that references to the principle should be inserted into the preamble to the convention.[53]

But an overly deferential understanding of subsidiarity could significantly advantage a state party wishing to argue that its domestic institutions were of supreme importance in determining moral positions, which is a problem with the more deferential justifications for subsidiarity. Paolo Carozza illustrates this line of argument thus; just because "the obligations [of international human rights law] leave the parties a great deal of room for a diversity of systems" to implement international human rights law, this would not be "compatible with a government set on destroying rights and liberties or systematically discriminating against minorities."[54] But many questions about the limits or application of human rights do not meet this threshold; they relate to complex questions about the limits of morality and social power. As Føllesdal argues, when many of the state parties to the ECtHR had evolved into functioning democracies where most rights were protected in domestic law, it led to the ECtHR's role changing "to helping correct their minor flaws as regards human-rights violations."[55] Protocol 15 of the ECHR enshrined the margin of appreciation test into the text of the convention, but was part of a package of measures to reassert the supremacy of national authorities. In certain areas, such as the protection of political speech under Article 10 of the ECHR, there have been signs in ECtHR jurisprudence of an approach which is more deferential.[56] This often ends up implicitly favoring the incumbent political party in a state which can take decisions regarding the scope of political speech which limits its political opponents. As some scholars note, there is every prospect of these effects being enhanced by further reform of the subsidiarity doctrine.[57] The notion of review mechanisms serving as a mechanism for correcting or enhancing democracy has been adopted by liberal theorists of international law as well as others seeking to explain how the legal protection of human rights can be compatible with democratic sovereignty.[58] Those arguing for a democratic grounding for the review powers of international courts and tribunals are, however, more wary of the notion that courts can serve as a corrective to the democratic process. Instead, they often conclude, as Andreas von Staden does in the case of the ECtHR, that deference to state authority through a maximal notion of subsidiarity is a means of enhancing the stated mission of the ECHR to promote human rights and democracy.[59] This argument does, however, lead to some difficult assumptions regarding the meaning of democracy, and when a majoritarian democratic system limits a set of rights for particular communities or sexes, or applies a completely different standard for certain religious communities, the ECtHR is put in the position of being countermajoritarian.[60] As Susanna Mancini puts it, at "its maximalist application" the margin of appreciation operates in a manner which would thwart the effectiveness of the ECtHR turning into a mechanism for "uncritical adherence to majority decisions."[61] Mancini and Føllesdal, while acknowledging how an unrestricted approach to the margin of appreciation could lead to unchecked majoritarianism constricting rights protection, are nevertheless cautious about the overall legitimacy of the court and its capacity to act as an arbitrator of quite difficult constitutional questions.

States that approach international human rights courts in order to defend their domestic laws and practices are unrestrained in arguing for as maximal a version of subsidiarity as possible, justifying it with defensive relativist argumentation. This can be illustrated by reference to the ECtHR's jurisprudence on Article 8 (the right to private and family life) in relation to discriminatory treatment against the LGBT community. The more extreme versions of maximal subsidiarity can be seen in cases such as *Alekseyev v.*

Russia, where the applicant had sought to hold an LGBT pride march to call more broadly for tolerance towards the LGBT community in Russia, and the domestic authorities had not only refused permission for the march but had refused permission for any public activity connected with LGBT rights. They eventually arrested the applicant when he and others tried to demonstrate without permission.[62] At the ECtHR, where the applicant claimed that his right to freedom of association under Article 11 of the ECHR had been violated, the submission for the government claimed the march "had to be banned for the protection of morals" because homosexuality was incompatible with the "religious doctrines for the majority of the population," and allowing these parades would be "perceived by believers as an intentional insult to their religious feelings."[63] The government, which was ultimately unsuccessful in *Alekseyev*, pursued arguments with an overtly majoritarian conclusion. As the court had indicated elsewhere, banning activities such as speech and association because the majority would be offended would do a "disservice to democracy and often even endanger it."[64] These cases involved the banning or restriction of protest with criminal or administrative sanctions, which makes it easier to reconcile the decision of the ECtHR in relation to an area of considerable sensitivity to the state in question, because of the disproportionate use of police power against an individual. Where the courts have had to make decisions heavily focused on the discriminatory nature of a domestic authority's decision making, they are arguably directly affecting a state's domestic-legal sovereignty. For example, in *Salgueiro da Silva Mouta v. Portugal*, a gay man contested the decision of Portuguese courts to restrict his Article 8 rights in connection with visiting his children. The courts had concluded that children had a right to "a traditionally Portuguese family, which is certainly not the set-up the father has decided to enter into."[65] In the domestic court's decision, it was clear that the applicant's sexual orientation was a factor in making a decision, in spite of claims by the state authorities at the ECtHR that the assessment had been made in a nondiscriminatory fashion and that it was the state's right to make such decisions. In other cases where concern for the rights of the child was wrapped up in broader cultural considerations, the ECtHR was unwilling to defer to the state party.[66]

Yet, the EctHR has allowed for considerable divergence between state parties over the issue of legal structures for the recognition of same sex relationships, concluding in 2016 that there was no right to equal marriage under the ECHR.[67] In much of the case law in this area, states have advanced arguments defending not just the notion of substantive cultural values, as represented by their marriage laws, but also their right to take such decisions in the exercise of the principle of subsidiarity.[68] Often, the argument playing out at the ECtHR is about the level of abstraction a state may be granted with respect to the identification of cultural values in relation to measures restricting rights.[69] In *Vallianatos v. Greece*, the court clarified that the "aim of protecting the family in the traditional sense is rather abstract," and that any determination of traditional values as a legitimate aim for restricting rights, such as the right to enter into a civil union as a homosexual couple, must acknowledge "there is not just one way or one choice when it comes to leading one's family or private life."[70] In *Orlandi v. Italy*, a case where domestic authorities were resisting recognizing same-sex marriages abroad, the Italian courts had justified the domestic authority's position, cautioning that a "creative interpretation" of domestic marriage laws risked undermining references to "marriage in its traditional sense."[71] The ECtHR, finding a violation of Article 8, noted that the Italian government had failed to "put forward a prevailing community interest" against which to balance the applicants' "momentous interests," instead relying on increasingly vague conceptions, such as the need to protect Italian "public order," while upholding domestic defenses of "traditional" marriage.[72] A defense of the ability to make rights restrictions in relation to a generalized conception of majority cultural values is a defense of maximal subsidiarity. It puts the state party in control of determining what the majority's values are and resists having to justify restrictions of rights stemming from that determination to an international body. The state parties pushing for maximal subsidiarity are implicitly appealing to majoritarianism—something the ECtHR has rejected, finding that generalized assumptions about majority values and their defenses are insufficient to justify discriminatory measures against the LGBT community.[73]

These arguments focus on both defending the decision that a domestic authority made in relation to the limitation of a particular right, and defending the authority of domestic institutions to restrict rights. The appeals to vague, tradition-orientated terminology are designed to create a situation where international courts can't review the substance of the decision making to limit particular rights. This favors the state party's construction of cultural values by design, and utilizes the antiuniversalist mechanism of subsidiarity to advance an argument where the conclusion is maximal subsidiarity, in an attempt to protect domestic legal sovereignty. Protecting sovereignty by making defensive relativist arguments can be a way of giving what Rebecca Bryant and Madeleine Reeves term "sovereign agency" to communities in a state that favor rights restriction.[74] Sovereign agency is an "aspiration" for recognition of a given political order or a form of "state desire" stemming from a "sense of loss . . . of political legibility."[75] The end-state of human rights law envisaged in these arguments is where the interpretation of a state's obligations and any limitations on those obligations rests with state authorities, who are then free to claim that their actions are representative of a broader state desire. It envisages a more deferential and limited role for human rights law and the bodies designed to enforce it, and as a consequence also envisages domestic authorities being able to use interpretations of human rights law to preserve cultural or traditional values.

Taming Facilitative Enforcement Mechanisms

Facilitative enforcement refers to procedures established by an international instrument designed to persuade states to comply with their obligations through so called "soft" mechanisms of enforcement, such as naming and shaming or political sanctions.[76] International human rights instruments and organizations have no directly coercive mechanisms of their own, but instead rely on the normative power of international law and the existence of legal obligation to alter a state's behavior. It is something of an article of faith among legal scholars, Andrew Guzman notes, that international instruments have an effect on state behavior, although many social scientists and international relations theorists are more skeptical as to why this happens.[77] There is relatively little evidence of "carrot and stick"–type behavior where preferential trade deals follow because of a state's commitment to an international human rights treaty, which explains commitment to the treaty but not subsequent compliance with that treaty.[78] Socialization theories of international law maintain that state behavior is shaped by the ongoing process of socialization within an international framework, such as an international organization.[79] This is often associated with constructivist theorists, who argue that legal obligation arises through the generation of interactions between states and organizations.[80] There are some deficits of explanation within this theoretical framework, not least the way it reduces states into interacting like individuals and dilutes the range of complexities involved in many international regimes.[81]

It is instead important to read in the role of reputation and reputation cost associated with socialized interactions in order to get a fuller picture of facilitative enforcement. As Oona Hathaway notes, the existence of collateral consequences on a state, which are associated with, but not necessarily directly generated by, an international legal regime, can affect compliance.[82] This can include a broader positional concern about the way a state is perceived by other states and institutions in the international community at large, not just in a facilitative sense but also in terms of its overall existential legitimacy. This is a combination of two factors: Firstly, existential equality, which, Gerry Simpson argues, arises out of "recognition by the international community" that an entity is entitled to sovereignty which exists in "a form of the state's own choosing."[83] Secondly, as argued in the first section above, it involves relational legitimacy—the notion that the way a state is governed should be measured with reference to some exterior standard, one of the most significant being the standards contained in international human rights law.[84] States are, in sum, concerned both about the maintenance of their own system of government and whether it is judged legitimate by the external metric of human rights law, allowing a regime such as a human rights tribunal or treaty body to impose an existential cost. This is a form of collateral consequence on states, as that body determines whether a state's actions are compatible with human rights standards, and in cases where they aren't, the body issues declarations or decisions with the intention or assumption of creating some kind of reputational sanction on the state.[85] Although varying in impact—an ECtHR judgment is legally binding and has the political structure of the Council of Europe to assist with enforcement, whereas the Committee on the Rights of the Child only goes so far as to frame its concluding observations as guidelines—all bodies designed to monitor and enforce international human rights law have a notional impact on the existential legitimacy of states, or at least operate with the presumption that a state ought to act in response to its decisions. Unpicking this is important for positioning what defensive relativism does to facilitative enforcement. This is well illustrated by the issues surrounding reservations which, as chapter 3 and 6 outline, remain an important but contested part of international human rights law, because of the way that reservations can remove the protection of the rights contained within human rights treaties.[86]

Blanket reservations can create situations of nonprotection where a state is party to an international instrument which nominally purports to afford a level of protection for a particular set of rights within that state's jurisdiction, but resists the implementation of those rights because of defensive relativist claims. Malawi's reservation upon accession to the Convention on the Elimination of all forms of Discrimination Against Women (CEDAW) in 1987 stated that "owing to the deep-rooted nature of some traditional customs and practices" it did not consider itself bound by a CEDAW provision requiring the eradication of "traditional customs and practices," which effectively rendered moot Articles 2 and 5 of CEDAW.[87] This was particularly significant, as both of these are provisions relating to state duty, directly connected to the implementation of other rights in CEDAW. Significant dialogue and negotiation led Malawi to withdraw its reservation a few years later with the government claiming thatit had had a "change of heart."[88] Yet, other reservations to Article 2 persist, effectively neutering any obligation that a state party might have under the treaty; for example, Bahrain's reservation to Article 2 upon accession to CEDAW renders the obligation to implement rights contained within CEDAW "within the bounds of the provisions of the Islamic sharia."[89] A coalition of Bahraini human rights groups noted in 2013 that the presence of reservations was having an "echo back" effect, allowing the government to justify a discriminatory legal framework because the reservations existed.[90] Although frequently raised with state parties in the process of their CEDAW review, as Marsha Freeman notes, the issue is often not "belaboured" even though the presence of reservations of this sort effectively bar the implementation of most if not all of CEDAW's provisions.[91] Studies of reputation cost in international law have identified that states place a premium on whether a norm is legal or not in terms of whether they comply with it, and that the existence of legality in and of itself is seen as a reason for compliance.[92] This contextualizes why reservations, rather than simple noncompliance, are important to states in terms of existential legitimacy. Reservations are a legal mechanism, and because a norm or mechanism's legality is perceived by states in general as a reason for compliance with it (regardless of its nature or content), a state that is acting in accordance with a reservation, even if it is engaging in an "echo back," can be said to be acting legally, hence preserving its relational sovereignty and, notionally at least, limiting any reputation cost.

Reservations which do not follow the International Law Commission's (ILC) guidance that reservations should not be "vague or general" in nature also limit both the legal obligation on a state party and facilitative enforcement.[93] For example, Bangladesh's reservation to Articles 13 and 16 of CEDAW imposed unlimited restrictions on both the right to participate in the economic and social life of the state as well the right to divorce, because of what the government deemed to be their "conflict with Sharia law based on Holy Quran."[94] In its concluding observations, the CEDAW Committee not only noted that these reservations, in particular the reservation to

Article 16, were incompatible with the object and purpose of the convention, but also that discriminatory domestic laws surrounding marriage and inheritance persisted.[95] A coalition of Bangladeshi NGOs, writing in support of the withdrawal of CEDAW reservations, argued that Bangladesh did not have a formal system of Sharia law, only "family issues" which were governed by laws "based on religious provisions in the absence of a Uniform Family Code," and that, in any event, not all the population was Muslim.[96] Bangladesh Mahila Parishad, a women's rights NGO which has been active for over forty years, observed in its shadow report to the CEDAW Committee that a number of other countries with majority Muslim populations did not have reservations of the sort that Bangladesh had in relation to Article 2, and concluded it remained "an important barrier against review and revision of all laws" relating to CEDAW implementation.[97] One of the most tangible impacts of a treaty like CEDAW is its ability to shape domestic laws with respect to women's rights by the existence of an international legal obligation being an active consideration in the law- and policy-making process. Reservations which give an open-ended exemption to a state party nullify this impact.[98] There is no obligation to accept all the terms of a treaty, and reservations are perfectly legal, but reservations which are vague in nature limit the ability of treaty bodies to scrutinize a state's compliance with a treaty.[99] Treaty bodies, when considering state reports in these cases, often focus on persuading states to remove reservations or declaring that reservations are impermissible.[100] Sometimes treaty bodies have even been aggressive in their responses to vague reservations—in 1994, the CEDAW Committee criticized Libya's reservation, which referenced Sharia, for being framed in a way which suggested Sharia had come to a "standstill three centuries ago."[101] But in such situations state responses are often characterized by silence, or by claims that such reservations are necessary for the state's participation in the treaty.[102] The consequences for reservations, therefore, heavily depend on the state's own position toward the committee; Bangladesh, for example, in its 2010 state report, responded to committee pressure and took some action toward removing its reservations, whereas Bahrain, in its 2018 report, simply restated its position in relation to reservations.[103]

Crucially, reservations can, if they are sufficiently vague, allow states to weaken the overall "moral appeal" of human rights treaties, as the reputational signaling they provide to a signatory state is created without concomitant improvement in actual rights protection for the individuals living within the signatory state.[104] As one study identified, reservations are most likely to be entered by a state when it anticipates that the treaty it is signing is likely to have legal effects in its jurisdiction, either from its own courts or from external bodies.[105] The end-state of human rights envisaged by defensive relativists in arguments about reservations is one where human rights treaties give the maximum reputational benefit with minimum legal cost. Reservations, even though they may carry an initial reputational cost, by virtue of their legal status and signaling benefits to other states who have not ratified the agreement or who wish to enter a similar type of reservation, are a means of reaching that end-state.[106] This end-state preserves the domestic legal sovereignty of states by minimizing their obligations in an open-ended way, but it also maintains their relational sovereignty through membership of human rights agreements.

Defensive Relativism and the Fragmentation of International Law

The fragmentation of international law describes the proliferation of international courts, tribunals, and other bodies with overlapping authority and uncertain boundaries, which has led to concern about both the ineffectiveness of legal regimes and the increasing lack of legitimacy of different regimes.[107] The growth of different regional human rights regimes has been part of the overall story of fragmentation.[108] The ILC report on fragmentation notes that there is no specific normative value in regionalism, but that regionalism assists with "functional differentiation," enabling the recognition of the different forces driving the law's creation.[109] The ILC report highlighted the sociological context of the creation of the law, but, crucially, for the purposes of analyzing defensive relativism, noted that one meaning of regionalism was that it was an argument about the "limitation to the sphere of validity of a universal rule or principle."[110] In the context of human rights law and the universalism-relativism debate, regionalism is often presented as a justification for the "the varying, context-sensitive implementation of human rights standards" which, as the reports concludes, can morph into a debate about whether the regional standard constitutes a *lex specialis*.[111] The wider problem with treating any form of human rights instrument as either a regional "limitation" of the law or *lex specialis* is, as Langlois argues, that the concept of human rights gets "watered down."[112] In its comments on the potential conflict between different legal rules, the ILC study group made the important observation that legal regimes are about "protecting rights and enforcing obligations," and warned that "in a decentralized and spontaneous institutional world" there was a real danger of the dilution of the sense that international law existed to serve common overall goods.[113] These concerns have been articulated in other literature critical of the notion of fragmentation, cautioning that different legal regimes could fundamentally alter the nature of legal obligations or weaken the overall responsibilities of states in specialized areas.[114] In the context of international human rights law, the benefit of fragmentation for the protection of human rights is that a localized substantive conception of human rights can make an institution more legitimate, by promoting a conception of human rights more attuned to regional needs and providing an enforcement mechanism with greater local legitimacy.[115] However, as Monica Pinto notes, human rights regimes can vary in their "reliability or trustworthiness" and differ considerably on whether they are able to meaningfully contribute in the struggle against the impunity of state authorities.[116] The development of regional legal regimes could, as Gerhard Hafner argues, enhance the overall prospect of compliance with international law; however, Gerhard adds that the uncertainty and inconsistent application of rules could allow states to escape their responsibilities, making regionalism "not necessarily [an] unmitigated" success for the development of international law.[117] It is, in short, possible that regimes can be designed to appear to be legal but not contain any legal obligations or capacity to protect rights, resulting in what can be described as a false fragmentation, as while there appears to be normative continuity from one regime to another, it is largely superficial.

The Arab League's Arab Charter on Human Rights is an example of how regionalism led to a form of fragmentation in international law, which resulted in a defensive relativist instrument in a similar fashion to ASEAN's Human Rights Declaration. Like the ASEAN Declaration, the Arab Charter has no enforcement body and does not create formal legal obligations on state parties. Like the ASEAN Declaration, even if the charter were to possess both of these features, the way that rights are substantively constructed in the charter would, if used to enforce rights against a state party, provide the party with a complete defensive relativist justification for restricting most substantive rights contained in the charter. Since its creation in 1945, the Arab League has been committed to noninterference, and the league's organizational design, as Michael Barnett and Etel Solingen note, was specifically intended to produce a highly constrained institution.[118] Declaratory statements about rights were favored by the league instead, including strong support for self-determination in Palestine, but this set only a limited political precedent in terms of creating rights that could be used by individuals living in its member states.[119] The league's actions in relation to recalcitrant member states, such as suspending member states or taking some other administrative action—as was the case with the suspension of Iraq in 1990 and the 2011 suspension of Libya—were framed less in terms of signaling condemnation of worsening human rights abuses within the state and more as a reflection of the collective institutional desire to maintain interorganizational stability. After a somewhat complicated political process in 1994, an Arab human rights charter was drafted and opened for signature, although it was never actually ratified. As An-Na'im notes, Article 4 of the 1994 charter allowed all rights contained in it to be subject to restrictions in order to protect "national security and economy, public order health and morals," which went far further than any equivalent provisions in other regional instruments, allowing unlimited restrictions of rights by states.[120]

A renewed attempt at creating an Arab human rights charter began, and in 2004 a revised version of the Arab charter was adopted by the league and came into force in 2008. Its substantive provisions were formulated in a framework that appeared to favor the operation of laws restricting the operation of human rights in a manner that favored state interests. For example, under the 2004 charter the right to freedom of speech is set out in a provision which limits free speech to being exercised within the "framework of society's fundamental principles."[121] Equally, an individual's nationality can be removed from that individual if there is "a legally valid reason" for doing so, again potentially allowing a wide scope for state parties to have legally valid reasons for restricting rights.[122] The charter specifically references Sharia as a source of the principle of equality but does not contain any real acknowledgment of the different schools of scholarship within Sharia law or dissenting traditions within various Muslim communities. Instead, it is formulated in a way which prioritizes the interests of state authorities or state-aligned groups in defining religious traditions.[123] The framing of the right to marriage in Article 33 reflects this, saying that the right to marry exists "according to the rules and conditions of marriage" in force in society at the time, again effectively giving the state party an unlimited veto over any prospective claim against a domestic rule restricting rights which was justified on the grounds of protecting tradition.[124] Theoretically, some of these issues could have been determined by robust adjudication, and the charter did contain references that its text was subject to an ongoing process of modification and progress.[125]

However, the Arab Commission set up by the 2004 charter has no powers of scrutiny over an individual state's human rights records, and other bodies created to enforce the charter, such as the Arab Court of Human Rights (set up in 2014), have been criticized for their lack of impartiality and independence.[126] As a 2021 study on the rights of women under the charter noted, the frameworks set up by the charter were powerless to tackle entrenched perceptions of gender roles found in the laws and policies of signatory states, and as a consequence there was effective mass noncompliance with the charter's substantive provisions.[127]

Claims that restrictions on human rights could be justified by reference to pan-regional cultural values do not necessarily reflect broader pan-regional opinions. Public surveys in a number of states in the league, including Jordan, Lebanon, and Algeria, showed divergence on a number of different questions relating to democracy and democratic governance but a relatively high level of agreement on questions relating to the importance of civil liberties and human rights.[128] Equally, the political developments in some states, such as the changes which occurred in some countries after the Arab Spring in 2011, helped cement political rights in domestic law which go further than the rights protected in the charter.[129] What drove the league's development of human rights mechanisms was not a desire to reflect common cultural or legal standards on human rights but, as Vera Van Hüllen argues, the "rational"—not "normative"—demand to confirm to international expectations.[130] There was an additional rational advantage in having a set of standards to which the political and legal behavior of a state could be assessed by the league organs, in order to provide further political justifications for actions against member states.[131] Yet, these rational incentives also had to be reconciled with the league's institutionalized commitment to defending sovereignty, hence the charter was designed to prioritize a state's interpretation of rights, and the commission and court as institutions were designed not to enforce the charter's provisions.[132]

Defensive relativism played less of a role in the design of the Arab Charter than it did in the ASEAN Declaration. But in both cases the end-state of a human rights body, which was defensive relativist by design, was actually reached—unlike the first and second end-states described above. This was a human rights regime which did not function as a legal regime but as a political vehicle to signal to an external audience about the nature and identity of its parent regional grouping.[133] As Avery Poole's account of the ASEAN Declaration's formation demonstrates, concerns about institutional recognition were central to the formation of inter-institutional consensus in ASEAN on the role of a human rights instrument.[134] Both instruments are framed in what Anna Grear describes as "normative continuity" with the Universal Declaration of Human Rights (UDHR), claiming to represent the regional-cultural implementation of the UDHR's standards.[135] This makes them appear to be equivalent to other regional groupings which have human rights mechanisms as part of their legal structure, while at the same time not providing any human rights remedies.[136] Chaloka Beyani, acknowledging some of the weaknesses in both the ASEAN Declaration and the Arab Charter, argues that regional human rights bodies "breathe life into the notion of universality," but this argument sidesteps how both instruments were designed so as to make it nearly impossible for either body to enforce human rights and give practical substance to an alternate notion of universality.[137] The absence of any enforcement mechanisms allows both instruments to defend both the domestic legal sovereignty and reputational sovereignty of their member states, creating what amounts to a false fragmentation, as what looks like a set of obligations is simply an unenforceable set of statements. This end-state of defensive relativism is the construction of a human rights regime which is purposefully ineffective at protecting human rights.

Conclusion: The End-States of Defensive Relativism and the Protection of Sovereignty

Maximal subsidiarity, limited facilitative enforcement, and the pursuit of false fragmentation are the "end-states" of defensive relativism in that they describe how defensive relativists advocate the law should operate. The three end-states allow for the simultaneous preservation of a state's domestic legal sovereignty while not compromising the overall perception of its relational sovereignty. Sovereignty, as Koskenniemi, notes does not have a fixed determinate content or precise definition. If it did, then a dispute over "whether an act falls within the state's legitimate sphere of action could always be solved by simply applying it to the case" under dispute.[138] Sovereignty as a juridical concept has had a fragmented history with a complex evolution, with different states being denied sovereignty on an equal footing with one another and the scope of what would constitute the legitimate exercise of a state's sovereign authority evolving over time.[139] Unlike a dispute about the physical presence of sovereignty, such as, say, a maritime boundary, where the question at issue is about the exercise of authority and power over a particular landmass, the contestation of sovereignty in international human rights law is a dispute about the authority an international institution possesses to make conclusions about a state's domestic lawmaking.[140] This is not just an abstract dispute—international human rights bodies can impact a state's relational sovereignty in their decisions about a state's compliance with the law or the compatibility of their actions to an agreed-upon human rights standard. Beyond the mere legal fact of state consent, the institutions and instruments of international human rights law can claim their power is legitimate by invoking the cosmopolitan sense that the rights of an individual are, or ought to be, transcendental, or by references to a teleological political justification that human rights are the best way of shaping society.[141] One of the central tenants of cosmopolitanism, which, as chapter 1 outlines, is a core part of the antiuniversalist case, is a form of teleological vision about the end-state of society, which is implicit in human rights instruments.[142] Although this version of human rights is often contested, defensive relativism seeks to directly challenge the cosmopolitan notion of rights.[143] It does this both explicitly, by the structure of its argument, as set out in chapters 1 to 3, and implicitly, by the advocacy of an end-state of the law which prioritizes the authority of the state over the perceived external interference of international human rights law.

All three would-be end-states see human rights law more as a declaratory set of statements, or aspirational labels, rather than a system of obligations that can affect the legal and material conditions of an individual living within a state that is party to a human rights instrument. The enforcement of international human rights law requires a complex series of interactions between the institutions of international law, interstate politics, and the overall sense of authority that the existence of a legal obligation upon states brings.[144] All three would-be end-states of human rights law crucially weaken some element of the legal obligation that an instrument purports to place on a state, or, as in the case of false fragmentation, claims to represent a notion of obligation that does not impose an obligation on a state to an action to protect human rights. Defensive relativist arguments can be unsuccessful at achieving these end-states. Often, the real impact of defensive relativism is that international human rights law continues on a day-to-day basis to afford a patchwork of limited rights protections, while falling short of the utopic promises advanced by the instruments which make up international human rights law.[145] The end-states of defensive relativism show how defensive relativism serves the strategic goal of protecting different forms of sovereignty in international human rights law. Some states use defensive relativism as a transitory justification, in that a state uses defensive relativist arguments to justify its difficulty in implementing particular rights. This was the case with some of the justifications for reservations under CEDAW, with the stated assumption being that these difficulties might cease. However, the end-states described above are descriptions of how the law should function indefinitely, and because defensive relativism is a form of argument which utilizes the normative vocabulary of international law to try and achieve specific outcomes, it is important to evaluate where, by implication, defensive relativist arguments want to take international human rights law.[146]

CONCLUSION

Defensive Relativism: The Human Rights Practitioner's Conundrum

Throughout this book, the majority of examples and case studies present defensive relativism as something hostile to human rights protection. Some of the examples presented, such as the claims to an unlimited margin of appreciation, which effectively allow a state to maintain that it is human rights compliant while doing little to implement certain rights, make it easy to see defensive relativism as antithetical to human rights protection. Human rights, as Joseph Raz puts it, exist to be enforced as a system of law. This means providing a framework for institutions to find that the laws of a state are incompatible with protections that state owes to individuals as a matter of international obligation.[1] When human rights law fails to be enforced, Katarina Tomaševski argues, it becomes "emptied of contents," transformed into "a weasel-word" to be "filled with new contents with every change of the political fashion of the season."[2] In the same way that "development" exists to cover any form of changing ideological trend in macroeconomic practice, protecting human rights can be justification for any and every moral practice, even not protecting human rights.[3]

The above paragraph can be read as a neat statement of principles that might have some readers nodding along in agreement, and likely represents the author's personal view—of the sort that he would almost certainly hold forth about over a coffee or a beer. But this does not deal with the world as it is. Defensive relativism is not a "bug" in the system of international human rights law; it is a feature of it. To understand this, it is important to reflect firstly on the broader conundrum of universality in international law, of which defensive relativism is a part, before going on, by way of conclusion, to give some reflections on human rights practice and defensive relativism.

The Contestation of the Universal

It was the "crisis of the mid-twentieth century," as Mark Mazower terms it, which led to a rethinking of the notion of the universal and universality in international law that went beyond the imperial-colonial assumptions that had characterized international law since the early nineteenth century.[4] Both the Bretton Woods Conference in 1944 and the San Francisco Conference in 1945 attempted a structural reimagination of the international order, creating institutions which would be in charge of defining universality in international law. Another development, following the Potsdam Conference in July 1945, was the creation of the International Military Tribunal in Nuremberg, which was to assume universal jurisdiction over war crimes committed by the Nazis.[5] The end of the Second World War became one of the "turning point" years in international law's history along with 1648 (Peace of Westphalia) and 1815 (Congress of Vienna). During the process of drafting the Universal Declaration of Human Rights (UDHR) in 1947, the Soviet delegate to the drafting convention subjected the delegates from the United States and the United Kingdom to a fierce critique of the notion of universality. The Soviets drew a link between the abuses of democracy by fascism and drew attention to colonialism and the Western powers' hypocrisy in relation to human rights—seeking the recognition of rights in international law while denying them to colonial territories.[6] The Soviet strategy was centered around attacking the contradictions of the Western powers in relation to racism and colonialism and advancing a clear agenda in relation to antidiscrimination and self-determination, which was conceived in explicitly revolutionary terms.[7] However, in these and earlier discussions, the Soviets were also advancing their own version of universality, one which focused on a Marxist teleology and envisaged a different form of society, emphasizing the importance of economic rights and questioned the role of democracy—or at least the role of democracy as understood by Western European societies.[8] Even then, the difference between those arguing against the UDHR on sovereignty-related grounds and those making a substantive critique of the origins or substance of human rights was not that significant, and most of these different schools of thought in opposition to the UDHR came to revolve around the right of a state to accord different priorities to rights protection.[9] When it came to drafting the instrument that would turn the UDHR into law, the Soviet arguments about universality were highlighted by the U.S. State Department and U.S. lawyers as a justification for resisting the new covenant; a 1951 article in the *American Bar Association Journal* described the draft covenant as a "danger to America."[10]

Meanwhile, in discussions about the new Geneva Conventions, a further split opened up between the United States and the British, who opposed universal jurisdiction for war crimes, and the Netherlands and Belgium, who supported universal jurisdiction.[11] Arguments about the forum in which universal crimes such as genocide should be prosecuted were not easily resolved during the drafting of the Genocide Convention in 1948, and fierce disagreements between the Soviet Union and France had to be resolved by a reaching a series of compromise positions regarding the justiciability of the convention.[12] The cosmopolitan aspirations of some of the leading intellectual backers of the creation of international crimes, such as Raphael Lemkin, were to be progressively dashed; later in his life, Lemkin would spend a lot of effort attempting to get the convention adopted as a national law in order to account for the seeming shortcomings of its universality.[13] The period between 1945 and 1957 in the history of international law—prior to the advent of decolonization—saw the contestation of universality in terms of its substance, form, and forum of interpretation. Writing in 1951, shortly after the outbreak of the Korean War, Kurt Wilk drew a distinction between the universal validity and efficacy of international law and—critiquing international law's positivism—observed that it could gain acceptance through regularized interaction between states.[14] A form of law, Wilk noted, would only "be accepted within any group" where there was "some common understanding of values within that group." The problem international law had, as he saw it, was that it was becoming increasingly particularized, as different states with different ideologies projected their own interpretations of how universality ought to be understood onto international law.[15] Wilk, although he didn't know it, was writing about defensive relativism before the first human rights treaty had even been ratified; as he observed, sovereignty would be used as a defense to universal principles of international law.[16]

The contestation over universality, described above, was not just a reflection of the political forces of the time. As the international political context changed, the contestation over universality evolved in tandem. The contestation over universality is a feature of international law's form, which, as Emmanuelle Jouannet notes, both "transcribes the values of those that create it" and is characterized by a desire to "harmonize the values" of the actors within it.[17] Individual states will therefore seek to project their ideology both in the process of law creation and the process of recognizing certain values as universal, but at the same time present the end process as a unified conception of universal law founded on common values.[18] This makes the process of constructing an international human rights instrument intrinsically ideological, as it involves making choices about which rights to include and how to frame rights, which will, as Jean-Luc Nancy observes, involve the projection of a "latent" ideology.[19] To an extent, therefore, the universality of a legal instrument that places obligations on states to change their laws and policies is contingent.[20] The universal is a construction of a particular time and place, and its codification within a particular instrument is in fact a codification of the time and place of the universal construction.[21] But on a practical level, rights which are framed in abstract terms reflecting a universal norm need to be translated into domestic laws and practices that citizens can use in their day to day lives—this is a basic requirement of all forms of international human rights law.[22] For example, a universal right guaranteeing the freedom to marry, of the sort contained in Article 16 of the Convention on the Elimination of all forms of Discrimination Against Women (CEDAW), requires states to pass a set of domestic laws about very basic things—where you and the person you love can go to register your union, how you will be able to get a legal status for any name change you wish to make, and clarification of the formal procedure for ending a union. In most countries, the physical realization of these rights is in forms or administrative buildings; in the United Kingdom, for example, the forms created by the 1949 Registration of Marriages Act and the often-grey concrete office blocs of local government registry services are the physical and tangible realization of the state party's discharge of its obligations under Article 16 of CEDAW.

International human rights law does not prescribe how to construct such forms or institutions; instead, it sets out principles which then have to be applied. These can then guide the creation of the laws and institutions, and there is likely to be considerable diversity about how these rights manifest themselves in different jurisdictions. This is sometimes referred to as the "claimability problem" by philosophers, where the abstract text describing a right has to be turned into a set of tangible actions by a duty holder.[23] Yet, international human rights law's specific version of the claimability problem is to assess the duty holder of an obligation in international law—the state—and its role in discharging its obligations. Legal doctrines, such as subsidiarity, are deployed by international human rights bodies in part as a means of acknowledging that states are the ones who actually have to facilitate the rights contained in a human rights instrument and resolve the claimability problem.[24] It has been noted in the literature on human rights implementation that agreeing to be party to a human rights instrument does not mean states have reconciled themselves to a definition of the universal, as the mere act of legal commitment does not subsequently equate to compliance.[25] State motivations in relation to committing to human rights law and protecting human rights are complex, as demonstrated at multiple points throughout this book, but even the most liberal of theorists about human rights law would not posit that the universal realization of rights should, or ought to, result in identical practices for realizing those rights in different countries.[26] There will, for example, be differences in realizing the right to marriage from one country to another—as the European Court of Human Rights (ECtHR) held in *Schalk and Kopf v. Austria*, "the non-existence of common ground between the laws of the Contracting States" justified different standards when it came to recognizing marriage between same sex couples.[27] Therefore, while the nature of universality will vary from one state to the other, the universal is in human rights law providing an aspiration and defining the contours of state decision making. As Pieter van Dijk notes in a commentary on the discussion of relativism at the second World Conference on Human Rights at Vienna in 1993, the difference between states appeared to be "not so much the universal validity of human rights" norms but the question of whether a norm "results in an obligation for universal interpretation and implementation."[28]

Defensive relativism is therefore a natural consequence of having a regime of universal human rights, as states will want to both define the way international human rights law and human rights bodies define the substance of rights and, seemingly, attempt to influence the contours of their decision making. The desire for control stems from the fact that states, which are both obligation holders and the targets of international human rights bodies, are tasked with seeing that those obligations are implemented. States are also concerned about both their reputational sovereignty on the international plane and domestic constituencies whose opinions they have to take into account in relation to the reform of laws to protect rights.[29] As noted earlier in this book, some scholars have called what happens next backlash, and defensive relativism definitely has played a role in backlash.[30] But a more common form of defensive relativism is simply a contestation of the nature of universality from states that wish to remain part of a human rights regime. In the event that there is tension surrounding the implementation of a specific right in circumstances which are politically difficult for the state in question, defensive relativism involves states utilizing an argumentative technique within the existing legal frameworks of international human rights law to carve out an exemption to the law. From the perspective of a human rights advocate or lawyer, the issue here is not the legal frameworks in question. While reservations and the margin of appreciation are explicitly antiuniversal, they are necessary to encourage states to commit to the law. Rather, it is the state construction and definition of culture in the use of these mechanisms, as this allows these mechanisms to be used to gain a legal exemption. Although this weakens human rights protection, defensive relativism does not occur in a vacuum. It is a manifestation of the contestation of the universal in international human rights law. Universality historically had its origins in the colonial-imperial project.[31] Yet, contestations of universality occur not just because of international law's historical provenance but also because of different conceptions of power and control in international law, and because of disagreement over the substance of universality.[32] The arguments between the Soviet Union and United States about the UDHR and the Genocide Convention in the 1940s were contestations of the form, substance, and control of universality in different emerging fields of international law. The broader argument that took place among political scientists and theorists at the end of the Cold War about the triumph of "Western values"—which Samuel Huntington rebuts in *The Clash of Civilizations*—is an object lesson in how notions of how what is and is not universal are always the subject of some form of ideological contest.[33] Defensive relativism describes the precise manifestation of the contestation of universality in international human rights law following the growth of regional mechanisms and human rights treaty bodies. Perhaps more importantly, defensive relativism represents the triumph of international human rights as an ideology; it is a strategic argument used by states wishing to appear rights compliant and often implicitly or explicitly accepts the permeance of legal institutions and the desirability of the language of human rights. Yet at the same time it often represents the failure of international human rights law to achieve substantial changes to people's lives.

Defensive Relativism in Practice

Even though defensive relativism is a feature of international human rights law's form as a universal system of law, where it is used as a form of argument in legal practice it is not always successful. Defensive relativism does not necessarily have to be detrimental to the protection of human rights. It illustrates that international human rights law serves an important instrumental function for states, giving them recognition in the international order, and highlights how states respect international human rights law as a system of belief in that they believe that they need to prove their conduct is legal.[34] Were states unable to make any form of defensive relativist argument, it might even exacerbate backlash or calls for withdrawal from human rights treaties over the seeming intolerance of universalism as applied by international human rights bodies. Yet, in a number of cases where defensive relativism is successful for the state party, as discussed in chapter 8, the net result is a weakening of human rights protection. To improve the protection of human rights, there are three areas where lawyers, human rights defenders and activists could mitigate the adverse impact of defensive relativism for human rights protection with either the deployment of certain counterarguments or by simply recognizing the systemic presence of defensive relativism.

1. Using Defensive Relativism as a Structural Validity Test

One chief problem with the way reservations to treaties are considered is that the state is required to use a legal test which evaluates the object and purpose of the treaty and then holds the reservations up to that treaty to assess to what extent it runs contrary to the object and purpose of the treaty. There has been a wide range of literature critical of the way the object and purpose test has been used in relation to human rights treaties.[35] Vassilis Pergantis summarizes the problems with the object and purpose test, observing that it quickly "lapses into 'anything goes' and is transformed into a 'claim' about substantive morality. . . . [creating] more problems than it resolves."[36] The CEDAW Committee has become increasingly interventionist over the substance of reservations, detailing how certain reservations are incompatible with the version of the object and purpose test contained in Article 28 of CEDAW.[37] However, this can be quite variable, and there is little by way of consistency in the level of detail given by the committee about what substantive changes should be made to reservations to meet the test. This is where defensive relativism could offer a substantive framework for scrutinizing the construction of reservations, not just their permissibility under the object and purpose test or their impact. As outlined in chapters 2, 3, and 6, the construction of reservations with intentionally vague terms is designed to create a legal exemption and points to an overall end-state, as chapter 8 argues, where the facilitative enforcement of human rights is weakened.[38]

Using all three elements of defensive relativism in sequence as a form of test would offer guidance as to how reservations ought to be framed, so as to allow for antiuniversalist divergence over particular issues without undermining rights protection as a whole. If, for example, all three elements of defensive relativism could be identified in the text of a reservation or human rights instrument, this would be grounds for concluding that a reservation or instrument was designed in manner that would be actively detrimental to the protection of human rights. If all three elements weren't clearly present, this might be more indicative of divergence over the nature of universality or substance of human rights. The increasing number of states withdrawing and resubmitting reservations, sometimes following their review by a treaty body or their Universal Periodic Review with the UN Human Rights Council, would be where the application of such a test might be potentially beneficial. Beyond enhancing the assessment of the permissibility of reservations, using the elements of defensive relativism as a means of assessing the potential efficacy of a human rights instrument would be a means of ascertaining whether or not it was structurally defensive relativism. The capacity of rights instruments to be used to create external legitimacy, either for a state or, as in the case of the Association of Southeast Asian Nations (ASEAN) Human Rights Declaration, a regional human rights body to be used as a reputation-shaping instrument rather than an instrument for rights protection, shows why such an approach might be useful for the purpose of assessing human rights protection.[39] While the academic literature on this process is often able to identify these issues in the comparative, by comparing such bodies to their European counterparts there is a less-clear objective standard.[40] Understandably, comparative work of this nature risks enhancing Western-centric understandings of human rights and diminishing genuine attempts to pursue different approaches to human rights law.[41] Yet, in order for the fragmentation of international law not to result in an increasing proliferation of regimes and standards, which could have a detrimental impact on rights protection, there would need to be some form of framework for recognizing different regimes.[42] Thinking about defensive relativism, and the ends those arguments point to, offers a mechanism for thinking about the way rights are limited and provides a form of coherent framework for regime recognition. This could occur without having to simultaneously contest the substance of universality or who controls universality, which, as outlined above, is always going to be the site of ideological contest.

2. Recognizing the Way the Margin of Appreciation is Used by Defensive Relativists

As outlined in chapters 3, 5, and 8, the way that states practicing defensive relativism have attempted to use the margin of appreciation has been to claim maximal subsidiarity. This maintains that the balancing of rights should be the unchecked prerogative of state institutions and authorities. Some form of balancing of rights is necessary due to the diverse nature of societies and the different interests within them, in order to give meaning to human rights in different countries.[43] As the ECtHR puts it, sometimes institutions need to weigh rights against other interests because "pluralism and democracy [are] based on a compromise that requires various concessions by individuals or groups of individuals, who must sometimes agree to limit some of the freedoms they enjoy."[44] The Human Rights Committee (HRC) does not use the margin of appreciation doctrine when interpreting the International Covenant on Civil and Political Rights (ICCPR), and has gone so far as to disavow the very concept; however, it still operates a principle of subsidiarity and requires states to demonstrate how they have balanced different interests when limiting rights.[45] Increasing skepticism has surrounded the application of the margin of appreciation by the ECtHR and the Inter-American Court of Human Rights (IACtHR).[46] Writing in 2011, Jan Kratochvíl noted that the inconsistency surrounding the application of the doctrine was in fact masking an increasingly deferential approach in its use.[47] The adoption of Protocol 15, incorporating the margin of appreciation into the text of the European Convention on Human Rights (ECHR), did not fundamentally alter the doctrine and was principally designed to address concerns that member states had about the legitimacy of the ECtHR as an institution.[48] In fact, some concern was expressed that Protocol 15 could have the effect of making the application of the doctrine even more deferential to the interests of certain state parties by having a less-rigorous standard of review for states with more established legal systems.[49]

The width of the margin of appreciation, the latitude granted for states to restrict rights under the doctrine, remains considerable in some areas where defensive relativism is an issue. In cases relating to the protection of speech, religious freedom, and privacy, there can be, as Oddný Mjöll Arnardóttir argues, a problem in the ECtHR's failure to distinguish between "deference to others for non-merits reasons and variable standards of review."[50] Janneke

Gerards, criticizing the margin of appreciation in a 2018 article, describes it as an increasingly "empty rhetorical device" and proposes an alternative mechanism of "incrementalism."[51] The danger with the margin of appreciation is that its approach to deference becomes circular, because, as Gerards argues, it relies on a "precedent based approach" which results in the ECtHR according "a certain margin of appreciation because it has already done so in earlier cases on a similar topic."[52] Instead, incrementalism, which involves focusing on the facts at hand, developing the meaning of the rights in a manner limited to a case's facts and not departing from precedent without clearly stated reasons, offers a more comprehensive and accountable framework for assessing a state's laws limiting rights. As Gerards notes, there is a line of case law on abortion and euthanasia which has shown how the ECtHR can "gradually provide a higher level of protection" for certain rights but engage with a state party to acknowledge its different legal and cultural traditions.[53] By taking a "gradual, step-by-step approach" before formulating general principles, the court is allowed to be as "deferential as it thinks is necessary" without blocking the substantive review of the individual practice or the state's balance of rights in the issue in question.[54] Other scholars have noted the way that the ECtHR, following cases such as *Animal Defenders International v. UK*, is increasingly looking at the substantive way decisions are made balancing rights, and is willing to make qualitative assessments of the way states balance rights.[55] This makes it harder for defensive relativists to advance state constructions of culture, although the margin of appreciation doctrine can still be applied in a highly deferential manner, as cases such as *SAS v. France* demonstrate.[56] The ECtHR's case law in this area is also quite influential on other interpretative bodies.[57] While the ECtHR might have the tools to develop an approach to the margin of appreciation that would limit defensive relativism, the institutional context within which it operates can make it wary about taking actions which may further exacerbate backlash from its member states.[58]

3. Treating "Culture" the Same as Security when Justifying the Restrictions of Rights

One of the themes of this book has been that cultural arguments are not really any different from other forms of argument advanced by states in relation to their limitations of human rights law. A cultural argument can be an appeal by a state to respect its domestic-legal sovereignty in general, such as when a state argues that a domestic institution has already made a determination in relation to the balancing of a particular right.[59] It also can be an appeal by a state motivated by the presence of a noncompliance constituency within the state—for example, a religious group with majority support could argue in favor of restricting the right to religious pluralism in order to protect its social status, as explored in chapter 5.[60] National security or security concerns have often intertwined with the question of sovereignty, as detailed in chapter 8, as a justification for the limitations of human rights. Human rights limitations can be justified on national security grounds both through the mechanism of derogation clauses, which involve suspending rights in times of emergency (as discussed in chapter 3), and through other limitation mechanisms.[61] Both security and defensive relativist claims are part of a wider construction of the public interest by the state which then serves as a justification for limiting rights.

Aileen McHarg conceptually divides the notion of the public interest into three categories. First, the preponderance interest, which assesses the notion of the interests that a population holds in aggregate, such as, for example, the notion that a certain religion ought to be treated in a particular way by the law.[62] Secondly, the unitary interest sees the broader public interest as overriding individual concerns, which, as McHarg notes, is often used in cases involving national interests such as security, resulting in rights being used as "trumps"—both by claimants to protect their individual interests and with state authorities pushing back and claiming that individual interests need to be "balanced" with the "unitary" public interest, with the public interest usually being favored in such arguments.[63] Defensive relativists have also used similar claims, as detailed in chapter 4; the construction of the ASEAN Human Rights Declaration fused together national authority with cultural symbolism that predated many of ASEAN's nation-states to create a form of unitary public interest which overrides the rights of individuals in the declaration.[64] Finally, there is the common interest conception of the public interest which "refers to interests which all members of the public have in common" distinct from individuals or groups, which McHarg argues carries "no moral authority" in and of itself.[65] Yet states may still cite the existence of a common interest as evidence of a moral concern that justifies the restriction of rights, in the way that some states use the existence of a common interest in relation to the general protection of public order, or the upholding of traditional interpretations on the nature of marriage to restrict LGBT rights.[66]

Yet, in all of these conceptions of the public interest, whether invoked in the interest of security or in the interest of cultural values, there is a clear construction on the part of state parties of that interest. In cases where a state derogates from a particular right in a time of emergency, there is some (albeit often quite deferential to the state party) scrutiny of the state's prerogative in relation to national security—either by an analysis of whether or not a state was right to declare an emergency or on the measures taken.[67] Review of a state party's construction of values in relation to relativism occurs mainly indirectly, such as in an analysis of whether a particular practice falls into a state's margin of appreciation or whether a reservation is permissible, which is concerned with whether a decision a state party has made fits into a particular template of legality.[68] Rarely does a state need to justify before a review body how it has constructed culture or what kind of values it has relied on in formulating a restriction of rights. Even though the level of scrutiny afforded by human rights of the exercise of security as a justification for the restriction of rights is limited, it nevertheless enables a more precise discourse around the legitimacy of government action in restricting rights in circumstances where defensive relativism is used. Defensive relativism's cultural claims, which often come in the form of black box references to "cultural values," "tradition," or references to religious authority in highly generalized terms (such as "Sharia") are too often treated as fact claims rather than constructed assumptions about society which can be interrogated. This is not just a suggestion for legal reform but a broader suggestion to those who advocate for human rights to be more skeptical about the use of blanket cultural references by state parties. The importance of remaining critical about the state construction of the public interest in relation to security is highlighted by Rosa Ehrenreich Brooks, who notes that terms such as "war" or "emergency" can be altered or reinterpreted by states, and hence the calculations involved in balancing rights would alter.[69] In similar fashion, bracketing defensive relativism uncritically as a public interest concern could have a direct impact on the way certain rights are perceived and certain rights claims are assessed. Civil society organizations and NGOs based in particular countries, as well as anthropologists and sociologists, have gone this way in responding to the culturally relativist claims made by states—by trying to unpick the factual veracity of these claims and challenging the construction of common interests at the heart of such arguments.

The End(s) of Defensive Relativism

In the final chapter of this book, the end or ends of defensive relativism are shown to be the defense of different forms of sovereignty within the framework of human rights law. In the mid-1990s, both Adamantia Pollis and Anne Bayefsky independently drew the link between the increasing use of arguments premised on culture or cultural values as a defense of sovereignty.[70] Other scholars in the late 1990s and early 2000s located this within the discourse on globalization and the role of the "local" as a form of resistance to universalizing and global values.[71] As Guyora Binder noted, international human rights law's reliance on its universalized morality as a proxy for legitimacy meant that it was almost inevitable that despite some of its logical contradictions, relativism would be used to defend state sovereignty.[72] The dilution sovereignty as the *Letztbegründung* (first principle) of international law was a result of many different factors, one of which was the spread of international human rights law and rising numbers of states signing up to human rights treaties.[73] The move to a more human-centric conception of international law, however, was not value neutral, and as cosmopolitan critics of human rights law frequently insisted, this was the extension of a particular philosophy of the individual, leading to claims that international human rights law was a form of imperialism from some states or represented a hidden political ideology from others.[74] Concerns about sovereignty can also be seen elsewhere in literature on the future of human rights reflecting anxieties that the idea of universal norms were unsuited to supranational legal forms.[75] As much of this literature can be traced back to the 1990s, it is illustrative of how large a factor contestations over sovereignty were in shaping the debate about cultural relativism and international human rights law.[76]

The protection of sovereignty is an inescapable part of the way that arguments about cultural relativism and human rights have played out. The local, the communal, or the cultural are in the system of international law located in the state, which is itself the subject of international law. By its very form, international law universalizes concepts across cultures because it seeks to provide sets of norms that operate as an independent constraint on states. As the state represents cultural and moral norms in the process of its domestic lawmaking or its domestic-legal sovereignty, the subset of international law of international human rights law represents a challenge to domestic-legal sovereignty, as it aims to create both shared morals and shared subjects of the law outside of the state. Management, pushback, or even backlash to that implicit challenge to sovereignty from the state party is a regular feature of international human rights law, both because of its challenge to sovereign authority and because of the indeterminacy of the law's substantive provisions and its claim to universality.[77] Defensive relativism is an attempt to systematize how this process happens in practice.

But in systematizing this process, defensive relativism's near inevitability has also been highlighted. It is possible that a system of human rights law, with interpretative bodies and an enforcement mechanism, could be created to function above the nation state without defensive relativism being a feature in its operation, but this has not yet happened. Furthermore, it is unlikely to ever happen, because of the inherent conceptual tensions in the whole idea of universality described above. It might be tempting to take refuge in teleology and assume that defensive relativism is used in relation to issues where there is a gradual social change occurring, and that defensive relativism is simply a transitional reaction from the state. LGBT rights over the previous thirty years have advanced in many countries, despite governments using defensive relativist arguments against international human rights bodies and instruments which have helped facilitate these advances. But this would be to confuse subject with form—defensive relativism is a reaction to the law, and what it attempts to do the subject matter explains the reason why a state may have decided to utilize defensive relativism to resist human rights in that specific incident. It also takes a "Whig" view of the history of human rights, where societies are in a constant movement toward some form of progressive ideal. Societies evolve, and new issues emerge which may be rights claims—or they may bring new claims. In the 1970s, as the evolutive interpretation of the ECHR was being developed by the ECtHR, it was hard to foresee how multiculturalism would develop in some Western European societies, leading to new battles over laws restricting Article 9 (freedom of religion) of the ECHR.

The end or ends of defensive relativism are the preservation of a state of equilibrium where international human rights law retains its overall function for providing public order norms and a standard for assessing the legitimate actions of states, but gives legal mechanisms to states to resist the application of rights in an open-ended fashion. This can quickly stray into outright discrimination in the application of certain rights, or the removal of rights protection altogether. But it can also simply operate as a background feature to a human rights regime, unnoticed until it becomes an issue for a state as it responds to a changing social situation. In a world of cultural difference but increasing interconnection, the need to define difference has become more important for states and the communities living within them. In tandem with this, the 2010s saw a growth of skepticism about international law and its institutions. All of this has made defensive relativism in international human rights law more likely than ever. Managing which end or ends of defensive relativism actually occur thus remains the unenviable task of the individual legal practitioner or human rights defender.

NOTES

Introduction

All links accessed 21 July 2019 unless stated otherwise.

1. Undule Mwakasungula, "The LGBT Situation in Malawi: An Activist Perspective," in Corinne Lennox and Matthew Waites (eds.) *Human Rights, Sexual Orientation and Gender Identity in The Commonwealth: Struggles for Decriminalisation and Change* (School of Advanced Study, University of London, 2013) 261.

2. BBC News, "Malawi Gay Couple Get Maximum Sentence of 14 Years," 20 May 2010, http://www.bbc.co.uk/news/10130240.

3. Mwakasungula (n. 1).

4. Kim Yi Dionne and Boniface Dulani, "This One Graph Shows the Biggest Threat to LGBT Rights in Malawi," Washington Post 1 March 2016, https://www.washingtonpost.com/news/monkey-cage/wp/2016/03/01/this-one-graph-shows-the-biggest-threat-to-lgbt-rights-in-malawi/?utm_term=.30a7d2c970bb.

5. *Toonen v. Australia*, No. 488/1992, UN Doc. CCPR/C/50/D/488/1992 (1994).

6. Mwakasungula (n. 1).

7. *Ms. Juliet Joslin et al. v. New Zealand*, Communication No. 902/1999, UN Doc. A/57/40 at 214 (2002) para. 4.

8. *Lautsi v. Italy*, Application No. 30814/06 (Grand Chamber, 18 March 2011) para. 30-36. The initial 2009 decision was later overturned in the Grand Chamber of the European Court of Human Rights.

9. Lynn Hunt, *Inventing Human Rights: A History* (Norton, 2010) Introduction.

10. This school and other schools of thought on this point are discussed in Marie-Benedicte Dembour, "What are Human Rights? Four Schools of Thought" (2010) 32 Human Rights Quarterly (HRQ) 1.

11. For an example, see Upendra Baxi, "Voices of Suffering and the Future of Human Rights" (1998) 8 Transnational Law and Contemporary Problems 125.

12. Janet Holl Madigan, *Truth, Politics, and Universal Human Rights* (Palgrave Macmillan, 2007) 54.

13. Alison Dundes Renteln, "The Unanswered Challenge of Relativism and the Consequences for Human Rights" (1985) 7 Human Rights Quarterly (HRQ) 514.

14. Stanford Encyclopedia of Philosophy, "Moral Relativism," first published 19 Feb 2004, substantive revision 9 Dec 2008, http://www.science.uva.nl/~seop/archives/win2008/entries/moral-relativism/ accessed 11 December 2012.

15. Neil Levy, *Moral Relativism: A Short Introduction* (Oneworld, 2002) 4-8.

16. Steven Lukes, *Moral Relativism* (Profile, 2009) 20.

17. For this specific example, see Richard Shweder, "In Defense of Moral Realism: Reply to Gabennesch" (1990) 61 Child Development 2060.

18. D. Loeb, "Moral Realism and the Argument from Disagreement" (1998) 90 Philosophical Studies: An International Journal for Philosophy in the Analytic Tradition 281.

19. Franz Boas, *The Mind of Primitive Man* (Macmillan Company, 1911) 5-20.

20. See Ruth Benedict, *Patterns of Culture* (Houghton Mifflin, 1934) 278.

21. Lévi-Strauss noted this was a fictitious story designed to prove a point. Claude Lévi-Strauss, *Myth and Meaning: Cracking the Code of Culture* (Schocken Books, 1979) 18-22.

22. Melville Herskovits, "Some Further Comments on Cultural Relativism" (1958) 60 American Anthropologist New Series 266.

23. Antony Anghie, *Imperialism, Sovereignty and the Making of International Law* (Cambridge University Press, 2004) 40-70.

24. Herskovits (n. 22) 543.

25. See Johannes Morsink, *Inherent Human Rights: Philosophical Roots of the Universal Declaration* (University of Pennsylvania Press, 2009) chp. 2.

26. Christos Galanos, "Universal Human Rights in the Face of Cultural Relativism and Moral Objectivity: Preaching or Teaching?" (2010) 16 UCL Jurisprudence Review 29, 31.

27. For two of the leading studies making this argument, see Jack Donnelly, "Cultural Relativism and Universal Human Rights" (1984) 6 Human Rights Quarterly (HRQ) 400; Fernando Teson, "International Human Rights and Cultural Relativism" (1984) 25 Virginia Journal of International Law 869.

28. For an example, see Chris Brown, 'Universal Human Rights: A Critique" (1997) 1 International Journal of Human Rights 41.

29. Abdullahi Ahmed An-Na'im, "Towards a Cross-Cultural Approach to Defining International Standards of Human Rights: The Meaning of Cruel, Inhuman or Degrading Treatment," in An-Na'im (ed.) *Human Rights in Cross-Cultural Perspectives: A Quest for Consensus*, 2nd ed. (Princeton University Press, 1995) 37. See also Josiah Cobbah, "African Values and the Human Rights Debate: An African Perspective" (1987) 9 Human Rights Quarterly (HRQ) 303.

30. Federico Lenzerini, *The Culturalization of Human Rights Law* (Oxford University Press, 2014).

31. See Mark Goodale, "Introduction: Locating Rights, Envisioning Law between the Global and the Local," as well as Sally Engle Merry, "Introduction," in Mark Goodale and Sally Engle Merry (eds.) *The Practice of Human Rights: Tracking Law between the Global and the Local* (Cambridge University Press, 2007).

32. Yale H. Ferguson and Richard W. Mansbach, *Remapping Global Politics: History's Revenge and Future Shock* (Cambridge University Press, 2004) 44.

33. Ibid., 46.

34. Kamari Maxine Clarke, "Internationalizing the Statecraft: Genocide, Religious Revivalism, and the Cultural Politics of International Criminal Law" (2006) 28 Loyola Los Angeles International and Comparative Law Review 279, 290.

35. Alexander Hinton, "The Dark Side of Modernity: Toward an Anthropology of Genocide," in Alexander Hinton (ed.) *Annihilating Difference: The Anthropology of Genocide* (University of California Press, 2002) 2.

36. Andrew Harding, "Comparative Law and Legal Transplantation in South East Asia," in David Nelken and Johannes Feest (eds.) *Adapting Legal Cultures* (Hart Publishing, 2001) 200.

37. Belinda Clark, "The Vienna Convention Reservations Regime and the Convention on Discrimination Against Women" (1991) 85 American Journal of International Law (AJIL) 281.

38. Ibid.

39. For examples, see Oona Hathaway, "Why Do Countries Commit to Human Rights Treaties?' (2007) 51 Journal of Conflict Resolution 588; Richard Nielsen and Beth Simmons, "Rewards for Ratification: Payoffs for Participating in the International Human Rights Regime?" (2015) 59 International Studies Quarterly 197.

40. Office of the United Nations High Commissioner for Human Rights, "Monitoring the Core International Human Rights Treaties," https://www.ohchr.org/EN/HRBodies/Pages/WhatTBDo.aspx accessed 20 February 2021.

41. These nine treaties are: the 1951 Refugee Convention, the 1965 International Convention on the Elimination of All Forms of Racial Discrimination, ICCPR, ICESCR, CEDAW, the UN Convention Against Torture (CAT), the 1989 Convention on the Rights of the Child, 2006 Convention on the Rights of Persons with Disabilities, and the 2006 International Convention for the Protection of All Persons from Enforced Disappearance.

42. Vienna Convention on the Law of Treaties (opened for signature 23 May 1969, entered into force 27 January 1980) 115 UNTS 331.

43. UN Human Rights Committee, General Comment No. 31, Nature of the General Legal Obligation Imposed on States Parties to the Covenant, (26 May 2004) CCPR/C/21/Rev.1/Add.13, para.12.

44. Oscar Garibaldi, "General Limitations on Human Rights: The Principle of Legality" (1976) 17 Harvard International Law Journal 503, 518.

45. Ibid.

46. See Steven Greer, *The European Convention on Human Rights: Achievements, Problems and Prospects*, 2nd ed. (Cambridge University Press, 2008) 8-40.

47. See Chidi Anselm Odinkalu, "The Individual Complaints Procedures of the African Commission on Human and Peoples' Rights: A Preliminary Assessment" (1998) 8 Transnational Law and Contemporary Problems 359.

48. Vienna Convention (n. 42) Art. 19.

49. Concerning Reservations to the Genocide Convention (Advisory Opinion) ICJ Rep 1, 23 (1951).

50. Ryan Goodman, "Human Rights Treaties, Invalid Reservations, and State Consent" (2002) 96 American Journal of International Law (AJIL) 531.

51. Steven Greer, *The Margin of Appreciation: Interpretation and Discretion under the European Convention on Human Rights* (Council of Europe Publishing, 2000) 5.

52. Dominic McGoldrick, "A Defence of the Margin of Appreciation and an Argument for Its Application by the Human Rights Committee" (2016) 65 International and Comparative Law Quarterly 21.

53. Ibid.

54. Christian Reus-Smit, "Politics and International Legal Obligation" (2003) 4 European Journal of International Relations 591. Barbara Koremenos et al., "The Rational Design of International Institutions," in Barbara Koremenos, Charles Lipson, and Duncan Snidal (eds.) *The Rational Design of International Institutions* (Cambridge University Press, 2004).

55. Douglas Irvin-Erickson, *Raphaël Lemkin and the Concept of Genocide* (University of Pennsylvania Press, 2017) 201.

56. See Anton Weiss-Wendt, *The Soviet Union and the Gutting of the UN Genocide Convention* (University of Wisconsin Press, 2016) chp. 6; Douglas Irvin-Erickson, "From Gena to Nuremberg to New York: Andrei Vyshinsky, Raphaël Lemkin, and the Struggle to Outlaw Revolutionary Violence, State Terror, and Genocide," in David Crowe, *Stalin's Soviet Justice: 'Show' Trials, War Crimes Trials, and Nuremberg* (Bloomsbury Academic, 2019).

57. Ida Bostian, "Cultural Relativism in International War Crimes Prosecutions: The International Criminal Tribunal for Rwanda" (2005) 12 ILSA Journal of International and Comparative Law 1; Mireille Delmas-Marty, "Interactions between National and International Criminal Law in the Preliminary Phase of Trial at the ICC" (2006) Journal of International Criminal Justice 2.

58. Jane E. Stromseth, "The International Criminal Court and Justice on the Ground" (2011) 43 Arizona State Law Journal 427, 436.

59. Luis E. Rodriguez-Rivera, "Is the Human Right to Environment Recognized under International Law? It Depends on the Source" (2001) 12 Colorado Journal of International Environmental Law and Policy 1; Roda Mushkat, "Contextualizing Environmental Human Rights: A Relativist Perspective" (2009) 26 Pace Environmental Law Review 119.

60. Kathryn Hochstetler, Ann Marie Clark, and Elisabeth Friedman, "Sovereignty in the Balance: Claims and Bargains at the UN Conferences on the Environment, Human Rights, and Women" (2000) 44 International Studies Quarterly 591.

61. Anthony Langlois, "Human Rights: The Globalisation and Fragmentation of Moral Discourse" (2002) 28 Review of International Studies 479.

62. Upendra Baxi, *Human Rights in a Posthuman World: Critical Essays* (Oxford University Press, 2008) 31.

63. Ibid.

64. Ibid.

65. Emilie Hafner-Burton, *Making Human Rights A Reality* (Princeton University Press, 2013) 5.

66. Andrew Vincent, *The Politics of Human Rights* (Oxford University Press, 2010) 158 and 165.

67. Samuel Moyn, "Plural Cosmopolitanism and the Origin of Human Rights," in Costas Douzinas and Conor Gearty, *The Meanings of Rights: The Philosophy and Social Theory of Human Rights* (Cambridge University Press 2014) 208-211.

68. For an account of this history, see Lynn Hunt, *Inventing Human Rights: A History* (Norton, 2008) chp. 1-3.

69. Sharon Detrick, Jaap Doek, and Nigel Cantwell, *The United Nations Convention on the Rights of the Child: A Guide to the "Travaux Préparatoires"* (Martinus Nijhoff 1992) 155-156, 392-393.

70. Katarina Tomaševski, *Responding to Human Rights Violations, 1946-1999* (Martinus Nijhoff, 2012) xi.

71. Illan rua Wall, *Human Rights and Constituent Power: Without Model or Warranty* (Routledge, 2012) 27-34.

72. See Bina Obinna Okere, "The Protection of Human Rights in Africa and the African Charter on Human and Peoples' Rights: A Comparative Analysis with European and American Systems" (1984) 6 Human Rights Quarterly (HRQ) 141.

73. Alison Dundes Renteln, *International Human Rights: Universalism Versus Relativism*, 3rd ed. (Quid Pro Books, 2013) Introduction.

74. See Tomaševski (n. 70) and Joseph Raz, "Human Rights in the Emerging World Order" (2010) 1 Transnational Law Review 31, 46.

75. William Paul Simmons, *Human Rights Law and the Marginalised Other* (Cambridge University Press, 2014).

76. For an overview, see Christian Djeffal, *Static and Evolutive Treaty Interpretation: A Functional Reconstruction* (Cambridge University Press, 2016).

77. Jean d'Aspremont, *International Law as a Belief System* (Cambridge University Press, 2018) 55.

78. Ibid.; The idea that state behavior is affected by international law is derived from a set of liberal presumptions about the law. See Martti Koskenniemi, *From Apology to Utopia: The Structure of International Legal Argument* (Cambridge University Press, 2005) 218-223; Anne-Marie Slaughter, "International Law in a World of Liberal States" (1995) 6 European Journal of International Law (EJIL) 503.

79. Onuma Yasuaki, "International Law in and with International Politics: The Functions of International Law in International Society" (2003) 14 European Journal of International Law (EJIL) 105.

80. Ibid.

81. Andrew Guzman, "Reputation and International Law" (2005) 34 Georgia Journal of International and Comparative Law 379; Dana Zartner and Jennifer Ramos, "Human Rights as Reputation Builder: Compliance with the Convention against Torture" (2011) 12 Human Rights Review 71.

82. For a comprehensive overview, see Erica Chenoweth et al., "Struggles from Below: Literature Review on Human Rights Struggles by Domestic Actors" (USAID/DCHA/DRG Working Papers Series, 21 February 2017) https://www.usaid.gov/sites/default/files/documents/2496/Struggles_from_Below_-_Literature_Review_on_Human_Rights_Struggles_by_Domestic_Actors.pdf

83. See Thomas Risse and Stephen Ropp, "Introduction and Overview," in Thomas Risse, Stephen Ropp, and Kathryn Sikkink (eds.) *The Persistent Power of Human Rights: From Commitment to Compliance* (Cambridge University Press, 2013).

84. For an explanation of this concept, see Sonia Cardenas, *Conflict and Compliance: State Responses to International Human Rights Pressure* (University of Pennsylvania Press, 2010) 27-29.

85. *Mellet v. Ireland*, CCPR/C/116/D/2324/201317 (November 2016).

86. See Michele Brandt and Jeffrey Kaplan, "The Tension between Women's Rights and Religious Rights: Reservations to CEDAW by Egypt, Bangladesh and Tunisia" (1995) 12 Journal of Law and Religion 105.

87. See Brooke Ackerly, *Universal Human Rights in a World of Difference* (Cambridge University Press, 2008) 1-39.

88. See Lenzerini (n. 30) and Tom Zwart, "Using Local Culture to Further the Implementation of International Human Rights: The Receptor Approach" (2012) 34 Human Rights Quarterly (HRQ) 546.

89. Jack Donnelly, "The Relative Universality of Human Rights" (2007) 29 Human Rights Quarterly (HRQ) 282, 283.

90. Renteln (n. 13) 527.

91. Donnelly (n. 89).

92. Rhoda Howard, "Human Rights and the Culture Wars: Globalization and the Universality of Human Rights" (1997) 53 International Journal 94, 95

93. Ibid., 97.

94. The mean number of treaties ratified increased most sharply in the ten-year period from 1987 to 1997. For details of this data, see Christine Min Wotipka and Kiyoteru Tsutsui, "Global Human Rights and State Sovereignty: State Ratification of International Human Rights Treaties, 1965-2001" (2008) 23 Sociological Forum 724, 729.

95. In general, see Eric Posner *The Twilight of Human Rights Law* (Oxford University Press, 2014); Leslie Vinjamuri, "Human Rights Backlash," in Stephen Hopgood, Jack Snyder, and Leslie Vinjamuri (eds.) *Human Rights Futures* (Cambridge University Press, 2017) 114; Wayne Sandholtz, Yining Bei, and Kayla Caldwell, "Backlash and International Human Rights Courts," in Alison Brysk and Michael Stohl (eds.) *Contracting Human Rights: Crisis, Accountability, and Opportunity* (Edward Elgar, 2018).

96. David Penna and Patricia Campbell, "Human Rights and Culture: Beyond Universality and Relativism" (1998) 19 Third World Quarterly 7, 18.

97. Adamantia Pollis, "Cultural Relativism Revisited: Through a State Prism" (1996) 18 Human Rights Quarterly (HRQ) 316, 320.

98. See *SAS v. France*, ECHR 695 (2014); *Belcacemi and Oussar v. Belgium*, ECHR 655 (2017).

99. Renteln (n. 13).

100. See Richard Wike, "Global Opinion Varies Widely on Use of Torture against Suspected Terrorists," Pew Research Centre 9 February 2016, http://www.pewresearch.org/fact-tank/2016/02/09/global-opinion-use-of-torture/. Amnesty International, "Stop Torture Global Survey: Attitudes to Torture," Amnesty International May 2014, https://www.amnestyusa.org/pdfs/GlobalSurveyAttitudesToTorture2014.pdf.

101. William Jordan, "Scepticism about human rights as well as the ECHR," YouGov 20 July 2014, https://yougov.co.uk/news/2014/07/20/scepticism-about-human-rights-well-echr/.

102. Tony Evans, "International Human Rights Law as Power/Knowledge" (2005) 27 Human Rights Quarterly (HRQ) 1046.

Chapter 1

1. Declaration by the United Nations, 1 January 1942, http://avalon.law.yale.edu/20th_century/decade03.asp accessed 31 March 2019.

2. See Roland Burke, "From Individual Rights to National Development: The First UN International Conference on Human Rights, Tehran, 1968" (2008) 19 Journal of World History 275.

3. See Diane Otto, "Rethinking the 'Universality' of Human Rights Law" (1997) 29 Human Rights Law Review 1.

4. International Covenant on Civil and Political Rights (ICCPR) (adopted 16 December 1966, entered into force 23 March 1976) 999 UNTS 171, Art. 2(1).

5. On this argument, see Abram Chayes and Antonia Handler Chayes, "On Compliance" (1993) 47 International Organization, 175. See also Oona A. Hathaway, "Do Human Rights Treaties Make a Difference?" (2002) 111 The Yale Law Journal 1935.

6. See Prosper Weil, "Towards Relative Normativity in International Law?" (1983) 77 American Journal of International Law (AJIL) 413.

7. See, respectively, Legality of the Threat or Use of Nuclear Weapons (Advisory Opinion) ICJ Rep 226, 395 (Dissenting Opinion of Judge Shahabuddeen) (1996); Case Concerning the Application of the Convention of 1902 Governing the Guardianship of Infants (Netherlands v. Sweden), ICJ Reports 95 (Separate Opinion of Judge Lauterpacht) (1958).

8. Elena Proukaki, *The Problem of Enforcement in International Law: Countermeasures, the Non-Injured State and the Idea of International Community* (Routledge, 2010) 16. William Conklin, "The Peremptory Norms of the International Community" (2012) 23 European Journal of International Law (EJIL) 837.

9. Jane E. Stromseth, "The International Criminal Court and Justice on the Ground" (2011) 43 Arizona State Law Journal 427.

10. Seyla Benhabib, *Dignity in Adversity: Human Rights in Troubled Times* (Polity, 2011) 11.

11. Philip Alston, "The Best Interests Principle: Towards a Reconciliation of Culture and Human Rights." (1994) 8 International Journal of Law, Policy and the Family 1, 8.

12. Donnelly describes this argument as "International Legal Universality." Jack Donnelly "The Relative Universality of Human Rights" (2007) 29 Human Rights Quarterly (HRQ) 281.

13. Alison Dundes Renteln "The Unanswered Challenge of Relativism and the Consequences for Human Rights." (1985) 7 Human Rights Quarterly (HRQ) 514.

14. Universal Declaration of Human Rights (UDHR) (1948) UNGA Res 217A (III), preamble.

15. See Johannes Morsink, *The Universal Declaration of Human Rights: Origins, Drafting, and Intent* (University of Pennsylvania Press, 1999) 4-6.

16. Seyla Benhabib, "Another Universalism: On the Unity and Diversity of Human Rights" (2007) 81 Proceedings and Addresses of the American Philosophical Association 7, 13.

17. See David Held, *Cosmopolitanism: Ideas and Realities* (Polity, 2010) 67-70.

18. Convention on the Elimination of All Forms of Discrimination against Women (CEDAW) (adopted 18 December 1979, entered into force 3 September 1981) 1249 UNTS 13, preamble.

19. Ibid.

20. Arvonne Fraser, "Becoming Human: The Origins and Developments of Women's Human Rights" (1999) 21 Human Rights Quarterly (HRQ) 853.

21. Wade Mansell and Karen Openshaw, *International Law: A Critical Introduction* (Hart, 2013) 135.

22. Alison Dundes Renteln "The Concept of Human Rights." (1988) 83 Anthropos 343.

23. Shirley Scott, "International Law as Ideology: Theorizing the Relationship between International Law and International Politics (1994) 5 European Journal of International Law (EJIL) 313, 319-321.

24. Steven Lukes, *Moral Relativism* (Profile, 2009) 16.

25. For key literature on state consent in relation to human rights treaties, see Ryan Goodman, "Human Rights Treaties, Invalid Reservations, and State Consent." (2002) 96 American Journal of International Law (AJIL) 531; Gerald Neuman, "Import, Export, and Regional Consent in the Inter-American Court of Human Rights." (2008) 19 European Journal of International Law (EJIL) 101.

26. This is explored further in chapter 3, but as several scholars have noted, the fact that human rights law confers benefits to citizens in a state but not to states themselves creates an inverse legitimacy conundrum requiring a high level of state acquiescence in the realization of the obligation. See Beth Simmons, *Mobilizing for Human Rights: International Law in Domestic Politics* (Cambridge University Press, 2009) 126.

27. Mark Balaguer, "Bare Bones Moral Realism and the Objections from Relativism," In Steven Hales (ed.) *A Companion to Relativism* (Wiley-Blackwell, 2011) 376.

28. Ibid.

29. Jack Donnelly, "Cultural Relativism and Universal Human Rights" (1984) 6 Human Rights Quarterly (HRQ) 400, 403.

30. Robert Meister, *After Evil: A Politics of Human Rights* (Columbia University Press, 2011) 114-115.

31. Carl Schmitt, *The* Nomos *of the Earth in the International Law of* the Jus Publicum Europaeum (Telos, 2003) 86. First published 1950.

32. Neil Levy, *Moral Relativism: A Short Introduction* (Oneworld, 2002) 30.

33. José-Manuel Barreto, "Imperialism and Decolonization as Scenarios of Human Rights History," in José-Manuel Barreto (ed.) *Human Rights from a Third World Perspective: Critique, History and International Law* (Cambridge Scholars Publishing, 2013) 142-143.

34. Ibid.

35. Daniel Brunstetter, "Sepúlveda, Las Casas, and the Other: Exploring the Tension between Moral Universalism and Alterity" (2010) 72 Review of Politics 409.

36. Michael Hardt and Antonio Negri, *Empire* (Harvard University Press, 2000) 115.

37. Antony Anghie, *Imperialism, Sovereignty and the Making of International Law* (Cambridge University Press, 2004) 19-20.

38. See Turan Kayaoglu, "Westphalian Eurocentrism in International Relations Theory" (2010) 12 International Studies Review 193.

39. This argument is made by Shelley Wright, *International Human Rights, Decolonisation and Globalisation: Becoming Human* (Routledge, 2001) chp. 2.

40. Hannes Cannie and Dirk Voorhoof, "The Abuse Clause and Freedom of Expression in the European Human Rights Convention: An Added Value for Democracy and Human Rights Protection?" (2011) 29 Netherlands Quarterly of Human Rights 54, 56-58.

41. Michael Banton, *International Action against Racial Discrimination* (Clarendon Press, 1996) 60.

42. Ibid., 61.

43. Committee on the Elimination of Discrimination Against Women, Consideration of Reports Submitted by States Parties under Article 18 of the Convention, China (8 February 2002) CEDAW/C/SR.421, para 3.

44. Convention on the Rights of the Child, India Reservations on Accession (11 December 1992) C.N.457.1992.TREATIES-19.

45. Committee on the Rights of the Child, Summary Record of 489th Meeting (2 October 1998) CRC/C/SR.489, para. 12.

46. Edward Said, *Culture and Imperialism* (Vintage, 1994) 9.

47. See Lewis Gordon, "Problematic People and Epistemic Decolonization: Toward the Postcolonial in Africana Political Thought," in Nalini Persram (ed.) *Postcolonialism and Political Theory* (Rowman & Littlefield, 2007) 121-142.

48. On the point of alterity, see, among others, Enrique Dussel, "Alterity and Modernity: Las Casas, Vitoria, and Suárez, 1514–1617," in Nalini Persram (ed.) *Postcolonialism and Political Theory* (Rowman & Littlefield, 2007).

49. John Hobson, *The Eurocentric Conception of World Politics: Western International Theory, 1760–2010* (Cambridge University Press, 2012) 72-75.

50. Howard Williams, "Colonialism in Kant's Political Philosophy" (2014) 39 Diametros 154. See also Andreas Føllesdal and Reidar Maliks, "Kantian Theory and Human Rights," in Føllesdal and Maliks (eds.) *Kantian Theory and Human Rights* (Routledge, 2014).

51. For an outline of this, see Domenico Losurdo *Liberalism: A Counter History*, trans. Gregory Elliot (Verso, 2011) 42-44.

52. Alexander Orakhelashvili, "The Idea of European International Law" (2006) 17 European Journal of International Law (EJIL) 315.

53. Michael Mann "'Torchbearers upon the Path of Progress': Britain's Ideology of a 'Moral and Material Progress' in India," in Harald Fischer-Tiné and Michael Mann (eds.) *Colonialism as Civilizing Mission: Cultural Ideology in British India* (Anthem, 2004) 4.

54. Nasser Hussain, *The Jurisprudence of Emergency: Colonialism and the Rule of Law* (University of Michigan Press, 2009) 141-143.

55. Michael Hardt and Antonio Negri, *Empire* (Harvard University Press, 2001) 35-38.

56. UDHR, Art. 28.

57. Karen Engle, "From Scepticism to Embrace: Human Rights and the American Anthropological Association from 1947–1999" (2001) 23 Human Rights Quarterly (HRQ) 536, 538.

58. See Terence Turner, "Human Rights, Human Difference: Anthropology's Contribution to an Emancipatory Cultural Politics" (1997) 53 Journal of Anthropological Research 273; Christos Galanos, "Universal Human Rights in the Face of Cultural Relativism and Moral Objectivity: Preaching or Teaching?" (2010) 16 UCL Jurisprudence Review 29.

59. See the preamble of the ICCPR (n. 4) and the International Covenant on Economic, Social, and Cultural Rights (ICESCR) (adopted 16 December 1966, entered into force 3 January 1976) 993 UNTS 3, preamble.

60. Makau Mutua, "Savages, Victims, and Saviours: The Metaphor of Human Rights" (2001) 42 Harvard International Law Journal 201, 206.

61. Abdullahi Ahmed An-Na'im (ed.) *Human Rights in Cross-Cultural Perspectives: A Quest for Consensus* (University of Pennsylvania Press, 1995).

62. Sonia Harris-Short, "International Human Rights Law: Imperialist, Inept and Ineffective? Cultural Relativism and the UN Convention on the Rights of the Child" (2003) 25 Human Rights Quarterly (HRQ) 130, 153.

63. Committee on the Rights of the Child, Summary Record of the 318th Meeting (22 October 1996) CRC/C/SR.318, para. 43.

64. Committee on the Rights of the Child, Summary Record of the 543rd Meeting (31 May 1999) CRC/C/SR.543, para. 42.

65. Committee on the Rights of the Child, Summary Record of the 489th Meeting (2 October 1998) CRC/C/SR.489 para. 12.

66. William Schabas, "Reservations to the Convention on the Rights of the Child" (1996) 18 Human Rights Quarterly (HRQ) 472, 478.

67. Committee on the Rights of the Child, Summary Record of the 132nd Meeting (12 April 1994) CRC/C/SR.132, para. 15.

68. Committee on the Rights of the Child, Summary Record of the 1444th Meeting (6 April 2010) CRC/C/SR.1444, para. 60.

69. Peter Fitzpatrick, *Modernism and the Grounds of Law* (Cambridge University Press, 2001) 211.

70. Judith Butler, Ernesto Laclau and Slavoj Žižek, *Contingency, Hegemony, Universality: Contemporary Dialogues on the Left* (Verso, 2000) 37.

71. Alison Dundes Renteln, "Relativism and the Search for Human Rights" (1998) 90 American Anthropologist 56.

72. B. G. Ramcharan, "The Universality of Human Rights" (1997) 58 International Commission of Jurists Review 105.

73. For an example of right-wing criticism, see A. Eilan,"*The General Assembly: Can It Be Salvaged?* (Heritage Foundation, 1984). For a historical assessment, see Paul Kennedy, *The Parliament of Man* (Penguin, 2006) 188-191.

74. Charles Beitz, "Human Rights as a Common Concern" (2001) 95 *American Political Science Review* 269.

75. Turner (n. 58) 273, 284.

76. For a summary of this history, see Larry Sidentop, *Inventing the Individual: The Origins of Western Liberalism* (Penguin, 2015) 128-140, 208-220.

77. Costas Douzinas, *Human Rights and Empire: The Political Philosophy of Cosmopolitanism* (Routledge, 2008) 57.

78. Rom Harré, "The 'Self' as a Theoretical Concept," in Michael Krausz (ed.) *Relativism: Interpretation and Confrontation* (University of Notre Dame Press, 1989) 387, 396.

79. Alan Gewirth, "The Epistemology of Human Rights" (1984) 1 Social Philosophy and Policy 1.

80. Daniel Whelan, "The United States and Economic and Social Rights: Past, Present . . . and Future? (2005) 5 Human Rights and Human Welfare 60.

81. For an account of the Russian position, see this Russian state–sponsored paper: Nataliya Semenova et al., "Traditional Values and Human Rights of LGBT under the Contemporary International Law" (2015) 6 Mediterranean Journal of Social Sciences 305; Alekseyev v. Russia (2010) ECHR 1562.

82. For examples of this outside of Russia, see Phillip Ayoub, "Perils of Success: Backlash and Resistance to LGBT Rights in Domestic and International Politics." in Alison Brysk and Michael Stohl (eds.) *Contracting Human Rights: Crisis, Accountability, and Opportunity* (Edward Elgar, 2018).

83. Momin Rahman, "Queer Rights and the Triangulation of Western Exceptionalism (2014) 13 Journal of Human Rights 274; Hendri Yulius, Shawna Tang, and Baden Offord, "The Globalization of LGBT Identity and Same-Sex Marriage as a Catalyst of Neo-institutional Values: Singapore and Indonesia in Focus," in Bronwyn Winter, Maxime Forest, and Réjane Sénac (eds) *Global Perspectives on Same-Sex Marriage: A Neo-Institutional Approach* (Palgrave Macmillan, 2018).

84. Linda Hart, "Anthropology of Kinship Meets Human Rights Rationality: Limits of Marriage and Family Life in the European Court of Human Rights" (2018) 20 Societies 816, 819.

85. Paul Johnson, "Marriage, Heteronormativity, and the European Court of Human Rights: A Reappraisal" (2015) 29 International Journal of Law, Policy and the Family 56.

86. Joslin v. New Zealand, Communication No. 902/1999, UN Doc. A/57/40 at 214 (2002).

87. Ibid., para. 4.14.

88. Ibid., para. 4.11.

89. See Carlos Nino, "The Communitarian Challenge to Liberal Rights" (1989) 8 Law and Philosophy 37.

90. Upendra Baxi, *The Future of Human Rights* (Oxford University Press, 2002) 92-97.

91. Homi Bhabha *The Location of Culture*, 2nd ed. (Routledge, 2004) xxii.

92. Pheng Cheah, "The Physico-Material Bases of Cosmopolitanism," in Sigal Ben-Porath and Rogers Smith (eds.) *Varieties of Sovereignty and Citizenship* (University of Pennsylvania Press, 2012) 192.

93. For a discussion in relation to the World Bank, see Stephen Humphreys, *Theatre of the Rule of Law: Transnational Legal Intervention in Theory and Practice* (Cambridge University Press, 2010) 131-148.

94. Martha Nussbaum, *The Cosmopolitan Tradition: A Noble but Flawed Idea* (Belknap Press, 2019) 219-220.

95. Alexander Hinton *The Justice Façade: Trials of Transition in Cambodia* (Oxford University Press 2018) 13-16.

96. Ibid. for the literature that is the focus of Hinton's argument. Kathryn Sikkink, *The Justice Cascade: How Human Rights Prosecutions Are Changing World Politics* (W.W. Norton, 2011) 8-20.

97. David Chandler, "The Limits of Human Rights and Cosmopolitan Citizenship," in David Chandler (ed.) *Rethinking Human Rights: Critical Approaches to International Politics* (Palgrave Macmillan, 2002) 134.

98. CEDAW, Art. 5 (1).

99. Committee on the Elimination of Discrimination against Women, declarations, reservations, objections and notifications of withdrawal of reservations relating to the Convention on the Elimination of All Forms of Discrimination against Women (10 April 2006) CEDAW/SP/2006/2, p. 13.

100. Committee on the Elimination of Discrimination against Women, "Consideration of Reports Submitted by States Parties Under Article 18 of the Convention on the Elimination of All Forms of Discrimination against Women: India" (10 March 1999) CEDAW/C/IND/1 para. 113.

101. UN General Assembly, "Report of the Committee on the Elimination of Discrimination against Women 21st Session UNGA Supplement No. 38" (17 August 2000) UN Doc. A/55/38 para. 60.

102. CEDAW Committee, Summary Record of the 462nd Meeting (31 January 2000) CEDAW/C/SR.462, para. 36.

103. CEDAW Committee, Summary Record of the 761st Meeting (26 January 2007) CEDAW/C/SR.761(A), para. 17.

104. Rikki Holtmaat, "Article 5," In Marsha Freeman, Christine Chinkin, and Beate Rudolf (eds.) *The UN Convention on the Elimination of All Forms of Discrimination against Women: A Commentary* (Oxford University Press, 2013) 156-158.

105. Ibid., 150.

106. Handyside v. United Kingdom 1 EHRR 737 (1976).

107. See Marie-Bénédicte Dembour, *Who Believes in Human Rights? Reflections on the European Convention* (Cambridge University Press, 2006) 159-160.

108. Handyside (n. 106) [48]-[49].

109. On Article 10 and the margin of appreciation, Karatas v. Turkey, Application No. 23168/94 (8 July 1999), where the restriction was not covered by the margin of appreciation. See also Giniewski v. France 45 EHRR 589 (2007).

110. Convention on the Elimination of All Forms of Discrimination against Women, "Singapore: Depository Notification" c.N.358.1995.TREATIES-5 (21 November 1995).

111. Linda Keller, "The Impact of State Parties': Reservations to the Convention on the Elimination of all Forms of Discrimination Against Women" (2014) Michigan State Law Review 309, 319.

112. CEDAW, Art. 28(2).

113. Commission on the Status of Women, Report on the Twenty Sixth and Resumed Twenty Sixth Sessions, Economic and Social Council E/5909E/CN.6/608 (13 September–1 October 1976) p. 26.

114. Paul Schiff Berman, *Global Legal Pluralism: A Jurisprudence of Law Beyond Borders* (Cambridge University Press, 2012) 10-13. Legal pluralism is discussed in more detail in chapters 3 and 8.

115. John Tilley, "Cultural Relativism" (2000) 22 Human Rights Quarterly (HRQ) 501, 505.

116. Berman (n. 114) 57.

117. Claudio Corradetti, *Relativism and Human Rights: A Theory of Pluralistic Universalism* (Springer, 2009) 13.

118. Tilley (n. 115).

119. Alasdair MacIntyre, *Whose Justice? Which Rationality?* (University of Notre Dame Press, 1988) 366.

120. CEDAW Committee, Reservations to the Convention on the Elimination of All Forms of Discrimination against Women (12 November 1996) CEDAW/C/1997/4, para. 6.

121. Belinda Clark, "The Vienna Convention Reservations Regime and the Convention on Discrimination against Women" (1991) 85 American Journal of International Law (AJIL) 281.

122. CEDAW Committee, Summary Report of the 412th Meeting (6 February 2002) CEDAW/C/SR.412. paras. 3, 9-11. See also Concluding Observations on the Third and Fourth Periodic Reports [submitted in a single document] of Algeria (29 May 2015) CEDAW/C/DZA/CO/3-4/Add.1, para. 13-15.

123. Louis Henkin, "The Universality of the Concept of Human Rights" (1989) 506 The Annals of the American Academy of Political and Social Science 10. For an explanation linking the universality of human rights with globalization, see Rhoda Howard, "Human Rights and the Culture Wars: Globalization and the Universality of Human Rights" (1997) 53 International Journal 94. For an explanation of universality based on liberal philosophy, see Robert D. Sloane, "Outrelativizing Relativism: A Liberal Defense of the Universality of International Human Rights" (2001) 34 Vanderbilt Journal of Transnational Law 527. For explanations of universality built on an analysis of non-Western traditions, see Makau Mutua "The Complexity of Universalism in Human Rights," in András Sajó (eds.) *Human Rights with Modesty: The Problem of Universalism* (Martinus Nijhoff, 2004).

Chapter 2

1. Michael Brown, "Cultural Relativism 2.0" (2008) 49 Current Anthropology 363, 364.

2. This comparison is drawn by Caroline Dodds Pennock in "Mass Murder or Religious Homicide? Rethinking Human Sacrifice and Interpersonal Violence in Aztec Society" (2012) 37 Historical Social Research 276, 277.

3. John Tilley, "Cultural Relativism" (2000) 22 Human Rights Quarterly (HRQ) 501, 514.

4. Ibid., 531.

5. Brown (n. 1).

6. Edward Tylor, *Primitive Culture* (John Murray Publishers, 1871).

7. David Perusek, "Grounding Cultural Relativism" (2007) 80 Anthropological Quarterly 821, 824.

8. For a history of the early anthropology in this period, see Thomas Hylland Eriksen and Finn Sivert Nielsen, *A History of Anthropology*, vol. 2 (Pluto Press, 2001) 29-45. About the

construction of the nation more generally, see Robert Foster, "Making National Cultures in the Global Ecumene" (1991) 20 Annual Review of Anthropology 235.

9. UNESCO, Universal Declaration on Cultural Diversity (3 November 2001) UNESCO General Conference 31st Session, preamble.

10. Federico Lenzerini, *The Culturalization of Human Rights Law* (Oxford University Press, 2014) 118.

11. David Wong, *Moral Relativity* (University of California Press, 1984) 37-40.

12. For philosophical explorations, see John Cook, *Morality and Cultural Differences* (Oxford University Press, 1999) 51-92; Patrick Phillips, *The Challenge of Relativism: Its Nature and Limits* (Continuum International, 2007) 27-47. For a general overview of relativism in the Western philosophical tradition, see Martin Kusch (ed.), *The Routledge Handbook of Philosophy of Relativism* (Routledge, 2019) 40-133. A useful overview of anthropological work on cultural relativism and human rights can be found in Jane Cowan, Marie-Bénédicte Dembour, and Richard Wilson (eds.), *Culture and Rights: Anthropological Perspectives* (Cambridge University Press, 2001).

13. Derek Robbins, *Cultural Relativism and International Politics* (Sage, 2014) Introduction.

14. George Stocking, "The Background of Boas' Anthropology," in George Stocking (ed.) *A Franz Boas Reader: The Shaping of American Anthropology, 1883–1911*, 3rd ed. (University of Chicago Press, 1989) 22.

15. For an overview of this work and a compendium of papers in this area, see Franz Boas, *Race, Language, and Culture* (University of Chicago Press, 1940).

16. Kwame Anthony Appiah, "The Defender of Differences," New York Review of Books, 28 May 2020, https://www.nybooks.com/articles/2020/05/28/franz-boas-anthropologist-defender-differences/.

17. Ruth Benedict, *Patterns of Culture* (Houghton Mifflin, 1934) 20.

18. Douglas Irvin-Erickson, *Raphaël Lemkin and the Concept of Genocide* (University of Pennsylvania Press, 2017) 245-246.

19. Ibid., 246

20. Melville Herskovits, "Some Further Comments on Cultural Relativism" (1958) 60 American Anthropologist New Series 256.

21. For an overview of the history of twentieth century anthropology in this respect, see Marshall Sahlins, "What is Anthropological Enlightenment? Some Lessons of the Twentieth Century" (1999) 28 Annual Review of Anthropology i.

22. Peter Winch, "Understanding a Primitive Society" (1964) 1 American Philosophical Quarterly 307, 321.

23. Mark Goodale, "Toward a Critical Anthropology of Human Rights" (2006) 47 Current Anthropology 485.

24. Ibid., 540.

25. Ibid., 542.

26. Ibid.

27. For examples, see Karen Engle, "From Skepticism to Embrace: Human Rights and the American Anthropological Association from 1947–1999 (2001) 23 Human Rights Quarterly (HRQ) 536, 546-547.

28. Wilcomb Washburn, "Cultural Relativism, Human Rights, and the AAA" (1987) 89 American Anthropologist 939, 940.

29. Elvin Hatch, "The Good Side of Relativism" (1997) 53 Journal of Anthropological Research 371, 372.

30. Elizabeth Zechenter, "In the Name of Culture: Cultural Relativism and the Abuse of the Individual" (1997) 53 Journal of Anthropological Research 319, 325.

31. Renato Rosaldo, "Grief and a Headhunter's Rage: On the Cultural Force of Emotions" (1984); ibid., Zechtner, 326.

32. Cook called this cultural relativism as epistemology. Cook (n. 12) 11.

33. Duncan Pritchard, "Defusing Epistemic Relativism" (2009) 166 Synthese 397.

34. Ibid., 399.

35. Tilley, "Cultural Relativism," 501, 530.

36. See Bernard Williams, *Moral Luck* (Cambridge University Press, 1981) chp. 2.

37. For studies on the different contexts within which polygamy occurs and the complex ethical questions it raises, see Janet Bennion and Lisa Fishbayn Joffe (eds.), *The Polygamy Question* (Utah State University Press, 2016).

38. Richard Shweder, "Ethical Relativism: Is there a Defensible Version?" (1990) 18 Ethos 205, 209-210.

39. Xiaorong Li *Ethics, Human Rights and Culture: Beyond Relativism and Universalism* (Palgrave Macmillan, 2006) Preface.

40. Rhoda Howard, "Cultural Absolutism and the Nostalgia for Community" (1993) 15 Human Rights Quarterly (HRQ) 315. For the point about the concept of absolutism and relativism, see Seungbae Park, "Defence of Cultural Relativism" (2011) 8 Cultura: International Journal of Philosophy of Culture and Axiology 159.

41. Ibid., Howard.

42. Ibid., 321.

43. Peter Fitzpatrick, *Modernism and the Grounds of Law* (Cambridge University Press, 2001) 211.

44. Ann-Belinda S. Preis, "Human Rights as Cultural Practice: An Anthropological Critique" (1996) 18 Human Rights Quarterly (HRQ) 286, 292.

45. See Ronald Cohen, "Human Rights and Cultural Relativism: The Need for a New Approach" (1989) 91 American Anthropologist 1014, 1016.

46. Alison Dundes Renteln, "Relativism and the search for human rights" (1988) 90 American Anthropologist 56.

47. Margaret Jolly, " Woman Ikat Raet Long Human Raet O No? Women's Rights, Human Rights and Domestic Violence in Vanuatu" (1996) 52 Feminist Review 169.

48. Tom Zwart, "Using Local Culture to Further the Implementation of International Human Rights: The Receptor Approach" (2012) 34 Human Rights Quarterly (HRQ) 546.

49. Ibid., 558-562.

50. Sally Engle Merry, "Transnational Human Rights and Local Activism: Mapping the Middle" (2006) 108 American Anthropologist 38, 39.

51. Clifford Geertz, "Distinguished Lecture: Anti Anti-Relativism" (1984) 86 American Anthropologist: New Series 263, 275.

52. For a summary of this critique, see Robert Ulin, "Revisiting Culture Relativism: Old Prospects for a New Cultural Critique" (2007) 80 Anthropological Quarterly 803, 814.

53. James Fernandez, "Tolerance in a Repugnant World and Other Dilemmas in the Cultural Relativism of Melville J. Herskovits" (1990) 18 Ethos 140; For a summary of this general argument, see John Bishop, "Cultural Relativism and the Virtue of Tolerance" in Donald M. Topping, Doris C. Crowell, Victor N. Kobayashi (eds.) *Thinking Across Cultures* (Routledge, 1989) 232-234.

54. Hye-Kyung Kim and Michael Wreen, "Relativism, absolutism, and tolerance" (2003) 34 Metaphilosophy 447, 459.

55. Benedict Anderson, *Imagined Communities*, 2nd ed. (Verso, 2006) chp. 7.

56. Azar Gat, *Nations* (Cambridge University Press, 2013) 24-34.

57. Martti Koskenniemi, *The Politics of International Law* (Hart, 2011) chp. 11.

58. Peter Wilson, *The Holy Roman Empire* (Allen Lane, 2016) 128. For a critical overview of this history, see Andreas Osiander, "Sovereignty, International Relations, and the Westphalian Myth" (2001) 55 International Organization 251; Stéphane Beaulac, "The Westphalian Legal Orthodoxy: Myth or Reality?" (2000) 2 Journal of the History of International Law 148.

59. Stephen Krasner, *Sovereignty: Organized Hypocrisy* (Princeton University Press, 1999) 12.

60. Antony Anghie, *Imperialism, Sovereignty and the Making of International Law* (Cambridge University Press, 2004) chp. 2; Osiander (n. 58) 251.

61. Ibid., Anghie, 52-64.

62. The notion of Westphalia was in fact something of a myth exported into international law. See Stéphane Beaulac, *The Power of Language in the Making of International Law: The Word Sovereignty in Bodin and Vattel and the Myth of Westphalia* (Martinus Nijhoff, 2004) 68-75.

63. *Island of Palmas* case, Perm. Ct. Arb. 1928, 2 UN Rep. Intl. Arb. Awards 829 p. 8.

64. *Norway v. Denmark*, PCIJ Ser. A/B NO. 53 (1933).

65. For a summary of this, see Jack Donnelly, "State Sovereignty and Human Rights" (working paper no. 21, Human Rights and Human Welfare, Josef Korbel School of International Studies, University of Denver, 2004)https://pdfs.semanticscholar.org/9985/e868940474e0f8ec517ddaeaf9b600add797.pdf.

66. This summary of the dominant understanding of sovereignty is described in Kurt Mills, *Human Rights in the Emerging Global Order: A New Sovereignty?* (Palgrave, 1998) 10-18.

67. James Crawford, "Sovereignty as a Legal Value," in James Crawford and Martti Koskenniemi (eds.) *The Cambridge Companion to International Law* (Cambridge University Press, 2012).

68. Krasner (n. 59); Richard Steinberg, "Who is Sovereign?" (2004) 40 Stanford Journal of International Law 329, 332.

69. Neil MacCormick, *Questioning Sovereignty: Law, State, and Nation in the European Commonwealth* (Oxford University Press, 1999) 124.

70. Carl Schmitt, *Political Theology: Four Chapters on the Concept of Sovereignty*, trans. George Schwab (University of Chicago Press, 2005).

71. For an analysis of Schmitt's work on this point, see Renato Cristi, "Carl Schmitt on Sovereignty and Constituent Power" (1997) 10 Canadian Journal of Law & Jurisprudence 18.

72. Lior Barshack, "Constituent Power as Body: Outline of a Constitutional Theology" (2006) 56 University of Toronto Law Journal 185, 192-197.

73. Schmitt (n. 70) 48-49.

74. Annette Marfording, "Cultural Relativism and the Construction of Culture: An Examination of Japan" (1997) 19 Human Rights Quarterly (HRQ) 431.

75. Phil Chan, "Shared values of Singapore: Sexual Minority Rights as Singaporean Value" (2009) 13 International Journal of Human Rights 279.

76. Anne Bayefsky, "Cultural Sovereignty, Relativism, and International Human Rights: New Excuses for Old Strategies" (1996) 9 Ratio Juris 42.

77. Ibid., 55.

78. Ibid.

79. See Michael Addo, "Practice of United Nations Human Rights Treaty Bodies in the Reconciliation of Cultural Diversity with Universal Respect for Human Rights" (2010) 32 Human Rights Quarterly (HRQ) 601.

80. See David Murray, "Representation and Cultural Sovereignty: Some Case Studies," in Gretchen M. Bataille (ed.) *Native American Representations: First Encounters, Distorted Images, and Literary Appropriations* (University of Nebraska Press, 2001) 81-82.

81. Convention on the Elimination of All Forms of Discrimination against Women (CEDAW) (adopted 18 December 1979, entered into force 3 September 1981) 1249 UNTS 3, Art. 16.

82. Reproduced in Ann Elizabeth Mayer, "Rhetorical Strategies and Official Policies on Women's Rights: The Merits and Drawbacks of the New World Hypocrisy" (1998) Al-Raida Journal 12-21, 13.

83. Belinda Clark, "The Vienna Convention Reservations Regime and the Convention on Discrimination Against Women" (1991) 85 American Journal of International Law (AJIL) 281.

84. Ann Elizabeth Mayer, "Cultural Particularism as a Bar to Women's Rights: Reflections on the Middle Eastern Experience," in Julie Peters and Andrea Wolper (eds.) *Women's Rights, Human Rights: International Feminist Perspectives* (Routledge, 1995).

85. Committee on the Elimination of Discrimination against Women, Third Periodic Reports of States Parties: Egypt (25 July 1996) CEDAW/C/EGY/3, p. 3.

86. Lila Abu-Lughod, "The Active Social Life of 'Muslim Women's Rights': A Plea for Ethnography, Not Polemic, with Cases from Egypt and Palestine" (2010) 6 Journal of Middle East Women's Studies 1, 5-6.

87. CEDAW Committee, Combined Fourth and Fifth Periodic Reports of States Parties: Egypt (30 March 2000) CEDAW/C/EGY/4-5, p. 88-90.

88. The Egyptian Association for Community Participation Enhancement, "Second Shadow Report for the CEDAW Coalition Egypt 2009," https://www.ecoi.net/en/document/1183276.html

89. CEDAW Committee (n. 87) p. 56.

90. Jasmine Moussa, "The Reform of Shari'a-Derived Divorce Legislation in Egypt: International Standards and the Cultural Debate" (2005) 1 Human Rights Law Commentary 1.

91. CEDAW Committee, Concluding Observations of the Committee on the Elimination of Discrimination against Women: Egypt (5 February 2010) CEDAW/C/EGY/CO/7, para. 13-14.

92. Mayer (n. 84).

93. Yvonne Donders and Vincent Vleugel, "Universality, Diversity and Legal Certainty: Cultural Diversity in the Dialogue between CEDAW and States Parties," in Machiko Kanetake and André Nollkaemper (eds.) *The Rule of Law at the National and International Levels: Contestations and Deference* (Oxford University Press, 2016).

94. See the introduction and chapter 8 in this volume for state motivations on membership. See also, more generally, Eric Neumayer, "Do International Human Rights Treaties Improve Respect for Human Rights?" (2005) 49 Journal of Conflict Resolution 925.

95. Alison Dundes Renteln, "The Use and Abuse of the Cultural Defense" (2005) 20 Canadian Journal of Law and Society 47.

96. Cheikh Mbacke Gueye, "Human Rights and Cultural Diversity: Some Criticisms of Alison Renteln's Theory of Cultural Defence," in Andreas Oberprantacher and Anne Siegetsleitner (eds.) *Mensch sein–Fundament, Imperativ oder Floskel?* (Innsbruck University Press, 2017).

97. Preis (n. 44) 289. Andrew J. Nathan, "Universalism: A Particularistic Account," in Lynda Bell, Andrew J. Nathan, and Ilan Peleg (eds.) *Negotiating Culture and Human Rights* (Columbia University Press, 2001).

98. For a major study on this process, see Ronald Inglehart and Wayne E. Baker, "Modernization, Cultural Change, and the Persistence of Traditional Values" (2000) 65 American Sociological Review 19.

99. For an account and explanation of the causes of the change of attitudes to violence over time, see Steven Pinker, *The Better Angels of Our Nature* (Penguin, 2011) chp. 2.

100. Seyla Benhabib, *The Claims of Culture: Equality and Diversity in the Global Era* (Princeton University Press, 2002) 36.

101. Neil Walker, "Universalism and Particularism in Human Rights," in Cindy Holder and David Reidy, *Human Rights: The Hard Questions* (Cambridge University Press, 2013) 41.

102. Bhikhu Parekh, *Rethinking Multiculturalism* (Harvard University Press, 2000) 157.

103. James Rachels, "The Challenge of Cultural Relativism," in Paul Moser and Thomas Carson (eds.) *Moral Relativism: A Reader* (Oxford University Press, 2001) 58.

104. Dudgeon v. United Kingdom, Appl. No. 7525/76 (ECtHR 22 October 1981).

105. Ibid., [26] and [56].

106. Human Rights Watch, *More Than a Name: State-Sponsored Homophobia and its Consequences in Southern Africa* (Human Rights Watch, 2003). See also Ignacio Saiz, "Bracketing Sexuality: Human Rights and Sexual Orientation; A Decade of Development and Denial at the UN" (SPW Working Papers, no. 2, November 2005).

107. UN Human Rights Council, National Report Submitted in Accordance with Paragraph 15 (A) of the Annex to Human Rights Council Resolution 5/1: Nigeria (5 January 2009) A/HRC/WG.6/4/NGA/1, para. 76.

108. Bernard Williams, *Ethics and the Limits of Philosophy*, 3rd ed. (Routledge, 2006) 174.

109. This is discussed further in chapter 6. Rosa Freedman, "The United Nations Human Rights Council's Backwards Step on LGBT Rights" INTLAWGRRLS, 7 June 2013, https://ilg2.org/2013/06/07/the-united-nations-human-rights-councils-backwards-step-on-lgbt-rights/.

110. United Nations Economic and Social Council, Proposed Amendments by Saudi Arabia, Pakistan, Egypt, Libya, and Malaysia (2003) E/CN.4/2003/L.106-110.

111. Williams (n. 108) 176.

112. Howard (n. 40).

113. David Held, "Principles of Cosmopolitan Order," in Garrett Wallace Brown and David Held (eds.) *The Cosmopolitanism Reader* (Polity 2010) 229.

114. Costas Douzinas, *Human Rights and Empire: The Political Philosophy of Cosmopolitanism* (Routledge-Cavendish 2007) 182-183.

115. Pheng Cheah, *Inhuman Conditions: On Cosmopolitanism and Human Rights* (Harvard University Press, 2006) 60-61.

116. Ibid., 145-146.

117. Mark Lilla, *The Shipwrecked Mind: On Political Reaction* (New York Review of Books, 2016) 4.

118. Howard (n. 39) 323.

119. See Teson (n. 20) 895. See also Reza Afshari, *Human Rights in Iran: The Abuse of Cultural Relativism* (University of Pennsylvania Press, 2011) 236-240.

120. Lilla (n. 117) 5.

121. International Convention on the Elimination of All Forms of Racial Discrimination (Adopted 4 January 1969, entered into force 12 March 1969) 660 UNTS 195, Art. 1(1).

122. This is traced in Addo (n. 79) 655-666.

123. See Clifford Bob, "'Dalit Rights Are Human Rights': Caste Discrimination, International Activism, and the Construction of a New Human Rights Issue" (2007) 29 Human Rights Quarterly (HRQ) 167.

124. Committee on the Elimination of Racial Discrimination, Concluding Observations of the Committee on the Elimination of Racial Discrimination: India (5 May 2007) CERD/C/IND/CO/19.

125. Statement by Omar Abdullah, World Conference Against Racism, Racial Discrimination, Xenophobia and Related Intolerance, Durban, South Africa, 2 September 2011, http://www.un.org/WCAR/statements/indiaE.htm.

126. Amar Khade, "India Upholds Caste System at the U.N." India Cultural Forum, 11 May 2016, http://indianculturalforum.in/2016/05/11/india-upholds-caste-system-at-the-u-n .

127. This newspaper article gives an idea as to internal differences in India on the subject: Shobhan Saxena, "Caste: Racism in All but Name?" *Times of India*, 26 April 2009, http://timesofindia.indiatimes.com/home/sunday-times/deep-focus/Caste-Racism-in-all-but-name/articleshow/4449716.cms.

128. Economist, "Caste in India: No Escape" (print edition) 25 July 2020.

129. Adamantia Pollis, "Cultural Relativism Revisited: Through a State Prism" (1996) 18 Human Rights Quarterly (HRQ) 316, 319.

130. Fernando Tesón, "International Human Rights and Cultural Relativism" (1985) 25 Virginia Journal of International Law 870, 895.

131. Ibid., 898.

132. Anjesh Prasad, "Cultural Relativism in Human Rights Discourse" (2007) 19 A Journal of Social Justice 589, 589.

133. Li (n. 39) 4.

134. Charles Beitz, *The Idea of Human Rights* (Oxford University Press, 2009) 85.

135. See Alain Pellet, "The ILC Guide to Practice on Reservations to Treaties: A General Presentation by the Special Rapporteur" (2013) 24 European Journal of International Law (EJIL) 1061.

136. Indeterminacy will be discussed in more depth in chapter 3, but for a general overview of defining concepts in human rights law, see Francesco Maiani, "The Concept of 'persecution' in Refugee Law: Indeterminacy, Context-Sensitivity, and the Quest for a Principled Approach" (2010) Les dossiers du Grihl, https://journals.openedition.org/dossiersgrihl/3896; Heikki Patomäki, "Rethinking Global Parliament: Beyond the Indeterminacy of International Law" (2006) 13 Widener Law Review 375.

137. Thomas Hylland Eriksen, "Between Universalism and Relativism: A Critique of the UNESCO Concept of Culture," in Cowan et al. (n. 12) 143.

138. United Nations Human Rights Council (UNHRC) Resolution, Promoting Human Rights and Fundamental Freedoms through a Better Understanding of Traditional Values of Humankind, A/HRC/12/L.13/Rev.1, 2009, 5.

139. Ibid., preamble and Art. 1.

140. UNHRC, Report of the United Nations High Commissioner for Human Rights: Workshop on Traditional Values of Humankind, A/HRC/16/37, 2010.

141. Andrew Fagan and Hans Fridlund, "Relative Universality, Harmful Cultural Practices and the United Nations' Human Rights Council" (2016) 34 Nordic Journal of Human Rights 21.

142. UNHRC Resolution, Promoting Human Rights and Fundamental Freedoms through a Better Understanding of Traditional Values of Humankind (24 March 2011) GE.A/HRC/16/37. 1-12492.

143. Ibid., Art. 5.

144. Ibid., preamble.

145. International Justice Research Center, "Why the Fuss? Understanding the Human Rights Council's Resolution on Traditional Values, 8 October 2012, https://ijrcenter.org/2012/10/08/why-the-fuss-understanding-the-human-rights-councils-resolution-on-traditional-values/.

146. Cai Wilkinson, "Putting 'Traditional Values' into Practice: The Rise and Contestation of Anti-Homopropaganda Laws in Russia" (2014) 13 Journal of Human Rights 363.

147. Frances Raday, "Recent Developments in the UN Human Rights Council: Traditional Values and Women's Right to Equality in the Family," Oxford Human Rights Hub, 2 September 2015, https://ohrh.law.ox.ac.uk/recent-developments-in-the-un-human-rights-council-traditional-values-and-womens-right-to-equality-in-the-family/.

148. Wilkinson (n. 146)

149. International Covenant on Civil and Political Rights (ICCPR) (adopted 16 December 1966, entered into force 23 March 1976) 999 UNTS 171, Art. 6.

150. Dodds-Pennock (n. 2). See also Azar Gat, *The Causes of War and The Spread of Peace* (Oxford University Press, 2017) loc 1398.

Chapter 3

1. Hans Kelsen, *Principles of International Law* (Law Book Exchange, 2003) 3-4. First published 1952.

2. Antony Anghie, *Imperialism, Sovereignty and the Making of International Law* (Cambridge University Press, 2004) 115-136.

3. Alexander Orakhelashvili, "The Position of the Individual in International Law" (2000) 31 California Western International Law Journal 241, 243-249.

4. Rosalyn Higgins, "Conceptual Thinking about the Individual in International Law" (1978) 4 British Journal of International Studies 1; P. K. Menon, "The International Personality of Individuals in International Law: A Broadening of the Traditional Doctrine" (1992) 1 Journal of Transnational Law and Policy 151.

5. Martti Koskenniemi, *From Apology to Utopia: The Structure of International Legal Argument*, 2nd ed. (Cambridge University Press,) 28-45.

6. Ibid., 39.

7. Philip Alston, "The Best Interests Principle: Towards a Reconciliation of Culture and Human Rights" (1994) 8 International Journal of Law, Policy and the Family 1, 18-19.

8. Jan Engberg and Dorothee Heller, "Vagueness and Indeterminacy in International Law," in Vijay K. Bhatia, Christopher N. Candlin, and Jan Engberg (eds.) *Legal Discourse across Cultures and Systems* (Hong Kong University Press, 2008) 149-153.

9. Andrea Bianchi, *International Law Theories: An Inquiry into Different Ways of Thinking* (Oxford University Press, 2016) 151-153.

10. Alberto Puppo, "Reasonable Stability vs. Radical Indeterminacy: A Disanalogy between Domestic Rule of Law and Humanity-Based International Law" (2016) 30 Journal for Constitutional Theory and Philosophy of Law 81, 91.

11. Ibid. See also Jean d'Aspremont, *Formalism and the Sources of International Law: A Theory of the Ascertainment of Legal Rules* (Oxford University Press, 2011) 12-28.

12. Jason Beckett, "Countering Uncertainty and Ending Up/Down Arguments: *Prolegomena* to a Response to NAIL" (2005) 16 European Journal of International Law (EJIL) 213, 224.

13. Upendra Baxi, *Human Rights in a Posthuman World* (Oxford University Press, 2008) 31.

14. Daniel Peat and Matthew Windsor, "Playing the Game of Interpretation: On Meaning and Metaphor in International Law," in Andrea Bianchi, Daniel Peat, and Matthew Windsor (eds.) *Interpretation in International Law* (Oxford University Press, 2015) 19-24.

15. This form of authority challenge to international bodies is described by Karen J. Alter, Laurence R. Helfer, and Mikael Rask Madsen, "How Context Shapes the Authority of International Courts," (2016) 79 Law and Contemporary Problems 1.

16. For a discussion of interpretation as persuasion, see John Tobin, "Seeking to Persuade: A Constructive Approach to Human Rights Treaty Interpretation" (2010) 23 Harvard Human Rights Journal 1.

17. Hugo Grotius, *Inleiding tot de Hollandsche Rechts-geleertheyd*, cited in James Crawford *State Responsibility: The General Part* (Cambridge University Press, 2013) 10.

18. Heinz Duchhardt, "From the Peace of Westpahlia to the Congress of Vienna," ixn Bardo Fassbender and Anne Peters (eds.) *The Oxford Handbook of the History of International Law*, 2nd ed. (Oxford University Press, 2014).

19. Spanish Zone of Morocco Claims case, 2 RIAA 615 (1925), cited in Martin Dixon and Robert McCorquodale, *Cases and Materials on International Law*, 3rd ed. (Blackstone Limited, 2001) 429.

20. UN General Assembly Resolution, (24 October 1970) A/RES/25/2625 (XXV).

21. Kenneth Abbott and Duncan Snidal, "Hard and Soft Law in International Governance" (2000) 54 International Organization 421, 423.

22. Christine Chinkin, "The Challenge of Soft Law: Development and Change in International Law" (1989) 38 International and Comparative Law Quarterly (ICLQ) 850.

23. Advisory Opinion Concerning Reservations to the Genocide Convention ICJ 1 (1951) 23. See also A. de Hoogh, "The Relationship between Jus Cogens, Obligations Erga Omnes and International Crimes: Peremptory Norms in Perspective," (1991) 42 Austrian Journal of Public and International Law 183.

24. William Conklin, "The Peremptory Norms of the International Community," (2012) 23 European Journal of International Law (EJIL) 837.

25. Oscar Schachter, "Towards a Theory of International Obligation," (1968) 8 Virginia Journal of International Law 300. Illustrative cases on this point cited by Schachter include Advisory Opinion on Certain Expenses of the United Nations, ICJ 151 (1962); Columbian-Peruvian Asylum case, ICJ 266 (1950).

26. Karen Parker, "Jus Cogens: Compelling the Law of Human Rights" (1988) 12 Hastings International and Comparative Law Review 411.

27. See Bridget Quitter, "Culture or Condemnation? The Status of Female Genital Mutilation in International Law" (2014) http://dx.doi.org/10.2139/ssrn.2498201.

28. Hadijatou Mani Koraou v. The Republic of Niger, ECW/CCJ/JUD/06/08, Economic Community of West African States (ECOWAS): Community Court of Justice (27 October 2008).

29. Vienna Convention on the Law of Treaties (VCLT) (adopted 23 May 1969, entered into force 27 January 1980) 115 UNTS 331, Art. 31(1)-(3).

30. Humphrey Waldock, Third Report *Yearbook of the International Law Commission*, vol. 2 (1964) 55.

31. International Covenant on Civil and Political Rights (ICCPR) (adopted 16 December 1966, entered into force 23 March 1976) 999 UNTS 171, Art. 2(3).

32. This was also in part due to the extensive reservations put in place by the U.S. to limit a number of obligations: Nadine Strossen, "United States Ratification of the International Bill of Rights: A Fitting Celebration of the Bicentennial of the U.S. Bill of Rights" (1992) 24 University of Toledo Law Review 203.

33. Matthew Craven, "The Ends of Consent," in Dino Kritsiotis and Michael J. Bowman (eds.) *Conceptual and Contextual Perspectives on the Modern Law of Treaties* (Cambridge University Press, 2014).

34. Fernando Tesón, "International Obligation and the Theory of Hypothetical Consent" (1990) 15 Yale Journal of International Law 84; Basak Çali, *The Authority of International Law* (Oxford University Press, 2015) 31.

35. Brown v. Stott, 1 AC 681 at 703 (2003).

36. As cited in Igor Lukashuk, "The Principle *Pacta Sunt Servanda* and the Nature of Obligation under International Law," (1989) 83 American Journal of International Law (AJIL) 513, 514.

37. Frédéric Mégret, "Nature of Obligations," in Daniel Moeckli, Sangeeta Shah, and Sandesh Sivakumaran (eds.) *International Human Rights Law* (Oxford University Press, 2014).

38. Osman v. United Kingdom, ECRR 101 (1998).

39. Oneryildiz v. Turkey, 41 EHRR 20 (2005).

40. International Covenant on Economic, Social, and Cultural Rights (ICESCR) (adopted 16 December 1966, entered into force 3 January 1976) 993 UNTS 3, Art. 2.

41. Committee on Economic, Social, and Cultural Rights (CESCR), General Comment No. 9, The Domestic Application of the Covenant (3 December 1998) E/C.12/1998/24, para. 2.

42. Jonathan Brown, "Diplomatic Immunity: State Practice under the Vienna Convention on Diplomatic Relations" (1988) 37 International and Comparative Law Quarterly (ICLQ) 53.

43. Effect of Reservations on the Entry into Force of the American Convention (Arts. 74 and 75) Advisory Opinion OC-2/82, IACHR Series A no. 2 IHRL 3398 (IACHR 1982) [29].

44. Beth Simmons, *Mobilizing for Human Rights: International Law in Domestic Politics* (Cambridge University Press 2009) 126.

45. Andrea Bianchi, "The Game of Interpretation in International Law: The Players, the Cards and Why the Game Is Worth the Candle," in Andrea Bianchi, Daniel Peat, and Matthew Windsor (eds.) *Interpretation in International Law* (Oxford University Press, 2015) 34.

46. Tyrer v. United Kingdom, 2 EHRR 1 (1978) [31].

47. Fernando Tesón, "International Human Rights and Cultural Relativism" (1985) 25 Virginia Journal of International Law 869, 878.

48. For an outline of this point, see Patricia Hyndman, "Cultural Legitimacy in the Formulation and Implementation of Human Rights Law in Australia," in Abdullahi Ahmed An-Na'im (ed.) *Human Rights in Cross-Cultural Perspectives: A Quest for Consensus* (University of Pennsylvania Press, 1995) 295-298.

49. Jean Grugel and Enrique Peruzzotti, "The Domestic Politics of International Human Rights Law: Implementing the Convention on the Rights of the Child in Ecuador, Chile, and Argentina" (2012) 34 Human Rights Quarterly (HRQ) 178.

50. Kerstin Mechlem, "Treaty Bodies and the Interpretation of Human Rights" (2009) 42 Vanderbilt Journal of Transnational Law 905.

51. Koskenniemi (n. 5) 9-15.

52. Alexander Orakhelashvili, "Restrictive Interpretation of Human Rights Treaties in the Recent Jurisprudence of the European Court of Human Rights" (2003) 14 European Journal of International Law (EJIL) 529.

53. David Brown, "Making Room for Sexual Orientation and Gender Identity in International Human Rights Law: An Introduction to the Yogyakarta Principles" (2010) 31 Michigan Journal of International Law (MJIL) 821, 875.

54. Bianchi (n. 45) 49-51.

55. Jean d'Aspremont, "The Multidimensional Process of Interpretation: Content-Determination and Law-Ascertainment Distinguished," in Andrea Bianchi, Daniel Peat, and Matthew Windsor (eds.) *Interpretation in International Law* (Oxford University Press, 2015) 114-116.

56. Convention on the Elimination of All Forms of Discrimination against Women (CEDAW), Saudi Arabia: Ratification (7 September 2000) C.N.925.2000.TREATIES-8.

57. Committee on the Elimination of Discrimination against Women, Concluding Observations on the Combined Third and Fourth Periodic Reports of Saudi Arabia (14 March 2018) CEDAW/C/SAU/CO/3-4, para. 10. See also Sifa Mtango, "A State of Oppression? Women's Rights in Saudi Arabia" (2004) 5 Asia-Pacific Journal on Human Rights and the Law 49, 62.

58. See, for example, Ed Bates, "Avoiding Legal Obligations Created by Human Rights Treaties" (2008) 57 International and Comparative Law Quarterly (ICLQ) 751.

59. For examples of this behavior from states, see Andreas Føllesdal, "Subsidiarity and International Human-Rights Courts: Respecting Self-Governance and Protecting Human Rights—or Neither?' (2016) 79 Law and Contemporary Problems 147; Alexandra Huneeus, "Courts Resisting Courts: Lessons from the Inter-American Court's Struggle to Enforce Human Rights" (2011) 44 Cornell International Law Journal 493.

60. Koskenniemi (n. 5) 300.

61. For an exploration, see David Cole, "Judging the Next Emergency: Judicial Review and Individual Rights in Times of Crisis." (2003) 101 Michigan Law Review 2565; For a more critical perspective, see Stephen Humphreys, "Legalizing Lawlessness: On Giorgio Agamben's *State of Exception*" (2006) 17 European Journal of International Law (EJIL) 677.

62. Dominic McGoldrick, "The Interface between Public Emergency Powers and International Law" (2004) 2 International Journal of Constitutional Law 380.

63. Rolando Gaete, *Human Rights and the Limits of Critical Reason* (Dartmouth, 1993) 91.

64. The Greek case (1969) 12 YB 1. The ICCPR takes a more restrictive view, still saying that derogations should not apply in times of war. See McGoldrick (n. 62) 386-389.

65. Claudio Grossman, "A Framework for the Examination of States of Emergency under the American Convention on Human Rights" (1986) 1 American University International Law Review 35.

66. Brannigan and McBride v. UK, 17 EHRR 539 (1993).

67. Emilie Hafner-Burton, Laurence Helfer, and Christopher Fariss, "Emergency and Escape: Explaining Derogations from Human Rights Treaties" (2011) 65 International Organization 673.

68. Report of the International Law Commission (ILC), Guide to Practice on Reservations to Treaties (12 August 2011) 63rd Session A/66/10/Add.1, para. 1.1(1).

69. Eric Neumayer, "Qualified Ratification: Explaining Reservations to International Human Rights Treaties" (2007) 36 Journal of Legal Studies 397.

70. ILC (n. 68) para. 3.1.5.2.

71. For a concise overview of this debate, see Bruno Simma and Gleider Hernández, "Legal Consequences of an Impermissible Reservation to a Human Rights Treaty: Where Do We Stand?" in Enzo Cannizzaro (ed.) *The Law of Treaties beyond the Vienna Convention* (Oxford University Press, 2011).

72. See Kasey Lowe McCall-Smith, "Reservations to Human Rights Treaties" (Ph.D thesis, submitted, University of Edinburgh, 2012) chp. 2.

73. UN Human Rights Committee (HRC) General Comment 24, General Comment on Issues Relating to Reservations Made upon Ratification or Accession to the Covenant or the Optional Protocols thereto, or in Relation to Declarations under Article 41 of the Covenant (4 November 1994) UN Doc. CCPR/C/21/Rev.1/Add.6, para. 4.

74. See The Effect of Reservations on the Entry into Force of the American Convention on Human Rights (Arts. 74 and 75), Advisory Opinion OC-2/82, Inter-Am. Ct. H.R. (Ser. A) No. 2 (24 September 1982); Austria v. Italy, Application No. 7881/60 (1960).

75. HRC (n. 73) para. 8.

76. D. W. Bowett, 'Reservations to Non-Restricted Multilateral Treaties.' (1977) 48 British Yearbook of International Law 1976-77 67.

77. Catherine Piper, "Reservations to Multilateral Treaties: The Goal of Universality" (1985) 71 Iowa Law Review 295, 296.

78. Martha Finnemore, *National Interests in International Society* (Cornell University Press, 1996) 6.

79. See William Schabas, *The European Convention on Human Rights: A Commentary* (Oxford University Press, 2015) 414.

80. Polys Modinos, "Effects and Repercussions of the European Convention on Human Rights" (1962) 11 International and Comparative Law Quarterly (ICLQ) 1097.

81. For an example, see Yannis Stivachtis and Mike Habegger, "The Council of Europe: The Institutional Limits of Contemporary European International Society?" (2011) 33 Journal of European Integration 159; Andrew Moravcsik, "The Origins of Human Rights Regimes: Democratic Delegation in Postwar Europe" (2000) 54 International Organization 217.

82. HRC (n. 73).

83. Jan Klabbers, "On Human Rights Treaties, Contractual Conceptions and Reservations," in Ineta Ziemele (ed.) *Reservations to Human Rights Treaties and the Vienna Convention Regime: Conflict, Harmony or Reconciliation* (Martinus Nijhoff, 2004).

84. Ibid., 181.

85. Jane Connors, "The Women's Convention in the Muslim World," in Mai Yamani (ed.) *Feminism and Islam: Legal and Literary Perspectives* (Ithaca Press, 1996).

86. Elena Baylis, "General Comment 24: Confronting the Problem of Reservations to Human Rights Treaties" (1999) 17 Berkeley Journal of International Law 277, 296-298; Elizabeth Lijnzaad, *Reservations to Un-Human Rights Treaties: Ratify and Ruin?* (Martinus Nijhoff, 1995) 80-90.

87. Belilos v. Switzerland, 10 EHRR 466 (1988) [55].

88. Rawle Kennedy v. Trinidad and Tobago, Communication No. 845/1999, CCPR/C/67/D/845/1999 (2 November 1999).

89. Roberto Baratta, 'Should Invalid Reservations to Human Rights Treaties Be Disregarded?' (2000) 11 European Journal of International Law (EJIL) 413.

90. Ibid., 413; VCLT Art. 20(4).

91. Matthew Craven, "Legal Differentiation and the Concept of the Human Rights Treaty in International Law" (2000) 11 European Journal of International Law (EJIL) 489, 497.

92. Roslyn Moloney, "Incompatible Reservations to Human Rights Treaties: Severability and the Problem of State Consent" (2004) 5 Melbourne Journal of International Law 155, 159; Rosalyn Higgins, "Human Rights: Some Questions of Integrity" (1989) 15 Commonwealth Law Bulletin 598.

93. Ibid., Moloney, 159.

94. Vassilis Pergantis, *The Paradigm of State Consent in the Law of Treaties: Challenges and Perspectives* (Edward Elgar, 2017) 239-242.

95. For further indicative literature on the difficulty of balancing human rights reservations with the VCLT regime, see Konstantin Korkelia, "New Challenges to the Regime of Reservations under the International Covenant on Civil and Political Rights" (2002) 13 European Journal of International Law (EJIL) 437; Kasey McCall-Smith, "Mind the Gaps: The ILC Guide to Practice and Reservations to Human Rights Treaties" (2014) 16 International Community Law Review 263.

96. Yuval Shany, "Toward a General Margin of Appreciation Doctrine in International Law?" (2005) 16 (European Journal of International Law (EJIL) 907, 910.

97. Handyside v. United Kingdom, ECHR 5 (1976) [48].

98. Eirik Bjorge, "Been There, Done That: The Margin of Appreciation and International Law" (2015) 4 Cambridge Journal of International and Comparative Law 181.

99. *Lansman et al. v. Finland*, Communication No. 511/1992, UN Doc. CCPR/C/52/D/511/1992 (1994) para. 9.4.

100. Sarah Joseph, *The International Covenant on Civil and Political Rights: Cases, Materials, and Commentary* (Oxford University Press, 2015) 527-528.

101. *Vo v. France*, Application No. 53924/00 (Grand Chamber, 8 July 2004) [82]-[83].

102. *Tammer v. Estonia*, Application No. 41205/98 (ECtHR 6 February 2001).

103. Ibid.

104. Ibid., [53].

105. James Sweeney, "Margins of Appreciation: Cultural Relativity and the European Court of Human Rights in the Post–Cold War Era" (2005) 54 International and Comparative Law Quarterly (ICLQ) 459.

106. Yutaka Arai-Takahashi, "The Margin of Appreciation Doctrine: A Theoretical Analysis of Strasbourg's Variable Geometry," in Andreas Føllesdal, Birgit Peters, and Geir Ulfstein (eds.) *Constituting Europe: The European Court of Human Rights in a National, European and Global Context* (Cambridge University Press, 2013) 71.

107. *Jahn v. Germany*, ECHR 444 (2005) [91].

108. See *Ricardo Canese v. Paraguay*, IACHR Series C No. 111, IACHR 7 (2004).

109. Pieter van Dijk, Godefridus and G. J. H. van Hoof, *Theory and Practice of the European Convention on Human Rights*, 3rd ed. (Kluwer Law International, 1998) 95.

110. This aspect of the margin of appreciation doctrine has come in for some criticism. See Başak Çalı, "Balancing Human Rights? Methodological Problems with Weights, Scales and Proportions" (2007) 29 Human Rights Quarterly (HRQ) 251.

111. Tobin (n. 16) 1, 4.

112. Ibid.

113. Nina Reiners, "Transnational Lawmaking Coalitions for Human Rights" (paper presentation, European Society of International Law Conference, Stockholm, Sweden, 10 September 2021.

114. Exemptions are usually explicitly designed and regulated by legal doctrine. See Bates (n. 58); Exemptions rely on the relatively patchwork nature of the way that various rights limiting mechanism and interpretation rules work. Martin Scheinin and Mathias Vermeulen, "Unilateral Exceptions to International Law: Systematic Legal Analysis and Critique of Doctrines that Seek to Deny or Reduce the Applicability of Human Rights Norms

in the Fight against Terrorism" (EUI Working Papers LAW no. 2010/08, European University Institute, 30 October 2010) https://scholar.google.com/scholar_url?url=https://papers.ssrn.com/sol3/papers.cfm%3Fabstract_id%3D1699152&hl=en&sa=T&oi=gsb&ct=res&cd=0&d=4606333729059890325&ei=DFg7YbTEGoOCy9YPj6WikAY&scisig=AAGBfm0_Fa6uG-Qf5FDgYMYiL0y-O8sEuA.

115. Often this takes the form of motivated reasoning from state parties. See Lorand Bartels and Federica Paddeu, "Introduction," in Bartels and Paddeu (eds.) *Exceptions in International Law* (Oxford University Press, 2020) 2-3.

116. For an example of this argument, see Laurence Helfer, "Overlegalizing Human Rights: International Relations Theory and the Commonwealth Caribbean Backlash against Human Rights Regimes" (2002) 102 Columbia Law Review 1832.

117. The political benefits of treaty participation in terms of external reputation benefits are well documented; Emilie Hafner-Burton, Kiyoteru Tsutsui, and John Meyer, "International Human Rights Law and the Politics of Legitimation: Repressive States and Human Rights Rreaties" (2008) 23 International Sociology 115; Richard Nielsen and Beth Simmons, "Rewards for Ratification: Payoffs for Participating in the International Human Rights Regime?" (2015) 59 International Studies Quarterly 197.

118. Darren Hawkins and Wade Jacoby, "Partial Compliance: A Comparison of the European and Inter-American Courts for Human Rights" (2010) 6 Journal of International Law and International Relations 35.

119. Giselle Corradi, "Introduction: Human Rights and Legal Pluralism; Four Research Agendas," in Giselle Corradi, Eva Brems, and Mark Goodale (eds.) *Human Rights Encounter Legal Pluralism: Normative and Empirical Approaches* (Hart, 2017) 3.

120. Giselle Corradi, "Indigenous Justice and the Right to a Fair Trial," in Corradi et al., Ibid.

121. VCLT, Art. 46.

122. Anthony Aust, *Modern Treaty Law and Practice* (Cambridge University Press, 2013) 160-161.

123. HRC General Comment 31, The Nature of the General Legal Obligation Imposed on States Parties to the Covenant (May 2004) CCPR/C/21/Rev.1/Add. 1326, para. 4.

124. Ibid. [17].

125. Jack Goldsmith, "Should International Human Rights Law Trump US Domestic Law?" (2000) 2 Chicago Journal of International Law 327.

126. Kenneth Roth, "The Charade of US Ratification of International Human Rights Treaties" (2000) 1 Chicago Journal of International Law 347; Laurence Rothenberg, "International Law, U.S. Sovereignty, and the Death Penalty" (2003) 35 Georgetown Journal of International Law 547.

127. For examples of states using these arguments in different contexts, see Michael Kirby, "Asia and Oceania LGBTI Law Reform: Breaking the Log-Jam" (2016) 46 Hong Kong Law Journal 151; Abadir Ibrahim, "LGBT Rights in Africa and the Discursive Role of International Human Rights Law" (2015) 15 African Human Rights Law Journal 263.

128. For a summary, see Anita Weiss, "Interpreting Islam and Women's Rights: Implementing CEDAW in Pakistan" (2003) 18 International Sociology 581.

129. Siobhan Fenton, "Anti-Domestic Violence Law to Protect Women is Un-Islamic, Pakistani Advisory Group Rules," *The Independent*, 4 March 2016, https://www.independent.co.uk/news/world/asia/bill-protecting-women-against-domestic-violence-is-un-islamic-pakistani-advisory-group-rules-a6911161.html.

130. Manar Waheed, “Domestic Violence in Pakistan: The Tension between Intervention & Sovereign Autonomy in Human Rights Law” (2004) 29 Brooklyn Journal of International Law 939, 947-948.

131. The distinction between the two is explored in Wade Cole, “Mind the Gap: State Capacity and the Implementation of Human Rights Treaties” (2015) 69 International Organization 405.

132. Ulf Linderfalk, “Doing the Right Thing for the Right Reason: Why Dynamic or Static Approaches Should Be Taken in the Interpretation of Treaties (2008) 10 International Community Law Review 109, 113.

133. Sondre Helmersen, “Evolutive Treaty Interpretation: Legality, Semantics and Distinctions” (2013) 6 European Journal of Legal Studies 127.

134. Eirik Bjorge, *The Evolutionary Interpretation of Treaties* (Oxford University Press, 2014) 5.

135. *The Right to Information on Consular Assistance in the Framework of the Guarantees of Due Process of Law*, Advisory Opinion OC-16/99, IACHR Series A No. 16 (1999) [114].

136. The Mayagna (Sumo) Awas Tingni Community v. Nicaragua (2008) 136 ILR 73 [146].

137. Christian Djeffal, *Static and Evolutive Treaty Interpretation: A Functional Reconstruction* (Cambridge University Press, 2016) 301-306.

138. Ibid.

139. See *Consular Assistance* (n. 135); Gerald Neuman, “Import, Export, and Regional Consent in the Inter-American Court of Human Rights” (2008) 19 European Journal of International Law (EJIL) 101, 106-7.

140. Artavia Murillo et al. v. Costa Rica, Preliminary Objections, Merits, Reparations, and Costs, Judgment, Inter-Am. Ct. H.R. (ser. C) No. 257 (28 November 2012); For a critique, see Ligia De Jesus, “A Pro-Choice Reading of a Pro-Life Treaty: The Inter-American Court on Human Rights’ Distorted Interpretation of the American Convention on Human Rights in Artavia v Costa Rica” (2014) 32 Wisconsin International Law Journal 223.

141. Lynn Morgan, “‘Human Life is Inviolable’: Costa Rica’s Human Rights Crucible” (2019) 38 Medical Anthropology 493; Julieta Lemaitre and Rachel Sieder, “The Moderating Influence of International Courts on Social Movements: Evidence from the IVF Case Against Costa Rica” (2017) 19 Health and Human Rights 149.

142. Ibid.

143. *Atala Riffo and Daughters v. Chile*, Inter-Am. Comm. HR, Case 12.502 (24 February 2012).

144. Ibid., [98].

145. See Pedro Garcia, “Chilean Paradoxes: LGBT Rights in Latin America,” Outright: Action International, 2012, https://www.outrightinternational.org/content/chilean-paradoxes-lgbt-rights-latin-america; see also Javier Corrales, “The Politics of LGBT Rights in Latin America and the Caribbean: Research Agendas” (2015) 100 European Review of Latin American and Caribbean Studies 53.

146. *Atala Riffo* [74].

147. This is discussed in chapter 8. See also Laurence Helfer and Erik Voeten, “International Courts as Agents of Legal Change: Evidence from LGBT Rights in Europe” (2014) 68 International Organization 77.

148. See Michael Hutchinson, “The Margin of Appreciation Doctrine in the European Court of Human Rights” (1999) 48 International and Comparative Law Quarterly (ICLQ) 638.

149. See Begum Bulak and Alain Zysset, "'Personal autonomy' and 'democratic society' at the European Court of Human Rights: Friends or Foes?" (2013) 2 UCL Journal of Law and Jurisprudence 230.

150. *Marckx v. Belgium*, ECHR 2 (1979).

151. Ibid., [40].

152. *Leo Hertzberg et al. v. Finland*, Communication No. 61/1979, UN Doc. CCPR/C/OP/1 (1985).

153. Viljam Engström, "Deference and the Human Rights Committee" (2016) 34 Nordic Journal of Human Rights 73.

154. HRC, General Comment No. 34, Article 19: Freedoms of Opinion and Expression (12 September 2011) CCPR/C/GC/34.

155. Dean Spielmann, "Allowing the Right Margin: The European Court of Human Rights and the National Margin of Appreciation Doctrine: Waiver or Subsidiarity of European Review?" (2012) 14 Cambridge Yearbook of European Legal Studies 381, 394.

156. International Committee of Jurists, "UN Human Rights Committee: 'Homosexual Propganda' Conviction Violated Freedom of Expression," International Justice Resource Center, 3 December 2012, https://ijrcenter.org/2012/12/03/un-human-rights-committee-homosexual-propaganda-conviction-violated-freedom-of-expression/.

157. Irina Fedotova v. Russian Federation, Communication No. 1932/2010, UN Doc. CCPR/C/106/D/1932/2010 (2012) [2.6] and [5.6].

158. Helmersen (n. 133) 314-320.

159. Convention on the Elimination of All Forms of Discrimination against Women (CEDAW), Art. 28(2).

160. Belinda Clark, "The Vienna Convention Reservations Regime and the Convention on Discrimination Against Women" (1991) 85 American Journal of International Law (AJIL) 281.

161. CEDAW Committee, Report of the Committee on the Elimination of Discrimination against Women (Eighteenth and Nineteenth sessions), (14 May 1998) 19th Session A/53/38/Rev.1., p. 47-50.

162. Ibid., p. 50.

163. Marsha Freeman, "Reservations to CEDAW: An Analysis for UNICEF," UNICEF: Policy and Practice, UNICEF December 2009.

164. Alain Pellet, "The ILC Guide to Practice on Reservations to Treaties: A General Presentation by the Special Rapporteur" (2013) 24 European Journal of International Law (EJIL) 1061.

165. Ibid., 1088.

166. Nisrine Abiad, *Sharia, Muslim States and International Human Rights Treaty Obligations: A Comparative Study* (British Institute of International and Comparative Law, 2008) 70-81.

167. Ibid.

168. CEDAW, Accession by Malaysia (5 July 1995) UNTC C.N.250.1995.TREATIES-3.

169. CEDAW Committee, Consideration of Reports Submitted by States Parties under Article 18 of the Convention on the Elimination of All Forms of Discrimination against Women: Malaysia (12 April 2004) CEDAW/C/MYS/1-2, para. 68-69.

170. CEDAW, Objection by France and Communication by the Netherlands to the Partial Withdrawal and Modification of a Reservation Made by Malaysia (7 September 1998) UNTC C.N. 318.2.998.

171. Marina Girshovich, "Classifications of Objections Based on the Legal Assessment of a Reservation by Objecting States" (2014) 16 International Community Law Review 333, 369.

172. CEDAW Committee, Concluding Observations on the Combined Third to Fifth Periodic Reports of Malaysia (14 March 2018) CEDAW/C/MYS/CO/3-5, para. 9-10.

173. For a basic summary of this point, see Louis Henkin, "Human Rights and State Sovereignty" (1996) 25 Georgia Journal of International and Comparative Law 31.

174. Jack Donnelly, "Human Rights: A New Standard of Civilization?" (1998) 74 International Affairs 1.

175. Jean d'Aspremont, *International Law as a Belief System* (Cambridge University Press, 2018) 31-34.

176. For an example of a states engaging in backlash toward an institution after interpretation/demarcation games not involving defensive relativism, see Wayne Sandholtz, Yining Bei, and Kayla Caldwell, "Backlash and International Human Rights Courts, In Alison Brysk and Michael Stohl (eds.) *Contracting Human Rights: Crisis, Accountability, and Opportunity* (Edward Elgar, 2018).

Chapter 4

All links accessed 18 February 2019 unless otherwise indicated.

1. For a contemporary insight, see Paul Harris, "An Opinion on the Depayin Massacre, "Asian Human Rights Commission, 10 January 2004, http://www.humanrights.asia/resources/journals-magazines/article2/special-edtion-the-depayin-massacre-burma/an-opinion-on-the-depayin-massacre/; for a retrospective account, see Peter Popham "'They Were Screaming: Die, Die, Die!': The Dramatic Inside Story of Aung San Suu Kyi's darkest hour," *The Independent* 16 October 2011, https://www.independent.co.uk/news/people/profiles/they-were-screaming-die-die-die-the-dramatic-inside-story-of-aung-san-suu-kyis-darkest-hour-2369492.html.

2. Association of Southeast Asian Nations (ASEAN), Joint Communiqué of the 36th ASEAN Ministerial Meeting, Phnom Penh, 16-17 June 2003, https://asean.org/?static_post=joint-communique-of-the-36th-asean-ministerial-meeting-phnom-penh-16-17-june-2003 para. 15.

3. Sanae Suzuki, "Why Is ASEAN Not Intrusive? Non-Interference Meets State Strength" (2019) 8 Journal of Contemporary East Asia Studies 157, 164; Mikio Oishi and Nina Ghani, "Developing a Way to Influence the Conduct of the Government in Intrastate Conflict: The Case of Myanmar," in Mikio Oishi (ed.) *Contemporary Conflicts in Southeast Asia: Towards a New ASEAN Way of Conflict Management* (Springer, 2015) 100.

4. See James Munro, "The Relationship between the Origins and Regime Design of the ASEAN Intergovernmental Commission on Human Rights (AICHR)" (2011) 15 International Journal of Human Rights 1185.

5. Ian Hurd, *International Organizations: Politics, Law, Practice* (Cambridge University Press, 2017) 17-18; Dan Sarooshi, *The United Nations and the Development of Collective Security* (Clarendon Press, 1999) 5.

6. José Alvarez, "International Organizations: Then and Now" (2006) 100 American Journal of International Law (AJIL) 324; B. S. Chimni, "International Institutions Today: An Imperial Global State in the Making" (2014) 15 European Journal of International Law (EJIL) 1.

7. Hurd (n. 5); Viljam Engström, "Reasoning on Powers of Organizations," in Jan Klabbers and Åsa Wallendahl (eds.) *Research Handbook on the Law of International Organizations* (Edward Elgar 2011) 61-65.

8. See Jan Klabbers, "The Emergence of Functionalism in International Institutional Law: Colonial Inspirations (2014) 25 European Journal of International Law (EJIL) 645.

9. Jan Klabbers, *An Introduction to International Organizations Law* (Cambridge University Press, 2015) 32-35.

10. Thomas Gehring, "Integrating Integration Theory: Neo-Functionalism and International Regimes" (1996) 10 Global Society 225; Anne-Marie Burley and Walter Mattli, "Europe before the Court: A Political Theory of Legal Integration" (1993) 47 International Organization 41.

11. In the context of European Union integration, see Andrew Moravcsik, "Preferences and Power in the European Community: A Liberal Intergovernmentalist Approach" (1993) 31 JCMS: Journal of Common Market Studies 473; Mark A Pollack, "International Relations Theory and European Integration (2001) 39 JCMS: Journal of Common Market Studies 221.

12. Kenneth W. Abbott and Duncan Snidal, "Why States Act through Formal International Organizations" (1998) 42 Journal of Conflict Resolution 3.

13. For an overview of different theories, see Victor Ayeni, "Why States Comply with Decisions of International Human Rights Tribunals: A Review of the Principal Theories and Perspectives" (2019) 10 Nnamdi Azikiwe University Journal of International Law and Jurisprudence 1.

14. Barbara Koremenos, "Institutionalism and International Law," ian Jeffrey Dunoff and Mark Pollack (eds.) *Interdisciplinary Perspectives on International Law and International Relations: The State of the Art* (Cambridge University Press, 2013) 62-63.

15. Barbara Koremenos, Charles Lipson, and Duncan Snidal, "The Rational Design of International Institutions" (2001) 55 International Organization 761, 762.

16. Ibid.

17. John Duffield, "The Limits of 'Rational Design' (2003) 57 International Organization 411.

18. Ernst Haas *Beyond the Nation State: Functionalism and International Organization*, 2018 ed. (ECPR Press, 2018) 124.

19. Barbara Koremenos, "If Only Half of International Agreements Have Dispute Resolution Provisions, Which Half Needs Explaining?" (2007) 36 Journal of Legal Studies 189.

20. See Koremenos (n. 14) 70-75.

21. Mikael Madsen, "From Cold War Instrument to Supreme European Court: The European Court of Human Rights at the Crossroads of International and National Law and Politics" (2007) 32 Law and Social Inquiry 137.

22. Rudolf Bernhardt, "Reform of the Control Machinery under the European Convention on Human Rights: Protocol No. 11" (1995) 89 American Journal of International Law (AJIL) 145; Steven Greer, "What's Wrong with the European Convention on Human Rights?" (2008) 30 Human Rights Quarterly (HRQ) 680.

23. Gina Bekker, "The African Court on Human and Peoples' Rights: Safeguarding the Interests of African States" (2007) 51 Journal of African Law 151.

24. Beth Simmons, "Capacity, Commitment and Compliance: International Institutions and Territorial Disputes" (2002) 46 Journal of Conflict Resolution 829.

25. Ramesh Thakur and Luk Van Langenhove, "Enhancing Global Governance through Regional Integration" (2006) 12 Global Governance 233.

26. Abbott and Snidal (n. 12); Kripa Sridharan, "Regional Organisations and Conflict Management: Comparing ASEAN and SAARC" Crisis States Research Centre Working Papers Series No. 2, March 2008) https://scholar.google.com/scholar_url?url=http://citeseerx.ist.psu.edu/viewdoc/download%3Fdoi%3D10.1.1.460.4351%26rep%3Drep1%26type%3Dpdf&hl=en&sa=T&oi=gsb-gga&ct=res&cd=0&d=8401593685303441135&ei=jkg_YZa7FtqUy9YPwseosAQ&scisig=AAGBfm1musoUAghA8JmGNMzcTG5MbIWoag.

27. Simon Chesterman, "Does ASEAN Exist? The Association of Southeast Asian Nations as an International Legal Person" (New York University Public Law and Legal Theory Working Papers) 83.

28. International Law Commission (ILC), "Fragmentation of International Law: Difficulties Arising from the Diversification and Expansion of International Law," Report of the Study Group of the International Law Commission, finalized by Martti Koskenniemi (13 April 2006) UN Doc. A/CN.4/L.682, p. 244.

29. See David Cohen, "The Rule of Law and Human Rights in ASEAN: Towards a 'rules-based' community?" in Diane Desierto and David Cohen (eds.) *ASEAN Law and Regional Integration: Governance and the Rule of Law in Southeast Asia's Single Market* (Routledge, 2020).

30. George Downs, Kyle Danish, and Peter Barsoom, "The Transformational Model of International Regime Design: Triumph of Hope or Experience?" (2000) 38 Columbia Journal of Transnational Law 465.

31. Anthony Langlois, "Human Rights, 'Orientation,' and ASEAN" (2014) 13 Journal of Human Rights 307; Mathew Davies, "ASEAN and Human Rights Norms: Constructivism, Rational Choice, and the Action-Identity Gap" (2013) 13 International Relations of the Asia-Pacific 207.

32. Mathew Davies, "The ASEAN Synthesis: Human Rights, Non-Intervention, and the ASEAN Human Rights Declaration.' (2013) 14 Georgetown Journal of International Affairs 51.

33. Attilio Pisanò, "Human Rights and Sovereignty in the ASEAN Path towards a Human Rights Declaration" (2014) 15 Human Rights Review 391.

34. B. Obinna Okere, "The Protection of Hman Rights in Africa and the African Charter on Human and Peoples' Rights: A Comparative Analysis with the European and American Systems" (1984) 6 Human Rights Quarterly (HRQ) 141.

35. Steven Greer, *The European Convention on Human Rights: Achievements, Problems and Prospects* (Cambridge University Press 2006); Karen Alter, "The Multiplication of International Courts and Tribunals after the End of the Cold War," in Cesare Romano, Karen J. Alter, and Yuval Shany (eds.) *The Oxford Handbook of International Adjudication* (Oxford University Press, 2013).

36. The ASEAN Declaration (Bangkok Declaration), Thailand (8 August 1967), https://agreement.asean.org/media/download/20140117154159.pdf.

37. Roland Burke, *Decolonization and the Evolution of International Human Rights* (University of Pennsylvania Press, 2009) chp. 1.

38. Yuen Foong Khong, "ASEAN and the Southeast Asian Security Complex," in David A. Lake and Patrick N. Morgan (eds.) *Regional Orders: Building Security in a New World* (Pennsylvania State University Press, 1997) 326-330.

39. Robin Ramcharan, "ASEAN and Non-Interference: A Principle Maintained" (2000) 22 Contemporary Southeast Asia 60.

40. Amitav Acharya, "ASEAN and Burma/Myanmar: Past and Prologue," DC Sigur Centre for Asian Studies Policy Brief, April 2012.

41. Ruukun Katanyuu, "Beyond Non-Interference in ASEAN: The Association's Role in Myanmar's National Reconciliation and Democratization (2006) 46 Asian Survey 825.

42. John Funston, "ASEAN: Out of its Depth?" (1998) 20 Contemporary Southeast Asia 22.

43. Hiro Katsumata, "Reconstruction of Diplomatic Norms in Southeast Asia: The Case for Strict Adherence to the 'ASEAN Way.'" (2003) 25 Contemporary Southeast Asia 104.

44. Tobias Ingo Nischalke, "Insights from ASEAN's Foreign Policy Co-operation: The 'ASEAN Way,' a Real Spirit or a Phantom?" (2000) 22 Contemporary Southeast Asia 89; Michael Vatikiotis, "ASEAN 10: The Political and Cultural Dimensions of Southeast Asian Unity" (1999) 27 Southeast Asian Journal of Social Science 77.

45. See Katsumata (n. 43); William Jones, "Universalizing Human Rights The ASEAN Way" (2014) 3 International Journal of Social Science 73.

46. Brian Massey and Li-jing Arthur Chang, "Locating Asian Values in Asian Journalism: A Content Analysis of Web Newspapers" (2002) 52 Journal of Communication 987.

47. Inoue Tatsuo, "'Liberal Democracy and Asian Orientalism," in Joanne Bauer and Daniel Bell (eds.) *The East Asian Challenge for Human Rights* (Cambridge University Press, 1999) 34.

48. Gillian Goh, "The 'ASEAN Way': Non-Intervention and ASEAN's Role in Conflict Management" (2003) 3 Stanford Journal of East Asian Affairs 113, 114.

49. Amitav Acharya, *Whose Ideas Matter? Agency and Power in Asian Regionalism* (Cornell University Press, 2011) chp. 2.

50. Goh (n. 48) 114.

51. Tan Sri Ahmad Fuzi bin Abdul Razak, "Facing Unfair Criticisms," in Tommy Koh, Rosario G. Manalo, and Walter Woon (eds.) *The Making of the ASEAN Charter* (World Scientific Publishing, 2009) 18.

52. See Lee Jones, *ASEAN, Sovereignty and Intervention in Southeast Asia* (Palgrave Macmillan, 2012) 2-5, 28-31.

53. Daniel Seah, "The ASEAN Charter (2009) 58 International and Comparative Law Quarterly (ICLQ) 197, 200.

54. John Arendshorst, "The Dilemma of Non-Interference: Myanmar, Human Rights, and the ASEAN Charter" (2009) 8 Northwestern Journal of Human Rights 102, 115-116.

55. Stefano Inama and Edmund Sim, *The Foundation of the ASEAN Economic Community: An Institutional and Legal Profile* (Cambridge University Press, 2015) 20-24.

56. For example, see Giovanni Molano-Cruz, "Addressing Human Rights in the Court of Justice of the Andean Community and the Tribunal of the Southern African Development Community" (2014) 81 Colombia Internacional 99, 109.

57. Anja Jetschke and Jürgen Rüland, "Decoupling Rhetoric and Practice: The Cultural Limits of ASEAN Cooperation" (2009) 22 The Pacific Review 179.

58. For an overview of this doctrine, see David Martin Jones, "Security and Democracy: The ASEAN Charter and the Dilemmas of Regionalism in South-East Asia" (2004) 84 International Affairs 735.

59. Declaration of ASEAN Concord II (Bali Concord II) (7 October 2003), Art. A.4, https://asean.org/declaration-of-asean-concord-ii-bali-concord-ii/.

60. There is no official citation system for ASEAN instruments, so they are cited with reference to their place of publication. ASEAN Charter 2007, https://asean.org/wp-content/uploads/2021/09/21069.pdf.

61. ASEAN, Terms of Reference of ASEAN Intergovernmental Commission on Human Rights (AICHR), July 2009, http://www.refworld.org/docid/4a6d87f22.html accessed 25 July 2016.

62. Ibid., Arts. 1.4 and 2.1(b).

63. Tan Hsien-Li, *The ASEAN Intergovernmental Commission on Human Rights: Institutionalising Human Rights in Southeast Asia* (Cambridge University Press, 2011) 169.

64. AICHR, Terms of Reference (n. 61), Para 2.4.

65. ASEAN Human Rights Declaration (ASEAN Secretariat Jakarta, February 2013), Art. 40.

66. Mathew Davies, "An Agreement to Disagree: The ASEAN Human Rights Declaration and the Absence of Regional Identity in Southeast Asia" (2014) 33 Journal of Current Southeast Asian Affairs 107, 114.

67. Hein Bui, "The ASEAN Human Rights System: A Critical Analysis" (2016) 11 Asian Journal of Comparative Law 111.

68. Yuyun Wahyuningrum, "A Decade of Institutionalizing Human Rights in ASEAN: Progress and Challenges" (2021) 20 Journal of Human Rights 158, 159.

69. Shaun Narine, "Human Rights Norms and the Evolution of ASEAN: Moving without Moving in a Changing Regional Environment" (2012) 34 Contemporary Southeast Asia 356, 371.

70. James Munro, "The Relationship between the Origins and Regime Design of the ASEAN Intergovernmental Commission on Human Rights (AICHR)" (2011) 15 The International Journal of Human Rights 1185, 1190. See more recently Nurhidayatuloh and Febrian, "ASEAN and European Human Rights Mechanisms, What Should be Improved?" (2019) 6 Padjadjaran Journal of Law 151, 164.

71. AICHR, Terms of Reference (n. 61), Paras. 4.2 and 4.6.

72. Hao Duy Phan, "Promotional Versus Protective Design: The Case of the Asean Intergovernmental Commission on Human Rights" (2019) 23 International Journal of Human Rights 915.

73. Ibid., 927.

74. Harsh Mahaseth and Karthik Subramaniam, "Binding or Non-Binding: Analysing the Nature of the ASEAN Agreements" (2021) 14 International and Comparative Law Review 100.

75. ASEAN Declaration (n. 65) Art 6.

76. Ibid., Art. 24.

77. See chapter 3 and Handyside v. United Kingdom (1976) ECHR 5.

78. ASEAN Declaration, Art. 27(1).

79. See Gino Naldi, "The African Union and the Regional Human Rights System," in Malcolm Evans and Rachel Murray (eds.) *The African Charter on Human and Peoples' Rights: The System in Practice 1986-2006*, 2nd ed. (Cambridge University Press, 2008) 244-288.

80. Diane Mauzy, "The Human Rights and 'Asian Values' Debate in Southeast Asia: Trying to Clarify the Key Issues" (1997) 10 The Pacific Review 210.

81. Vijay Prashad, *The Darker Nations: A People's History of the Third World* (New Press, 2007) 245-50.

82. Yvonne Tew, "Beyond 'Asian Values': Rethinking Rights" (CGHR Working Paper 5, University of Cambridge Centre of Governance and Human Rights, November 2012) https://www.repository.cam.ac.uk/handle/1810/245115.

83. For an overview of the origins of the oriental despotism thesis, see Jenifer Pitts, *Boundaries of the International: Law and Empire* (Harvard University Press, 2018) chp. 2. For a critique in the context of the Asian values debate, see John Ingelson, "The Asian Values Debate: Accommodating Dissident Voices" (1998) 8 Social Semiotics 227.

84. M. Sani, "Mahathir Mohamad as a Cultural Relativist: Mahathirism on Human Rights," (paper presentation, 17th Biennial Conference of the Asian Studies Association of Australia, Melbourne, Australia, 1-3 July 2008) http://arts.monash.edu.au/mai/asaa/mohdazizuddinmohdsani.pdf.

85. Mark Thompson, "Whatever Happened to 'Asian Values'?" (2001) 12 Journal of Democracy 154, 156.

86. Wan Manan, "A Nation in Distress: Human Rights, Authoritarianism, and Asian Values in Malaysia" (1999) 14 Sojourn: Journal of Social Issues in Southeast Asia 359; Terence Chong, "Asian Values and Confucian Ethics: Malay Singaporeans' Dilemma" (2002) 32 Journal of Contemporary Asia 394.

87. Mark Thompson, "Pacific Asia after 'Asian Values': Authoritarianism, Democracy, and 'Good Governance' (2004) 25 Third World Quarterly 1079.

88. Amartya Sen, "Human Rights and Asian Values" (16th Morgenthau Memorial Lecture on Ethics and Foreign Policy, Carnegie Council on Ethics and International Affairs, 1997) p. 18, http://rarre.org/documents/sen/Sen-%20Human%20Rights%20and%20Asian%20Values.pdf.

89. Tatsuo (n. 47) 28.

90. Michael Barr, *Cultural Politics and Asian Values: The Tepid War* (Routledge, 2004) 5-6.

91. Leigh Jenco, "Revisiting Asian Values" (2013) 74 Journal of the History of Ideas 237, 239.

92. So Yong Kim, "Do Asian Values Exist? Empirical Tests of the Four Dimensions of Asian Values" (2010) 10 Journal of East Asian Studies 315.

93. Alison Duxbury and Hsien-Li Tan, *Can ASEAN Take Human Rights Seriously?* (Cambridge University Press, 2019) 111-144.

94. Mathew Davies, "Explaining the Vientiane Action Programme: ASEAN and the Institutionalisation of Human Rights" (2013) 26 The Pacific Review 385, 399.

95. Gerard Clarke, "The Evolving ASEAN Human Rights System: The ASEAN Human Rights Declaration of 2012" (2012) 11 Northwestern Journal of Human Rights 1.

96. Ibid.

97. Amnesty International, "Postpone Deeply Flawed ASEAN Human Rights Declarations," Amnesty International Thailand Press Release, 5 November 2012, https://www.amnesty.org/en/press-releases/2012/11/postpone-deeply-flawed-asean-human-rights-declaration .

98. An Open Letter from the Coordination Committee of the Special Procedures of the Human Rights Council on the Draft ASEAN Human Rights Declaration, UN Office of the High Commissioner for Human Rights, 14 November 2012, https://www.ohchr.org/EN/NewsEvents/Pages/DisplayNews.aspx?NewsID=14864&LangID=E.

99. ICJ Press Release, "ICJ Condemns Fatally Flawed ASEAN Human Rights Declaration," 19 Nov 2012, http://www.icj.org/icj-condemns-fatally-flawed-asean-human-rights-declaration/.

100. Seth Kaplan, *Human Rights in Thick and Thin Societies: Universality without Uniformity* (Cambridge University Press, 2013) 23-24; Tan Hsien-Li (n. 63) 66.

101. For an overview, see T. Jeremy Gunn, "Deconstructing Proportionality in Limitations Analysis" (2005) 19 Emory International Law Review 465.

102. Human Rights Watch, "Creating a Culture of Fear: The Criminalization of Peaceful Expression in Malaysia," Human Rights Watch, 26 October 2015, https://www.hrw.org/report/2015/10/26/creating-culture-fear/criminalization-peaceful-expression-malaysia; Shad Saleem Faruqi, "Constitution, Courts and Free Speech," The Star Online, 12 April 2018 https://www.thestar.com.my/opinion/columnists/reflecting-on-the-law/2018/04/12/constitution-courts-and-free-speech-some-judges-have-already-planted-the-seeds-of-human-rights-activ/.

103. ASEAN Declaration (n. 65) Art. 8.

104. See Grace Poore, "Time to Get It Right: Southeast Asian Nations Human Rights Declaration," Huffington Post, 26 November 2012, https://www.huffingtonpost.com/grace-poore/time-to-get-it-right-sout_b_1914604.html.

105. ASEAN Declaration (n. 65) Art. 7.

106. Preamble, Bangkok Declaration, in Ko Swan Sik, M. C. W. Pinto, J. J. G. Syatauw (eds.) *Asian Yearbook of International Law 1993* (Martinus Nijhoff, 1994) 488-491.

107. Christina Cerna, "Universality of Human Rights and Cultural Diversity: Implementation of Human Rights in Different Socio-Cultural Contexts" (1994) 16 Human Rights Quarterly (HRQ) 740, 749.

108. Kevin Boyle, "Stock-Taking on Human Rights: The World Conference on Human Rights, Vienna 1993" (1995) 43 Political Studies 79.

109. UN General Assembly, Vienna Declaration and Programme of Action (12 July 1993) A/CONF.157/23, para. 5.

110. For an overview, see Cees Flinterman, "Vienna Declaration and Programme of Action: 20 Years Later" (2017) 31 Netherlands Quarterly of Human Rights 129.

111. Thomas Buergenthal, "The Normative and Institutional Evolution of International Human Rights" (1997) 19 Human Rights Quarterly (HRQ) 703, 714.

112. A copy of this letter can be found at UN Watch, "Letter from UN's Islamic Group to UNHRC President Opposing Panel on Violence against Gays," *UN Watch*, 17 February 2012, http://blog.unwatch.org/index.php/2012/02/17/letter-from-uns-islamic-group-to-unhrc-president-opposing-panel-on-violence-against-gays/.

113. Vienna Declaration (n. 110) para. 5.

114. Catherine Renshaw, *Human Rights and Participatory Politics in Southeast Asia* (University of Pennsylvania Press, 2019) 78-82.

115. Ole Bruun and Michael Jacobson, "Introduction," in Michael Jacobsen and Ole Bruun (eds.) *Human Rights and Asian Values: Contesting National Identities and Cultural Representations in Asia* (Routledge, 2000) 12.

116. N. A. Englehart, "Rights and Culture in the Asian Values Argument: The Rise and Fall of Confucian Ethics in Singapore" (2000) 22 Human Rights Quarterly (HRQ) 548.

117. Jack Donnelly, *Universal Human Rights: In Theory and Practice*, 2nd ed. (Cornell University Press, 2003) 113.

118. Brian Massey and Li-Jing Arthur Chang, "Locating Asian Values in Asian Journalism: A Content Analysis of Web Newspapers" (2002) 52 Journal of Communication 987.

119. See Anna Meijknecht and Byung Sook de Vries, "Is There a Place for Minorities' and Indigenous Peoples' Rights within ASEAN?: Asian Values, ASEAN Values and the Protection of Southeast Asian Minorities and Indigenous Peoples" (2010) 17 International Journal on Minority and Group Rights 75.

120. Davies (n. 94) 114.

121. Anthony Langlois, "Human Rights in Southeast Asia: ASEAN's Rights Regime after Its First Decade (2021) 20 Journal of Human Rights 151, 153.

122. Randy W. Nandyatama, *Indonesian Civil Society and Human Rights Advocacy in ASEAN: Power and Normative Struggles* (Palgrave Macmillan, 2021) 3-5.

123. Renshaw (n. 114) 80-81.

124. Ibid.

125. For an overview of this discourse, see Herman Joseph Kraft, "Human Rights, ASEAN and Constructivism: Revisiting the 'Asian Values' Discourse (2001) 22 Philippine Political Science Journal 33.

126. Sriprapha Petcharamesree, "The ASEAN Human Rights Architecture: Its Development and Challenges" (2013) 11 Equal Rights Review 46, 50.

127. Anja Jetschke, "Why Create a Human Rights Regime? The ASEAN Intergovernmental Commission for Human Rights," in Tanja A. Börzel and Vera van Hüllen (eds.) *Governance Transfer by Regional Organizations: Patching Together a Global Script* (Palgrave Macmillan, 2015).

128. Mathew Davies, "The Perils of Incoherence: ASEAN, Myanmar and the Avoidable Failures of Human Rights Socialization?" (2012) 34 Contemporary Southeast Asia 1.

129. Lee Jones, "ASEAN's Albatross: ASEAN's Burma Policy, from Constructive Engagement to Critical Disengagement" (2008) 4 Asian Security 271.

130. Other aspects of ASEAN constitutionalization seem to back up the preference for informal dispute resolution mechanisms. See Anja Jetschke, "What Drives Institutional Reforms in Regional Organisations? Diffusion, Contextual Conditions, and the Modular Design of ASEAN" (2017) 5 TRaNS: Trans-Regional and -National Studies of Southeast Asia 173.

131. Jack Donnelly, "Human Rights: A New Standard of Civilization?" (1998) 74 International Affairs 1; See also Duxbury and Hsien-Li Tan (n. 92) 346.

132. Mathew Davies, "How Regional Organizations Respond to Human Rights: ASEAN's Ritualism in Comparative Perspective" (2021) 20 Journal of Human Rights 262.

133. Nattapat Limsiritong, "Why ASEAN Fails to Play Role in the Rohingya Situation from the Perspective of ASEAN Charter" (2017) 1 Asian Political Science Review 73.

134. See Monica Pinto, "Fragmentation or Unification among International Institutions: Human Rights Tribunals" (1998) 31 New York University Journal of International Law and Policy 833.

135. Phan (n. 72).

Chapter 5

1. *Şahin v. Turkey*, ECHR 819 (2005) [16].

2. Michael Goldhaber, *A People's History of the European Court of Human Rights* (Rutgers University Press, 2009) 94-95.

3. *Lautsi v. Italy*, 54 EHRR (2012) 3.

4. See Jeffrey Brauch, "The Margin of Appreciation and the Jurisprudence of the European Court of Human Rights: Threat to the Rule of Law" (2005) 11 Columbia Journal of European Law 113; Jan Kratochvíl, "The Inflation of the Margin of Appreciation by the European Court of Human Rights" (2011) 29 Netherlands Quarterly of Human Rights 324.

5. Marie-Bénédicte Dembour, *Who Believes in Human Rights? Reflections on the European Convention* (Cambridge University Press, 2006) 159-161.

6. European Court of Human Rights, "Your Application to the ECHR: How to Apply and How Your Application is Processed," Council of Europe, https://www.echr.coe.int/Documents/Your_Application_ENG.pdf.

7. Philip Leach, *Taking a Case to the European Court of Human Rights* (Oxford University Press, 2011) 75-77.

8. Steven Greer, *The European Convention on Human Rights: Achievements, Problems and Prospects* (Cambridge University Press, 2006) 197-198.

9. Gerhard van der Schyff, "Interpreting the Protection Guaranteed by Two-Stage Rights in the European Convention on Human Rights," in Eva Brems and Janneke Gerards (eds.) *Shaping Rights in the ECHR* (Cambridge University Press, 2013).

10. European Convention on Human Rights (ECHR) (1950) Art. 8.

11. Ibid.

12. Greer (n. 8) 199.

13. Başak Çalı, "Balancing Human Rights? Methodological Problems with Weights, Scales and Proportions" (2007) 29 Human Rights Quarterly (HRQ) 251, 253.

14. Oddný Mjöll Arnardóttir, "Rethinking the Two Margins of Appreciation" (2016) 12 European Constitutional Law Review 27.

15. See Janneke Gerards, "Pluralism, Deference and the Margin of Appreciation Doctrine" (2011) 17 European Law Journal 80; Bosko Tripkovic, "A New Philosophy for the Margin of Appreciation and European Consensus (2021) Oxford Journal of Legal Studies, gqab031, https://doi.org/10.1093/ojls/gqab031.

16. Abbey Burke, "Is the Whole Point of Human Rights Their Universal Character? A, B & C v Ireland and SAS v France" (2018) 3 London School of Economics Law Review 45.

17. Dean Spielmann, "Whither the Margin of Appreciation?" (2014) 67 Current Legal Problems 49, 59.

18. George Letsas 'Two Concepts of the Margin of Appreciation' (2006) 26 Oxford Journal of Legal Studies 705, 706; ibid., Spielmann (n. 17) 49.

19. Ibid., Letsas.

20. Lord Lester, as cited in Michael R. Hutchinson, "The Margin of Appreciation Doctrine in the European Court of Human Rights" (1999) 48 International and Comparative Law Quarterly (ICLQ) 638, 641.

21. M. Lutfi Chakim, "The Margin of Appreciation and Freedom of Religion: Assessing Standards of the European Court of Human Rights" (2020) 24 International Journal of Human Rights 850.

22. See James T. Richardson, "The Sociology of Religious Freedom: A Structural and Socio-Legal Analysis" (2006) 67 Sociology of Religion 27.

23. Benjamin Straumann, "The Peace of Westphalia (1648) as a Secular Constitution" (2008) 15 Constellations 173.

24. William Schabas, *The European Convention on Human Rights: A Commentary* (Oxford University Press, 2017) 413.

25. Franklin D. Roosevelt, "Annual Address to Congress—'The Four Freedoms,'" 6 January 1941, Franklin D. Roosevelt Presidential Library and Museum, http://docs.fdrlibrary.marist.edu/od4frees.html.

26. Abdulaziz Alwasil, "Saudi Arabia's Engagement in, and Interaction with, the UN Human Rights System: An Analytical Review" (2010) 14 International Journal of Human Rights 1072, 1075.

27. UN General Assembly, Declaration on the Elimination of All Forms of Intolerance and of Discrimination Based on Religion or Belief, UNGA Res 36/55, A/RES/36/55 (25 November 1981).

28. Carolyn Evans, *Freedom of Religion Under the European Convention on Human Rights* (Oxford University Press, 2001) 70.

29. UN Human Rights Council (HRC), General Comment No. 22, The Right to Freedom of Thought, Conscience and Religion (30 July 1993) CCPR/C/21/Rev.1/Add.4, Art. 18, para. 3.

30. Isaiah Berlin, "Two Concepts of Liberty," in Henry Hardy (ed.) *Isaiah Berlin: Liberty* (OUP 2002); For the specific argument in relation to religious freedom, see Douglas Laycock, "Religious Liberty as Liberty" (1996) 7 Journal of Contemporary Legal Issues 313.

31. See Gila Stopler, "Hobby Lobby, S.A.S., and the Resolution of Religion-Based Conflicts in Liberal States" (2017) 14 International Journal of Constitutional Law 941.

32. Sylvie Langlaude Doné, "Indoctrination, Secularism, Religious Liberty and the ECHR" (2006) 55 International and Comparative Law Quarterly (ICLQ) 929.

33. Council of Europe, *Collected Edition of the 'Travaux Préparatoires' of the European Convention on Human Rights*, vol. 1 (Martinus Nijhoff, 1975) 124.

34. Evans (n. 28) 40.

35. Council of Europe, *Collected Edition of the 'Travaux Préparatoires' of the European Convention on Human Rights*, vol. 3 (Martinus Nijhoff, 1975) 266.

36. Ed Bates, *The Evolution of the European Convention on Human Rights: From Its Inception to the Creation of a Permanent Court of Human Rights* (Oxford University Press, 2010) 114-115.

37. Marco Duranti, *The Conservative Human Rights Revolution: European Identity, Transnational Politics, and the Origins of the European Convention* (Oxford University Press, 2017) 375-380.

38. Marco Duranti, "'A Blessed Act of Oblivion': Human Rights, European Unity and Postwar Reconciliation," in Birgit Schwelling (ed.) *Reconciliation, Civil Society, and the Politics of Memory: Transnational Initiatives in the 20th and 21st Century* (Transcript Verlag, 2012) 135-138.

39. A. W. Brian Simpson, *Human Rights and the End of Empire: Britain and the Genesis of the European Convention on Human Rights* (Oxford University Press, 2001) 4.

40. European Court of Human Rights: Statistics, "Violations by Article and By State 1959-2018," https://www.echr.coe.int/Documents/Stats_violation_1959_2018_ENG.pdf accessed 12 February 2019.

41. Alex Stone Sweet, "On the Constitutionalisation of the Convention: The European Court of Human Rights as a Constitutional Court" (2009) 71 Yale Law School Legal Scholarship Repository 1.

42. Zachary Calo, "Pluralism, Secularism and the European Court of Human Rights" (2010) 26 Journal of Law and Religion 261.

43. *Moscow Branch of the Salvation Army v. Russia* (2006) ECHR 828 [62].

44. *X v. United Kingdom*, ECHR 9 (1981) [33].

45. Ian Leigh, "The European Court of Human Rights and Religious Neutrality," in Gavin D'Costa, Malcolm Evans, Tariq Modood, and Julian Rivers (eds.) *Religion in a Liberal State* (Cambridge University Press, 2013) 39-41.

46. Tony Judt, *Postwar: A History of Europe since 1945*, 2nd ed. (Pimlico, 2007) 263-270.

47. HRC, Concluding Observations: Argentina (2000) CCPR/C/70/ARG, para. 16; HRC, Concluding Observations: Chile (1999) CCPR/C/79/ Add. 104, para. 24.

48. *Buscarini and Others v. San Marino*, Application No. 24645/94 (ECtHR 18 February 1999) [8].

49. Ibid., para. 32.

50. Ibid., para. 34.

51. See A. Papadakis. "The Historical Tradition of Church-State Relations under Orthodoxy," in Pedro Ramet (ed.) *Eastern Christianity and Politics in the Twentieth Century* (Duke University Press, 1998) 51-52; Daniela Kalkandjieva, " Comparative Analysis on Church-State Relations in Eastern Orthodoxy: Concepts, Models, and Principles" (2011) 53 Journal of Church and State 587.

52. Adamantia Pollis, "Greek National Identity: Religious Minorities, Rights, and European Norms" (1992) 10 Journal of Modern Greek Studies 171, 176.

53. Kyriakos Kyriazopoulos "The 'Prevailing Religion' in Greece: Its Meaning and Implications' (2001) 43 Journal of Church and State 511, 524.

54. *Kokkinakis v. Greece*, Application No. 14307/88 (ECtHR 25 May 1993) [49].

55. Ibid., para. 17.

56. This point is made in the Partially Concurring Opinion of Judge Pettiti in Kokkinakis, who argued that the court members were "confining themselves to the particular case [which] is tantamount to supervising the national court in respect of the degree of severity of the sentence passed" rather than looking at the law itself, going on to observe that "[some] may regret that, on such a serious matter, on the eve of the United Nations World Year for Tolerance, and given the United Nations Declaration against religious intolerance, the Court has failed to make explicit its interpretation of proselytism."

57. K. A. Dunne, "Addressing Religious Intolerance in Europe: The Limited Application of Article 9 of the European Convention of Human Rights and Fundamental Freedoms" (1999) 30 California Western International Law Journal 117, 138.

58. Metropolitan Church of Bessarabia v. Moldova, Application No. 45701/99 (ECtHR 13 December 2001).

59. Ibid.

60. See Church of Scientology Moscow v. Russia, ECHR 258 (2007); Religionsgemeinschaft der Zeugen Jehovas and Others v. Austria, Application. No. 40825/98 (ECtHR 31 July 2008) [92].

61. *Savez Crkava "Riječ Života" v. Croatia*, 54 EHRR 36 (2012) [73]-[75].

62. *Manoussakis v. Greece*, 23 EHRR 387 (1997) [39].

63. Lance S. Lehnhof, "Freedom of Religious Association: The Right of Religious Organizations to Obtain Legal Entity Status under the European Convention" (2002) BYU Law Review 561, 607-608.

64. *Lautsi* (n. 3).

65. Andrea Pin, "Public Schools, the Italian Crucifix, and the European Court of Human Rights: The Italian Separation of Church and State" (2011) 25 Emory International Law Review 95.

66. *Lautsi v. Italy*, ECHR 1901 (2009).

67. Ibid., para. 42.

68. Dominic McGoldrick, "Religion in the European Public Square and in European Public Life: Crucifixes in the Classroom?" (2011) 11 Human Rights Law Review 451.

69. *Lautsi* (n. 3) [68].

70. Malcolm Evans and Peter Petkoff, "Marginal Neutrality: Neutrality and the Margin of Appreciation in the Jurisprudence of the European Court of Human Rights" in Jeroen Temperman, T. Jeremy Gunn, and Malcolm D. Evans (eds.) *The European Court of Human Rights and the Freedom of Religion or Belief* (Brill, 2019) 136.

71. András Sajó, "Preliminaries to a Concept of Constitutional Secularism" (2008) 6 International Journal of Constitutional Law 605, 610.

72. Ibid.

73. *Wingrove v. United Kingdom*, 24 EHRR 1 (1997); *Otto-Preminger-Institut v. Austria*, Application. No. 13470/87 (ECtHR 20 September 1994).

74. Ibid., *Otto-Preminger-Institut.*

75. Peter Danchin, "Islam in the Secular Nomos of the European Court of Human Rights" (2010) 32 Michigan Journal of International Law 663.

76. Ann Power-Forde, "Freedom of Religion and 'Reasonable Accommodation' in the Case Law of the European Court of Human Rights" (2016) 5 Oxford Journal of Law and Religion 575.

77. Matthias Koenig, "The Governance of Religious Diversity at the European Court of Human Rights," in Jane Boulden and Will Kymlicka (eds.) *International Approaches to Governing Ethnic Diversity* (Oxford University Press, 2015) 51, 60-64.

78. *Kalaç v. Turkey*, 27 EHRR 552, 560 (1999).

79. *Dahlab v. Switzerland*, App. no. 42393/98 (ECtHR 15 February 2001).

80. *Dogru v. France*, 49 EHRR 8 (2009); *Şahin* (n. 1).

81. Some scholars have analyzed these arguments in decisions such as *Şahin*; see Jill Marshall, "Conditions for Freedom? European Human Rights Law and the Islamic Headscarf Debate" (2008) 30 Human Rights Quarterly (HRQ) 631; Anastasia Vakulenko, "'Islamic Headscarves' and the European Convention on Human Rights: An Intersectional Perspective" (2007) 16 Social and Legal Studies 183.

82. Amelie Barras, *Refashioning Secularisms in France and Turkey: The Case of the Headscarf Ban* (Routledge, 2014) 31, 76.

83. *Şahin* [35].

84. Yussef Al Tamimi, "Human Rights and the Excess of Identity: A Legal and Theoretical Inquiry into the Notion of Identity in Strasbourg Case Law" (2018) 27 Social and Legal Studies 283, 294.

85. Benjamin Bleiberg, "Unveiling the Real Issue: Evaluating the European Court of Human Rights' Decision to Enforce the Turkish Headscarf Ban in Leyla Sahin v. Turkey" (2005) 91 Cornell Law Review 129, 155.

86. *Eweida v. UK*, ECHR 37 (2013) [94].

87. Jill Marshall, "S.A.S. v France: Burqa Bans and the Control or Empowerment of Identities" (2015) 15 Human Rights Law Review 377.

88. Dissenting Opinion of Judge Tulkens, *Şahin* (n. 1) [7].

89. Patrick Weil, "Why the French *Laïcité* is Liberal" (2009) 30 Cardozo Law Review 2699.

90. Stéphanie Hennette Vauchez, "Is French *Laïcité* Still Liberal? The Republican Project under Pressure (2004–15)" (2017) 17 Human Rights Law Review 285.

91. Abdullahi An-Na'im, "Human Rights and Islamic Identity in France and Uzbekistan: Mediation of the Local and Global" (2000) 22 Human Rights Quarterly (HRQ) 906.

92. *SAS v. France*, 60 EHRR 11 (2015) [25].

93. Ibid. [82].

94. Esther Erlings, "'The Government Did Not Refer to It': SAS v France and Ordre Public at the European Court of Human Rights" (2015) 16 Melbourne Journal of International Law 587.

95. Ibid.; Lori Beaman, "Living Together v. Living Well Together: A Normative Examination of the SAS Case (2016) 4 Social Inclusion 3.

96. For background, see Naima Bouteldja, "The Reality of l'affaire du foulard," *The Guardian*, 25 February 2005 https://www.theguardian.com/world/2005/feb/25/france.religion; See also Hakeem Yusuf, "S.A.S v France: Supporting 'Living Together' or Forced Assimilation?" (2014) 3 International Human Rights Law Review 277.

97. Thomas Hammarberg, *Human Rights in Europe: No Grounds for Complacency; Viewpoints by Thomas Hammarberg, Council of Europe Commissioner for Human Rights* (Council of Europe Publishing, 2011) 40-41.

98. *SAS* [141].

99. *Ebrahimian v. France*, ECHR 1041 (2015) [42] and [67].

100. Eva Brems, "Ebrahimian v France: Headscarf Ban Upheld for Entire Public Sector," Strasbourg Observers, 27 November 2015, https://strasbourgobservers.com/2015/11/27/ebrahimian-v-france-headscarf-ban-upheld-for-entire-public-sector/.

101. Melanie Adrian, "The Principled Slope: Religious Freedom and the European Court of Human Rights" (2017) 45 Religion, State and Society 174.

102. Eva Brems, "The European Court of Human Rights and Face Veil Bans,'" E-International Relations, 21 Feb 2018, https://www.e-ir.info/2018/02/21/the-european-court-of-human-rights-and-face-veil-bans/.

103. Malcolm Evans, "The Freedom of Religion or Belief in the ECHR since *Kokkinakis*. Or 'Quoting *Kokkinakis*'" (2017) 12 Religion and Human Rights 83, 83.

104. Ibid., 84

105. Matthew Nicholson, "Majority Rule and Human Rights: Identity and Non-Identity in SAS v France" (2016) 67 Northern Ireland Legal Quarterly 115, 125.

106. James McCauley, "France Mandates Masks to Control the Coronavirus. Burqas Remain Banned" Washington Post, 10 May 2020, https://www.washingtonpost.com/world/europe/france-face-masks-coronavirus/2020/05/09/6fbd50fc-8ae6-11ea-80df-d24b35a568ae_story.html.

107. Brems (n. 100).

108. Van de Graaf, Cathérine, "The Human Rights Centre Submitted a Joint Third Party Intervention in a Case before the ECTHR against Belgium Concerning a Ban of Religious Symbols in Public High Schools," Strasbourg Observers, 1 September 2021, https://strasbourgobservers.com/2021/09/01/the-human-rights-centre-submitted-a-joint-third-party-intervention-in-a-case-before-the-ecthr-against-belgium-concerning-a-ban-of-religious-symbols-in-public-high-schools/.

109. See Janneke Gerards, "Margin of Appreciation and Incrementalism in the Case Law of the European Court of Human Rights" (2018) 18 Human Rights Law Review 495; Richard Pildes, "Supranational Courts and The Law of Democracy: The European Court of Human Rights" (2018) 9 Journal of International Dispute Settlement 154; Clare Ryan, "Europe's Moral Margin: Parental Aspirations and the European Court of Human Rights" (2018) 56 Columbia Journal of Transnational Law 468.

110. On ECtHR compliance, see Courtney Hillebrecht, "The Power of Human Rights Tribunals: Compliance with the European Court of Human Rights and Domestic Policy Change" (2014) 20 European Journal of International Relations 1100.

111. Chakim (n. 21).

112. *SAS*, [130].

Chapter 6

1. Safeeyah Kharsany, "Saudi Accepts 181 UN Human Rights Proposals," Al Jazeera, 19 March 2014, https://www.aljazeera.com/indepth/features/2014/03/saudi-accepts-181-un-human-rights-proposals-201431816474653255 8.html.

2. See Alan Desmond, "The Triangle that Could Square the Circle? The UN International Convention on the Protection of the Rights of All Migrant Workers and Members of Their Families, the EU and the Universal Periodic Review" (2015) 17 European Journal of Migration and Law 39; James Gomez and Robin Ramcharan (eds.) *The Universal Periodic Review of Southeast Asia* (Palgrave Macmillan, 2018) 97-99.

3. Nazila Ghanea, "From UN Commission on Human Rights to UN Human Rights Council: One Step Forwards or Two Steps Sideways?" (2006) 55 International and Comparative Law Quarterly 695.

4. Convention on the Elimination of All Forms of Discrimination against Women (CEDAW) (adopted 18 December 1979, entered into force 3 September 1981) 1249 UNTS 3, Art. 28(2).

5. Ronagh McQuigg, "The Responses of States to the Comments of the CEDAW Committee on Domestic Violence" (2007) 11 International Journal of Human Rights 461, 475.

6. Jennifer Riddle, "Making CEDAW Universal: A Critique of CEDAW's Reservation Regime under Article 28 and the Effectiveness of the Reporting Process" (2002) 34 George Washington International Law Review 605.

7. Frank Horn, *Reservations and Interpretative Declarations to Multilateral Treaties* (Elsevier Science, 1988) 153.

8. A full list of CEDAW reservations can be found at the United Nations Treaty Collection website, Convention on the Elimination of All Forms of Discrimination against Women, https://treaties.un.org/pages/ViewDetails.aspx?src=IND&mtdsg_no=IV-8&chapter=4&clang=_en accessed 12 January 2022.

9. Report of the UN Secretary-General, "In Larger Freedom: Towards Development, Security and Human Rights for All" (21 March 2005) A/59/2005, para. 182.

10. Ibid., para. 147.

11. Elvira Redondo, "The Universal Periodic Review of the UN Human Rights Council: An Assessment of the First Session" (2008) 7 Chinese Journal of International Law 721.

12. Edward McMahon and Marta Ascherio, "A Step Ahead in Promoting Human Rights? The Universal Periodic Review of the UN Human Rights Council" (2012) 18 Global Governance 231.

13. Allehone Abebe, "Of Shaming and Bargaining: African States and the Universal Periodic Review of the United Nations Human Rights Council" (2009) 9 Human Rights Law Review 1.

14. UN General Assembly, RES 60/251 (13 April 2006) UN Doc. A/RES/60/251.

15. Helen Upton, "The Human Rights Council: First Impressions and Future Challenges (2007) 7 Human Rights Law Review 29, 34.

16. 26th Regular Session of the Human Rights Council (10–27 June 2014).

17. "Written Statement Submitted by the International Rehabilitation Council for Torture Victims (IRCT), a Non-Governmental Organization in Special Consultative Status" (9 March 2007) A/HRC/4/NGO/144.

18. Ying Hooi Khoo, "Malaysia's Human Rights Performance: Assessment of its First Session of Universal Periodic Review in the United Nations Human Rights Council" (2014) 6 Cosmopolitan Civil Societies Journal 19.

19. Jane Cowan, "The Universal Periodic Review as a Public Audit Ritual: An Anthropological Perspective on Emerging Practices in the Global Governance of Human Rights," in Hilary Charlesworth and Emma Larking (eds.) *Human Rights and the Universal Periodic Review: Rituals and Ritualism* (Cambridge University Press, 2014) 44.

20. Valentina Carraro 'The United Nations Treaty Bodies and Universal Periodic Review: Advancing Human Rights by Preventing Politicization?" (2017) 39 Human Rights Quarterly (HRQ) 943, 952-953.

21. Hanna Beate Schöpp-Schilling, "Reservations to the Convention on the Elimination of All Forms of Discrimination against Women: An Unresolved Issue or (No) New Developments?" in Ineta Ziemele (ed.) *Reservations to Human Rights Treaties and the Vienna Convention Regime: Conflict, Harmony or Reconciliation* (Martinus Nijhoff, 2004) 12-17.

22. Report prepared by Alain Pellet, special rapporteur of the International Law Commission, "Second Report on Reservations to Treaties" (13 June 1996) UN Doc. A/CN.4/477/Add1.

23. Ibid., para. 211.

24. Ineta Ziemele and Lāsama Liede, "Reservations to Human Rights Treaties: From Draft Guideline 3.1.12 to Guideline 3.1.5.6" (2013) 24 European Journal of International Law (EJIL) 1135, 1149.

25. Ibrahim Salama, "Remarks by Ibrahim Salama: Proliferation of Treaty Bodies or Expansion of Protection?" (2011) 105 Proceedings of the Annual Meeting: American Society of International Law 515; Frederick Cowell, "Understanding the Legal Status of Universal Periodic Review Recommendations" (2018) 7 Cambridge International Law Journal 164.

26. For an overview of the literature on this point, see Elizabeth Bates, "Sophisticated Constructivism in Human Rights Compliance Theory" (2015) 25 European Journal of International Law (EJIL) 1169.

27. Friedrich Kratochwil "Making sense of 'international practices,'" in Emanuel Adler and Vincent Pouliot (eds.) *International Practices* (Cambridge University Press, 2011) 36; Kal Raustiala, "Form and Substance in International Agreements" (2005) 99 American Journal of International Law (AJIL) 581, 582.

28. Damian Etone, "Theoretical Challenges to Understanding the Potential Impact of the Universal Periodic Review Mechanism: Revisiting Theoretical Approaches to State Human Rights Compliance" (2019) 18 Journal of Human Rights 36.

29. Walter Kälin, "Ritual and Ritualism at the Universal Periodic Review: A Preliminary Appraisal," in Hilary Charlesworth and Emma Larking (eds.) *Human Rights and the Universal Periodic Review: Rituals and Ritualism* (Cambridge University Press, 2014).

30. See Edward McMahon and Marta Ascherio, "A Step Ahead in Promoting Human Rights? The Universal Periodic Review of the UN Human Rights Council" (2012) 18 Global Governance 231, 235-236.

31. Gareth Sweeney and Yuri Saito, "An NGO Assessment of the New Mechanisms of the UN Human Rights Council" (2009) 9 Human Rights Law Review 203.

32. Ibid.

33. Natalie Baird, "The Role of International Non-Governmental Organisations in the Universal Periodic Review of Pacific Island States: Can 'Doing Good' Be Done Better?" (2015) 16 Melbourne Journal of International Law 550, 557.

34. Constance de la Vega and Tamara Lewis, "Peer Review in the Mix: How the UPR Transforms Human Rights Discourse," in M. C. Bassiouni and W. A. Schabas (eds.) *New challenges for the UN human rights machinery* (Intersentia 2012) 375.

35. Kari Lerum, Kiesha McCurtis, Penelope Saunders, and Stephanie, "Using Human Rights to Hold the US Accountable for its Anti-Sex Trafficking Agenda: The Universal Periodic Review and New Directions for US Policy" (2012) 1 Anti-Trafficking Review 1 (2012) 80.

36. Kate Gilmore, Luis Mora, Alfonso Barragues, and Ida Mikkelsen, "The Universal Periodic Review: A Platform for Dialogue, Accountability, and Change on Sexual and Reproductive Health and Rights" (2015) 17 Health and Human Rights 167.

37. Sarah Tufano, "The 'Holy Trinity' of the United Nations Universal Periodic Review: How to Make an Effective Recommendation Regarding Women's Rights" (2018) 21 University of Pennsylvania Journal of Law and Social Change 187.

38. Gayatri Patel, "Smoke and Mirrors at the United Nations' Universal Periodic Review Process" (2017) 10 International Journal of Human Rights in Healthcare 310.

39. Christina Szurlej, "Universal Periodic Review: A Step in the Right Direction?" 169, (PhD thesis, submitted to Middlesex University, London, UK, July 2013, http://eprints.mdx.ac.uk/13763/1/CSzurlej_thesis.pdf.

40. Patel (n. 38).

41. Jeremy Sarkin, "How to Better Infuse Gender into the Human Rights Council's Universal Periodic Review Process" (2010) 2 Jindal Global Law Review 172.

42. Cosette Creamer and Beth Simmons, "The Dynamic Impact of Periodic Review on Women's Rights" (2018) 81 Law and Contemporary Problems 31.

43. Roger Lloret Blackburn, "Cultural Relativism in the Universal Periodic Review of the Human Rights Council" (working paper 2011/03, International Catalan Institute for Peace [ICIP], 2011) http://ssrn.com/abstract=2033134.

44. Edward McMahon and Marta Ascherio, "A Step Ahead in Promoting Human Rights? The Universal Periodic Review of the UN Human Rights Council" (2012) 18 Global Governance 231.

45. See Gayatri Patel, "How 'Universal' Is the United Nations' Universal Periodic Review Process? An Examination of the Discussions Held on Polygamy" (2017) 18 Human Rights Review 459; Mari Dahl Schlanbusch, "Sexual Orientation and Gender Identity Rights in the Universal Periodic Review" (master's thesis, Department of Archaeology and Social Anthropology, University of Tromsø, Tromsø, Norway, 2013) https://munin.uit.no/bitstream/handle/10037/5326/thesis.pdf?sequence=2&isAllowed=y.

46. For a more general study of reservations in the UPR process, see Frederick Cowell, "Reservations to Human Rights Treaties in Recommendations from the Universal Periodic Review: An Emerging Practice?" (2021) 25 International Journal of Human Rights 274.

47. For two detailed studies in this area, see Amira el-Azhary Sonbol, "A Response to Muslim Countries' Reservations against Full Implementation of CEDAW" (2010) 8 Hawwa 348; Anjali Sara Bonner, "Muslim States' Reservations to CEDAW and Possibilities for the Reconciliation of Shariah Law with International Women's Rights Norms" (2009) 3 Hong Kong Journal of Legal Studies 27.

48. UN Human Rights Committee (HRC), Report of the Working Group on the Universal Periodic Review: Mauritania" (4 January 2011) A/HRC/16/17, paras. 54, 92.11. and 92.13.

49. Mauritania: Partial Withdrawal of Reservation (30 July 2014) C.N.505.2014. TREATIES-IV.8.

50. See, for example, Niger across cycles 1 & 2, HRC, Report of the Working Group on the Universal Periodic Review: Niger (25 March 2011) A/HRC/17/15, paras. 78.7 and 78.12; HRC, Report of the Working Group on the Universal Periodic Review: Niger (12 April 2016) A/HRC/32/5, para. 120.18.

51. CEDAW, Bahrain Reservations on Accession (15 July 2002) C.N.717.2002. TREATIES-20 (Depositary Notification).

52. Supreme Council for Women, "International Cooperation and Follow up of International Agreements," June 2015, http://www.scw.bh/en/CooperationandPartnership/International/Pages/InternationalAgreements.aspx accessed 18 December 2018.

53. NGOs in Bahrain, "The Shadow Report on Implementation of the Convention on the Elimination of All Forms of Discrimination against Women (CEDAW)," (September 2008) 12, https://tbinternet.ohchr.org/Treaties/CEDAW/Shared%20Documents/BHR/INT_CEDAW_NGO_BHR_42_8141_E.pdf accessed 19 Dec 2020, as are all subsequent links.

54. Bahrain Human Rights Society (BHRS), "Bahrain: The Impact of Reservations to CEDAW," Coalition Eaglité Sans Réserve.

55. CEDAW Committee, Concluding Observations of the Committee on the Elimination of Discrimination against Women: Bahrain" (14 November 2008) CEDAW/C/BHR/CO/2, para. 16.

56. HRC, Report of the Working Group on the Universal Periodic Review: Bahrain" (22 May 2008) A/HRC/8/19, para. 60.2.

57. HRC, National Report Submitted in Accordance with Paragraph 5 of the Annex to Human Rights Council Resolution 16/21: Bahrain (30 March 2012) A/HRC/WG.6/13/BHR/1, p. 5.

58. HRC, Report of the Working Group on the Universal Periodic Review: Bahrain (6 March 2012) A/HRC/21/6, paras. 115.9-115.10.

59. "Bahrain Approves Women's Rights Law Amendment," Trade Arabia, 17 March 2014, http://www.tradearabia.com/news/MISC_254144.html.

60. CEDAW, Bahrain: Modification of Reservations Made upon Accession (5 August 2016) C.N.578.2016.TREATIES-IV.8.

61. CEDAW Committee, Fourth Periodic Report Submitted by Bahrain under Article 18 of the Convention (11 October 2018) CEDAW/C/BHR/4, para. 52.

62. CEDAW Committee, Concluding Observations on the Third Periodic Report of Bahrain (10 March 2014) CEDAW/C/BHR/CO/3, paras. 9-10.

63. HRC, Report of the Working Group on the Universal Periodic Review: Bahrain (10 July 2017) A/HRC/36/3, para. 9.

64. Ibid., para. 114.2.

65. HRC, Report of the Working Group on the Universal Periodic Review: Singapore (15 April 2016) A/HRC/32/17, para. 11.

66. Ibid.

67. Ibid., para. 76.

68. CEDAW, Accession of Maldives (26 October 1993) C.N.2.51.19.

69. CEDAW, Objection by Finland Concerning Reservations Made by Maldives upon Accession (28 July 1994) C.N.205.1994.TREATIES-4.

70. HRC, Report of the Working Group on the Universal Periodic Review: Maldives (4 January 2011) A/HRC/16/7, para. 100.21.

71. HRC, National Report Submitted in Accordance with Paragraph 15(a) of the Annex to Human Rights Council Resolution 5/1: Maldives (30 August 2010) A/HRC/WG.6/9/MDV/1/Rev.1, para. 39.

72. UN Development Programme (UNDP), Written Contribution for the UPR Documentation of Maldives by United Nations Development Programme Country Office, Maldives, 2015, https://www.refworld.org/docid/553a25c14.html.

73. CEDAW, Maldives: Withdrawal of Reservation Regarding Article 7(A) (1 April 2010) C.N.195.2010.TREATIES-2.

74. Hope for Women, "Maldives NGO Shadow Report to the Committee on the Elimination of Discrimination against Women, 2012" September 2012, https://www2.ohchr.org/english/bodies/cedaw/docs/ngos/hopeforwomen_maldivesforpswg.pdf.

75. CEDAW Committee, Concluding Observations on the Combined Fourth and Fifth Periodic Reports of Maldives (11 March 2015) CEDAW/C/MDV/CO/4-5, paras. 8-9.

76. HRC, Report of the Working Group on the Universal Periodic Review: Maldives (13 July 2015) A/HRC/30/8, para. 11.

77. Ibid., para. 12.

78. Final Declaration of the Regional Meeting for Asia of the World Conference on Human Rights, 2 April 1993, https://www.ru.nl/publish/pages/688605/bangkok-eng.pdf.

79. Rhona Smith, "The Pacific Island States: Themes Emerging from the United Nations Human Rights Council's Inaugural Universal Periodic Review?" (2012) 13 Melbourne Journal of International Law 569.

80. Frederick Cowell and Angelina Milon, "Decriminalisation of Sexual Orientation through the Universal Periodic Review" (2012) 12 Human Rights Law Review 341.

81. Sweeney and Saito (n. 31).

82. Blackburn (n. 43).

83. Jarvis Matiya, "Repositioning the International Human Rights Protection System: The UN Human Rights Council" (2010) 36 Commonwealth Law Bulletin 313.

84. CEDAW, Denmark: Objection (10 March 2003) C.N.215.2003.TREATIES-4.

85. Ibid.

86. CEDAW Committee, Concluding Observations of the Committee on the Elimination of Discrimination against Women: United Arab Emirates, (5 February 2010) CEDAW/C/ARE/CO/1, para. 17.

87. CEDAW Committee, Concluding Observations on the Combined Second and Third Periodic Reports of the United Arab Emirates (24 November 2015) CEDAW/C/ARE/CO/2-3, para. 10.

88. CEDAW Committee, Consideration of Reports Submitted by States Parties under Article 18 of the Convention: United Arab Emirates (3 December 2014) CEDAW/C/ARE/2-3, para. 17.

89. Ibid., para. 89.

90. HRC, Report of the Working Group on the Universal Periodic Review: United Arab Emirates (12 January 2009) A/HRC/10/75, para. 30.

91. HRC, Report of the Working Group on the Universal Periodic Review: United Arab Emirates (21 March 2013) A/HRC/23/13, para. 15-16.

92. Ibid., para 54.

93. Edward, McMahon, "Herding Cats and Sheep: Assessing State and Regional Behavior in the Universal Periodic Review Mechanism of the United Nations Human Rights Council," UPR Info, September 2010, https://www.researchgate.net/profile/Edward_Mcmahon2/publication/267561571_Herding_Cats_and_Sheep_Assessing_State_and_Regional_Behavior_in_the_Universal_Periodic_Review_Mechanism_of_the_United_Nations_Human_Rights_Council/links/59074b34aca272116d36615a/Herding-Cats-and-Sheep-Assessing-State-and-Regional-Behavior-in-the-Universal-Periodic-Review-Mechanism-of-the-United-Nations-Human-Rights-Council.pdf.

94. Gayatri Patel, *Women and International Human Rights Law: Universal Periodic Review in Practice* (Routledge, 2020) 13-15.

95. See Hilary Charlesworth and Christine Chinkin, *The Boundaries of International Law: A Feminist Analysis* (Manchester University Press, 2000) 218-240; Darren Rosenblum, 'Unsex CEDAW, or What's Wrong with Women's Rights" (2011) 20 Columbia Journal of Gender and Law 98.

Chapter 7

1. Susan Marks, "Nightmare and Noble Dream: The 1993 World Conference on Human Rights" (1994) 53 Cambridge Law Journal 54.

2. For historical commentary, see Christina Cerna, "Universality of Human Rights and Cultural Diversity: Implementation of Human Rights in Different Socio-Cultural Contexts" (1994)

16 Human Rights Quarterly (HRQ) 740. Cees Flinterman, "Vienna Declaration and Programme of Action: 20 Years Later" (2013) 31 Netherlands Quarterly of Human Rights 129.

3. For the original Christopher quote, see David Ottaway, "Universality of Rights is Defended by U.S.," *Washington Post*, 15 June 1993. For an account on the difficulty of drafting the declaration, see Laurie Wiseberg, "The Vienna World Conference on Human Rights," in Eric Fawcett and Hanna Newcombe (eds.) *United Nations Reform: Looking Ahead After Fifty Years* (Dundurn, 1995) 175-180.

4. Kevin Boyle, "Stock-Taking on Human Rights: The World Conference on Human Rights, Vienna 1993" (1995) 43 Political Studies 79, 81.

5. For contemporary sources supporting this view, see Patricia Feeney, "The UN World Conference on Human Rights, Vienna, June 1993" (1993) 3 Development in Practice 218.

6. Upendra Baxi, *Human Rights in a Posthuman World* (Oxford University Press, 2008) 31.

7. Anthony Pagden, "Human Rights, Natural Rights, and Europe's Imperial Legacy" (2003) 31 Political Theory 171.

8. Balakrishnan Rajagopal, *International Law from Below: Development, Social Movements and Third World Resistance* (Cambridge University Press, 2003).

9. Makau Mutua, "Savages, Victims, and Saviors: The Metaphor of Human Rights" (2001) 42 Harvard International Law Journal 201, 206.

10. Opeoluwa Badaru, "Examining the Utility of Third World Approaches to International Law for International Human Rights Law" (2008) 10 International Community Law Review 379.

11. See Antony Anghie, "'Colonial Origins of International Law' in Laws of the Postcolonial," in Eve Darian-Smith and Peter Fitzpatrick (eds.) *Laws of the Postcolonial* (University of Michigan Press, 1999).

12. Francisco de Vitoria, *Vitoria: Political Writings*, ed. Anthony Pagden and Jeremy Lawrance (Cambridge University Press, 1991) 232.

13. Paolo Carozza, "From Conquest to Constitutions: Retrieving a Latin American Tradition of the Idea of Human Rights" (2003) 25 Human Rights Quarterly (HRQ) 281, 289-291.

14. David Kennedy, "Primitive Legal Scholarship" (1986) 27 Harvard Journal of International Law 1.

15. Antony Anghie, *Imperialism, Sovereignty and the Making of International Law* (Cambridge University Press, 2004) chp. 1.

16. Brett Bowden, "The Colonial Origins of International Law: European Expansion and the Classical Standard of Civilization" (2005) 7 Journal of the History of International Law / Revue d'histoire du droit international 1571.

17. Antony Anghie, "Colonialism and the Birth of International Institutions: Sovereignty, Economy, and the Mandate System of the League of Nations" (2002) 34 NYU Journal of International Law and Policy 513.

18. José-Manuel Barreto, "Decolonial Strategies and Dialogue in the Human Rights Field: A Manifesto" (2012) 3 Transnational Legal Theory 1.

19. Aníbal Quijano, "Coloniality and Modernity/Rationality" (2007) 21 Cultural Studies 168, 177.

20. Peter Fitzpatrick, "The Revolutionary Past: Decolonizing Law and Human Rights" (2014) 2 Metodo: International Studies in Phenomenology and Philosophy 117, 120.

21. José-Manuel Barreto, 'Imperialism and Decolonization as Scenarios of Human Rights History.' In José-Manuel Barreto (ed.) *Human Rights from a Third World Perspective: Critique, History and International Law* (Cambridge Scholars Publishing, 2013) 141-149.

22. Abdullahi An-Na'im, "Toward a Cross-Cultural Approach to Defining International Standards of Human Rights: The Meaning of Cruel, Inhuman, or Degrading Treatment or Punishment.' In Abdullahi An-Na'im (ed.) *Human Rights in Cross-Cultural Perspectives: A Quest for Consensus*, 2nd ed. (University of Pennsylvania Press, 1995).

23. Walter Mignolo, "Citizenship, Knowledge, and the Limits of Humanity" (2006) 18 American Literary History 312, 314.

24. Walter Mignolo, "Epistemic Disobedience, Independent Thought and De-Colonial Freedom" (2009) 26 Theory, Culture and Society 1, 3. See also Kishore Mahbubani, *Can Asians Think? Understanding the Divide Between East and West* (Steerforth Press, 2001).

25. Macarena Gómez-Barris, "Mapuche Hunger Acts: Epistemology of the Decolonial" (2012) 3 Transmodernity 120, 127.

26. Vijay Prashad, *The Poorer Nations: A Possible History of the Global South* (Verso, 2013) 49.

27. For related scholarly work on this point, see Dianne Otto, "Postcolonialism and Law?" (1999) 15 Third World Legal Studies vi; Owen Brown, "Rights from the Other Side of the Line: Postcolonial Perspectives on Human Rights" (2014) 25 Politikon: The IAPSS Journal of Political Science 5.

28. Chidi Odinkalu, "Analysis of Paralysis or Paralysis by Analysis? Implementing Economic, Social, and Cultural Rights Under the African Charter on Human and Peoples' Rights (2001) 23 Human Rights Quarterly (HRQ) 327, 336.

29. Richard Kiwanuka 'The Meaning of "People" in the African Charter on Human and Peoples' Rights.' (1988) 82 American Journal of International Law (AJIL) 80.

30. The Social and Economic Rights Action Centre and the Centre for Economic and Social Rights v. Nigeria, Communication 155/96 in the 15th Activity Report of the African Commission on Human and Peoples Rights 2001–2002, ACHPR/RPT 15 Annex V, para. 56.

31. Makau Mutua, "The Banjul Charter and the African Cultural Fingerprint: An Evaluation of the Language of Duties" (1995) 35 Virginia Journal of International Law 339.

32. Melissa Robbins, "Powerful States, Customary Law and the Erosion of Human Rights through Regional Enforcement" (2005) 35 California Western International Law Journal 275.

33. Philip Amoah, "The African Charter on Human and Peoples' Rights: An Effective Weapon for Human Rights?" (1992) 4 African Journal of International and Comparative Law 226.

34. See Mutua (n. 31); Richard Gittleman, "The African Charter on Human and Peoples' Rights: A Legal Analysis" (1982) 22 Virginia Journal of International Law 667.

35. See Daniel Whelan, *Indivisible Human Rights: A History* (University of Pennsylvania Press, 2010) chp. 6.

36. For examples, see Claude Ake, "The African Context of Human Rights" (1987) 34 Africa Today 5 and Mark Anikpo, "Human Rights and Self-Reliance in Africa," in George Shepherd and Mark Anikpo (eds.) *Emerging Human Rights:Tthe African Political Economy Context* (Greenwood Press, 1990).

37. See Odinkalu (n. 28); Rowland Cole, "The African Court on Human and Peoples' Rights: Will Political Stereotypes Form an Obstacle to the Enforcement of its Decisions?" (2010) 43 Comparative and International Law Journal of Southern Africa 23.

38. Bonny Ibhawoh, "Between Culture and Constitution: Evaluating the Cultural Legitimacy of Human Rights in the African State" (2000) 22 Human Rights Quarterly (HRQ) 838, 853.

39. Ibid., 854

40. Joint Separate Opinion of Judges A. A. Canqado Trindade, M. Pacheco Gomez, and A. Abreu Burelli, Mayagna (Sumo) Awas Tingni Community v. Nicaragua, Judgment, Inter-Am. Ct. H. R. (Ser. C) No. 79, T 14 (31 August 2001) para. 14.

41. Boaventura de Sousa Santos, "Toward a Multicultural Conception of Human Rights," in Felipe Gómez Isa and Koen de Feyter (eds.) *International Protection of Human Rights: Achievements and Challenges* (University of Deusto, 2006) 58.

42. Amnesty International, Comité Loosli Bachelard, Lawyers' Committee for Human Rights, Association of Members of the Episcopal Conference of East Africa v. Sudan (1999) Application No. 48/90-50/91-52/91-89/93, para. 72-78.

43. African Commission on Human and Peoples' Rights, Consideration of Reports Submitted by States Parties under the Terms of Article 62 of the African Charter on Human and Peoples' Rights: Concluding Observations and Recommendations on the Periodic Report of the Republic of Sudan (4 June 2004) para. 12.

44. Julia Ernst, "Religious Law and Women's Human Rights: Reflections upon the African Human Rights System" (2016) 39 Hastings International and Comparative Law Review 1.

45. APDF & AMP v Mali (046/2016) [2018] AFCHPR 15; (11 MAY 2018) para. 66.

46. Frans Viljoen, "An Introduction to the Protocol to the African Charter on Human and Peoples' Rights on the Rights of Women in Africa" (2009) 16 Washington and Lee Journal of Civil Rights and Social Justice 11, 31.

47. Carl Schmitt, *Political Theology: Four Chapters on the Concept of Sovereignty*, trans. and ed. George Schwab (University of Chicago Press, 2005) chp. 4; On the history of the concept more generally, see Martin Loughlin, "On Constituent Power," in Michael Dowdle and Michael Wilkinson (eds.) *Constitutionalism beyond Liberalism* (Cambridge University Press, 2017).

48. Andreas Kalyvas, "Popular Sovereignty, Democracy, and the Constituent Power" (2005) 12 Constellations 223.

49. For a discussion of this and other tensions in the notion of constituted power in international law, see Bardo Fassbender, "'We the Peoples of the United Nations': Constituent Power and Constitutional Form in International Law," in Martin Loughlin and Neil Walker (eds.) *The Paradox of Constitutionalism: Constituent Power and Constitutional Form* (Oxford University Press, 2008) 268.

50. Beth Simmons, *Mobilizing for Human Rights: International Law in Domestic Politics* (Cambridge University Press, 2009) 126. Evidence also shows that treaty commitments can be effective at mobilizing political opinion against governments. See Adam Chilton, "The Influence of International Human Rights Agreements on Public Opinion: An Experimental Study" (2014) 15 Chicago Journal of International Law 110.

51. See Thomas Risse and Kathryn Sikkink, "The Socialization of International Human Rights Norms into Domestic Practices: Introduction," in Thomas Risse, Stephen C. Ropp, and Kathryn Sikkink (eds.) *The Power of Human Rights: International Norms and Domestic Change* (Cambridge University Press, 1999).

52. Boaventura de Sousa Santos and César A. Rodríguez-Garavito, "Law, Politics, and the Subaltern in Counter-Hegemonic Globalization," in Boaventura de Sousa Santos and César A. Rodríguez-Garavito (eds.) *Law and Globalization from Below: Towards a Cosmopolitan Legality* (Cambridge University Press, 2005).

53. Kay Warren, "The 2000 UN Human Trafficking Protocol: Rights, Enforcement, Vulnerabilities," in Mark Goodale and Sally Engle Merry (eds.) *The Practice of Human Rights: Tracking Law Between the Global and the Local* (Cambridge University Press, 2007) 243.

54. Neil Stammers, "Social Movements and the Social Construction of Human Rights" (1999) 21 Human Rights Quarterly (HRQ) 980.

55. Ibid.

56. Sylvia Vatuk, "The 'Women's Court' in India: An Alternative Dispute Resolution Body for Women in Distress" (2013) 45 Journal of Legal Pluralism and Unofficial Law 76.

57. Veronica Magar, "Empowerment Approaches to Gender-Based Violence: Women's Courts in Delhi Slums" (2003) 26 Women's Studies International Forum 509.

58. Laura Arriaza and Naomi Roht-Arriaza, "Social Repair at the Local Level: The Case of Guatemala," in Kieran McEvoy and Lorna McGregor (eds.) *Transitional Justice from Below: Grassroots Activism and the Struggle for Change* (Hart Publishing, 2008) 164-165.

59. Megan Davis, "Indigenous Struggles in Standard-Setting: The United Nations Declaration on the Rights of Indigenous Peoples" (2008) 9 Melbourne Journal of International Law 439.

60. See, respectively, César A. Rodríguez-Garavito and Luis Arenas, "Indigenous Rights, Transnational Activism, and Legal Mobilization: The Struggle of the U'wa People in Colombia," in Santos and Rodríguez-Garavito (n. 52); Peggy Levitt and Sally Merry, "Vernacularization on the Ground: Local Uses of Global Women's Rights in Peru, China, India and the United States" (2009) 9 Global Networks 441, 449.

61. Steven Wheatley, *Democracy, Minorities and International Law* (Cambridge University Press, 2005) 15.

62. As Choudhury argues, relativist arguments are often characterized by culture as a bounded and unchanging entity, making it less of an appropriate vehicle for these sorts of claims. Cyra Akila Choudhury, "Beyond Culture: Human Rights Universalisms versus Religious and Cultural Relativism in the Activism for Gender Justice" (2015) 30 Berkeley Journal of Gender, Law and Justice 226, 231.

63. For a summary, see Jamie Mayerfeld, "The Democratic Legitimacy of International Human Rights Law" (2009) 19 Indiana International and Comparative Law Review 49.

64. Adamantia Pollis, "A New Universalism," in Adamantia Pollis and Peter Schwab (eds.) *Human Rights: New Perspectives, New Realities* (Lynne Rienner, 2000).

65. For example, see criticism of the ECtHR in Richard Bellamy, "The Democratic Legitimacy of International Human Rights Conventions: Political Constitutionalism and the European Convention on Human Rights" (2015) 25 European Journal of International Law (EJIL) 1019.

66. Jed Rubenfeld, "Unilateralism and Constitutionalism" (2004) 79 NYU Law Review 1971, 1978.

67. See Conor Gearty, *On Fantasy Island: Britain, Europe, and Human Rights* (Oxford University Press, 2016) 81-95.

68. John O. McGinnis and Ilya Somin, "Democracy and International Human Rights Law" (2009) 84 Notre Dame Law Review 1739, 1741.

69. Jean Cohen, "Rethinking Human Rights, Democracy, and Sovereignty in the Age of Globalization" (2008) 36 Political Theory 578.

70. See Sanjaya Wilson Jayasekera, "Democratic Legitimacy of International Human Rights Law: A Reply to Professor Rubenfeld" (March 22, 2017). Available at SSRN: https://ssrn.com/abstract=3007132.

71. Janneke Gerards, "Margin of Appreciation and Incrementalism in the Case Law of the European Court of Human Rights" (2018) 18 Human Rights Law Review 495.

72. Open Door and Dublin Well Woman v. Ireland, ECHR 68 (1992).

73. Jorge Contesse, “Resisting the Inter-American Human Rights System” (2019) 44 Yale Journal of International Law 1.

74. Mayerfeld (n. 63) 63.

75. Ellen Messer, “Pluralist Approaches to Human Rights” (1997) 53 Journal of Anthropological Research 293.

76. Roberto Unger, *The Critical Legal Studies Movement: Another Time, A Greater Task*, 3rd ed. (Verso, 2015).

77. Theodor Adorno and Max Horkheimer, *Dialectic of Enlightenment*, 7th ed., trans. John Cumming (Verso, 2016).

78. Balakrishnan Rajagopal, “Counter-Hegemonic International Law: Rethinking Human Rights and Development as a Third World Strategy” (2006) 27 Third World Quarterly 767.

79. For a discussion of this point, see Ben Golder, “Beyond Redemption? Problematising the Critique of Human Rights in Contemporary International Legal Thought” (2014) 2 London Review of International Law 77.

80. Costas Douzinas, *The End of Human Rights: Critical Legal Thought at the Turn of the Century* (Hart Publishing, 2000) 7.

81. Marie-Bénédicte Dembour, “What are Human Rights? Four Schools of Thought? (2010) 32 Human Rights Quarterly (HRQ) 1.

82. Illan rua Wall, *Human Rights and Constituent Power: Without Model or Warranty* (Routledge, 2012).

83. Elizabeth Iglesias, “International Law, Human Rights, and LatCrit Theory” (1996) 28 University of Miami Inter-American Law Review 177, 184.

84. Jean-Luc Nancy, “On Human Rights: Two Simple Remarks,” trans. Gilbert Leung, in Costas Douzinas and Conor Gearty (eds.) *The Meanings of Rights: The Philosophy and Social Theory of Human Rights* (Cambridge University Press, 2014) 16.

85. John Laughland, “Human Rights and the Rule of Law: Achieving Universal Justice?” in David Chandler (ed.) *Rethinking Human Rights: Critical Approaches to International Politics* (Palgrave Macmillan, 2002) 38, 44.

86. Ben Golder, “Foucault and the Unfinished Human of Rights” (2010) 6 Law, Culture and the Humanities 354.

87. Jessica Whyte, “Human Rights: Confronting Governments? Michel Foucault and the Right to Intervene,” in Matthew Stone, Illan rua Wall, and Costas Douzinas (eds.) *New Critical Legal Thinking: Law and the Political* (Routledge, 2012) 14.

88. Paul Patton, “Government, Rights and Legitimacy: Foucault and Liberal Political Normativity” (2015) 15 European Journal of Political Theory 1.

89. Pheng Cheah, *Inhuman Conditions: On Cosmopolitanism and Human Rights* (Harvard University Press, 2006) 146-147.

90. Tony Evans, *Human Rights in the Global Political Economy* (Lynne Rienner, 2011) 40.

91. Illan rua Wall, “On a Radical Politics for Human Rights,” in Costas Douzinas and Conor Gearty (eds.) *The Meanings of Rights: The Philosophy and Social Theory of Human Rights* (Cambridge University Press, 2014) 113.

92. Stewart Motha and Thanos Zartaloudis, “Law, Ethics and the Utopian End of Human Rights” (2003) 12 Social and Legal Studies 243.

93. Whyte (n. 87).

94. Costas Douzinas, *Human Rights and Empire: The Political Philosophy of Cosmopolitanism* (Routledge-Cavendish, 2007) 53-59.

95. UN General Assembly, Vienna Declaration and Programme of Action (12 July 1993) A/CONF.157/23, para. 5.

96. Tony Evans, "International Human Rights Law as Power/Knowledge" (2005) 27 Human Rights Quarterly (HRQ) 1046-1068.

97. Dianne Otto, "Rethinking Universals: Opening Transformative Possibilities in International Human Rights Law" (1997) 18 Australian Yearbook of International Law 1, 10.

98. Sylvia Tamale, "The Right to Culture and the Culture of Rights: A Critical Perspective on Women's Sexual Rights in Africa" (2008) 16 Feminist Legal Studies 47, 64.

99. L. and V. v. Austria, Application Nos. 39392/98 and 39829/98. (ECtHR 9 January 2003).

100. Hope Lewis, "Embracing Complexity: Human Rights in Critical Race Feminist Perspective" (2003) 12 Columbia Journal of Gender and Law 510.

101. Martti Koskenniemi, *The Politics of International Law* (Hart, 2011) 299.

102. Emmanuelle Jouannet, "A Critical Introduction to Koskenniemi," in Martti Koskenniemi, *The Politics of International Law* (Hart, 2011) 13.

103. See Steven Ratner, "Persuading to Comply: On the Deployment and Avoidance of Legal Argumentation," in Jeffrey Dunoff and Mark Pollack, *Interdisciplinary Perspectives on International Law and International Relations: The State of the Art* (Cambridge University Press, 2013).

104. For a definition of content-independent legitimacy, see Lynn Dobson, "Legitimacy, Institutional Power, and International Human Rights Institutions: A Conceptual Enquiry," in Andreas Føllesdal, Johan Karlsson Schaffer, and Geir Ulfstein (eds.) *The Legitimacy of International Human Rights Regimes: Legal, Political and Philosophical Perspectives* (Cambridge University Press, 2013) 195-202.

105. Christian Reus-Smit, *The Politics of International Law* (Cambridge University Press, 2004) 25.

106. For clarification of these terms, see Thomas Risse and Stephen Ropp, "Introduction and Overview," in Thomas Risse, Stephen Ropp, and Kathryn Sikkink (eds.) *The Persistent Power of Human Rights: From Commitment to Compliance* (Cambridge University Press, 2013).

107. Christian Reus-Smit, "Politics and International Legal Obligation" (2003) 9 European Journal of International Relations 591, 611.

108. See Jana von Stein, "Making Promises, Keeping Promises: Democracy, Ratification and Compliance in International Human Rights Law" (2015) 46 British Journal of Political Science 655; Zachary Elkins, Tom Ginsburg, and Beth Simmons, "Getting to Rights: Treaty Ratification, Constitutional Convergence, and Human Rights Practice" (2013) 54 Harvard International Law Journal 61.

109. Reus-Smit (n. 107) 613.

110. For an example, see James Hollyer and B. Peter Rosendorff, "Why Do Authoritarian Regimes Sign the Convention against Torture? Signaling, Domestic Politics and Non-Compliance" (2011) 6 Quarterly Journal of Political Science 275.

111. Sonia Cardenas, *Conflict and Compliance: State Responses to International Human Rights Pressure* (University of Pennsylvania Press, 2010) 27-29.

112. This moment is identified by Goodman and Jinks in response to their theory of acculturation as a form of human rights change; Ryan Goodman and Derek Jinks, "Incomplete Internalization and Compliance with Human Rights Law" (2008) 19 European Journal of International Law (EJIL) 275.

113. Surabhi Ranganathan, *Strategically Created Treaty Conflicts and the Politics of International Law* (Cambridge University Press, 2014) 96-97.

114. Johns describes in some detail how legal regimes are self-reproducing; see Fleur Johns, *Non-Legality in International Law: Unruly Law* (Cambridge University Press, 2013) chp. 1.

115. On the point of compliance, see Abram Chayes and Antonia Handler Chayes, "On Compliance" (1993) 47 International Organization 175.

116. Jana von Stein, "The Engines of Compliance," in Jeffery Dunoff and Mark Pollack (eds.) *Interdisciplinary Perspectives on International Law and International Relations: The State of the Art* (Cambridge University Press, 2013) 486-487.

117. See Messer (n. 75).

118. For this definition of sovereignty, see Richard Steinberg, "Who is Sovereign?" (2004) 40 Stanford Journal of International Law 329, 332.

119. For an overview, see Courtney Hillebrecht, *Domestic Politics and International Human Rights Tribunals: The Problem of Compliance* (Cambridge University Press, 2014) 44-60.

120. Cardenas (n. 111).

121. Douglas Lee Donoho, "The Democratic Legitimacy in Human Rights: The Future of International Decision-Making" (2003) 21 Wisconsin International Law Journal 1.

122. For literature on this point, see Susanne Zwingel, "From Intergovernmental Negotiations to (Sub)National Change" (2005) 7 International Feminist Journal of Politics 400; Neil A. Englehart and Melissa K. Miller, "The CEDAW Effect: International Law's Impact on Women's Rights" (2014) 13 Journal of Human Rights 22.

123. Andrew Novak, "Using International and Foreign Law in Human Rights Litigation: The Decriminalization of Homosexuality in Belize" (2018) 10 Journal of Human Rights Practice 346.

124. Marks (n. 1) 56.

Chapter 8

1. *Shin v. Republic of Korea*, Communication No. 926/2000, CCPR/C/80/D/926/2000 (2004) para. 2.1.

2. Ibid., para. 2.2.

3. See *Keun-Tae Kim v. Republic of Korea*, Communication No. 574/1994, CCPR/C/64/D/574/1994 (1999); *Jung v. Republic of Korea*, Communication No. 1593, CCPR/C/98/D/1593-1603/2007 (2010).

4. Shin (n. 1) para. 7.3 .

5. Jacques Derrida, *The Beast and the Sovereign*, vol. 1, trans. Geoffrey Bennington (Chicago University Press, 2011) 70.

6. See Carl Schmitt, *The Leviathan in the State Theory of Thomas Hobbes: Meaning and Failure of a Political Symbol*, trans. George Schwab and Erna Hilfstein (Greenwood Press, 1996) 34-32. For a critique of the image of the Leviathan as an image of the sovereign in Hobbes's work, see Arash Abizadeh, "The Representation of Hobbesian Sovereignty: *Leviathan* as Mythology," in S. A. Lloyd (ed.) *Hobbes Today: Insights for the Twenty First Century* (Cambridge University Press, 2013).

7. See Kate Parlett, *The Individual in the International Legal System: Continuity and Change in International Law* (Cambridge University Press, 2011) 338-339; Brad Roth, *Sovereign Equality and Moral Disagreement: Premises of a Pluralist International Legal Order* (Oxford University Press, 2011) Introduction.

8. Michael Stohl, "It Was the Best of Times, It Was the Worst of Times: Conclusions on Contesting Human Rights," in Alison Brysk and Michael Stohl (eds.) *Contesting Human Rights: Norms, Institutions and Practice* (Edward Elgar, 2018).

9. Sonia Cardenas, *Conflict and Compliance: State Responses to International Human Rights Pressure* (University of Pennsylvania Press, 2010) 27-29.

10. See Diane Kraft, "South Korea's National Security Law: A Tool of Oppression in an Insecure World" (2006) 24 Wisconsin International Law Journal 627.

11. Surabhi Ranganathan, *Strategically Created Treaty Conflicts and the Politics of International Law* (Cambridge University Press, 2014) 96-97.

12. Robert Howse and Ruti Teitel, "Beyond Compliance: Rethinking Why International Law Really Matters" (2010) 1 Global Policy 127; Geoff Dancy and Christopher J. Fariss, "Rescuing Human Rights Law from International Legalism and its Critics" (2017) 39 Human Rights Quarterly (HRQ) 1.

13. Jean d'Aspremont, *International Law as a Belief System* (Cambridge University Press, 2017) 9-17.

14. Giselle Corradi, 'Introduction: Human Rights and Legal Pluralism; Four Research Agendas," inn Giselle Corradi, Eva Brems, and Mark Goodale (eds.) *Human Rights Encounter Legal Pluralism: Normative and Empirical Approaches* (Hart, 2017) 3.

15. Louis Henkin, "That 'S' Word: Sovereignty, and Globalization, and Human Rights, Et Cetera" (1999) 68 Fordham Law Review 1, 6.

16. Robert Jackson, "Sovereignty in World Politics: A Glance at the Conceptual and Historical Landscape" (1999) 47 Political Studies 431, 433.

17. J. Samuel Barkin, *The Sovereignty Cartel* (Cambridge University Press, 2021) 68-77.

18. Stephen Krasner, *Sovereignty: Organized Hypocrisy* (Princeton University Press, 1999) 12.

19. Wendy Brown, *Walled States, Waning Sovereignty* (Zone, 2010) 22.

20. Carmen Pavel, *Divided Sovereignty: International Institutions and the Limits of State Authority* (Oxford University Press, 2015) 55.

21. See Holning Lau, "Rethinking the Persistent Objector Doctrine in International Human Rights Law" (2005) 6 Chicago Journal of International Law 495.

22. Vassilis Pergantis, *The Paradigm of State Consent in the Law of Treaties: Challenges and Perspectives* (Edward Elgar, 2017) 64.

23. Roslyn Moloney, "Incompatible Reservations to Human Rights Treaties: Severability and the Problem of State Consent" (2004) 5 Melbourne Journal of International Law 155.

24. Pergantis (n. 22) 66.

25. Alan Brudner, "The Domestic Enforcement of International Covenants on Human Rights: A Theoretical Framework" (1985) 35 University of Toronto Law Journal 219; Johannes van Aggelen, "State Obligations Under Universal Human Rights Treaties," in Stefan Kadelbach, Thilo Rensmann, and Eva Rieter (eds.) *Judging International Human Rights* (Springer, 2019).

26. See Gino Naldi and Konstantinos Magliveras, "Human Rights and the Denunciation of Treaties and Withdrawal from International Organisations" (2013) 33 Polish Yearbook of International Law 95.

27. Stephen Gardbaum, "Human Rights as International Constitutional Rights" (2008) 19 European Journal of International Law (EJIL) 749.

28. See Kiyoteru Tsutsui, Claire Whitlinger, and Alwyn Lim, "International Human Rights Law and Social Movements: States' Resistance and Civil Society's Insistence" (2012) 8 Annual Review of Law and Social Science 367.

29. These might relate to concerns about the future. See Andrew Guzman, *How International Law Works: A Rational Choice Theory* (Oxford University Press, 2008) 40-41.

30. Andrew Legg, *The Margin of Appreciation in International Human Rights Law: Deference and Proportionality* (Oxford University Press, 2012) 61-65; Yuval Shany "Toward a General Margin of Appreciation Doctrine in International Law?" (2006) 16 European Journal of International Law (EJIL) 907.

31. For examples, see Stohl (n. 8); Philip Alston, "The Populist Challenge to Human Rights" (2017) 9 Journal of Human Rights Practice 1.

32. Helen Stacy, "Relational Sovereignty" (2003) 55 Stanford Law Review 2029.

33. Ibid., 2030.

34. For the argument, see Allan Rosas, "State Sovereignty and Human Rights: Towards a Global Constitutional Project, in David Beetham (ed.) *Politics and Human Rights* (Blackwell, 1995) 74; Luke Glanville "The antecedents of 'sovereignty as responsibility'" (2011) 17 European Journal of International Relations 233.

35. Christian Reus-Smit, "Human Rights and the Social Construction of Sovereignty" (2001) 27 Review of International Studies 519.

36. See Thomas J. Biersteker and Cynthia Weber, "The Social Construction of State Sovereignty," in Thomas J. Biersteker and Cynthia Weber (eds.) *State Sovereignty as Social Construct* (Cambridge University Press, 1996) 6-10.

37. Jean Cohen, "Rethinking Human Rights, Democracy, and Sovereignty in the Age of Globalization" (2008) 36 Political Theory 578.

38. Jutta Brunnée and Stephen J. Toope, "International Law and Constructivism: Elements of an International Theory of International Law" (2000) 39 Columbia Journal of Transnational Law 19; Ann Marie Clark, "The Normative Context of Human Rights Criticism: Treaty Ratification and UN Mechanisms" in Thomas Risse, Stephen Ropp, and Kathryn Sikkink (eds.) *The Persistent Power of Human Rights: From Commitment to Compliance* (Cambridge University Press 2013); For a more critical analysis, see Rolf Schwartz, "The Paradox of Sovereignty, Regime Type and Human Rights Compliance" (2004) 8 International Journal of Human Rights 199.

39. For an example of this argument, see Christine Min Wotipka and Kiyoteru Tsutsui, "Global Human Rights and State Sovereignty: State Ratification of International Human Rights Treaties, 1965–2001" (2008) 23 Sociological Forum 724.

40. Michael Fowler and Julie Bunck, *Law, Power, and the Sovereign State: The Evolution and Application of the Concept of Sovereignty* (Pennsylvania State University Press, 1995) 12.

41. Jack Donnelly, "Human Rights: A New Standard of Civilization?" (1998) 74 International Affairs 1.

42. See Alison Duxbury, The Participation of States in International Organisations: The Role of Human Rights and Democracy (Cambridge University Press, 2011) 27-58.

43. See Heather Smith-Cannoy, *Insincere Commitments: Human Rights Treaties, Abusive States, and Citizen Activism* (Georgetown University Press, 2012) 88; Xinyuan Dai, "The 'Compliance Gap' and the Efficacy of International Human Rights Institutions," in Thomas Risse, Stephen Ropp, and Kathryn Sikkink (eds.) *The Persistent Power of Human Rights: From Commitment to Compliance* (Cambridge University Press, 2013).

44. Emilie Hafner-Burton and Kiyoteru Tsutsui, "Human Rights in a Globalizing World: The Paradox of Empty Promises" (2005) 110 American Journal of Sociology 1373, 1378.

45. Christopher Fariss, "The Changing Standard of Accountability and the Positive Relationship between Human Rights Treaty Ratification and Compliance" (2017) 48 British Journal of Political Science 239; Alex Geisinger and Michael Ashley Stein, "Rational Choice, Reputation, and Human Rights Treaties (2007) 106 Michigan Law Review 1129.

46. Andreas Føllesdal, "Subsidiarity and the Global Order," in Michelle Evans and Augusto Zimmermann (eds.) *Global Perspectives on Subsidiarity* (Springer, 2014) 212.

47. Gareth Davies, "Subsidiarity as a Method of Policy Centralisation" in Tomer Broude and Yuval Shany (eds.) *The Shifting Allocation of Authority in International Law: Considering Sovereignty, Supremacy and Subsidiarity* (Hart, 2008) 83.

48. Jonas Christoffersen *Fair Balance: A Study of Proportionality, Subsidiarity and Primarity in the European Convention on Human Rights* (Brill, 2009) 229-232.

49. Luzius Wildhaber, "The European Court of Human Rights: The Past, The Present, The Future" (2007) 22 American University International Law Review 521, 526; Luzius Wildhaber, *The European Court of Human Rights 1998–2006: History, Achievements, Reform* (NP Engle, 2006) 95.

50. Belgian Linguistics cases (Belgium v. Belgium), Application Nos. 1474/62, 1677/62, 1691/62, 1769/63, 1994/63, and 2126/64, (ECtHR 23 July 1968) [10].

51. For examples, see Steven Greer, "The Margin of Appreciation: Interpretation and Discretion under the European Convention on Human Rights" (2000) Human Rights Files no. 17, Council of Europe Publishing; Dimitrios Tsarapatsanis, "The Margin of Appreciation as an Underenforcement Doctrine," In Petr Agha (ed.) *Human Rights Between Law and Politics: The Margin of Appreciation in Post-National Context.* (Hart, 2017).

52. Robert Spano, "Universality or Diversity of Human Rights? Strasbourg in the Age of Subsidiarity" (2014) 14 Human Rights Law Review 487.

53. Alistair Mowbray, "Subsidiarity and the European Convention on Human Rights" (2015) 15 Human Rights Law Review 313.

54. Paolo Carozza, "Subsidiarity as a Structural Principle of International Human Rights Law" (2003) 97 American Journal of International Law (AJIL) 38, 49.

55. Andreas Føllesdal, 'Subsidiarity and International Human-Rights Courts: Respecting Self-Governance and Protecting Human Rights—Or Neither?" (2016) 79 Law and Contemporary Problems 147, 152.

56. Ian Cram, "Protocol 15 and Articles 10 and 11 ECHR: The Partial Triumph of Political Incumbency Post-Brighton?' (2018) 67 International and Comparative Law Quarterly (ICLQ) 477.

57. Andreas Føllesdal and Geir Ulfstein, "The Draft Copenhagen Declaration: Whose Responsibility and Dialogue?' EJIL Talk! 22 February 2018, https://www.ejiltalk.org/the-draft-copenhagen-declaration-whose-responsibility-and-dialogue/.

58. Robert Keohane, Stephen Macedo, and Andrew Moravcsik, "Democracy-Enhancing Multilateralism" (2009) 63 International Organization 1.

59. Andreas von Staden, "The Democratic Legitimacy of Judicial Review beyond the State: Normative Subsidiarity and Judicial Standards of Review" (2010) 10 International Journal of Constitutional Law (ICON) 1023.

60. See Mattias Kumm, "Institutionalising Socratic Contestation: The Rationalist Human Rights Paradigm, Legitimate Authority and the Point of Judicial Review" (2007) 1 European Journal of Legal Studies 153; For a more cautious approach, see Andreas Føllesdal, "The

Legitimacy of International Human Rights Review: The Case of the European Court of Human Rights" (2009) 40 Journal of Social Philosophy 595.

61. Susanna Mancini, "The Crucifix Rage: Supranational Constitutionalism Bumps against the Counter-Majoritarian Difficulty" (2010) 6 European Constitutional Law Review 6, 26.

62. *Alekseyev v. Russia*, Application. Nos. 4916/07, 25924/08, and 14599/09 (ECtHR 21 October 2010).

63. Ibid., [59].

64. *Sergey Kuznetsov v. Russia*, ECHR 1170 (2008) [45].

65. *Salgueiro da Silva Mouta v. Portugal*, 31 EHRR 47 (2001) [34].

66. Kathleen A. Doty, "From Fretté to E. B.: The European Court of Human Rights on Gay and Lesbian Adoption" (2009) 18 Law and Sexuality 121, 125.

67. See Chapin and Charpentier v. France, Application. No. 40183/07 (ECtHR 9 June 2016); See also Grégor Puppinck, "The ECHR Unanimously Confirms the Non-Existence of a Right to Gay Marriage," European Centre for Law and Justice, 2016, https://eclj.org/marriage/the-echr-unanimously-confirms-the-non-existence-of-a-right-to-gay-marriage accessed 17 March 2021.

68. The ECtHR has been deferential to the argument that Article 12 of the ECHR (the right to marry) reflects the "traditional" notion of marriage in Schalk and Kopf v. Austria, 53 EHRR 20 (2011).

69. Helen Fenwick, "Same Sex Unions at the Strasbourg Court in a Divided Europe: Driving forward Reform or Protecting the Court's Authority via Consensus Analysis?" (2016) 3 European Human Rights Law Review 249.

70. *Vallianatos and Others v. Greece*, 59 EHRR 12 (2014) [84].

71. *Orlandi and Others v. Italy*, Application. No. 26431/12 (ECHR 14 Dec 2017) [76].

72. Ibid. [199]-[200].

73. *Karner v. Austria*, 38 EHRR 24 (2004) [41].

74. Rebecca Bryant and Madeleine Reeves, "Introduction: Toward an Anthropology of Sovereign Agency," in Rebecca Bryant and Madeleine Reeves (eds.) *The Everyday Lives of Sovereignty: Political Imagination beyond the State* (Cornell University Press, 2021) 4.

75. Ibid.

76. Gier Ulfstein, Thilo Marauhn, and Andreas Zimmermann, "Introduction," In Gier Ulfstein (ed.) *Making Treaties Work: Human Rights, Environment and Arms Control* (Cambridge University Press, 2007) 6.

77. Guzman (n. 29) 8-9.

78. Richard Nielsen and Beth Simmons, "Rewards for Ratification: Payoffs for Participating in the International Human Rights Regime?" (2015) 59 International Studies Quarterly 197.

79. Pu Xiaoyu, "Socialisation as a Two-Way Process: Emerging Powers and the Diffusion of International Norms" (2012) 5 Chinese Journal of International Politics 341.

80. Elizabeth Bates, "Sophisticated Constructivism in Human Rights Compliance Theory" (2015) 25 European Journal of International Law (EJIL) 1169.

81. For this point and a critical overview of constructivism, see Bill Bowring, "What is Realism in International Law and Human Rights?" in Jonathan Joseph and Colin Wight (eds.) *Scientific Realism and International Relations* (Palgrave Macmillan, 2010).

82. Oona Hathaway, "Why Do Countries Commit to Human Rights Treaties?" (2007) 51 Journal of Conflict Resolution 588.

83. Gerry Simpson, *Great Powers and Outlaw States: Unequal Sovereigns in the International Legal Order* (Cambridge University Press, 2006) 53-54.

84. Stacy (n. 32); See also Samantha Besson, "The Legitimate Authority of International Human Rights: On the Reciprocal Legitimation of Domestic and International Human Rights," in Andreas Føllesdal, Johan Schaffer, and Geir Ulfstein (eds.) *The Legitimacy of International Human Rights Regimes: Legal, Political and Philosophical Perspectives* (Cambridge University Press, 2014) 56-57.

85. Dana Zartner and Jennifer Ramos, "Human Rights as Reputation Builder: Compliance with the Convention Against Torture" (2011) 12 Human Rights Review 71.

86. Elizabeth Lijnzaad, *Reservations to Un-Human Rights Treaties: Ratify and Ruin?* (Martinus Nijhoff, 1995) 88-103.

87. Convention on the Elimination of All Forms of Discrimination against Women (CEDAW), Accession of Malawi and Paraguay (18 December 2017) C.N.78.1987.TREATIES-3.

88. Sylvia Tamale, "The Right to Culture and the Culture of Rights: A Critical Perspective on Women's Rights Sexual Rights in Africa," (2008) 16 Feminist Legal Studies 47, 57.

89. CEDAW, Bahrain Accession (18 June 2002) C.N.717.2002.TREATIES-20.

90. Bahrain Centre for Human Rights (BCHR), "Submission to the CEDAW Committee: On the Occasion of the Review of Bahrain's Third Periodic Report," July 2013, https://tbinternet.ohchr.org/Treaties/CEDAW/Shared%20Documents/BHR/INT_CEDAW_NGO_BHR_14750_E.pdf.

91. Marsha Freeman, "Reservations to CEDAW: An Analysis for UNICEF," UNICEF Policy and Practice, UNICEF 2009.

92. Michael Tomz, "Reputation and the Effect of International Law on Preferences and Beliefs" (working paper, Stanford University, 2008) https://tomz.people.stanford.edu/sites/g/files/sbiybj4711/f/tomz-intllaw-2008-02-11a.pdf.

93. International Law Commission (ILC), "Guide to Practice on Reservations to Treaties," *Yearbook of the ILC*, vol. 2 (2011) part 2, para. 3.1.5.2.

94. CEDAW, Accession of Bangladesh (27 November 1984) C.N.289.1984.TREATIES-11 (Depositary Notification).

95. CEDAW Committee, Concluding Observations of the Committee on the Elimination of Discrimination against Women Bangladesh (22 March 2011), CEDAW/C/BGD/CO/7, paras. 11-12 and 15-16.

96. Citizens' Initiatives on CEDAW, Bangladesh (CIC-BD), "Withdrawal of Reservation," Daily Star, 3 September 2015, https://www.thedailystar.net/op-ed/politics/withdrawal-reservation-136687.

97. Bangladesh Mahila Parishad (BMP), "Bangladesh CEDAW Alternative Report 2016," 19 January 2017, http://mahilaparishad.org/bangladesh-cedaw-alternative-report-2016/ p. 8.

98. Başak Çalı and Mariana Montoya, "The March of Universality? Religion-Based Reservations to the Core UN Treaties and What They Tell Us about Human Rights and Universality in the 21stCcentury" (working paper, Hertie School of Governance, 2017) https://www.universal-rights.org/wp-content/uploads/2017/05/Policy_report_march_universality_LR_spread.pdf.

99. Curtis A. Bradley and Jack L. Goldsmith, "Treaties, Human Rights, and Conditional Consent" (2000) 149 University of Pennsylvania Law Review 399.

100. William Schabas, "Reservations to the Convention on the Elimination of All Forms of Discrimination against Women and the Convention on the Rights of the Child" (1997) 3 William and Mary Journal of Women and the Law 79, 91-100.

101. Ibid., 99.

102. Eric Tistounet, "The Problem of Overlapping among Different Treaty Bodies," in Philip Alston (ed.) *The Future of UN Human Rights Treaty Monitoring* (Cambridge University Press, 2000) 396-399.

103. CEDAW Committee, Combined Sixth and Seventh Periodic Report of States Parties, Bangladesh (24 March 2010) CEDAW/C/BGD/6-7, para. 68.; CEDAW Committee, Fourth Periodic Report Submitted by Bahrain (11 October 2018) CEDAW/C/BHR/4, para. 50.

104. Eric Neumayer, "Qualified Ratification: Explaining Reservations to International Human Rights Treaties" (2007) 36 Journal of Legal Studies 397, 403.

105. Daniel Hill, "Avoiding Obligation: Reservations to Human Rights Treaties" (2015) 60 Journal of Conflict Resolution 1129.

106. Laurence Helfer, "Response: Not Fully Committed? Reservations, Risk, and Treaty Design" (2006) 31 Yale Journal of International Law 367.

107. Eyal Benvenisti and George Downs, "The Empire's New Clothes: Political Economy and the Fragmentation of International Law" (2007) 60 Stanford Law Review 595.

108. Monica Pinto, "Fragmentation or Unification among International Institutions: Human Rights Tribunals" (1998) 31 NYU Journal of International Law and Policy 833.

109. ILC, Report of the Study Group on the Ornamentation of International Law at the Fifty-Eighth Session of the International Law Commission [Koskenniemi Report], (2006) UN Doc. A/CN.4/L 682.

110. Ibid., para 212.

111. Ibid., para 216.

112. Anthony Langlois, "Human Rights: The Globalisation and Fragmentation of Moral Discourse" (2002) 28 Review of International Studies 479.

113. ILC (n. 109) para. 244.

114. See Bruno Simma and Dirk Pulkowski, "Of Planets and the Universe: Self-Contained Regimes in International Law" (2006) 17 European Journal of International Law (EJIL) 483.

115. For an argument in this vein, see Siobhán McInerney-Lankford, "Fragmentation of International Law Redux: The Case of Strasbourg" (2012) 32 Oxford Journal of Legal Studies 609.

116. Pinto (n. 108) 842.

117. Gerhard Hafner, "Pros and Cons Ensuing from Fragmentation of International Law" (2004) 25 Michigan Journal of International Law (MJIL) 849, 856.

118. Michael Barnett and Etel Solingen, "Designed to Fail or Failure of Design? The Origins and Legacy of the Arab League," in Amitav Acharya and Alastair Iain Johnston (eds.) *Crafting Cooperation: Regional International Institutions in Comparative Perspective* (Cambridge University Press, 2007) 181.

119. Naseer Aruri, "Disaster Area: Human Rights in the Arab World," MERIP Middle East Report, no. 149 Human Rights in the Middle East (1987) 6.

120. Abdullahi An-Na'im, "Human Rights in the Arab World: A Regional Perspective" (2001) 23 Human Rights Quarterly (HRQ) 701, 714.

121. Arab Charter on Human Rights, Art. 32 (2004). Full text available at League of Arab States, Arab Charter on Human Rights, 22 May 2004, https://www.unicef.org/tdad/arabcharterhumanrights.doc.

122. Ibid., Art. 29(1).

123. See CEDAW Committee, Reservations to the Convention on the Elimination of All Forms of Discrimination against Women (12 November 1996) CEDAW/C/1997/4, para. 6.

124. Arab Charter (n. 121), Art. 33.

125. This appears to be the view advanced by Elisa Grimi; Elisa Grimi, "A Universal Declaration?" in Luca Di Donato and Elisa Grimi (eds.) *Metaphysics of Human Rights 1948–2018: On the Occasion of the 70th Anniversary of the UDHR* (Vernon, 2019) 132.

126. Tom Gerald Daly, "Repression in Bahrain: The End of Any Hope for an Effective Arab Court of Human Rights?" I-CONnect: Blog of the International Journal of Constitutional Law, 22 July 2016, http://www.iconnectblog.com/2016/07/repression-in-bahrain-the-end-of-any-hope-for-an-effective-arab-court-of-human-rights; Konstantinos Magliveras and Gino Naldi, "The Arab Court of Human Rights: A Study in Impotence" (2016) 29 Quebec Journal of International Law 147.

127. Ahmed Almutawa and Konstantinos Magliveras, "Enforcing Women's Rights under the Arab Charter on Human Rights 2004" (2021) 25 International Journal of Human Rights 1258.

128. Fares Braizat, "What Arabs Think" (2010) 21 Journal of Democracy 131.

129. Konstantin Magliveras, "The Protection of Human Rights and Fundamental Freedoms in the League of Arab States and in the Arab-Islamic World: An Overview" (2018) 1 Diritti umani e diritto internazionale 105.

130. Vera Van Hüllen, "Just Leave Us Alone: The Arab League and Human Rights," In Tanja Börzel and Vera van Hüllen (eds.) *Governance Transfer by Regional Organizations: Patching Together a Global Script* (Springer, 2015) 126.

131. Ibid.

132. Magliveras and Naldi (n. 126).

133. For this point, see Daniel Farber, "Rights as Signals" (2002) 31 Journal of Legal Studies 83.

134. Avery Poole, "'The World is Outraged': Legitimacy in the Making of the ASEAN Human Rights Body" (2015) 37 Contemporary Southeast Asia 355.

135. Anna Grear, "'Framing the Project' of International Human Rights Law: Reflections on the Dysfunctional 'Family' of the Universal Declaration," in Conor Gearty and Costas Douzinas (eds.) *The Cambridge Companion to Human Rights Law* (Cambridge University Press, 2012) 21.

136. Anne van Aaken, "Making International Human Rights Protection More Effective: A Rational-Choice Approach to the Effectiveness of Ius Standi Provisions" (2005) MPI Collective Goods Preprint no. 2005-16, https://ssrn.com/abstract=802424.

137. Chaloka Beyani, "Reconstituting the Universal: Human Rights as a Regional Idea," in Conor Gearty and Costas Douzinas (eds.) *The Cambridge Companion to Human Rights Law* (Cambridge University Press, 2012) 178.

138. Martti Koskenniemi, *From Apology to Utopia: The Structure of International Legal Argument*, reissue with new epilogue (Cambridge University Press, 2005) 240.

139. See Hent Kalmo and Quentin Skinner, "Introduction: A Concept in Fragments," in Hent Kalmo and Quentin Skinner (eds.) *Sovereignty in Fragments: The Past, Present and Future of a Contested Concept* (Cambridge University Press, 2011); Antony Anghie, "The Evolution of International Law: Colonial and Postcolonial Realities," in Richard Falk, Balakrishnan Rajagopal, and Jacqueline Stevens (eds.) *International Law and the Third World: Reshaping Justice* (Routledge, 2008) 35.

140. See Emilie Hafner-Burton, Edward Mansfield, and Jon Pevehouse, 'Human Rights Institutions, Sovereignty Costs, and Democratization.' (ILAR working paper no. 8, Laboratory on International Law and Regulation, 2011) https://www.researchgate.net/profile/Emilie_Hafner-Burton/publication/228311609_Human_Rights_Institutions_Sovereignty_Costs_and

_Democratization/links/00b495390ac0b15513000000/Human-Rights-Institutions-Sovereignty-Costs-and-Democratization.pdf; On contested meanings of sovereignty see Jost Delbruck, "International Protection of Human Rights and State Sovereignty" (1982) 57 Indiana Law Journal 567.

141. See Besson (n. 84).

142. David Chandler, "The Limits of Human Rights and Cosmopolitan Citizenship,"iIn David Chandler (ed.) *Rethinking Human Rights: Critical Approaches to International Politics* (Palgrave Macmillan, 2002).

143. David Held, "Restructuring Global Governance: Cosmopolitanism, Democracy and the Global Order" (2009) 37 Millennium: Journal of International Studies 535

144. Harold Hongju Koh, "1998 Harris Lecture: How Is International Human Rights Law Enforced?" (1999). Faculty Scholarship Series 2103, https://digitalcommons.law.yale.edu/cgi/viewcontent.cgi?article=2882&context=fss_papers.

145. For a critique of human rights law in this respect, see Costas Douzinas, "Human Rights and Postmodern Utopia" (2000) 11 Law and Critique 219.

146. Koskenniemi has noted the way that fundamentally political questions are often fitted into a particular vocabulary of international law. See Martti Koskenniemi, "The Politics of International Law—20 Years Later" (2009) 20 European Journal of International Law (EJIL) 1, 11.

Conclusion

1. Joseph Raz, "Human Rights in the Emerging World Order" (2010) 1 Transnational Legal Theory 31, 46.

2. Katarina Tomaševski *Responding to Human Rights Violations, 1946–1999* (Martinus Nijhoff, 2012) xi.

3. Ibid.

4. Mark Mazower, "An International Civilization? Empire, Internationalism and the Crisis of the Mid-Twentieth Century" (2006) 82 International Affairs 553.

5. Willard Cowles, "Universality of Jurisdiction over War Crimes" (1945) 33 California Law Review 177.

6. Anton Weiss-Wendt, *The Soviet Union and the Gutting of the UN Genocide Convention* (University of Wisconsin Press, 2016) 122.

7. Ibid.

8. Åshild Samnøy, "Human Rights as International Consensus: The Making of the Universal Declaration of Human Rights 1945–1948" (1993) Chr. Michelsen Institute Report no. 4, 93, 105.

9. Mostafa Faghfoury, "Human Rights: 50 Years Later," in William Sweet (ed.) *Philosophical Theory and the Universal Declaration of Human Rights* (University of Ottawa Press, 2003).

10. William Fleming, "Danger to America: The Draft Covenant on Human Rights" (1951) 37 American Bar Association Journal 739.

11. Mark Lewis, *The Birth of the New Justice* (Oxford University Press, 2013) 235.

12. Ibid., 210-213.

13. Douglas Irvin-Erickson, *Raphaël Lemkin and the Concept of Genocide* (University of Pennsylvania Press, 2017) 10-15.

14. Kurt Wilk, "International Law and Global Ideological Conflict: Reflections on the Universality of International Law" (1951) 45 American Journal of International Law (AJIL) 648.

15. Ibid., 657

16. Ibid.

17. Emmanuelle Jouannet, "Universalism and Imperialism: The True-False Paradox of International Law?" (2007) 18 European Journal of International Law (EJIL) 379, 387.

18. Mégret describes this in terms of the debate of cosmopolitanism, but the principle of universal juridical construction remains the same. Frédéric Mégret, "International Law as Law," in James Crawford and Martti Koskenniemi (eds.) *The Cambridge Companion to International Law* (Cambridge University Press, 2012) 66-67.

19. Jean-Luc Nancy, "On Human Rights: Two Simple Remarks," trans. Gilbert Leung, in Costas Douzinas and Conor Gearty (eds.) *The Meanings of Rights: The Philosophy and Social Theory of Human Rights* (Cambridge University Press, 2014) 17.

20. Ibid.

21. Judith Butler, "Restaging the Universal," in Judith Butler, Ernesto Laclau, and Slavoj Žižek (eds.) *Contingency, Hegemony, Universality: Contemporary Dialogues on the Left* (Verso Books 2000) 37-38.

22. George Lestas, *A Theory of Interpretation of the European Convention on Human Rights* (Oxford University Press, 2007) 17-36.

23. For an overview of this critique, see Adam Etinson, "Human Rights, Claimability and the Uses of Abstraction" (2013) 25 Utilitas 463, 464.

24. Paolo Carozza, "Subsidiarity as a Structural Principle of International Human Rights Law" (2017) 97 American Journal of International Law (AJIL) 38.

25. This is called the compliance gap. For an explanation, see Emilie Hafner-Burton and Kiyoteru Tsutsui, "Human Rights in a Globalizing World: The Paradox of Empty Promises" (2005) 110 American Journal of Sociology 1373

26. For state motivations in relation to human rights treaties, see Oona Hathaway, "Why Do Countries Commit to Human Rights Treaties?" (2007) 51 The Journal of Conflict Resolution 588. Liberal theory posits the idea of shared interests within and between states leading to human rights commitment; see Andrew Moravcsik, "Explaining International Human Rights Regimes: Liberal Theory and Western Europe" (1995) 1 European Journal of International Relations 157.

27. Schalk and Kopf v. Austria, Application No. 30141/04 (ECtHR 20 June 2010) [98].

28. Pieter van Dijk, "A Common Standard of Achievement: About Universal Validity and Uniform Interpretation of International Human Rights Norms" (1995) 13 Netherlands Quarterly of Human Rights 105.

29. For an overview of this literature, see Ryan Goodman and Derek Jinks, "Incomplete Internalization and Compliance with Human Rights Law" (2008) 19 European Journal of International Law (EJIL) 725.

30. For an examination of human rights backlash in human rights courts, see Mikael Madsen, "The Challenging Authority of the European Court of Human Rights: From Cold War Legal Diplomacy to the Brighton Declaration and Backlash" (2016) 79 Law and Contemporary Problems 141; On the general point of backlash. see Leslie Vinjamuri, "Human Rights Backlash," in Stephen Hopgood, Jack Snyder, and Leslie Vinjamuri (eds.) *Human Rights Futures* (Cambridge University Press, 2017) 114.

31. Antony Anghie, "Finding the Peripheries: Sovereignty and Colonialism in Nineteenth-Century International Law" (1999) 40 Harvard International Law Journal 1; Pierre-Marie Dupuy, "Some Reflections on Contemporary International Law and the Appeal to Universal Values: A Response to Martti Koskenniemi" (2005) 16 European Journal of International Law (EJIL) 131.

32. Otto notes the association of universality with various forms of disciplinary projects beyond the historical period of colonial imperialism; see Dianne Otto, "Rethinking Universals: Opening Transformative Possibilities in International Human Rights Law" (1997) 18 Australian Yearbook of International Law 1.

33. Samuel Huntington, *The Clash of Civilizations and the Remaking of World Order* (Simon and Schuster, 1997).

34. Onuma Yasuaki, "International Law in and with International Politics: The Functions of International Law in International Society" (2003) 14 European Journal of International Law (EJIL) 105.

35. For examples of such literature, see William Schabas, "Reservations to Human Rights Treaties: Time for Innovation and Reform" (1995) 32 Canadian Yearbook of International Law 39; Konstantin Korkelia 'New challenges to the regime of reservations under the International Covenant on Civil and Political Rights.' (2002) 13 European Journal of International Law (EJIL) 437; Ryan Goodman, 'Human rights treaties, invalid reservations, and state consent.' (2002) 96 American Journal of International Law (AJIL) 531.

36. Vassilis Pergantis, *The Paradigm of State Consent in the Law of Treaties: Challenges and Perspectives* (Edward Elgar, 2017) 245.

37. For details about how this emerged over time, see William Schabas, "Reservations to the Convention on the Elimination of All Forms of Discrimination against Women and the Convention on the Rights of the Child" (1997) 3 William and Mary Journal of Women and the Law 79; Marijke De Pauw, "Women's Rights: From Bad to Worse? Assessing the Evolution of Incompatible Reservations to the CEDAW Convention" (2013) 29 Merkurious 51.

38. Daniel Hill, "Avoiding Obligation: Reservations to Human Rights Treaties" (2016) 60 Journal of Conflict Resolution 1129; Elena Baylis, "General Comment 24: Confronting the Problem of Reservations to Human Rights Treaties" (1999) 17 Berkeley Journal of International Law 277.

39. Avery Poole, "'The World is Outraged': Legitimacy in the Making of the ASEAN Human Rights Body" (2015) 37 Contemporary Southeast Asia 355.

40. For general comparisons of ASEAN to European regionalism, see Anja Jetschke and Jürgen Rüland, "Decoupling Rhetoric and Practice: The Cultural Limits of ASEAN Cooperation" (2009) 22 Pacific Review 181.

41. Scholars working on the African human rights system are wary about being too reliant on this type of comparative analysis because of its underlying Eurocentricity. However, there is still some utility in comparing both organizations in a functional sense. For examples of this scholarship, see Rachel Murray, "A Comparison between the African and European Courts of Human Rights" (2002) 2 African Human Rights Law Journal 195; Carolyn Shaw, "The Evolution of Regional Human Rights Mechanisms: A Focus on Africa" (2007) 6 Journal of Human Rights 209.

42. Writers on fragmentation are usually skeptical about the need for such criteria, arguing, as Simma does, that there is a "presumption that states, when creating new rules of international law, do not aim at violating their obligations under other, pre-existing rules." Simma at the same time acknowledges the need for a "sense of responsibility" by states about the issues posed by fragmentation. Bruno Simma, "Universality of International Law from the Perspective of a Practitioner" (2009) 20 European Journal of International Law (EJIL) 265, 276, and 292.

43. A summary of the principle of balancing in relation to Article 10 is set out in Yutaka Arai-Takahashi, *The Margin of Appreciation Doctrine and the Principle of Proportionality in the Jurisprudence of the ECHR* (Intersentia, 2002) 76-77. For a good summary of the reasoning

from a non–human rights perspective, see Erlend Leonhardsen, "Treaty Change, Arbitral Practice and the Search for Balance," in Lukasz Gruszczynski and Wouter Werner (eds.) *Deference in International Courts and Tribunals: Standard of Review and Margin of Appreciation* (Oxford University Press, 2014) 138-144.

44. Refah Partisi (The Welfare Party) and Others v. Turkey, App. no. 41340, 41342, and 41343/98 (Grand Chamber, 13 February 2003) [99].

45. Dominic McGoldrick, "A Defence of the Margin of Appreciation and an Argument for its Application by the Human Rights Committee" (2016) 65 International and Comparative Law Quarterly (ICLQ) 21.

46. Dean Spielmann, 'Allowing the Right Margin: The European Court of Human Rights and The National Margin of Appreciation Doctrine; Waiver or Subsidiarity of European Review?' (2012) 14 Cambridge Yearbook of European Legal Studies 381.

There is also some broader concern that the doctrine is not transportable outside of the specific European context.; Andreas Føllesdal, "Exporting the Margin of Appreciation: Lessons for the Inter-American Court of Human Rights" (2017) 15 International Journal of Constitutional Law (ICON) 359.

47. Jan Kratochvíl, "The Inflation of the Margin of Appreciation by the European Court of Human Rights" (2011) 29 Netherlands Quarterly of Human Rights 324.

48. Marisa Iglesias Vila, "Subsidiarity, Margin of Appreciation and International Adjudication within a Cooperative Conception of Human Rights" (2017) 15 International Journal of Constitutional Law (ICON) 393; Dean Spielmann, "Whither the Margin of Appreciation?" (2014) 67 Current Legal Problems 49.

49. Ian Cram, "Protocol 15 and Articles 10 and 11 ECHR: The Partial Triumph of Political Incumbency Post-Brighton?' (2018) 67 International and Comparative Law Quarterly (ICLQ) 477.

50. Oddný Mjöll Arnardóttir, "Rethinking the Two Margins of Appreciation" (2016) 12 European Constitutional Law Review 27, 51.

51. Janneke Gerards, "Margin of Appreciation and Incrementalism in the Case Law of the European Court of Human Rights" (2018) 18 Human Rights Law Review 495, 497.

52. Ibid., 503.

53. Ibid., 508.

54. Ibid., 512.

55. Animal Defenders International v. UK, Application no. 48876/08, 22 April 2013; Matthew Saul, "The European Court of Human Rights' Margin of Appreciation and the Processes of National Parliaments" (2015) 15 Human Rights Law Review 745.

56. SAS v. France, ECHR 695 (2014).

57. McGoldrick (n. 45).

58. Simon Paul, "Governing from the Margins: The European Court of Human Rights' Margin of Appreciation Doctrine as a Tool of Global Governance" (2016) 12 Croatian Yearbook of European Law and Policy 81.

59. For a specific example, see Monica Lugato, "The Margin of Appreciation and Freedom of Religion: Between Treaty Interpretation and Subsidiarity" (2013) 52 Journal of Catholic Legal Studies 49. For a general cases study, see Robert Spano, "Universality or Diversity of Human Rights? Strasbourg in the Age of Subsidiarity" (2014) 14 Human Rights Law Review 487.

60. This terminology is taken from Sonia Cardenas, *Conflict and Compliance: State Responses to International Human Rights Pressure* (University of Pennsylvania Press, 2010) 27-29.

61. On derogations, see Emilie Hafner-Burton, Laurence Helfer, and Christopher Fariss, "Emergency and Escape: Explaining Derogations from Human Rights Treaties" (2011) 65 International Organization 673.

62. Aileen McHarg, "Reconciling Human Rights and the Public Interest: Conceptual Problems and Doctrinal Uncertainty in the Jurisprudence of the European Court of Human Rights" (1999) 62 Modern Law Review 671.

63. Ibid. On the notion of balancing security interests, see Christopher Michaelsen, "Balancing Civil Liberties against National Security: A Critique of Counterterrorism Rhetoric" (2006) 29 UNSW Law Journal 1.

64. See the discussion in chapter 4 and the following illustrative literature: Catherine Shanahan Renshaw, "The ASEAN Human Rights Declaration 2012" (2013) 13 Human Rights Law Review 557; Mathew Davies, "An Agreement to Disagree: The ASEAN Human Rights Declaration and the Absence of Regional Identity in Southeast Asia" (2014) 33 Journal of Current Southeast Asian Affairs 107.

65. McHarg (n. 62) 676-677.

66. See Laurence Helfer and Erik Voeten, "International Courts as Agents of Legal Change: Evidence from LGBT Rights in Europe" (2014) 68 International Organization 77.

67. Oren Gross and Fionnuala Ní Aoláin, "From Discretion to Scrutiny: Revisiting the Application of the Margin of Appreciation Doctrine in the Context of Article 15 of the European Convention on Human Rights" (2001) 23 Human Rights Quarterly (HRQ) 625; Aly Mokhtar, "Human Rights Obligations v. Derogations: Article 15 of the European Convention on Human Rights" (2004) 8 International Journal of Human Rights 65.

68. For this explanation of how states use the margin of appreciation, see Jeffrey Brauch, "The Margin of Appreciation and the Jurisprudence of the European Court of Human Rights: Threat to the Rule of Law" (2005) 11 Columbia Journal of European Law 113, 129-139; Janneke Gerards, "Pluralism, Deference and the Margin of Appreciation Doctrine" (2011) 17 European Law Journal 80.

69. Rosa Ehrenreich Brooks, "War Everywhere: Rights, National Security Law, and the Law of Armed Conflict in the Age of Terror" (2004) 153 University of Pennsylvania Law Review 675.

70. Anne Bayefsky, "Cultural Sovereignty, Relativism, and International Human Rights: New Excuses for Old Strategies" (1996) 9 Ratio Juris 42; Adamantia Pollis, "Cultural Relativism Revisited: Through a State Prism" (1996) 18 Human Rights Quarterly (HRQ) 316.

71. For examples, see Michael Jacobsen and Stephanie Lawson, "Between Globalization and Localization: A Case Study of Human Rights Versus State Sovereignty" (1999) 5 Global Governance 203; Jack Donnelly, 'The relative universality of human rights.' (2007) 29 Human Rights Quarterly (HRQ) 281.

72. Guyora Binder, "Cultural Relativism and Cultural Imperialism in Human Rights Law" (1999) 5 Buffalo Human Rights Law Review 211.

73. Anne Peters, "Humanity as the A and Ω of Sovereignty" (2009) 20 European Journal of International Law (EJIL) 513.

74. Binder (n. 72); Costas Douzinas, *Human Rights and Empire: The Political Philosophy of Cosmopolitanism* (Routledge, 2007) chp. 3.

75. Christopher Joyner and John Dettling, "Bridging the Cultural Chasm: Cultural Relativism and the Future of International Law" (1989) 20 California Western International Law Journal 275; Elizabeth Zechenter, "In the Name of Culture: Cultural Relativism and the Abuse of the Individual" (1997) 53 Journal of Anthropological Research 319.

76. For illustrative literature, see Kathryn Hochstetler, Ann Marie Clark, and Elisabeth Friedman, "Sovereignty in the Balance: Claims and Bargains at the UN Conferences on the Environment, Human Rights, and Women" (2000) 44 International Studies Quarterly 591; Kimberly Schooley, "Cultural Sovereignty, Islam, and Human Rights: Toward a Communitarian Revision" (1994) 25 Cumberland Law Review 651.

77. For definitions of these different concepts, see Michael Stohl, "Conclusion: From Hope to Fear in the Millennium; Human Rights in an age of Backlash," in Alison Brysk and Michael Stohl (eds.) *Contracting Human Rights: Crisis, Accountability, and Opportunity* (Edward Elgar, 2018).

BIBLIOGRAPHY

Abbott, Kenneth, and Duncan Snidal. "Why States Act through Formal International Organizations" (1998) 42 Journal of Conflict Resolution 3.

———. "Hard and Soft Law in International Governance" (2000) 54 International Organization 421.

Acharya, Amitav. *Whose Ideas Matter? Agency and Power in Asian Regionalism* (Cornell University Press, 2011).

Ackerly, Brooke. *Universal Human Rights in a World of Difference* (Cambridge University Press, 2008).

Addo, Michael. "Practice of United Nations Human Rights Treaty Bodies in the Reconciliation of Cultural Diversity with Universal Respect for Human Rights" (2010) 32 Human Rights Quarterly (HRQ) 601.

Adrian, Melanie. "The Principled Slope: Religious Freedom and the European Court of Human Rights" (2017) 45 Religion, State and Society 174.

Akila Choudhury, Cyra. "Beyond Culture: Human Rights Universalisms versus Religious and Cultural Relativism in the Activism for Gender Justice" (2015) 30 Berkeley Journal of Gender Law and Justice 226.

Al Tamimi, Yussef. "Human Rights and the Excess of Identity: A Legal and Theoretical Inquiry into the Notion of Identity in Strasbourg Case Law" (2018) 27 Social and Legal Studies 283.

Anghie, Antony. "Colonialism and the Birth of International Institutions: Sovereignty, Economy, and the Mandate System of the League of Nations" (2002) 34 NYU Journal of International Law and Policy 513.

———. Colonial Origins of International Law' in Laws of the Postcolonial," in Eve Darian-Smith and Peter Fitzpatrick (eds.) *Laws of the Postcolonial* (University of Michigan Press, 1999).

———. *Imperialism, Sovereignty and the Making of International Law* (Cambridge University Press, 2004).

Badaru, Opeoluwa. "Examining the Utility of Third World Approaches to International Law for International Human Rights Law" (2008) 10 International Community Law Review 379.

Baird, Natalie. "The Role of International Non-Governmental Organisations in the Universal Periodic Review of Pacific Island States: Can 'Doing Good' Be Done Better?" (2015) 16 Melbourne Journal of International Law 550.

Balaguer, Mark. "Bare Bones Moral Realism and the Objections from Relativism," in Steven Hales (ed.) *A Companion to Relativism* (Wiley-Blackwell, 2011).

Baratta, Roberto. "Should Invalid Reservations to Human Rights Treaties Be Disregarded?" (2000) 11 European Journal of International Law (EJIL) 413.

Barkin, J. Samuel. *The Sovereignty Cartel* (Cambridge University Press, 2021).

Barreto, José-Manuel. "Decolonial Strategies and Dialogue in the Human Rights Field: A Manifesto" (2012) 3 Transnational Legal Theory 1.

———. "Imperialism and Decolonization as Scenarios of Human Rights History," in José-Manuel Barreto (ed.) *Human Rights from a Third World Perspective: Critique, History and International Law* (Cambridge Scholars Publishing, 2013).

Bates, Ed. *The Evolution of the European Convention on Human Rights: From Its Inception to the Creation of a Permanent Court of Human Rights* (Oxford University Press, 2010).

Bates, Elizabeth. "Sophisticated Constructivism in Human Rights Compliance Theory" (2015) 25 European Journal of International Law (EJIL) 1169.

Baxi, Upendra. *The Future of Human Rights* (Oxford University Press, 2002).

———. *Human Rights in a Posthuman World* (Oxford University Press, 2008).

Bayefsky, Anne. "Cultural Sovereignty, Relativism, and International Human Rights: New Excuses for Old Strategies" (1996) 9 Ratio Juris 42.

Baylis, Elena. "General Comment 24: Confronting the Problem of Reservations to Human Rights Treaties" (1999) 17 Berkeley Journal of International Law 277.

Beitz, Charles. "Cosmopolitan Ideals and National Sentiment" (1983) 80 Journal of Philosophy 591.

———. "Human Rights as a Common Concern" (2001) 95 American Political Science Review 269.

———. *The Idea of Human Rights* (Oxford University Press, 2009).

Bellamy, Richard. "The Democratic Legitimacy of International Human Rights Conventions: Political Constitutionalism and the European Convention on Human Rights" (2015) 25 European Journal of International Law (EJIL) 1019.

Bhabha, Homi. *The Location of Culture*, 2nd ed. (Routledge, 2004).

Bianchi, Andrea. *International Law Theories: An Inquiry into Different Ways of Thinking* (Oxford University Press, 2016).

Bjorge, Eirik. "Been There, Done That: The Margin of Appreciation and International Law" (2015) 4 Cambridge Journal of International and Comparative Law 181.

Bleiberg, Benjamin. "Unveiling the Real Issue: Evaluating the European Court of Human Rights' Decision to Enforce the Turkish Headscarf Ban in Leyla Sahin v. Turkey" (2005) 91 Cornell Law Review 129.

Bostian, Ida. "Cultural relativism in international war crimes prosecutions: The International Criminal Tribunal for Rwanda" (2005) 12 ILSA Journal of International and Comparative Law 1.

Bowden, Brett. "The Colonial Origins of International Law: European Expansion and the Classical Standard of Civilization" (2005) 7 Journal of the History of International Law / Revue d'histoire du droit international 1571.

Boyle, Kevin. "Stock-Taking on Human Rights: The World Conference on Human Rights, Vienna 1993" (1995) 43 Political Studies 79.

Buergenthal, Thomas. "The Normative and Institutional Evolution of International Human Rights" (1997) 19 Human Rights Quarterly (HRQ) 703.

Bui, Hein. "The ASEAN Human Rights System: A Critical Analysis" (2016) 11 Asian Journal of Comparative Law 111.

Burke, Roland. *Decolonization and the Evolution of International Human Rights* (University of Pennsylvania Press, 2009).

———. "From Individual Rights to National Development: The First UN International Conference on Human Rights, Tehran, 1968" (2008) 19 Journal of World History 275.

Butler, Judith, Ernesto Laclau, and Slavoj Žižek. *Contingency, Hegemony, Universality: Contemporary Dialogues on the Left* (Verso, 2000).

Brauch, Jeffrey. "The Margin of Appreciation and the Jurisprudence of the European Court of Human Rights: Threat to the Rule of Law" (2005) 11 Columbia Journal of European Law 113.

Brems, Eva. "Enemies or Allies? Feminism and Cultural Relativism as Dissident Voices in Human Rights Discourse" (1997) 19 Human Rights Quarterly (HRQ) 136.

———. *Human Rights: Universality and Diversity* (Martinus Nijhoff, 2001).

Brown, Michael. "Cultural Relativism 2.0" (2008) 49 Current Anthropology 363.

Bryant, Rebecca, and Madeleine Reeves. "Introduction: Toward an Anthropology of Sovereign Agency," in Rebecca Bryant and Madeleine Reeves (eds.) *The Everyday Lives of Sovereignty: Political Imagination beyond the State* (Cornell University Press, 2021).

Çalı, Başak. "Balancing Human Rights? Methodological Problems with Weights, Scales and Proportions" (2007) 29 Human Rights Quarterly (HRQ) 251.

Cardenas, Sonia. *Conflict and Compliance: State Responses to International Human Rights Pressure* (University of Pennsylvania Press, 2010).

Carozza, Paolo. "From Conquest to Constitutions: Retrieving a Latin American Tradition of the Idea of Human Rights" (2003) 25 Human Rights Quarterly (HRQ) 281.

———. "Subsidiarity as a Structural Principle of International Human Rights Law" (2017) 97 American Journal of International Law (AJIL) 38.

Carraro, Valentina. "The United Nations Treaty Bodies and Universal Periodic Review: Advancing Human Rights by Preventing Politicization." (2017) 39 Human Rights Quarterly (HRQ) 943.

Cheah, Pheng. *Inhuman Conditions: On Cosmopolitanism and Human Rights* (Harvard University Press, 2006).

Clark, Belinda. "The Vienna Convention Reservations Regime and the Convention on Discrimination against Women" (1991) 85 American Journal of International Law (AJIL) 281.

Clarke, Gerard. "The Evolving ASEAN Human Rights System: The ASEAN Human Rights Declaration of 2012" (2012) 11 Northwestern Journal of Human Rights 1.

Cohen, Jean. "Rethinking Human Rights, Democracy, and Sovereignty in the Age of Globalization" (2008) 36 Political Theory 578.

Cohen, Ronald. "Human Rights and Cultural Relativism: The Need for a New Approach" (1989) 91 American Anthropologist 1014.

Connors, Jane. "The Women's Convention in the Muslim World," in Mai Yamani (ed.) *Feminism and Islam: Legal and Literary Perspectives* (Ithaca Press, 1996).

Contesse, Jorge. "Resisting the Inter-American Human Rights System" (2019) 44 Yale International Law Journal 1.

Cook, John. *Morality and Cultural Differences* (Oxford University Press, 1999).

Corradetti, Claudio. *Relativism and Human Rights: A Theory of Pluralistic Universalism* (Springer, 2009).

Corradi, Giselle. "Introduction: Human Rights and Legal Pluralism; Four Research Agendas," in Giselle Corradi, Eva Brems, and Mark Goodale (eds.) *Human Rights Encounter Legal Pluralism: Normative and Empirical Approaches* (Hart, 2017).

Cowan, Jane. "The Universal Periodic Review as Public Audit Ritual: An Anthropological Perspective on Emerging Practices in the Global Governance of Human Rights," in Hilary Charlesworth and Emma Larking (eds.) *Human Rights and the Universal Periodic Review: Rituals and Ritualism* (Cambridge University Press, 2015).

Cram, Ian. "Protocol 15 and Articles 10 and 11 ECHR: The Partial Triumph of Political Incumbency Post-Brighton?" (2018) 67 International and Comparative Law Quarterly (ICLQ) 477.

Danchin, Peter. "Islam in the Secular Nomos of the European Court of Human Rights" (2010) 32 Michigan Journal of International Law (MJIL) 663.

d'Aspremont, Jean. *Epistemic Forces in International Law: Foundational Doctrines and Techniques of International Legal Argumentation* (Edward Elgar, 2015).

———. *International Law as a Belief System* (Cambridge University Press, 2017).

———. "The Multidimensional Process of Interpretation," in Andrea Bianchi, Daniel Peat, and Matthew Windsor (eds.) *Interpretation in International Law* (Oxford University Press, 2015).

Davies, Mathew. "ASEAN and Human Rights Norms: Constructivism, Rational Choice, and the Action-Identity Gap" (2013) 13 International Relations of the Asia-Pacific 207.

———. "The ASEAN Synthesis: Human Rights, Non-Intervention, and the ASEAN Human Rights Declaration." (2013) 14 Georgetown Journal of International Affairs 51.

———. "The Perils of Incoherence: ASEAN, Myanmar and the Avoidable Failures of Human Rights Socialization" (2012) 34 Contemporary Southeast Asia 1.

Davis, Megan. "Indigenous Struggles in Standard-Setting: The United Nations Declaration on the Rights of Indigenous Peoples" (2008) 9 Melbourne Journal of International Law 439.

De Pauw, Marijke. "Women's Rights: From Bad to Worse? Assessing the Evolution of Incompatible Reservations to the CEDAW Convention" (2013) 29 Merkurious 51.

de Sousa Santos, Boaventura, and César A. Rodríguez-Garavito. "Law, Politics, and the Subaltern in Counter-Hegemonic Globalization," in Boaventura de Sousa Santos and César A. Rodríguez-Garavito (eds.) *Law and Globalization from Below: Towards a Cosmopolitan Legality* (Cambridge University Press, 2005).

Dembour, Marie-Bénédicte. "What are Human Rights? Four Schools of Thought" (2010) 32 Human Rights Quarterly (HRQ) 1.

———. *Who Believes in Human Rights? Reflections on the European Convention* (Cambridge University Press, 2006).

Dobson, Lynn. "Legitimacy, Institutional Power, and International Human Rights Institutions: A Conceptual Enquiry," in Andreas Føllesdal, Johan Karlsson Schaffer, and Geir Ulfstein (eds.) *The Legitimacy of International Human Rights Regimes: Legal Political and Philosophical Perspectives* (Cambridge University Press, 2013).

Donnelly, Jack. "Cultural Relativism and Universal Human Rights" (1984) 6 Human Rights Quarterly (HRQ) 400.

———. "Human Rights and Human Dignity: An Analytic Critique of Non-Western Conceptions of Human Rights" (1982) 76 The American Political Science Review 303.

———. "Human Rights: A New Standard of Civilization?" (1998) 74 International Affairs 1.

———. "The Relative Universality of Human Rights" (2007) 29 Human Rights Quarterly (HRQ) 282.

———. *Universal Human Rights: In Theory and Practice*, 2nd ed. (Cornell University Press, 2003).

Dhare, Ulf Johansson. "Searching for a Middle Ground: Anthropologists and the Debate on the Universalism and the Cultural Relativism of Human Rights" (2017) 21 International Journal of Human Rights 1.

Douzinas, Costas. *The End of Human Rights: Critical Legal Thought at the Turn of the Century* (Bloomsbury, 2004).

———. *Human Rights and Empire: The Political Philosophy of Cosmopolitanism* (Routledge, 2007).

———. *The Radical Philosophy of Rights* (Routledge, 2019).

Dupuy, Pierre-Marie. "Some Reflections on Contemporary International Law and the Appeal to Universal Values: A Response to Martti Koskenniemi" (2005) 16 European Journal of International Law (EJIL) 131.

Duranti, Marco. "'A Blessed Act of Oblivion': Human Rights, European Unity and Postwar Reconciliation," in Birgit Schwelling (ed.) *Reconciliation, Civil Society, and the Politics of Memory: Transnational Initiatives in the 20th and 21st Century* (Transcript Verlag, 2012).

———. *The Conservative Human Rights Revolution: European Identity, Transnational Politics, and the Origins of the European Convention* (Oxford University Press, 2017).

Duxbury, Alison, and Hsien-Li Tan. *Can ASEAN Take Human Rights Seriously?* (Cambridge University Press, 2019).

Engle, Karen. "From Skepticism to Embrace: Human Rights and the American Anthropological Association from 1947–1999" (2001) 23 Human Rights Quarterly (HRQ) 536.

Englehart, Neil. "Rights and Culture in the Asian Values Argument: The Rise and Fall of Confucian Ethics in Singapore" (2000) 22 Human Rights Quarterly (HRQ) 548.

Englehart, Neil and Melissa K. Miller. "The CEDAW Effect: International Law's Impact on Women's Rights" (2014) 13 Journal of Human Rights 22.

Evans, Carolyn. *Freedom of Religion under the European Convention on Human Rights* (Oxford University Press, 2001).

Evans, Tony. "International Human Rights Law as Power/Knowledge" (2005) 27 Human Rights Quarterly (HRQ) 1046.

Faghfoury, Mostafa. "Human Rights: 50 Years Later," in William Sweet (ed.) *Philosophical and the Universal Declaration of Human Rights* (University of Ottawa Press, 2003).

Fassbender, Bardo. "'We the Peoples of the United Nations': Constituent Power and Constitutional Form in International Law," in Martin Loughlin and Neil Walker (eds.) *The Paradox of Constitutionalism: Constituent Power and Constitutional Form* (Oxford University Press, 2008).

Fernandez, James. "Tolerance in a Repugnant World and Other Dilemmas in the Cultural Relativism of Melville J. Herskovits" (1990) 18 Ethos 140.

Fraser, Arvonne. "Becoming Human: The Origins and Developments of Women's Human Rights" (1999) 21 Human Rights Quarterly (HRQ) 853.

Finnemore, Martha. *National Interests in International Society* (Cornell University Press, 1996).

Fitzpatrick, Peter. *Modernism and the Grounds of Law* (Cambridge University Press, 2001).

———. "The Revolutionary Past: Decolonizing Law and Human Rights" (2014) 2 Metodo: International Studies in Phenomenology and Philosophy 117.

Føllesdal, Andreas. "Exporting the Margin of Appreciation: Lessons for the Inter-American Court of Human Rights" (2017) 15 International Journal of Constitutional Law (ICON) 359.

———. "Subsidiarity and International Human-Rights Courts: Respecting Self-Governance and Protecting Human Rights—or Neither?" (2016) 79 Law and Contemporary Problems 147.

Galanos, Christos. "Universal Human Rights in the Face of Cultural Relativism and Moral Objectivity: Preaching or Teaching?" (2010) 16 UCL Jurisprudence Review 29.

Gat, Azar. *Nations* (Cambridge University Press, 2013).

Gayim, Eyassu. "The Discourse on Human Rights and the International Regime of Human Rights" (2016) 11 Nordicum-Mediterraneum 1.

Geertz, Clifford. "Distinguished Lecture: Anti Anti-Relativism" (1984) 86 American Anthropologist: New Series 263.

Gerards, Janneke. "Margin of Appreciation and Incrementalism in the Case Law of the European Court of Human Rights" (2018) 18 Human Rights Law Review 495.

———. "Pluralism, Deference and the Margin of Appreciation Doctrine" (2011) 17 European Law Journal 80.

Gewirth, Alan. "The Epistemology of Human Rights" (1984) 1 Social Philosophy and Policy 1.

Goh, Gillian. "The 'ASEAN Way'" (2000) 13 Pacific Review 439.

Goodale, Mark. "Introduction: Locating Rights, Envisioning Law between the Global and the Local," in Mark Goodale and Sally Engle Merry (eds.) *The Practice of Human Rights: Tracking Law Between the Global and the Local* (Cambridge University Press, 2007).

———. "Toward a Critical Anthropology of Human Rights" (2006) 47 Current Anthropology 485.

Goodman, Ryan. "Human Rights Treaties, Invalid Reservations, and State Consent" (2002) 96 American Journal of International Law (AJIL) 531.

Goodman, Ryan, and Derek Jinks. "Incomplete Internalization and Compliance with Human Rights Law" (2008) 19 European Journal of International Law (EJIL) 725.

Greer, Steven. *The European Convention on Human Rights: Achievements, Problems and Prospects*, 2nd ed. (Cambridge University Press, 2008).

Hafner-Burton, Emilie. *Making Human Rights a Reality* (Princeton University Press, 2013).

Hafner-Burton, Emilie, Kiyoteru Tsutsui, and John Meyer. "International Human Rights Law and the Politics of Legitimation: Repressive States and Human Rights Treaties." (2008) 23 International Sociology 115.

Hafner-Burton, Emilie, Laurence Helfer, and Christopher Fariss. "Emergency and Escape: Explaining Derogations from Human Rights Treaties." (2011) 65 International Organization 673.

Hardt, Michael, and Antonio Negri. *Empire* (Harvard University Press, 2001).

Hart, Linda. "Anthropology of Kinship Meets Human Rights Rationality: Limits of Marriage and Family Life in the European Court of Human Rights" (2018) 20 Societies 816.

Hatch, Elvin. "The Good Side of Relativism" (1997) 53 Journal of Anthropological Research 371.

Hathaway, Oona. "Why Do Countries Commit to Human Rights Treaties?" (2007) 51 Journal of Conflict Resolution 588.

Helfer, Laurence. "Overlegalizing Human Rights: International Relations Theory and the Commonwealth Caribbean Backlash against Human Rights Regimes" (2002) 102 Columbia Law Review 1832.

Helfer, Laurence, and Erik Voeten. "International Courts as Agents of Legal Change: Evidence from LGBT Rights in Europe" (2014) 68 International Organization 77.

Henkin, Louis. "The Universality of the Concept of Human Rights" (1989) 506 Annals of the American Academy of Political and Social Science 10.

Herskovits, Melville. "Some Further Comments on Cultural Relativism" (1958) 60 American Anthropologist New Series 266.

Hill, Daniel. "Avoiding Obligation: Reservations to Human Rights Treaties" (2016) 60 Journal of Conflict Resolution 1129.

Hillebrecht, Courtney. *Domestic Politics and International Human Rights Tribunals: The Problem of Compliance* (Cambridge University Press, 2014)

———. "The Power of Human Rights Tribunals: Compliance with the European Court of Human Rights and Domestic Policy Change" (2014) 20 European Journal of International Relations 1100.

Hobson, John. *The Eurocentric Conception of World Politics: Western International Theory, 1760–2010* (Cambridge University Press, 2012).
Holtmaat, Rikki. "Article 5," in Marsha Freeman, Christine Chinkin, and Beate Rudolf (eds.) *The UN Convention on the Elimination of All Forms of Discrimination against Women: A Commentary* (Oxford University Press, 2013).
Howard, Rhoda. "Cultural Absolutism and the Nostalgia for Community" (1993) 15 Human Rights Quarterly (HRQ) 315.
———. "Human Rights and the Culture Wars: Globalization and the Universality of Human Rights" (1997) 53 International Journal 94.
———. "Human Rights and the Search for Community" (1995) 32 Journal of Peace Research 1.
Huneeus, Alexandra. "Courts Resisting Courts: Lessons from the Inter-American Court's Struggle to Enforce Human Rights" (2011) 44 Cornell International Law Journal 493.
Hurd, Ian. *International Organizations: Politics, Law, Practice* (Cambridge University Press, 2017).
Hyndman, Patricia. "Cultural Legitimacy in the Formulation and Implementation of Human Rights Law and Policy in Australia," In Abdullahi Ahmed An-Na'im (ed.) *Human Rights in Cross-Cultural Perspectives: A Quest for Consensus* (University of Pennsylvania Press, 1995).
Ibhawoh, Bonny. "Between Culture and Constitution: Evaluating the Cultural Legitimacy of Human Rights in the African State" (2000) 22 Human Rights Quarterly (HRQ) 838.
Irvin-Erickson, Douglas. *Raphaël Lemkin and the Concept of Genocide* (University of Pennsylvania Press, 2017).
Jenco, Leigh. "Revisiting Asian Values" (2013) 74 Journal of the History of Ideas 273.
Jeske, Anja. "Why Create a Human Rights Regime? The ASEAN Intergovernmental Commission for Human Rights," in Tanja A. Börzel and Vera van Hüllen (eds.) *Governance Transfer by Regional Organizations: Patching Together a Global Script* (Palgrave Macmillan, 2015).
Johnson, Paul. "Marriage, Heteronormativity, and the European Court of Human Rights: A Reappraisal" (2015) 29 International Journal of Law, Policy and the Family 56.
Jouannet, Emmanuelle. "Universalism and Imperialism: The True-False Paradox of International Law?" (2007) 18 European Journal of International Law (EJIL) 379.
Kainz, Howard. "Natural Law and Natural Rights," in William Sweet (ed.) *Philosophical Theory and the Universal Declaration of Human Rights* (University of Ottawa Press, 2003).
Katsumata, Hiro. "Reconstruction of Diplomatic Norms in Southeast Asia: The Case for Strict Adherence to the 'ASEAN Way'" (2003) 25 Contemporary Southeast Asia 104.
Kayaoglu, Turan. "Westphalian Eurocentrism in International Relations Theory" (2010) 12 International Studies Review 193.
Keller, Linda. "The Impact of State Parties' Reservations to the Convention on the Elimination of All Forms of Discrimination against Women" (2014) Michigan State Law Review 309.
Kennedy, David. "Primitive Legal Scholarship" (1986) 27 Harvard Journal of International Law 1.
Kiwanuka, Richard. "The Meaning of 'People' in the African Charter on Human and Peoples' Rights" (1988) 82 American Journal of International Law (AJIL) 80.
Klabbers, Jan. "The Emergence of Functionalism in International Institutional Law: Colonial Inspirations" (2014) 25 European Journal of International Law (EJIL) 645.
———. An Introduction to International Organizations Law (Cambridge University Press, 2015).
Koenig, Matthias. "The Governance of Religious Diversity at the European Court of Human Rights," in Jane Boulden and Will Kymlicka (eds.) *International Approaches to Governing Ethnic Diversity* (Oxford University Press, 2015).

Korkelia, Konstantin. "New Challenges to the Regime of Reservations under the International Covenant on Civil and Political Rights" (2002) 13 European Journal of International Law (EJIL) 437.

Koremenos, Barbara. "Institutionalism and International Law," in Jeffrey Dunoff and Mark Pollack (eds.) *Interdisciplinary Perspectives on International Law and International Relations: The State of the Art* (Cambridge University Press, 2013).

Koremenos, Barbara, Charles Lipson, and Duncan Snidal. "The Rational Design of International Institutions" (2001) 55 International Organization 761.

Koskenniemi, Martti. *From Apology to Utopia: The Structure of International Legal Argument*, reissue with new epilogue (Cambridge University Press, 2005).

——. *The Politics of International Law* (Hart, 2011).

Kratochvíl, Jan. "The Inflation of the Margin of Appreciation by the European Court of Human Rights" (2011) 29 Netherlands Quarterly of Human Rights 324.

Langlois, Anthony. "Human Rights: The Globalisation and Fragmentation of Moral Discourse" (2002) 28 Review of International Studies 479.

Laughland, John. "Human Rights and the Rule of Law," in David Chandler (ed.) *Rethinking Human Rights: Critical Approaches to International Politics* (Palgrave Macmillan, 2002).

Leigh, Ian. "The European Court of Human Rights and Religious Neutrality," in Gavin D"Costa, Malcolm Evans, Tariq Modood, and Julian Rivers (eds.) *Religion in a Liberal State* (Cambridge University Press, 2013).

Lenzerini, Federico. *The Culturalization of Human Rights Law* (Oxford University Press, 2014).

Leonhardsen, Erlend. "Treaty Change, Arbitral Practice and the Search for Balance," in Lukasz Gruszczynski and Wouter Werner (eds.) *Deference in International Courts and Tribunals: Standard of Review and Margin of Appreciation* (Oxford University Press, 2014).

Letsas, George. "Two Concepts of the Margin of Appreciation" (2006) 26 Oxford Journal of Legal Studies 705.

Lévi-Strauss, Claude. *Myth and Meaning: Cracking the Code of Culture* (Schocken Books, 1979).

Levy, Neil. *Moral Relativism: A Short Introduction* (Oneworld, 2002).

Lewis, Mark. *The Birth of the New Justice* (Oxford University Press, 2013).

Li, Xiaorong. *Ethics, Human Rights and Culture: Beyond Relativism and Universalism* (Palgrave Macmillan, 2006).

Losurdo, Domenico. *Liberalism: A Counter History*, trans. Gregory Elliott (Verso, 2011).

Lukes, Steven. *Moral Relativism* (Profile, 2008).

Madigan, Janet Holl. *Truth, Politics and Universal Human Rights* (Palgrave Macmillan, 2007).

Madsen, Mikael. "From Cold War Instrument to Supreme European Court: The European Court of Human Rights at the Crossroads of International and National Law and Politics" (2007) 32 Law and Social Inquiry 137.

Marshall, Jill. "Conditions for Freedom? European Human Rights Law and the Islamic Headscarf Debate" (2008) 30 Human Rights Quarterly (HRQ) 631.

Mayerfeld, Jamie. "The Democratic Legitimacy of International Human Rights Law" (2009) 19 Indiana International and Comparative Law Review 49.

Mazower, Mark. "An International Civilization? Empire, Internationalism and the Crisis of the Mid-Twentieth Century" (2006) 82 International Affairs 553.

McGoldrick, Dominic. "A Defence of the Margin of Appreciation and an Argument for its Application by the Human Rights Committee" (2016) 65 International and Comparative Law Quarterly (ICLQ) 21.

———. Religion in the European Public Square and in European Public Life: Crucifixes in the Classroom? (2011) 11 Human Rights Law Review 451.

McHarg, Aileen. "Reconciling Human Rights and the Public Interest: Conceptual Problems and Doctrinal Uncertainty in the Jurisprudence of the European Court of Human Rights" (1999) 62 Modern Law Review 671.

Mechlem, Kirsten. "Treaty Bodies and the Interpretation of Human Rights" (2009) 42 Vanderbilt Journal of Transnational Law 905.

Mégret, Frédéric. "International Law as Law," in James Crawford and Martti Koskenniemi (eds.) *The Cambridge Companion to International Law* (Cambridge University Press, 2012).

Merry, Sally Engle. "Transnational Human Rights and Local Activism: Mapping the Middle" (2006) 108 American Anthropologist 38.

Messer, Ellen. "Pluralist Approaches to Human Rights" (1997) 53 Journal of Anthropological Research 293.

Mignolo, Walter. "Citizenship, Knowledge, and the Limits of Humanity" (2006) 18 American Literary History 312.

———. "Epistemic Disobedience, Independent Thought and De-Colonial Freedom" (2009) 26 Theory, Culture and Society 1.

Mjöll Arnardóttir, Oddný. "Rethinking the Two Margins of Appreciation" (2016) 12 European Constitutional Law Review 27.

Moloney, Roslyn. "Incompatible Reservations to Human Rights Treaties: Severability and the Problem of State Consent" (2004) 5 Melbourne Journal of International Law 155.

Moravcsik, Andrew. "Explaining International Human Rights Regimes: Liberal Theory and Western Europe" (1995) 1 European Journal of International Relations 157.

———. "The Origins of Human Rights Regimes: Democratic Delegation in Postwar Europe" (2000) 54 International Organization 217.

Morsink, Johannes *Inherent Human Rights: Philosophical Roots of the Universal Declaration* (University of Pennsylvania Press, 2009).

Moyn, Samuel. "Plural Cosmopolitanisms and the Origins of Human Rights," in Costas Douzinas and Conor Gearty (eds.) *The Meanings of Rights: The Philosophy of Social Theory of Human Rights* (Cambridge University Press, 2014).

Munroe, James. "The Relationship between the Origins and Regime Design of the ASEAN Intergovernmental Commission on Human Rights (AICHR)" (2011) 15 International Journal of Human Rights 1185.

Murray, Rachel. "A Comparison between the African and European Courts of Human Rights" (2002) 2 African Human Rights Law Journal 195.

Murray, Rachel, and Frans Viljoen. "Towards Non-Discrimination on the Basis of Sexual Orientation: The Normative Basis and Procedural Possibilities before the African Commission on Human and Peoples' Rights and the African Union" (2007) 29 Human Rights Quarterly (HRQ) 86.

Mutua, Makau. "The Banjul Charter and the African Cultural Fingerprint: An Evaluation of the Language of Duties" (1995) 35 Virginia Journal of International Law 339.

———. "The Complexity of Universalism in Human Rights," in András Sajó (ed) *Human Rights with Modesty: The Problem of Universalism* (Martinus Nijhoff, 2004).

———. "Savages, Victims, and Saviours: The Metaphor of Human Rights" (2001) 42 Harvard International Law Journal 201.

Nancy, Jean-Luc. "On Human Rights: Two Simple Remarks," trans. Gilbert Leung, from Costas Douzinas and Conor Gearty (eds.) *The Meanings of Rights: The Philosophy and Social Theory of Human Rights* (Cambridge University Press, 2014) 16.

Narine, Shaun. "Human Rights Norms and the Evolution of ASEAN: Moving without Moving in a Changing Regional Environment" (2012) 34 Contemporary Southeast Asia 356.

Neumayer, Eric. "Qualified Ratification: Explaining Reservations to International Human Rights Treaties" (2007) 36 Journal of Legal Studies 397.

Nicholson, Matthew. "Majority Rule and Human Rights: Identity and Non-Identity in SAS v France" (2016) 67 Northern Ireland Legal Quarterly 115.

Novak, Andrew. "Using International and Foreign Law in Human Rights Litigation: The Decriminalization of Homosexuality in Belize" (2018) 10 Journal of Human Rights Practice 346.

Nussbaum, Martha. *The Cosmopolitan Tradition: A Noble but Flawed Ideal* (Belknap Press, 2019).

Odinkalu, Chidi. "Analysis of Paralysis or Paralysis by Analysis? Implementing Economic, Social, and Cultural Rights under the African Charter on Human and Peoples' Rights" (2001) 23 Human Rights Quarterly (HRQ) 327.

———. "The Individual Complaints Procedures of the African Commission on Human and Peoples' Rights: A Preliminary Assessment" (1998) 8 Transnational Law and Contemporary Problems 359.

Okere, B. Obinna. "The Protection of Human Rights in Africa and the African Charter on Human and Peoples' Rights: A Comparative Analysis with the European and American Systems" (1984) 6 Human Rights Quarterly (HRQ) 141.

Orakhelashvili, Alexander. "Restrictive Interpretation of Human Rights Treaties in the Recent Jurisprudence of the European Court of Human Rights" (2003) 14 European Journal of International Law (EJIL) 529.

Otto, Dianne. "Rethinking the 'Universality' of Human Rights Law" (1997) 29 Human Rights Law Review 1.

Pagden, Anthony. "Human Rights, Natural Rights, and Europe's Imperial Legacy" (2003) 31 Political Theory 171.

Parker, Karen. "Jus Cogens: Compelling the Law of Human Rights" (1988) 12 Hastings International and Comparative Law Review 411.

Patel, Gayatri. "How 'Universal' Is the United Nations' Universal Periodic Review Process? An Examination of the Discussions Held on Polygamy" (2017) 18 Human Rights Review 459.

———. "Smoke and Mirrors at the United Nations' Universal Periodic Review Process" (2017) 10 International Journal of Human Rights in Healthcare 310.

Paul, Simon. "Governing from the Margins: The European Court of Human Rights' Margin of Appreciation Doctrine as a Tool of Global Governance" (2016) 12 Croatian Yearbook of European Law and policy 81.

Peat, Daniel, and Matthew Windsor. "Playing the Game of Interpretation: On Meaning and Metaphor in International Law" in Andrea Bianchi, Daniel Peat, and Matthew Windsor (eds.) *Interpretation in International Law* (Oxford University Press, 2015).

Pergantis, Vassilis. *The Paradigm of State Consent in the Law of Treaties: Challenges and Perspectives* (Edward Elgar, 2017).

Perusek, David. "Grounding Cultural Relativism" (2007) 80 Anthropological Quarterly 821.

Phillips, Patrick. *The Challenge of Relativism: Its Nature and Limits* (Continuum International, 2007).

Piper, Catherine. "Reservations to Multilateral Treaties: The Goal of Universality" (1985) 71 Iowa Law Review 295.
Pisanò, Attilio. "Human Rights and Sovereignty in the ASEAN Path towards a Human Rights Declaration" (2014) 15 Human Rights Review 391.
Pollis, Adamantia. "Cultural Relativism Revisited: Through a State Prism." (1996) 18 Human Rights Quarterly (HRQ) 316.
———. "Greek National Identity: Religious Minorities, Rights, and European Norms" (1992) 10 Journal of Modern Greek Studies 171.
———. "A New Universalism," in Adamantia Pollis and Peter Schwab (eds.) *Human Rights: New Perspectives, New Realities* (Lynne Rienner, 2000).
Poole, Avery. "'The World is Outraged': Legitimacy in the Making of the ASEAN Human Rights Body." (2015) 37 Contemporary Southeast Asia 355.
Prashad, Vijay. *The Darker Nations: A People's History of the Third World* (New Press, 2007).
———. *The Poorer Nations: A Possible History of the Global South* (Verso, 2013) 49.
Preis, Ann-Belinda. "Human Rights as Cultural Practice: An Anthropological Critique" (1996) 18 Human Rights Quarterly (HRQ) 286.
Puppo, Alberto. "Reasonable Stability vs. Radical Indeterminacy: A Disanalogy between Domestic Rule of Law and Humanity-Based International Law" (2016) 30 Journal for Constitutional Theory and Philosophy of Law 81.
Rahman, Momin. "Queer Rights and the Triangulation of Western Exceptionalism (2014) 13 Journal of Human Rights 274.
Rajagopal, Balakrishnan. *International Law from Below: Development, Social Movements and Third World Resistance* (Cambridge University Press, 2003).
Ramcharan, Robin. "ASEAN and Non-interference: A Principle Maintained" (2000) 22 Contemporary Southeast Asia 60.
Ranganathan, Surabhi. *Strategically Created Treaty Conflicts and the Politics of International Law* (Cambridge University Press 2014).
Ratner, Steven. "Persuading to Comply: On the Deployment and Avoidance of Legal Argumentation," in Jeffrey Dunoff and Mark Pollack, *Interdisciplinary Perspectives on International Law and International Relations: The State of the Art* (Cambridge University Press, 2013).
Raz, Joseph. "Human Rights in the Emerging World Order" (2010) 1 Transnational Legal Theory 31.
Redondo, Elvira. "The Universal Periodic Review of the UN Human Rights Council: An Assessment of the First Session" (2008) 7 Chinese Journal of International Law 721.
Renteln, Alison Dundes. "The Concept of Human Rights" (1988) 83 Anthropos 343.
———. "A Cross-Cultural Approach to Validating International Human Rights: the Case of Retribution Tied to Proportionality," in David Louis Cingranelli (ed.) *Human Rights: Theory and Measurement* (Palgrave Macmillan, 1988).
———. *International Human Rights: Universalism Versus Relativism*, 2nd ed. (Quid Pro, 2013).
———. "Relativism and the Search for Human Rights" (1998) 90 American Anthropologist 56.
———. "The Unanswered Challenge of Relativism and the Consequences for Human Rights" (1985) 7 Human Rights Quarterly (HRQ) 514.
Reus-Smit, Christian. "Politics and International Legal Obligation" (2003) 9 European Journal of International Relations 591.
———. *The Politics of International Law* (Cambridge University Press, 2004)

Richardson, James. "The Sociology of Religious Freedom: A Structural and Socio-Legal Analysis" (2006) 67 Sociology of Religion 27.

Riddle, Jennifer. "Making CEDAW Universal: A Critique of CEDAW's Reservation Regime under Article 28 and the Effectiveness of the Reporting Process" (2002) 34 George Washington International Law Review 605.

Roth, Kenneth. "The Charade of US Ratification of International Human Rights Treaties" (2000) 1 Chicago Journal of International Law 347.

rua Wall, Illan. *Human Rights and Constituent Power: Without Model or Warranty* (Routledge, 2012).

Ryan, Clare. "Europe's Moral Margin: Parental Aspirations and the European Court of Human Rights" (2018) 56 Columbia Journal of Transnational Law 468.

Said, Edward. *Culture and Imperialism* (Vintage, 1994).

Samnøy, Åshild. "Human Rights as International Consensus: The Making of the Universal Declaration of Human Rights 1945–1948" (1993) Chr. Michelsen Institute Report 4.

Scott, Shirley. "International Law as Ideology: Theorizing the Relationship between International Law and International Politics" (1994) 5 European Journal of International Law (EJIL) 313.

Schabas, William. *The European Convention on Human Rights: A Commentary* (Oxford University Press, 2017).

———. Reservations to the Convention on the Elimination of All Forms of Discrimination against Women and the Convention on the Rights of the Child" (1997) 3 William and Mary Journal of Women and the Law 79.

———. "Reservations to the Convention on the Rights of the Child" (1996) 18 Human Rights Quarterly (HRQ) 472.

———. "Reservations to Human Rights Treaties: Time for Innovation and Reform" (1995) 32 Canadian Yearbook of International Law 39.

Schmitt, Carl. *Political Theology: Four Chapters on the Concept of Sovereignty*, trans. and ed. George Schwab (University of Chicago Press, 2005).

Seah, Daniel. "The ASEAN Charter" (2009) 58 International and Comparative Law Quarterly 197.

Shany, Yuval. "Toward a General Margin of Appreciation Doctrine in International Law?" (2005) 16 European Journal of International Law (EJIL) 907.

Simma, Bruno, and Gleider Hernandez. "Legal Consequences of an Impermissible Reservation to a Human Rights Treaty: Where Do We Stand?" in Enzo Cannizzaro (ed.) *The Law of Treaties beyond the Vienna Convention* (Oxford University Press, 2011).

Simmons, Beth. "Capacity, Commitment and Compliance: International Institutions and Territorial Disputes" (2002) 46 Journal of Conflict Resolution 829.

———. *Mobilizing for Human Rights: International Law in Domestic Politics* (Cambridge University Press, 2009).

Sloane, Robert. "Outrelativizing Relativism: A Liberal Defense of the Universality of International Human Rights." (2001) 34 Vanderbilt Journal of Transnational Law 527.

Smith, Rhona. "The Pacific Island States: Themes Emerging from the United Nations Human Rights Council's Inaugural Universal Periodic Review?" (2012) 13 Melbourne Journal of International Law 569.

Spielmann, Dean. "Whither the Margin of Appreciation?" (2014) 67 Current Legal Problems 49.

Sweeney, James. "Margins of Appreciation: Cultural Relativity and the European Court of Human Rights in the Post–Cold War era" (2005) 54 International and Comparative Law Quarterly (ICLQ) 459.

Stammers, Neil. "Social Movements and the Social Construction of Human Rights" (1999) 21 Human Rights Quarterly (HRQ) 980.

Stivachtis, Yannis, and Mike Habegger. "The Council of Europe: The Institutional Limits of Contemporary European International Society?" (2011) 33 Journal of European Integration 159.

Stone-Sweet, Alex. "On the Constitutionalisation of the Convention: The European Court of Human Rights as a Constitutional Court" (2009) 71 Yale Law School Legal Scholarship Repository 1.

Tan Hsien-Li. *The ASEAN Intergovernmental Commission on Human Rights: Institutionalising Human Rights in Southeast Asia* (Cambridge University Press, 2011).

Tesón, Fernando. "International Human Rights and Cultural Relativism" (1985) 25 Virginia Journal of International Law 869.

———. "International Obligation and the Theory of Hypothetical Consent" (1990) 15 Yale International Law Journal 84.

Thompson, Mark. "Whatever Happened to 'Asian Values'?" (2001) 12 Journal of Democracy 154.

Tilley, John. "Cultural Relativism" (2000) 22 Human Rights Quarterly (HRQ) 501.

Tobin, John. "Seeking to Persuade: A Constructive Approach to Human Rights Treaty Interpretation" (2010) 23 Harvard Human Rights 1.

Tufano, Sarah. "The 'Holy Trinity' of the United Nations Universal Periodic Review: How to Make an Effective Recommendation Regarding Women's Rights" (2018) 21 University of Pennsylvania Journal of Law and Social Change 187.

Turner, Terence. "Human Rights, Human Difference: Anthropology's Contribution to an Emancipatory Cultural Politics" (1997) 53 Journal of Anthropological Research 273.

Unger, Roberto. *The Critical Legal Studies Movement: Another Time, A Greater Task*, 3rd ed. (Verso, 2015).

Vakulenko, Anastasia. "'Islamic Headscarves' and the European Convention on Human Rights: An Intersectional Perspective" (2007) 16 Social and Legal Studies 183.

van Dijk, Pieter. "A Common Standard of Achievement: About Universal Validity and Uniform Interpretation of International Human Rights Norms" (1995) 13 Netherlands Quarterly of Human Rights 105.

Vincent, Andrew. *The Politics of Human Rights* (Oxford University Press, 2010).

Vinjamuri, Leslie. "Human Rights Backlash," in Stephen Hopgood, Jack Snyder, and Leslie Vinjamuri (eds.) *Human Rights Futures* (Cambridge University Press, 2017).

von Stein, Jana. "Making Promises, Keeping Promises: Democracy, Ratification and Compliance in International Human Rights Law" (2015) 46 British Journal of Political Science 655.

Weil, Patrick. "Why the French *Laïcité* Is Liberal" (2009) 30 Cardozo Law Review 2699.

Weiss-Wendt, Anton. *The Soviet Union and the Gutting of the UN Genocide Convention* (University of Wisconsin Press, 2016).

Wheatley, Steven. *Democracy, Minorities and International Law* (Cambridge University Press, 2005).

———. "On the Legitimate Authority of International Human Rights Bodies," in Andreas Føllesdal, Johan Karlsson Schaffer, and Geir Ulfstein (eds.) *The Legitimacy of International*

Human Rights Regimes: Legal, Political and Philosophical Perspectives (Cambridge University Press, 2014).

Whyte, Jessica. "Human Rights: Confronting Governments? Michel Foucault and the Right to Intervene," in Matthew Stone, Illan rua Wall, and Costas Douzinas (eds.) *New Critical Legal Thinking: Law and the Political* (Routledge, 2012).

Wilk, Kurt. "International Law and Global Ideological Conflict: Reflections on the Universality of International Law" (1951) 45 American Journal of International Law (AJIL) 648.

Wong, David. *Moral Relativity* (University of California Press, 1984).

Wright, Shelley. *International Human Rights, Decolonisation and Globalisation: Becoming Human* (Routledge, 2001).

Yasuaki, Onuma. "International Law and International Politics: The Functions of International Law in International Society" (2003) 14 European Journal of International Law (EJIL) 105.

Zechenter, Elizabeth. "In the Name of Culture: Cultural Relativism and the Abuse of the Individual" (1997) 53 Journal of Anthropological Research 319.

Ziemele, Ineta, and Lāsma Liede. "Reservations to Human Rights Treaties: From Draft Guideline 3.1.12 to Guideline 3.1.5.6" (2013) 24 European Journal of International Law (EJIL) 1135.

Zwart, Tom. "Using Local Culture to Further the Implementation of International Human Rights: The Receptor Approach" (2012) 34 Human Rights Quarterly (HRQ) 546.

INDEX